contents

BASIC TOOLS and TIPS

TOOLS

I love collecting different bar shakers, mixers, and gadgets, including whipped cream chargers, water carbonators, and absinthe spoons. That being said, the only tools you need to start mixing at home are:

> Boston shaker
> Hawthorn strainer
> Julep strainer
> Bar spoon—cocktail spoon
> Bar knife—paring knife
> Muddler
> Citrus reamer
> Jigger

And of course you need glasses. The three most used glasses are rocks, Collins, and martini (also called a cocktail glass).

John's bar basics.

TIPS

How to juice

Always used freshly squeezed juice. And roll your citrus on the counter before cutting—rolling makes it juicier (I stole that tip from my wife).

How to make a citrus twist

Cut a quarter-size piece of peel from a lemon, lime, or other citrus fruit, trying to avoid as much of the bitter white pith as possible. Hold the disk skin side down by the edges with your thumb and index finger a few inches over the drink. Pinch the edges up and together, to bend the disk without breaking it, thereby releasing essential oils from the skin into the drink, and then drop it into the drink.

How to make a flamed twist

Cut a quarter-size piece of peel from a lemon, lime, or other citrus fruit, trying to avoid as much of the bitter white pith as possible. With your thumb and index finger, hold the disk by the edges, skin side facing out. Light a kitchen match and hold it in front of the citrus peel. Pinch the edges of the disk together to bend it without breaking it, which will release the essential oils from the peel. The oils will flare up the match (it is a pretty cool effect) and will be toasted. Then drop the peel into the drink.

How to muddle

Usually a few taps with the muddler (8 to 10) at the bottom of the glass part of a Boston shaker are enough to release the essential oils from fresh herbs—too much muddling will bruise the leaves. You can muddle more if you're muddling fruit or berries.

How to shake

A Boston shaker has two halves: a metal half and a glass half. Always build your drink in the glass part. When you have added all of the ingredients, add enough ice directly to the cocktail to almost fill the glass half, and then place the metal half upside down on top of the glass half and tap the bottom of the metal half to seal the two together. Shake vigorously for 17 seconds—the perfect amount of time to impart just the right amount of cold and dilution to the drink. Place the metal half upright on a counter and gently tap the side of the glass half to remove. Place the Hawthorn strainer on the opening of the metal half and pour the drink through the strainer into the serving glass.

How to stir

Same as above, except instead of shaking, stir with a bar spoon directly in the glass half. Twenty stirs should be fine. When straining into the serving glass, use the julep strainer. (You use a julep when straining from the glass half of the shaker, and a Hawthorn when straining from the metal half.)

When to shake and when to stir

If your cocktail has only liquor and no juices, you should stir. If you have fruit juice in the drink, you should shake. (Although James Bond likes his martinis shaken, and I'm not about to argue with him.) Whatever you prefer is fine.

How to chill a cocktail glass

Usually when serving drinks on the rocks, you fill a rocks glass to the top with ice, and immediately strain your drink in. If you are making a "tall" drink (for example, a drink "stretched" with seltzer) you would do the same with a Collins glass. For serving a drink "up" (i.e., no ice), use a martini glass and chill beforehand by filling the glass with ice and cold water before you mix your drink. When your drink is ready to be strained, toss the ice and water out of the martini glass and—voilà—your glass is chilled!

How to crush ice

Fill a plastic bag with ice, cover with a kitchen towel, and smash to bits with a mallet or the back of a small skillet.

How to salt-rim a glass (for a Margarita)

Rub a wedge of lime around the rim of the glass. Fill a small plate or saucer with coarse large-crystal salt (sea salts work well) or other rim salt mixture and twirl the wet rim in the salt so it sticks. If adding ice, do so after the glass is rimmed and be careful not to knock off the salt.

Cocktail techniques.

Frutti di Bosco Cooler

A couple of years ago, Rachael brought home a rather elegant bottle of St-Germain elderflower liqueur, which had been recommended by our local wineshop. Being averse to anything sweet, particularly in cocktails, I was initially suspicious of the clear, thin, syrupy liquid. However, after I used it for the first time, it immediately became one of my favorite cocktail ingredients. It is only slightly sweet and floral, with a subtle honeysuckle flavor that enhances stronger base spirits without overpowering them.

In many of my recipes, I use agave syrup as a sweetener. It is a great substitute in any drink that calls for simple syrup, and unlike simple syrup, which must be made ahead of time (by melting sugar into water), agave syrup comes ready to use, and often in a convenient squeeze bottle. It has a consistency not unlike honey or maple syrup, but with a simpler flavor profile.

This drink is the first of my many St-Germain cocktail recipes; indeed, countless drinks can be created using the basic recipe below and substituting different fruits and/or citrus.

2 **fresh mint leaves**, plus a sprig for garnish
3 or 4 **blackberries**
1 tablespoon **agave syrup**
Juice of ½ **lemon**
2 ounces **gin**
1 ounce **St-Germain elderflower liqueur**

Muddle the mint leaves at the bottom of a cocktail shaker. Add the blackberries and muddle as well. Add the remaining ingredients and shake well with ice. Strain into an ice-filled rocks glass and garnish with a sprig of mint.

2 **strawberries**, plus 1 for garnish
1½ ounces **vodka**
1 ounce **honey liqueur**
Juice of ½ **lime**
1 **egg white**

Muddle 2 strawberries at the bottom of a cocktail shaker. Add the remaining ingredients and shake well with ice. Strain into a chilled cocktail glass and garnish with another strawberry.

Strawberry Velvet

While it may seem counterintuitive, a raw egg white, which alone appears slimy and gloppy, when shaken into a cocktail imparts a velvety elegance and a supple mouthfeel, along with a pretty foam finish. And being rather flavorless, it does not alter the taste of the cocktail itself.

As far as health is concerned, I have been told that buying fresh eggs from a reliable source may reduce the risk of bacteria. You can also use pasteurized eggs. I am not a doctor, so if you are particularly concerned, skip the egg. Whatever you do, don't cook the egg and then add it to the cocktail. *That* would be gross.

This drink also has an unusual ingredient—honey liqueur. It was a gift from our friend Tommy Crudup. I am told it's big in Bavaria. It tastes like boozy honey.

Ginger Mule

Basically this is a minty Moscow Mule with gin instead of vodka. This drink is traditionally served in a copper mug, but a rocks glass is fine. Try to find ginger beer. It is spicier and has more body than ginger ale. Some supermarkets carry it, or you can order it on the Web (Reed's makes a good one).

5 **fresh mint leaves**
1½ ounces **gin**
½ ounce **agave syrup**
½ ounce **fresh lime juice**
1 ounce **ginger beer**
Lime wedge, for garnish

Muddle the mint at the bottom of a cocktail shaker. Add the gin, agave syrup, and lime juice and shake well with ice. Strain into a copper mug filled with crushed ice. Top with the ginger beer and stir gently. Garnish with a lime wedge.

Meyer Gin Fizz

Meyer lemons are thought to be a cross between a lemon and an orange. They look a lot like ordinary lemons, but are slightly sweeter and less acidic. They make a refreshing twist on the classic Gin Fizz.

1½ ounces **gin**
1 ounce fresh **Meyer lemon juice**
1 ounce **agave syrup**
Club soda

Shake all the ingredients except the club soda in an ice-filled cocktail shaker and strain into an ice-filled Collins glass. Top with club soda and stir gently.

Green Gin Fizz

Chartreuse is a liqueur that has been made since the 1700s by the Carthusian monks in France. There are two kinds, green and the slightly sweeter yellow. Green Chartreuse supposedly has the most herbal extracts of any liqueur—130. The recipe is a closely guarded secret, and the liqueur is assertive and vegetal; a little bit goes a long way. When used correctly, it imparts a brisk, verdant flavor to your drink.

3 **fresh mint leaves**
4 thin slices **seedless cucumber**, plus 1 for garnish
2 ounces **gin**
1 ounce **green Chartreuse**
Juice of 1 **lime**
1 tablespoon **agave syrup**
Club soda

Muddle the mint and cucumber at the bottom of a cocktail shaker. Add the gin, Chartreuse, lime juice, and agave syrup. Shake well with ice and strain into an ice-filled Collins glass. Top with club soda and stir gently. Garnish with a cucumber slice.

Bitter Sloe Fizz

Sloe gin is a liqueur traditionally made from infusing gin with sloe berries (sort of like plums). It's syrupy, kind of sweet, and slightly medicinal. You can't make a sloe gin fizz without it, and when made correctly, a sloe gin fizz is a great summertime drink. In my opinion, there is one—and only one—sloe gin brand you should ever buy: Plymouth.

> 1 ounce **gin**
> 1 ounce **sloe gin**
> 1 ounce **fresh lemon juice**
> Dash of **Angostura bitters**
> **Club soda**

Shake all the ingredients except the club soda in an ice-filled cocktail shaker and strain into an ice-filled Collins glass. Top with club soda.

Sex on an Italian Beach

The original version of this cocktail from the 1980s is too sweet for me. This version, featuring the bitter grapefruit-based Campari along with lemon sorbet, reminds me of kicking back on the Amalfi Coast in Italy.

> 2 ounces **gin**
> 1 ounce **Campari**
> Dash of **grapefruit bitters**
> 1 scoop **lemon sorbet**
> **Club soda**

Shake all the ingredients except the club soda in an ice-filled cocktail shaker and strain into an ice-filled Collins glass. Top with club soda.

Moroccan Nog

Rachael and I discovered almond milk at one of our favorite hotels, La Mamounia in Marrakesh. When you check in they greet you with fresh dates and a glass of cold, restorative almond milk. The addition of rum was my idea.

> 2 ounces **almond milk**
> 2 ounces **rum**
> Dash of **vanilla extract**
> Dash of **almond extract**
> 1 **egg white**
> Dash of **Amargo bitters**

Shake all the ingredients except the bitters in an ice-filled cocktail shaker and strain into a chilled martini glass. Garnish with the bitters.

Ginger Stinger

A pinch (or more) of cayenne pepper ratchets up the sizzle factor, while the cucumber cools it down in this spicy refresher.

    4 slices **cucumber**, plus 1 spear for garnish
    4 ounces **vodka**
    ½ teaspoon grated **fresh ginger**
    Juice of ½ **lime**
    Pinch of **cayenne pepper**, or more to taste
    Ginger beer

Muddle the cucumber slices at the bottom of a cocktail shaker. Add the remaining ingredients except the ginger beer and shake well with ice. Strain into an ice-filled Collins glass. Top with ginger beer and garnish with a cucumber spear.

Tea & Honey Tini

The main drink in Morocco is hot mint tea—about a bushel of fresh mint steeped in boiling water and poured ceremoniously into beautiful crystal teacups. Traditionally, booze would never, ever be mixed in mint tea, but I aim to break with tradition.

    3 ounces **brewed green tea**, steeped with lots
        of **fresh mint** sprigs and then cooled
    2 ounces **gin**
    2 ounces **honey liqueur**
    Juice of ½ **lemon**
    Mint sprig and **lemon wheel**, for garnish

Shake all the ingredients in an ice-filled cocktail shaker and strain into a chilled martini glass. Garnish with a fresh mint sprig and a thin lemon wheel floating on the drink.

Rachael's Cel-Ray

Dr. Brown's Cel-Ray® soda is a soft drink that has a celery flavor and is ubiquitous in Jewish delis (it pairs great with a corned beef sandwich). This is my boozy take on the beverage (and it happens to share half its name with my wife).

1 ounce **gin**
1 ounce **green Chartreuse**
1 ounce **St-Germain elderflower liqueur**
Juice of ½ **lime**
2 dashes of **celery bitters**
Seltzer
Celery rib, for garnish

Shake all the ingredients except the seltzer in an ice-filled cocktail shaker and strain into an ice-filled Collins glass. Top with seltzer and garnish with a celery rib.

Blue Ginger

This is an ode to tiki bar culture, but with gin instead of rum—the spirit of choice in many tiki drinks—mainly because my wife likes gin better than rum. I kept the flavors tart rather than overly sweet and would have put the drink in a coconut husk if I'd had one.

1½ ounces **gin**
1 ounce **blue curaçao**
2 ounces **pineapple juice**
Juice of ½ **lemon**
Juice of ½ **lime**
½ teaspoon grated **fresh ginger**
½ teaspoon **agave syrup**
Edible flowers, for garnish

Shake all the ingredients in an ice-filled cocktail shaker and strain into an ice-filled Collins glass or tiki mug (if you have one). Garnish with edible flowers.

Cucumber Sage Martini

Sage is one of my favorite herbs . . . and it tastes as delicious in a cocktail as it does stuffed in your Thanksgiving turkey!

  1 **fresh sage leaf**
  3 slices peeled **seedless cucumber**
  3 ounces **gin**
  2 ounces **St-Germain elderflower liqueur**
  Lime twist, for garnish

Muddle the sage and cucumber at the bottom of a cocktail shaker. Add the remaining ingredients and shake well with ice. Strain into a chilled cocktail glass. Garnish with a flamed lime twist.

Brandyvine

Brandy is made from grapes . . . so why not mix grapes with brandy? Grapes are sweet enough that the addition of simple syrup is not needed for this drink to be fresh and refreshing.

  2 **fresh mint leaves**, plus more for garnish
  3 **seedless green grapes**, plus more for garnish
  1½ ounces **brandy**
  ¾ ounce **St-Germain elderflower liqueur**
  Juice of ½ **lime**
  Club soda

Muddle the mint and grapes at the bottom of a cocktail shaker. Add the remaining ingredients except the club soda and shake well with ice. Strain into a Collins glass filled with crushed ice. Top with club soda and garnish with additional mint and grapes.

Ginger Snap

Domaine de Canton ginger liqueur is a great product. It makes this drink taste just like a gingersnap cookie.

    1 ounce **Domaine de Canton ginger liqueur**
    1½ ounces **vodka**
    1 ounce **fresh lemon juice**
    ¼ teaspoon grated **fresh ginger**
    ¼ teaspoon **agave syrup**
    Pinch of ground **cloves**
    Pinch of ground **cinnamon**
    Pinch of grated **nutmeg**
    Cinnamon stick, for garnish

Shake all the ingredients in an ice-filled cocktail shaker and strain into a chilled cocktail glass. Garnish with a cinnamon stick.

Rickey's Cherry Rickey

A boozy spin on a soda fountain classic: Cherry Lime Rickey.

    5 **fresh cherries**, plus 1 for garnish
    2 ounces **gin**
    2 ounces **St-Germain elderflower liqueur**
    Juice of 1 **lime**

Muddle 5 cherries at the bottom of a cocktail shaker. Add the remaining ingredients and shake well with ice. Strain into an ice-filled rocks glass. Garnish with a cherry.

My Tai

My version of the tiki classic Mai Tai features pineapple gum syrup produced by Small Hand Foods out of Berkeley, California, an artisanal company that makes small-batch high-quality syrups. This one adds viscosity and mouthfeel to your cocktails as well as a great acidic pineapple flavor.

 3 or 4 **fresh mint leaves**
 2 ounces **rum** (I use 10 Cane)
 1 ounce **Grand Marnier**
 ½ ounce **pineapple gum syrup**
 2 dashes of **Angostura orange bitters**
 Juice of 1 **lime**
 Mint sprig and **fresh cherry**, for garnish

Muddle the mint at the bottom of a cocktail shaker. Add the remaining ingredients and shake well with ice. Strain into an ice-filled rocks or hurricane glass (if you have it). Garnish with a mint sprig and a cherry.

Deep Purple

This one is for my bandmate Roto. He is a *huge* Richie Blackmore fan. It features crème de violette, which is a liqueur produced from violet flowers. Used judiciously, it adds haunting floral notes to a cocktail (it is a core ingredient in the classic Aviation Cocktail).

 5 **seedless black grapes**, plus 2 or 3 for garnish
 2 ounces **gin**
 1 ounce **crème de violette**
 Juice of ½ **lime**
 ½ teaspoon **agave syrup**

Muddle 5 grapes at the bottom of a cocktail shaker. Add the remaining ingredients and shake well with ice. Strain into an ice-filled rocks glass. Garnish with additional grapes.

Portly Punch

Typically, punch is presented in a large bowl to serve many guests. This recipe is for one cocktail. If you prefer, multiply the ingredients by 12 and serve in a punch bowl at your next party. (Tip: fill a large round plastic container with water and freeze for a large round ice cube to keep your punch bowl cold without diluting the punch as quickly as a lot of smaller ice cubes. Larger ice = less surface area = longer melt time.)

  2 ounces **port**
  2 ounces **gin**
  ½ teaspoon **agave syrup**
  2 dashes of **Angostura bitters**
  Club soda
  Lemon twist, for garnish

Shake all the ingredients except the club soda in an ice-filled cocktail shaker and strain into an ice-filled snifter. Top with club soda and garnish with a lemon twist.

Black and Blue

One of my wife's favorite brunch libations is simply a glass of bubbly with a few dashes of Angostura bitters (a Champagne Cocktail without the sugar cube). Since she also likes grapefruit, I tried a variation with Fee Brothers brand grapefruit bitters.

  ½ ounce **blue curaçao**
  3 or 4 dashes of **grapefruit bitters**
  Champagne
  Black raspberries, for garnish

Pour the curaçao and bitters into a champagne flute. Top with Champagne and garnish with black caps (black raspberries).

The Reviver

A hangover cure, but there's a possibility it will merely delay the pain.

  2 ounces **gin**
  1 ounce **St-Germain elderflower liqueur**
  1 ounce **green Chartreuse**
  ½ teaspoon **agave syrup**
  2 or 3 dashes of **Amargo bitters**
  1 **egg white**
  Juice of ½ **lemon**
  Club soda
  Lemon wheel, for garnish

Shake all the ingredients except the club soda in an ice-filled cocktail shaker. Strain into an ice-filled Collins glass. Top with club soda and garnish with a lemon wheel.

Ginger Pimm's Cup

Quintessentially British, Pimm's No. 1 is sort of a Gin Sling in a bottle, typically mixed with 7UP or lemonade and sipped at garden parties.

  3 ounces **Pimm's No. 1**
  6 ounces **diet ginger ale**
  4 or 5 slices peeled **seedless cucumber**, plus
     1 spear for garnish
  Dash of **grapefruit bitters**

Stir all ingredients in an ice-filled cocktail shaker and strain into an ice-filled mug. Garnish with a cucumber spear.

Strawberry Brunch Punch

4 or 5 **strawberries**, plus 1 for garnish
1½ ounces **rum**
1½ ounces **vodka**
Juice of 1 **lime**
2 dashes of **Angostura bitters**
1 **egg white**
¼ ounce **agave syrup**

Muddle 4 or 5 strawberries at the bottom of a cocktail shaker. Add the remaining ingredients and shake well with ice. Strain into a chilled cocktail glass. Garnish with a strawberry.

Bloody Clear Maria

This one takes some time, but it's worth it. It tastes like a gazpacho spin on the classic brunch cocktail.

To begin with, the day before assembling this I made tomato water, which tastes like tomato juice but is clear. First puree a bunch of fresh tomatoes (plums or vine-ripened are fine) in a food processor. Then line the bottom of a fine-mesh strainer with 10 layers of cheesecloth. Place the strainer over a large mixing bowl and pour the tomato puree into the strainer. Place in the fridge overnight until the tomatoes have drained beautiful, clear tomato water into the bowl.

5 to 10 **fresh cilantro leaves**
¼ **fresh jalapeño chile**, seeded
4 or 5 slices peeled **seedless cucumber**
2 ounces **tequila**
2½ ounces **tomato water**
Juice of ½ **lime**
¼ teaspoon **celery salt**
Freshly ground **black pepper**, to taste
Garnish: ½ **jalapeño** (sliced lengthwise),
    1 **cocktail onion**, 1 **pickled jalapeño slice**

Muddle the cilantro, fresh jalapeño, and cucumber at the bottom of a cocktail shaker. Add the remaining ingredients and shake well with ice. Strain into an ice-filled Collins glass. Garnish with the ½ jalapeño, cocktail onion, and pickled jalapeño on a cocktail spear.

Absinthe Minded

2 or 3 **fresh mint leaves**
2 ounces **vodka**
1 ounce **absinthe**
Juice of ½ **lime**
½ ounce **agave syrup**

Muddle the mint at the bottom of a cocktail shaker. Add the remaining ingredients and shake well with ice. Strain into an ice-filled rocks glass.

Cucumber Ginger Mojito

10 **fresh mint leaves**, plus 1 sprig for garnish
3 slices peeled **seedless cucumber**, plus 1 for garnish
3 ounces **rum**
2 ounces **Domaine de Canton ginger liqueur**
Juice of ½ **lime**
Club soda

Muddle the mint and 3 cucumber slices at the bottom of a cocktail shaker. Add the remaining ingredients except the club soda and shake well with ice. Strain into an ice-filled rocks glass. Top with club soda and garnish with fresh mint and a slice of cucumber.

Watermelon Cooler

To make fresh watermelon juice for this possibly most refreshing summer cocktail ever, simply push watermelon slices through a fine-mesh veggie strainer and voilà! You have juice! Use it immediately, as it does not store well.

2 **fresh mint leaves**
1½ ounces **vodka**
1½ ounces fresh **watermelon juice**
¼ teaspoon **agave syrup**
Pinch of **kosher salt**
Pinch of freshly ground **black pepper**
Mint sprig and **watermelon wedge**, for garnish

Muddle the mint at the bottom of a cocktail shaker. Add the remaining ingredients and shake well with ice. Strain into an ice-filled rocks glass. Garnish with a fresh mint sprig and a watermelon wedge.

Green Lantern

3 or 4 fresh **mint leaves**
3 slices peeled **seedless cucumber**
2 ounces **green Chartreuse**
1 ounce **Domaine de Canton ginger liqueur**
Juice of ½ **lime**
1 or 2 dashes of **mint bitters** (I use Fee
   Brothers)
Ginger ale

Muddle the mint and cucumber at the bottom
of a cocktail shaker. Add the remaining ingredients except the ginger ale and shake well with ice.
Strain into an ice-filled copper mug or rocks glass.
Top with ginger ale and stir gently.

Strawberry Lemonade

4 **fresh mint leaves**, plus 1 sprig for garnish
3 to 6 **strawberries** (depending on size)
2 ounces **gin**
1½ ounces **St-Germain elderflower liqueur**
Juice of ½ **Meyer lemon**
¼ ounce **agave syrup**

Muddle the mint and strawberries at the bottom of a cocktail shaker. Add the remaining
ingredients and shake well with ice. Strain into an
ice-filled rocks glass. Garnish with a mint sprig.

Berry Frothy Tini

5 **blackberries**
5 **blueberries**
3 ounces **gin**
Juice of ½ **Meyer lemon**
½ ounce **agave syrup**
1 **egg white**

Muddle the berries at the bottom of a cocktail shaker. Add the remaining ingredients and shake well with ice. Strain into a chilled cocktail glass.

Summer Sun Cooler

4 or 5 **fresh mint leaves**, plus 1 sprig for garnish
2 ounces **yellow Chartreuse**
Juice of ½ **lime**
2 dashes of **grapefruit bitters**
Brut Champagne

Muddle the mint at the bottom of a cocktail shaker. Add the remaining ingredients except the Champagne and shake well with ice. Strain into an ice-filled Collins glass. Top with cold Champagne, stir gently, and garnish with a mint sprig.

Sloe Bubbly

½ ounce **sloe gin**
1 **lemon wedge**
Brut Champagne
Lemon twist, for garnish

Pour the sloe gin into a champagne flute. Squeeze in the juice from the lemon wedge. Top with brut Champagne and garnish with a lemon twist.

Ginger Rail

2 ounces **rum**
1 ounce **Domaine de Canton ginger liqueur**
4 dashes of **lemon bitters** (I use Fee Brothers)
Club soda
Mint sprig and **lemon twist**, for garnish

Shake all the ingredients except the club soda in an ice-filled cocktail shaker and strain into an ice-filled rocks glass. Top with club soda and garnish with a mint sprig and a lemon twist.

Bitter Sun

Like its big brother Campari, Aperol is essentially a bitter orange–based aperitif. It is gentler on the palate than Campari, and with less than half the alcohol, it is refreshing without being overpowering.

1½ ounces **vodka**
1 ounce **Aperol**
1 or 2 dashes of **absinthe**

Stir all the ingredients with ice and strain into a chilled cocktail glass.

Halloween Fizz

Halloween is a big deal in our house, and Rachael goes all out with the creepy-but-fun decorations. I tried to make a cocktail that we could enjoy among the crazy witches, black cats, and jack-o'-lanterns. And what's scarier than green absinthe (made with wormwood, no less)?

1½ ounces **gin**
½ ounce **absinthe**
½ ounce **agave nectar**
1 **egg white**
Club soda

Shake all the ingredients except the club soda in an ice-filled cocktail shaker and strain into a chilled rocks glass. Top with club soda and garnish with something scary.

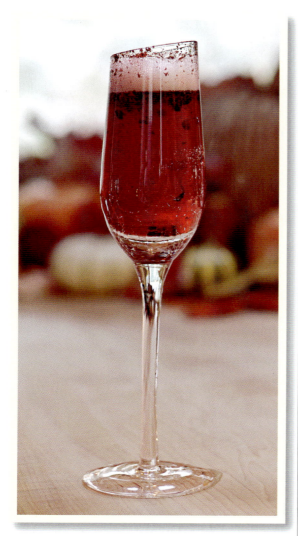

French Cheer

1 **blackberry**
¾ ounce **dry red wine** (a nice French if possible)
Brut Champagne

Gently muddle the blackberry at the bottom of a champagne flute. Add the wine and top with Champagne.

Blackberry Mule

3 **blackberries**
1½ ounces **vodka**
½ ounce **Domaine de Canton ginger liqueur**
Ginger beer
Mint sprig, for garnish

Muddle the blackberries at the bottom of a cocktail shaker. Add the vodka and liqueur and shake well with ice. Strain into an ice-filled copper mug or rocks glass. Top with ginger beer and garnish with a mint sprig.

Winter Cherry

We found some nice-looking cherries at the market this past winter, which I was happy to use as the base for this cocktail. It also features Maraschino liqueur, which is one of my favorite secret ingredients. Not to be confused with those sticky sweet red maraschino cherries, this bittersweet liqueur is made from Marasca cherries (from Croatia and northern Italy) and their pits lend it an almond-like flavor. A little bit adds a haunting, elusive flavor to the right cocktails.

2 **fresh sage leaves**
3 **fresh cherries**, plus 1 for garnish
2 ounces **bourbon**
½ ounce **Maraschino liqueur**
½ ounce **Benedictine**
Juice of ½ **lemon**

Muddle the sage and 3 cherries at the bottom of a cocktail shaker. Add the remaining ingredients and shake well with ice. Strain into a chilled cocktail glass. Garnish with a cherry.

Nod to Nog

I figured out a way to make a lighter and less fattening eggnog—with skim milk instead of heavy cream—but it requires purchasing a milk frother. I already had one lying around the house (I use it for cappuccino). It's called the Aeroccino (made by Nespresso), but probably any handheld wand-type frother would work. By frothing skim milk, you get a creamy, albeit much lighter, feel to the nog.

2 ounces **skim milk**, cold
2½ ounces **dark rum**
1 pinch of ground **cinnamon**
1 pinch of ground **cardamom**
1 whole **egg**
Nutmeg, for garnish

Froth the milk well as if for cappuccino. Shake the remaining ingredients in an ice-filled cocktail shaker and strain into a glass mug. Top with the frothed milk and garnish with freshly grated nutmeg.

Alamagoozlum

Huh? Let me explain . . .

I am obsessed with a book called *Vintage Spirits and Forgotten Cocktails* by Ted Haigh. It features a hundred classic cocktail recipes from the turn of and the early part of the twentieth century, many of which feature lost and rare ingredients that seem to be making a comeback in today's classic cocktail resurgence.

This is my version of the first cocktail in the book, originally created by none other than J. Pierpont Morgan. Please note that this recipe makes 2 or 3 drinks.

2 ounces **gin**
1½ ounces **dark rum**
1½ ounces **yellow Chartreuse**
½ ounce **Grand Marnier**
2 ounces **water**
½ **egg white**
1½ ounces **simple syrup**
½ ounce **Angostura bitters**

Shake all the ingredients in an ice-filled cocktail shaker and strain into 2 or 3 chilled martini glasses.

Corpse Reviver #2

(Adapted from *Drinks of all Kinds* by Harry Craddock, 1895)

Originally devised by the famous barman and author of the 1930 classic tome *The Savoy Cocktail Book*, this was meant to be a morning-after "hair of the dog" cure.

1 ounce **gin**
1 ounce **Grand Marnier**
1 ounce **Lillet blanc**
1 ounce **lemon juice**
3 drops of **absinthe**
Fresh cherry, for garnish

Shake all the ingredients in an ice-filled cocktail shaker and strain into a chilled cocktail glass. Garnish with a cherry.

Cherry Bomb

3 **cherries**
2 ounces **gin**
½ ounce **fresh lime juice**
½ ounce **Maraschino liqueur**
¼ ounce **agave syrup**
Rosé Champagne
Lime twist, for garnish

Muddle the cherries at the bottom of a cocktail shaker. Add the remaining ingredients except the Champagne and shake well with ice. Strain into a chilled cocktail glass. Top with rosé Champagne and garnish with a lime twist.

The First Word

This is adapted from Scott Beattie's version of the classic Prohibition-era cocktail The Last Word in his book, *Artisanal Cocktails*, which is filled with luxurious cocktails from California's wine country.

¾ ounce **yellow Chartreuse**
¾ ounce **vodka**
¾ ounce **Maraschino liqueur**
¾ ounce **fresh lime juice**
Fresh cherry, for garnish

Shake all the ingredients in an ice-filled cocktail shaker and strain into a chilled cocktail glass. Garnish with a cherry.

Bloody Johnny Bar

Bloody Marys are especially fun to make for a group if you create a "bloody station" in your kitchen. Prep a pitcher of bloody mix beforehand (mine is spicy and has a secret ingredient—citrus zest), put out a bottle of vodka, some garnishes, glasses, a bucket of ice, and a bar spoon, and your guests can mix their drinks to taste.

 48-ounce bottle of **Spicy Hot V8 vegetable juice**
 Grated zest and juice of 1 **lemon**
 Grated zest and juice of 1 **lime**
 2 tablespoons **prepared horseradish** (more or less to taste)
 13 (or more) dashes of **Tabasco sauce**
 2 ounces **Worcestershire sauce**
 1 teaspoon **celery salt**
 1 teaspoon freshly ground **black pepper**

Combine all the ingredients in a sealable pitcher or container. Shake well and chill.

To make one cocktail, combine 1½ ounces vodka and bloody mix in an ice-filled Collins glass. Stir and garnish with any or all of the following: celery rib, olives, lemon and lime wedges, pickled veggies, fresh cilantro sprigs, etc. Go crazy . . .

The Panettone

So named because it tastes like panettone, a sweet Italian loaf of bread eaten around the holidays (and great for French toast).

 1½ ounces **vodka**
 ½ ounce **Grand Marnier**
 ½ ounce **orgeat syrup**
 Brut Champagne
 Orange twist, for garnish

Shake all the ingredients except the Champagne in an ice-filled cocktail shaker and strain into a champagne flute. Top with Champagne and garnish with a flamed orange twist.

BB Sour

This is an adaptation of the classic Whiskey Sour so nicely presented in *Vintage Cocktails* by Brian Van Flandern. Instead of plain whiskey, I use Hudson Baby bourbon whiskey from New York State's own Tuthilltown Spirits (they also make a mean corn whiskey).

1½ ounces **Hudson Baby bourbon whiskey**
½ ounce **simple syrup**
Juice of 1 **lemon**
Orange wheel and **fresh cherries**, for garnish

Shake all the ingredients with ice and strain into an ice-filled rocks glass. Garnish with an orange wheel and cherries.

Blood Orange Margarita

Popular in Sicily, blood oranges are grown in this country in winter months and are sweet, with red flesh dark enough to stain your countertops (which is why I cut them on a washable cutting board).

2 ounces **tequila blanco**
1 ounce **Grand Marnier**
½ ounce **fresh lime juice**
1 ounce fresh **blood orange juice**

Shake all the ingredients in an ice-filled cocktail shaker and strain into an ice-filled rocks glass or chilled cocktail glass.

Blood Orange Negroni

It's winter . . . so we have a lot of blood oranges around the house. I used them in this classic Italian cocktail.

1½ ounces **gin**
1½ ounces **Campari**
½ teaspoon **sweet vermouth**
2 **blood orange** wedges
Club soda
Lemon twist, for garnish

Combine the gin, Campari, and vermouth in an ice-filled rocks glass. Squeeze and drop the orange wedges into the glass. Top with club soda, garnish with a lemon twist, and stir gently.

Blood Orange Kiss

½ ounce **gin**
½ ounce **dry vermouth**
½ ounce **Lillet blanc**
½ ounce fresh **blood orange juice**
2 teaspoons **Grand Marnier**
1 teaspoon **orange bitters**
Blood orange twist, for garnish

Shake all the ingredients in an ice-filled cocktail shaker and strain into a chilled cocktail glass. Garnish with a blood orange twist.

Whiskey Rickey

1½ ounces **rye whiskey**
½ ounce **green Chartreuse**
½ ounce **fresh lime juice**
¼ ounce **agave syrup**
Lime twist, for garnish

Shake all the ingredients in an ice-filled cocktail shaker and strain into an ice-filled rocks glass. Garnish with a lime twist.

Bittersweet Screwdriver

1½ ounces **vodka**
½ ounce **Grand Marnier**
3 dashes of **orange bitters**
2 ounces fresh **blood orange juice**
Blood orange wheel, for garnish

Shake all the ingredients in an ice-filled cocktail shaker and strain into an ice-filled Collins glass. Garnish with a blood orange wheel and serve with a straw.

Blackberry Margarita

My wife and I both love Margaritas—she says I make the best. For a plain Margarita I often use St-Germain elderflower liqueur in lieu of orange curaçao or Grand Marnier—there is something about it that pairs perfectly with equal parts tequila and lime, and it adds not too much sweetness and no syrupiness. I like my Margaritas tart and refreshing. Adding blackberries works great, too, and adds deep color.

Black sea salt
3 **blackberries**
¾ ounce **fresh lime juice**
1 ounce **St-Germain elderflower liqueur**
2 ounces **tequila blanco**

Rim a rocks glass with black sea salt. Muddle the blackberries at the bottom of a cocktail shaker. Add the remaining ingredients and shake well with ice. Strain into the salt-rimmed rocks glass, filled with ice.

Smokehouse Margarita

Mezcal is like tequila, but smoky. I like to pair it with the smokiness of ancho chiles in my home-made rim salt.

JC's Ancho Rim Salt Supremo (recipe follows)
2 ounces **mezcal**
1 ounce fresh **lime juice**
1 ounce orange **curaçao**

Rim a rocks glass with the ancho rim salt. Shake all the ingredients in an ice-filled cocktail shaker and strain into the rimmed rocks glass, filled with ice.

JC'S ANCHO RIM SALT SUPREMO

2 tablespoons **ancho chile powder**
2 teaspoons **light brown sugar**
½ teaspoon ground **cinnamon**
1 teaspoon **kosher salt**

Stir all the ingredients well and spread out on a saucer big enough to rim the rocks glass on.

Sherry/Cherry Cocktail

1½ ounces **rum**
1 ounce **dry sherry**
½ ounce **fresh lemon juice**
½ teaspoon **agave syrup**
5 dashes of **cherry bitters** (I use Fee Brothers)

Shake all the ingredients in an ice-filled cocktail shaker and strain into a cocktail glass or coupe.

Grapefruit Margarita

Pink sea salt
2 ounces **tequila blanco**
1 ounce **Grand Marnier**
½ ounce **fresh lime juice**
1 ounce **fresh grapefruit juice**

Rim a rocks glass with sea salt. Shake all the ingredients in an ice-filled cocktail shaker and strain into the rimmed rocks glass, filled with ice.

The Whiskey Rose

My wife bought me a small barrel of clear corn whiskey from upstate New York. It's funny how this stuff used to be made in people's backyards and called moonshine, and now it's well on its way to becoming a top-shelf product. In any event, it is delicious (it tastes sort of like an un-aged rye whiskey). As far as rosewater goes (available in many supermarkets and online), a little goes a long way—use too much and your cocktail will taste like a bar of soap.

1 **sugar cube**
Dash of **rosewater**
1 ounce **clear corn whiskey**
Rosé Champagne

Combine the sugar, rosewater, and whiskey in a champagne flute and top with rosé Champagne.

Spiced Apple

2 ounces **Calvados**
1 ounce **green Chartreuse**
¼ teaspoon **agave syrup**
Club soda

Shake all the ingredients except the club soda in an ice-filled cocktail shaker and strain into an ice-filled Collins glass. Top with club soda.

Saratoga Sling

1 ounce **dark rum**
1 ounce **light rum**
½ ounce **Kirschwasser**
½ ounce **orgeat syrup**
1 ounce **fresh lime juice**
1 ounce **pineapple juice**
Dash of **grenadine**
Lime wheel, for garnish

Shake all the ingredients in an ice-filled cocktail shaker and strain into an ice-filled Collins glass. Garnish with a lime wheel.

Catcher in the Rye

1½ ounces **rye whiskey**
1 ounce **yellow Chartreuse**
1 ounce **fresh lime juice**
Dash of **agave syrup**
Lime twist, for garnish

Shake all the ingredients in an ice-filled cocktail shaker and strain into a chilled cocktail glass. Garnish with a flamed lime twist.

Rome-a-Tini

1½ ounces **gin**
¼ ounce **Aperol**
¼ ounce **dry vermouth**
3 dashes of **orange bitters**
2 dashes of **Angostura bitters**
Lemon twist, for garnish

Shake all the ingredients in an ice-filled cocktail shaker and strain into a chilled cocktail glass. Garnish with a lemon twist.

Buenos Aires Fixer

My wife and I had the pleasure of visiting Argentina. Buenos Aires is a European and cosmopolitan city, with parts at once familiar if you live in New York City, and with wide boulevards reminiscent of Paris or Barcelona. Hang your veganism at the door—when you are there you will eat steak, steak, and more steak. And then some other grilled meats, all washed down with full-bodied delicious reds (malbec is a big grape there). All that powerful food needs a powerful digestif, and Fernet Branca is strong medicine. They consume it quite a bit in Argentina and usually combine it with Coca-Cola.

> 1 **orange wedge**
> 1 **lemon wedge**
> 1 **lime wedge**
> ½ ounce **agave syrup**
> 1½ ounces **Fernet Branca**
> **Club soda**

Squeeze and drop the orange, lemon, and lime into a rocks glass. Add the agave syrup and Fernet Branca. Fill with ice and top with club soda.

Caipir-Maria-nha

My sister-in-law, Maria, loves Champagne and loves caipirinhas. That made coming up with this cocktail easy—I simply combined the two!

> 1 **lime**, cut into wedges
> 1 teaspoon **superfine sugar**
> 1½ ounces **cachaça**
> **Champagne**

Muddle the lime wedges and sugar at the bottom of a rocks glass. Add ice to fill the glass. Add cachaça and stir well. Top with Champagne and stir gently.

Espresso Soda (Nonalcoholic)

For a boozy version, add 1½ ounces Kahlúa.

> 1 shot of **espresso**
> 1 ounce **simple syrup**
> 1½ ounces **half-and-half**
> **Club soda**

Combine all the ingredients in a Collins glass and fill with ice. Top with club soda and stir gently. Serve with a straw.

A Bronx Tail

(Adapted from *Vintage Spirits and Forgotten Cocktails* by Ted Haigh)

> 1½ ounces **gin**
> ¾ ounce **sweet vermouth**
> ¾ ounce **dry vermouth**
> Juice of ¼ **blood orange**
> 2 dashes of **Angostura bitters**
> **Blood orange twist**, for garnish

Shake all the ingredients in an ice-filled cocktail shaker and strain into a chilled cocktail glass. Garnish with a blood orange twist.

Elderflower Smash

Near our NYC home is the beautiful Gramercy Park Hotel. It's been there for years and recently underwent a massive renovation. The hotel is quiet, homey, and dog-friendly, and has wonderful room service, including artisanal cocktails.

Last year Rachael and I were flying back from a busy weekend in Chicago, promoting her line of tabletop items (plates, bowls, etc.). Our flight back to New York was delayed, and when we finally landed it was late at night, our nerves were frayed, and we were exhausted. We arrived home only to find that our building's hot water heater had broken and as a result, all of the water was shut off until the next day. Arrrgh!

Luckily, we had not yet unpacked, so we simply grabbed Isaboo, spun around on our heels, and rolled right out of there and over to the GPH, where we relaxed, watched in-room movies, and ordered several rounds of the cocktail I have adapted below.

4 or 5 fresh **mint leaves**, plus 1 sprig for garnish
2 ounces **gin**
1½ ounces **St-Germain elderflower liqueur**
Juice of ½ **lemon**
3 big dashes of **Angostura bitters**

Shake all the ingredients in an ice-filled cocktail shaker and strain into a rocks glass filled with crushed ice. Garnish with a mint sprig.

Thai Fizzy

3 **Thai basil leaves**
1 slice **fresh chile**
1½ ounces **vodka**
Juice of ½ **lemon**
½ teaspoon **agave syrup**
Club soda

Shake all the ingredients except the club soda in an ice-filled cocktail shaker. Strain into an ice-filled Collins glass. Top with club soda.

Spring Spritz

½ **orange**
½ **tangelo** or **tangerine**
1 ounce **vodka**
1 ounce **Lillet blanc**
Club soda

Squeeze and drop the fruits directly into a Collins glass. Add the vodka and Lillet, fill with ice, and top with club soda. Stir gently and serve with a straw.

Almond Rum Rickey

1½ ounces **dark rum**
Juice of 1 **lime**
½ ounce **orgeat syrup**
2 or 3 pinches of freshly grated **nutmeg**
Club soda
Mint sprig, for garnish

Shake all the ingredients except the club soda in an ice-filled cocktail shaker. Strain into an ice-filled Collins glass. Top with club soda and garnish with a mint sprig.

Negroni Spritzer

1½ ounces **gin**
1 ounce **Campari**
Juice of ½ **blood orange**
2 dashes of **sweet vermouth**
2 dashes of **Angostura bitters**
Club soda
Lemon twist, for garnish

Shake all the ingredients except the club soda in an ice-filled cocktail shaker. Strain into an ice-filled Collins glass. Top with club soda and garnish with a lemon twist.

New Orleans Smash

4 or 5 fresh **mint leaves**
2 ounces **gin**
1½ ounces **St-Germain elderflower liqueur**
Juice of ½ **lime**
3 dashes of **Peychaud's bitters**
Lime wheel, for garnish

Muddle the mint at the bottom of a cocktail shaker. Add the remaining ingredients and shake well with ice. Strain into a rocks glass filled with crushed ice. Garnish with a lime wheel.

Cocktail demonstration.

Chartreuse & Ginger

1 sprig fresh **rosemary**, plus 1 sprig for garnish
2 ounces **vodka**
1 ounce **green Chartreuse**
Juice of ½ **lime**
Fresh Ginger Ginger Ale (unfiltered; from Bruce Cost)

Muddle 1 sprig rosemary at the bottom of a cocktail shaker. Add all the remaining ingredients except the ginger ale and shake well with ice. Strain into an ice-filled Collins glass. Top with ginger ale and garnish with a rosemary sprig.

The "Jules"

3 or 4 **blackberries**, plus more for garnish
2 ounces **Armagnac**
1 ounce **green Chartreuse**
Juice of 1 **lemon**

Muddle 3 or 4 berries at the bottom of a cocktail shaker. Add the remaining ingredients and shake well with ice. Strain into an ice-filled rocks glass. Garnish with additional blackberries.

Thyme for a Cocktail

2 sprigs **thyme**
2 ounces **gin**
Juice of ½ **Meyer lemon**
½ ounce **agave syrup**
Club soda
Edible flowers, for garnish

Muddle the thyme at the bottom of a cocktail shaker. Add the remaining ingredients except the club soda and shake well with ice. Strain into an ice-filled Collins glass. Top with club soda and garnish with an edible flower.

Spiced Blackberry Sour

4 **blackberries**
1 ounce **vodka**
1 ounce **spiced dark rum**
1 ounce **fresh lime juice**
Grated zest of ½ **lemon**
1 **egg white**
½ ounce **simple syrup**
2 dashes of **Angostura bitters**
Edible flowers, for garnish

Muddle the blackberries at the bottom of a cocktail shaker. Add the remaining ingredients and shake well with ice. Strain into a chilled cocktail glass. Garnish with an edible flower.

Sage Whiskey Sour

Orange wedge
Bourbon-smoked sugar
2 or 3 **fresh sage leaves**
2 ounces **rye whiskey**
½ ounce **simple syrup**
1½ ounces **fresh lemon juice**
Orange slice, for garnish

Rub the rim of a chilled cocktail glass with an orange wedge and coat rim with bourbon-smoked sugar. Muddle the sage leaves at the bottom of a cocktail shaker. Add the remaining ingredients and shake well with ice. Strain into the rimmed cocktail glass. Garnish with a thin orange slice.

Primavera Cooler

Basil makes this refreshing and verdant libation taste like spring in the Italian countryside.

3 **fresh mint leaves**
2 **fresh basil leaves**
3 slices peeled **seedless cucumber**
1½ ounces **gin**
½ ounce **green Chartreuse**
½ ounce **fresh lemon juice**
½ ounce **fresh lime juice**
¼ ounce **agave syrup**
Club soda
Rosemary sprig, for garnish

Muddle the mint, basil, and cucumber at the bottom of a cocktail shaker. Add the remaining ingredients except the club soda and shake well with ice. Strain into an ice-filled Collins glass. Top with club soda and garnish with a rosemary sprig.

Pepper Berry

10 **arugula leaves**
3 or 4 **strawberries**
2 ounces **gin**
1½ ounces **St-Germain elderflower liqueur**
Pinch of freshly ground **pepper**
Juice of ½ **lemon**
¼ ounce **agave syrup**

Muddle the arugula well at the bottom of a cocktail shaker. Add the strawberries and muddle also. Add the remaining ingredients and shake well with ice. Strain into an ice-filled rocks glass.

Boozeberry Soda

5 **fresh mint leaves**, plus 1 sprig for garnish
1 **fresh basil leaf**
5 **blackberries**
2 ounces **gin**
1½ ounces **St-Germain elderflower liqueur**
½ ounce **agave syrup**
½ ounce **fresh lemon juice**
Seltzer

Muddle the mint, basil, and berries at the bottom of a cocktail shaker. Add the remaining ingredients except the seltzer and shake well with *no ice*. Strain into an ice-filled Collins glass. Top with seltzer, stir gently, and garnish with mint sprig.

Champagne Bouquet

Our buddy Rob, who owns Adirondack Wine Merchants in Queensbury, New York, insisted I try Esprit de June liqueur. It is made from a bouquet of different vine flowers, and is delicate and summery.

1 ounce **Esprit de June liqueur**
Champagne
Edible flowers, for garnish

Pour the Esprit de June into a champagne flute. Top with Champagne and garnish with edible flowers.

Lake George Iced Tea

Rachael and I have a little roundabout boat that we take on Lake George during the (typically short) summers upstate. I prepare a few of these drinks beforehand for sipping on the water.

1½ ounces **vodka**
1 ounce **dark-brewed unsweetened tea**, cooled
Juice of ¼ **lemon**
¼ ounce **agave syrup**
Lemon wheel, for garnish

Shake all the ingredients in an ice-filled cocktail shaker and strain into an ice-filled Collins glass. Garnish with a lemon wheel.

Morning Glory Fizz

(Adapted from Hugo Ensslin, who wrote *Recipes for Mixed Drinks*)

Scotch for breakfast? I'm in!

1½ ounces **Scotch**
Juice of ½ **lemon**
Juice of ½ **lime**
½ ounce **simple syrup**
¼ teaspoon **absinthe**
1 **egg white**
Club soda

Shake all the ingredients except the club soda in an ice-filled cocktail shaker and strain into a chilled Collins class. Top with club soda and stir gently.

The Eyepatch

2 ounces **rum**
½ ounce **pineapple gum syrup**
2 or 3 dashes of **lemon bitters**
Club soda

Shake the rum, pineapple gum syrup, and bitters in an ice-filled cocktail shaker and strain into an ice-filled rocks glass. Top with club soda.

Bittersweet Symphony

1½ ounces **vodka**
1 ounce **Lillet blanc**
½ ounce **simple syrup**
¼ teaspoon **sweet vermouth**
Dash of **absinthe**
Juice of ½ **lime**
3 dashes of **orange bitters**
Edible flowers, for garnish

Shake all the ingredients in an ice-filled cocktail shaker and strain into a chilled cocktail glass. Garnish with an edible flower.

Basil Fizz

3 or 4 **fresh basil leaves**
1 ounce **gin**
1 ounce **sloe gin**
Juice of ½ **lemon**
¾ ounce **agave syrup**
2 dashes of **plum bitters** (I use Fee Brothers)
Club soda
Lemon wedge and a **fresh cherry**, for garnish

Muddle the basil at the bottom of a cocktail shaker. Add the remaining ingredients except the club soda and shake well with ice. Strain into an ice-filled Collins glass. Top with club soda and garnish with a lemon wedge and a cherry.

Elderflower-Blackberry Foam

This recipe isn't technically a drink in itself, but rather a cocktail foam. Dispense it as you would whipped cream and it can be a great garnish to other cocktails. For starters, try it as a topping to a glass of Champagne.

8 to 10 **blackberries**, mashed through a fine-mesh sieve
4 **egg whites**
6 ounces **St-Germain elderflower liqueur**
2 ounces **water**

Place all the ingredients in a whipped cream dispenser. Charge the dispenser with two canisters and then refrigerate the entire dispenser for at least 2 hours until chilled. Shake well before dispensing.

The Purple Plum

2 fresh **mint leaves**
2 small **red plums**, quartered and pitted
2 ounces **vodka**
1 ounce **blue curaçao**
Juice of ½ **lemon**
Edible flowers, for garnish

Muddle the mint and then the plums at the bottom of a cocktail shaker. Add the remaining ingredients and shake well with ice. Strain into an ice-filled rocks glass. Garnish with edible flowers.

Plum Lucky

1 **fresh basil leaf**, plus finely shredded basil for garnish
2 small **red plums**, quartered and pitted, plus 1 plum slice for garnish
2 ounces **vodka**
1½ ounces **St-Germain elderflower liqueur**
Juice of ¼ **lemon**
¼ ounce **agave syrup**

Muddle the basil leaf and then the plums at the bottom of a cocktail shaker. Add the remaining ingredients and shake well with ice. Strain into an ice-filled rocks glass. Garnish with the shredded basil and a plum slice.

TOKYO PLUM LUCKY: Substitute shiso leaves for the basil and 1 ounce dry sake and 1 ounce soshiku (a Korean distilled beverage with a flavor similar to vodka) for the vodka.

Cherry Ginger Sling

3 **fresh cherries**
1 ounce **gin**
½ ounce **Kirschwasser**
1 ounce **yellow Chartreuse**
Juice of ½ **lemon**
½ ounce **agave syrup**
Ginger beer
Lime wheel, for garnish

Muddle the cherries at the bottom of a cocktail shaker. Add the remaining ingredients except the ginger beer and shake well with ice. Strain into an ice-filled Collins glass. Top with ginger beer and garnish with a lime wheel.

The Lower East Side

2 **fresh cherries**, plus 1 for garnish
1½ ounces **blended Scotch**
1½ ounces **Benedictine**
3 dashes of **Angostura bitters**

Muddle 2 cherries at the bottom of a cocktail shaker. Add the remaining ingredients and shake well with ice. Strain into a chilled cocktail glass and garnish with a cherry.

Gin Tiki

1 fresh **mint leaf**
Pinch of grated **fresh ginger**
2 ounces **gin**
1½ ounces **St-Germain elderflower liqueur**
1 ounce **pineapple juice**
Juice of ½ **lime**
Juice of ¼ **lemon**
¼ ounce **grenadine**
Fresh cherry and **lime wheel**, for garnish

Muddle the mint and ginger at the bottom of a cocktail shaker. Add the remaining ingredients and shake well with ice. Strain into a Collins glass filled with crushed ice. Garnish with a cherry and a lime wheel.

Italian Champer Spritzer

Leaves stripped from 1 sprig **rosemary**
1 or 2 **orange wedges**
2 ounces **gin**
1 ounce **Grand Marnier**
1 ounce **Campari**
3 dashes of **grapefruit bitters**
½ ounce **agave syrup**
Champagne
Orange twist, for garnish

Muddle the rosemary leaves and orange wedges at the bottom of a cocktail shaker. Add the remaining ingredients except the Champagne and shake well with ice. Strain into an ice-filled Collins glass. Top with Champagne, stir gently, garnish with a flaming orange twist, and serve with a straw.

The "Boop"

1 **orange wedge**
1½ ounces **gin**
½ ounce **honey liqueur**
Juice of ½ **lemon**
2 or 3 dashes of **grapefruit bitters**
Dash of **grenadine**

Muddle the orange at the bottom of a cocktail shaker. Add the remaining ingredients and shake well with ice. Strain into a chilled martini glass and slowly pour a dash of grenadine on top to garnish.

Sweet Aviator

2½ ounces **gin**
½ ounce **Maraschino liqueur**
Juice of 1 small **lemon**
Lemon twist and a dash of **grenadine**, for garnish

Shake all the ingredients in an ice-filled cocktail shaker and strain into a chilled cocktail glass. Garnish with a lemon twist and slowly pour a dash of grenadine on top for another garnish.

7½ Heaven

2 ounces **vodka**
½ ounce **Maraschino liqueur**
2 ounces **fresh grapefruit juice**
½ ounce **agave syrup**
Mint sprig, for garnish

Shake all the ingredients in an ice-filled cocktail shaker and strain into a chilled cocktail glass. Garnish with a mint sprig.

Klausner's Old-Fashioned

My buddy Dave Klausner loves bourbon. Naturally he makes a mean Old-Fashioned and did so at my house. He recommends using Woodford Reserve. I only had Knob Creek and neither of us minded.

1 **orange wedge**
Dash of **Angostura bitters**
½ teaspoon **superfine sugar**
Bourbon
Fresh cherry, for garnish

Muddle the orange wedge, bitters, and sugar at the bottom of a rocks glass. Fill the glass with ice, add bourbon to fill, and stir. Garnish with a cherry.

Berry Birthday

2 **blackberries**
5 **blueberries**
2 ounces **vodka**
½ ounce **blue curaçao**
Juice of ¼ **lemon**
Juice of ¼ **lime**
1 or 2 dashes of **grapefruit bitters**
¼ ounce **agave syrup**
1 **egg white**
Purple basil leaf, for garnish

Muddle the berries at the bottom of a cocktail shaker. Add the remaining ingredients and shake well with ice. Strain into a chilled cocktail glass. Garnish with a purple basil leaf.

The T.C.

Our friend Tommy (aka T.C.) likes this drink because it has Scotch in it. We drink it after a round of golf.

1½ ounces **Scotch**
½ ounce **Maraschino liqueur**
1 ounce **fresh lemon juice**
3 dashes of **Peychaud's bitters**
¼ ounce **agave syrup**
Lime twist, for garnish

Shake all the ingredients in an ice-filled cocktail shaker and strain into a chilled cocktail glass. Garnish with a flamed lime twist.

Maple Bacon Sazerac

I make my own bacon-infused rye whiskey, which I use in this cocktail. To infuse the rye, first pour a bottle of it into a glass container. Cook up some smoky bacon and reserve 2 ounces of the bacon fat. Strain the fat directly into the rye and let it stand and infuse overnight at room temperature. (Add in two slices of the cooked bacon, too, for extra smoky flavor.) Remove the bacon (if added) and freeze the container until the fat collects at the top and can be easily removed. Then strain the rye back into its original bottle (which you should clearly mark "bacon-infused").

1½ ounces **bacon-infused rye**
2 dashes of **Peychaud's bitters**
2 dashes of **Angostura bitters**
2 dashes of **absinthe**
¼ teaspoon **maple syrup**
Lemon twist, for garnish

Shake all the ingredients in an ice-filled cocktail shaker and strain into a rocks glass. Serve neat, garnished with a lemon twist.

Warm Skater's Toddy

This makes more whipped cream than you need for just 1 drink, but it's hard to whip less than ½ cup—and no doubt you'll be making more than one of these toddies!

½ cup **heavy cream**
¼ teaspoon **maple syrup**
¼ teaspoon **vanilla extract**
1½ ounces **dark rum**
3 ounces **boiling water**
Pinch of freshly grated **nutmeg**, plus more for garnish
Pinch of ground **cinnamon**
Pinch of ground **allspice**
¼ teaspoon **brown sugar**

Whip the cream in a cold bowl until stiff peaks form. Stir in the maple syrup and vanilla.

Combine the remaining ingredients in a heat-proof mug. Add the whipped cream mixture and stir until blended. Garnish with grated nutmeg.

Spiced Rum Daiquiri

1½ ounces **spiced dark rum**
Juice of 1 **lime**
½ ounce **simple syrup**
Lime wheel, for garnish

Shake all the ingredients in an ice-filled cocktail shaker and strain into an ice-filled rocks glass. Garnish with a lime wheel.

What's That Wasser?

1 ounce **vodka**
½ ounce **Kirschwasser**
½ ounce **honey liqueur**
½ ounce fresh **lime juice**
Lime twist, for garnish

Shake all the ingredients in an ice-filled cocktail shaker and strain into a small cocktail glass. Garnish with a lime twist.

The Ellis Island

Sort of like a Manhattan, this cocktail works just as well (albeit differently) with clear corn whiskey in place of rye. Carpano Antica is hands down the best red vermouth ever. Oh, *man*, it makes a cocktail good!

1½ ounces **rye whiskey**
¼ ounce **simple syrup**
½ ounce **Carpano Antica red vermouth**
3 dashes of **orange bitters**
Fresh cherry, for garnish

Shake all the ingredients in an ice-filled cocktail shaker and strain into a chilled cocktail glass. Garnish with a cherry.

Ginger Slip

There are several good-quality ginger simple syrups on the market, made by small companies in single batches. Or you can make your own by adding about an inch or two of thinly sliced fresh ginger to 1 cup water and 1 cup sugar, then boiling to dissolve the sugar. Let cool, then strain out the ginger and store the syrup in the fridge.

5 **fresh mint leaves**
4 **lime slices**
½ ounce **ginger simple syrup**
1½ ounces **vodka**
Juice of ½ **lemon**
Club soda

Muddle the mint and lime at the bottom of a Collins glass. Add all the remaining ingredients except the club soda, fill the glass with ice, stir well, and top with club soda. Serve with a straw.

Popcorn Ball

1 ounce **corn whiskey**
½ ounce **Grand Marnier**
7 dashes of **orange bitters**
7 dashes of **Angostura bitters**
Champagne
Lime twist, for garnish

Pour all the ingredients except the Champagne into a champagne coupe and stir. Top with Champagne and garnish with a lime twist.

Harvest Sparkler

1 sprig **thyme**
⅛ teaspoon grated **fresh ginger**
¼ **apple**, chopped
2½ ounces **Calvados**
Juice of ¼ **lemon**
¼ ounce **agave syrup**
Sparkling hard cider
Apple slice rubbed with **lemon juice** and
    sprinkled with **cinnamon**, for garnish

Muddle the thyme, ginger, and apple at the bottom of a cocktail shaker. Add the remaining ingredients except the cider and shake well with ice. Strain into an ice-filled Collins glass. Top with cider, stir gently, and garnish with the apple slice.

The Houston

Audrey Saunders owns an amazing back-in-the-day cocktail lounge, the Pegu Club, on Houston Street in downtown NYC. If I owned a cocktail lounge, I'd want it to be just like her place (I have the same wall covering as her club in my apartment). The Pegu Club itself is a classic cocktail and you can get a great one at Audrey's club. I swapped out lime for Meyer lemon in my version.

1½ ounces **gin**
½ ounce **Grand Marnier**
¾ ounce **Meyer lemon juice**
2 dashes of **Angostura bitters**

Shake all the ingredients in an ice-filled cocktail shaker and strain into a chilled cocktail glass.

Mulled Hot Cider

    6 ounces **cloudy apple cider**
    1 or 2 pinches of grated **lemon zest**
    2 **cinnamon sticks**
    1 or 2 whole **cloves**
    1 or 2 pinches of freshly grated **nutmeg**
    1 ounce **Calvados**

In a small saucepan, combine the cider, zest, 1 of the cinnamon sticks, the cloves, and nutmeg and simmer for about 10 minutes. Do not boil. Pour the Calvados into a heatproof mug and strain in the hot cider mix. Garnish with a cinnamon stick.

Lime Basil Martini

    2 **lime basil leaves**
    2 ounces **vodka**
    2 ounces **Lillet blanc**
    2 ounces **fresh lime juice**
    ½ teaspoon **superfine sugar**
    Lime twist, for garnish

Muddle the lime basil at the bottom of a cocktail shaker. Add the remaining ingredients and shake well with ice. Strain into a chilled cocktail glass. Garnish with flamed lime twist.

Grapefruit Negroni

    2 ounces **vodka**
    2 ounces **Aperol**
    ½ ounce **sweet vermouth**
    Juice of ½ **lime**
    Juice ¼ **grapefruit**
    ½ ounce **Rose's lime juice**
    2 dashes of **grapefruit bitters**
    Club soda
    Grapefruit wedges and **lime twist**, for garnish

Shake all the ingredients except the club soda in an ice-filled cocktail shaker and strain into an ice-filled rocks glass. Top with club soda and garnish with grapefruit wedges and a lime twist.

The Spicy Pineapple

1 sprig **cilantro**
2 ounces **Hangar 1 chipotle vodka**
1 ounce **fresh lime juice**
1 ounce **pineapple juice** or 1 ounce **pineapple gum syrup**
Fresh chile slice, for garnish

Muddle the cilantro at the bottom of a cocktail shaker. Add the remaining ingredients and shake well with ice. Strain into a chilled cocktail glass. Garnish with a slice of fresh chile.

The Grecian

3 slices peeled **seedless cucumber**
A palmful of coarsely chopped **fresh dill**, plus sprigs for garnish
2 ounces **vodka**
1 ounce **ouzo**
¼ ounce **agave syrup**
Juice of 1 **lime**

Muddle the cucumber and dill at the bottom of a cocktail shaker. Add the remaining ingredients and shake well with ice. Strain into an ice-filled rocks glass. Garnish with additional fresh dill sprigs.

Raspberry Beret

2 **raspberries**
1 ounce **St-Germain elderflower liqueur**
1 squeeze of **fresh lemon juice**
Rosé Champagne
Edible flowers, for garnish

Muddle the raspberries at the bottom of a cocktail shaker. Add the St-German and lemon juice, stir well, and pour into the bottom of a champagne flute. Top with chilled rosé Champagne and garnish with edible flowers.

Marina

2 ounces **gin**
1 ounce **Carpano Antica red vermouth**
Juice of ½ **lemon**
½ ounce **simple syrup**
Orange twist, for garnish

Shake all the ingredients in an ice-filled cocktail shaker and strain into a chilled cocktail glass. Garnish with an orange twist.

Ginger Swizzle

Alchemia makes a nice vodka infused with fresh ginger. If you can't find Alchemia, you can make your own by putting a 2-inch piece of fresh ginger, thinly sliced, into a bottle of vodka and letting it infuse for a few days.

3 **fresh sage leaves**
4 slices peeled **seedless cucumber**
1½ ounces **Alchemia ginger vodka**
½ ounce **green Chartreuse**
1 teaspoon **agave syrup**

Muddle the sage and cucumber at the bottom of a cocktail shaker. Add the remaining ingredients and shake well with ice. Strain into a rocks glass filled with crushed ice.

Manny's Cobbler

4 **blackberries**, plus 1 for garnish
2 ounces **bourbon**
½ ounce **Maraschino liqueur**
Juice of ½ **lemon**
½ ounce **simple syrup**

Muddle 4 blackberries at the bottom of a cocktail shaker. Add the remaining ingredients and shake well with ice. Strain into a rocks glass filled with crushed ice. Garnish with a blackberry.

Undertow

This is based on a cocktail my wife had at Maison Premiere in Brooklyn, New York, a turn-of-the-twentieth-century bar with artisanal cocktails and a fresh raw bar, and that's it. She had their version with oysters on the half shell and reported back to me, and I adapted as follows:

2 ounces **gin**
½ ounce **fresh lemon juice**
½ ounce **fresh lime juice**
1 ounce **Honey-Vanilla Simple Syrup** (recipe follows)
A few grinds of **sea salt**

Shake all ingredients well with ice and strain into an ice-filled rocks glass.

Honey-Vanilla Simple Syrup: In a small saucepan, simmer 1 cup water and 1 cup honey with 1 split and scraped vanilla bean until the honey is dissolved. Let cool, strain, and store in the refrigerator.

Pomegranate Margarita

Our friend Mary's parents own a farm in California. Fall and winter produce beautiful, juicy (and countertop-staining) pomegranates. Work on a washable rubber board in or near a sink when cutting open a pomegranate.

1½ ounces **tequila blanco**
½ ounce **orange curaçao**
1 ounce **fresh pomegranate juice**
½ ounce **fresh lime juice**
Pomegranate seeds, for garnish

Shake all the ingredients in an ice-filled cocktail shaker and strain into an ice-filled rocks glass. Garnish with pomegranate seeds.

Hibiscus Margarita

Wild hibiscus flowers in syrup are available at wildhibiscus.com, or you can make your own version by steeping wild hibiscus flowers in simple syrup. Either way, it's a dark red color, and the candied whole flowers make an impressive statement in a cocktail.

2 ounces **tequila blanco**
2 ounces **fresh lime juice**
1 ounce **hibiscus syrup**
Hibiscus flower from the syrup, for garnish

Shake all the ingredients in an ice-filled cocktail shaker and strain into an ice-filled rocks glass or into a chilled cocktail glass. Garnish with a hibiscus flower.

Gunga Din

A palmful of **fresh cilantro leaves**
2 ounces **vodka**
1 ounce **ginger simple syrup** (see page 43 for how to make)
Juice of 1 **lime**
Seltzer
Fresh chile slices, for garnish

Muddle the cilantro at the bottom of a cocktail shaker. Add the remaining ingredients except the seltzer and shake well with ice. Strain into an ice-filled Collins glass. Top with seltzer and garnish with up to 5 slices of fresh chile (seeds, too), depending on how hot you can take it.

Quince Sling

2 ounces **dry gin**
1 ounce **quince liqueur**
Club soda
Lemon twist, for garnish

Shake the gin and liqueur in an ice-filled cocktail shaker and strain into an ice-filled rocks glass. Top with club soda and garnish with a lemon twist.

Ford Cocktail

(From *Vintage Spirits and Forgotten Cocktails* by Ted Haigh)

1 ounce **gin**
1 ounce **dry vermouth**
3 dashes of **Benedictine**
3 dashes of **orange bitters**
Orange twist, for garnish

Shake all the ingredients in an ice-filled cocktail shaker and strain into a chilled cocktail glass. Garnish with an orange twist.

Christmas Cheer

About 5 **fresh grapes** or 1 ounce **grape juice**
2 ounces **vodka**
1 ounce **fresh lemon juice**
¼ ounce **agave syrup**
1 **egg white**
Rosemary sprig, for garnish

Muddle the grapes at the bottom of a cocktail shaker (if using). Add the remaining ingredients and shake well. Strain into a chilled cocktail glass and garnish with a rosemary sprig.

Pomegranate Martini

1½ ounces **vodka**
¾ ounce **fresh lemon juice**
½ ounce **simple syrup**
½ ounce **fresh pomegranate juice**
Pomegranate seeds, for garnish

Shake all the ingredients in an ice-filled cocktail shaker and strain into a chilled cocktail glass. Garnish with pomegranate seeds.

Bronx with Bittermens

Another back-in-the-day cocktail, the Bronx is rarely seen on cocktail menus these days. According to Ted Haigh, a Bronx with Bitters is also known as the Income Tax Cocktail. I used Bittermens Orange Cream Citrate (a sweet-tart extract) to add a hint of a Creamsicle flavor.

1½ ounces **dry gin** (I used Plymouth)
¾ ounce **dry vermouth**
¾ ounce **sweet vermouth**
Juice of ¼ **orange**
2 dashes of **Angostura bitters**
2 dashes of **Bittermens Orange Cream Citrate**
Orange slice, for garnish

Shake all the ingredients in an ice-filled cocktail shaker and strain into a cocktail glass. Garnish with an orange slice.

The Double Secret Probation

(Adapted from the Secret Cocktail recipe in *Vintage Spirits and Forgotten Cocktails* by Ted Haigh)

1½ ounces **gin**
½ ounce **Calvados**
Juice of ½ **lemon**
1 **egg white**
½ ounce good-quality **grenadine**

Shake all the ingredients in an ice-filled cocktail shaker and strain into a cocktail glass.

Chocolate Margarita

1½ ounces **blanco** or **silver tequila**
1½ ounces **Kahlúa**
1½ ounces **heavy cream**
2 dashes **Bittermens Xocolatl Mole bitters**

Shake all the ingredients in an ice-filled cocktail shaker and strain into an ice-filled rocks glass.

Pickled Ramp Martini

Early spring means ramps are in season and we buy and cook with a lot of them. I figured since an olive is basically pickled in brine, as is a cocktail onion, why not make a martini with a pickled ramp? Of course I first had to ask my wife to pickle some ramps for me, which she did (see below). Hint: Pickled ramps make a great garnish for a Bloody Mary, too.

Dry vermouth
4 ounces **dry gin**
Splash of **ramp pickling brine**
Pickled ramp, for garnish (recipe follows)

Fill a cocktail shaker with ice. Add a dash of dry vermouth, enough to coat the ice. Add the gin and splash of brine and shake well. Strain into a chilled cocktail glass. Garnish with a pickled ramp.

PICKLED RAMPS

You'll need enough ramps to fill, loosely packed, an 8-ounce resealable container. The container also needs to be heatproof because you'll be pouring hot brine into it.

Ramps, trimmed of roots and leaves, white tops and tender shoots only
1 handful of **fresh dill**
2 sprigs **thyme**
2 **fresh bay leaves**
¼ **fresh chile**, finely chopped
½ cup **white balsamic vinegar**
1 tablespoon **sugar**
1 teaspoon **kosher salt**

Place the ramps, dill, thyme, bay leaves, and chile in an 8-ounce heatproof container. In a small saucepan, combine the vinegar, ¼ cup water, the sugar, and salt and bring to a boil. Pour the boiling brine over the ramps. Let cool, then cover and refrigerate at least overnight.

The Midmorning Nap

Absinthe
1½ ounces **brandy**
Juice of ½ **lemon**
½ ounce **simple syrup**
3 dashes of **Angostura bitters**
Prosecco

Coat the inside of a champagne flute with absinthe. Shake the brandy, lemon juice, simple syrup, and bitters in an ice-filled cocktail shaker. Strain into the flute. Top with prosecco.

acknowledgments

Thanks to Judith Curr and Johanna Castillo and the great team at Atria Books. Thank you for sorting through my poorly organized and gargantuan file of photography. Thanks to Andrew Kaplan for reviewing the manuscript. A thank-you to my parents for imparting to me the genetic disposition to enjoy a good cocktail. And last but not least, thanks to the prettiest girl on two legs and the prettiest girl on four legs, Rachael and Isaboo, without whom this book would not even be a blog.

index

MY YEAR IN MEALS

ALSO BY RACHAEL RAY

The Book of Burger

MY YEAR IN MEALS

RACHAEL RAY

FOOD PHOTOGRAPHY BY
RACHAEL RAY AND JOHN CUSIMANO

ATRIA BOOKS

NEW YORK   LONDON   TORONTO   SYDNEY   NEW DELHI

ATRIA BOOKS

A Division of Simon & Schuster, Inc.
1230 Avenue of the Americas
New York, NY 10020

Photographs of Rachael on pages 46, 106, 158 © Melanie Dunea/CPi
Photographs of Rachael and John on pages 53 and 181 © Timothy White
Photograph on page 117 courtesy of The Ridge Terrace Restaurant, Lake George, N.Y.
Photographs of Rachael on page 132 © Jim Wright
Photograph of Rachael on page 273 © John Kernick

First Atria Books hardcover edition November 2012

ATRIA BOOKS and colophon are trademarks of Simon & Schuster, Inc.

For information about special discounts for bulk purchases,
please contact Simon & Schuster Special Sales at
1-866-506-1949 or business@simonandschuster.com.

The Simon & Schuster Speakers Bureau can bring authors
to your live event. For more information or to book an event,
contact the Simon & Schuster Speakers Bureau at
1-866-248-3049 or visit our website at www.simonspeakers.com.

Designed by Elizabeth Van Itallie

Manufactured in the United States of America

10   9   8   7   6   5   4   3   2   1

Library of Congress Cataloging-in-Publication Data

Ray, Rachael.
My year in meals / by Rachael Ray.
    p. cm.
1. Cooking. I. Title.
TX714.R385   2012
641.5—dc23   2012028785

ISBN: 978-1-4516-5972-6
ISBN: 978-1-4516-5974-0 (ebook)

**My Year in Meals:
An Atria Smart Book.**
Rachael talks about her new cookbook.

You will find tags like the ones below throughout this book. You can use them to access enhanced digital content. To do so, simply download the free app at gettag.mobi. Then hold your phone's camera a few inches away from the tag and enjoy what comes next. You can also visit pages.simonandschuster.com/MyYearinMealsTags to access this content.

If you access content through a mobile device, message and data rates may apply.

Choosing seasonal ingredients.
(Page 25) Rachael talks about gardening and shopping at your local farmers' markets.

Experience Rachael's Italy.
(Page 156) Rachael shares her passion for Italy.

Celebrate the season with Rachael and John. (Page 179) Rachael and John share holiday traditions and reveal their favorite season.

Rachael shares her seasonal favorites.
(Page 212) Rachael shares stories about some of the dishes in the book.

Rachael's tips on entertaining.
(Page 254) Rachael shares tips on what to serve and what to bring to a party.

John's bar basics.
(Page 1) John gives a crash course on basic bar equipment and utensils used throughout this section.

Cocktail techniques.
(Page 2) John demonstrates some basic techniques used in making cocktails.

Cocktail demonstration.
(Page 30) John demonstrates making some of the cocktails from the book.

Scan here for bonus recipes.
(On jacket flap) View bonus recipes as Rachael continues her *Year in Meals*.

Scan here for bonus recipes.
(On jacket flap) View bonus recipes as John continues his *Year in Cocktails*.

contents

guac top?
giardeniera?
pico?

SSG burgers w/ pickled fennel
and pepperonata relish
on garlic butter Rolls (ciabatta)
o + v garlic sweet peppers
tomato

White Bean & Tuna Salad + Potato
garlic minced or grated white onion, tuna
RWV, parsley EVOO - hot potatoes, use
celery + leaves fine chop 5.5.52

vegetable risotto
EVOO   fine
              1 ca
en baby   1 on
eas
2 cups   2 pinch
water & saffron
to use all)

9/10 Put
Raenb
Shred.
Shallo!
fenn
top

1/4 C
melt

magnifica shallot garlic
& orange zest
white wine

PEPPER HASH BROWN
a potatoes w/ oil
EVOO 2T Pepper
Pepper sliced frozen
chopped 1 red onion
45 call corn garnish
eggo Aracana
+ Parsley 1/4 C
PROVOLONE garnish
tend foil
can speck 2oz
or use plate to ba
scrape - 4
ry red onion 1/2
1 cup packed
d shredded 4
ggs s+p Butter

nerves of steel coffee ice cream
2 min 3T inst espresso 1 c
1/2 c superfine sugar milk
on low add 2 c cream 1 tsp van
transfer to mixer add
chopped coffee beans pinch
cinnamon · choc covered espresso
bean add 3T chopped butter
choc! Pickles for 4th
Slaw - 1 small red + 1 onion
celery salt · pepper, 3T each
Red wine vinegar + oil

1/2 C balsamic white
1 C water 1/4 C sugar 2T
6 kirby pickles Salt
1 onion 2 chilies 3-4
must pop coriander bay
3-4 stems dill 1 tsp each
4 cloves garlic
2 sweet yellow 2 fresno
1 sweet red long 3-4 stems parsley
1 c cider 1/2 c water 1/3 sug 2 bay
1T salt

habed
Baby
Yukon
Gold

Bfast Sandwiches
ciabatta
hot oil giardeniera w/ parsley
pepper   fried egg w (24/
    uncured bacon (Colema
        tomatoes
        arugula

3/12 PM Ck Shallot Spaghetti

out of town 3/15 - 19
    lemon
    Poppy seed egg tagliatelle
    Lamb w/ Tomato Jam (D

n's wine picks.

        thinly
        sliced
3/24 Lamb left over bon
        w/
    Tomato Jam
1/2 head Radicchio 1/4 small red
    all thin sliced
    1/2 lemon
        24/7 Seasone
            or s+p
        1T EVOO or to
Jam, Lamb,   toss
    Seau on Amos toast

3/24 PICI - 1/2 c fava bean
dinner   1/2 c parsley 1/2
        1/4 c tarragon
1/3 c parm or 1 lemon juice
    pecorino   About 1/3 c EVOO

introduction

My Year in Meals is our food and drink diary. This is the most meaningful book that I have written to date, because it involves my personal life with my family and friends. I've been coming into your homes for years, and now you get to come into mine and see what I put down on my own kitchen table for the people I love.

The idea for a food diary came about one day when John and I were at our home in upstate New York with a good friend of ours, Andrew Kaplan (we call him Kappy). I was cooking dinner for everyone when Kappy suggested that I share what I cook for John and myself with our readers and viewers; many people assume that with all the filming and cooking I do for my job, I would be too tired to cook at home. That definitely could not be further from the truth. It's on the longest, hardest days that I most look forward to coming home and cooking with John, regardless of how late it is. It's our quiet time to enjoy together, no matter how late dinner may be served.

Since childhood, I've had this habit of keeping a notebook and a Sharpie by my side so that when an idea comes to me, I can put it down on paper and look it over the next day and apply it to one of my dishes. The great thing is, I'm always cooking in my head; whether I'm in the middle of something or just sitting and relaxing, my mind is constantly thinking up new ideas for dishes.

My Year in Meals:
An Atria Smart Book.

Even if I'm waiting in line at the airport or shopping at a farmers' market, I can visualize myself using different ingredients, see the pots and pans going and the fire flaming, and can smell the makings of a delicious meal. So keeping a food diary and jotting down everything I cooked for us over the course of an entire year was really an organic process, and before I knew it, I had a stack of notebooks on my bedside table that I couldn't wait to share with all of you. You can see some of the pages of those notebooks opposite.

John and I drink wine with dinner, but my love for food is rivaled by his love of crafting cocktails. John is a weekend mixologist, and while I'm cooking, he spends time concocting new variations of classic drinks. John has included excellent guidelines, such as which tools to have on hand and how to use fresh ingredients to liven up any simple cocktail. There are more than one hundred cocktail recipes in this book, and when you flip over *My Year in Meals,* you'll get *My Year in Cocktails*—it's like getting two books for the price of one.

There are more than five hundred recipes in this book. A handful are not structured recipes; they're meant to give you inspiration and to help your imagination run wild so you can go off and create your own dishes. You'll know them when you see them; they're written on what look like recipe cards.

All the photos in this book were taken by us, no professional photographer, no food stylists. We hope you love this book as much as we do.

—Rachael and John

APRIL

FRIDAY/1

DINNER
Sicilian sauce, homemade spinach garganelli

SATURDAY/2

SUNDAY/3

BREAKFAST
dandelion greens with eggs & potatoes

MONDAY/4

DINNER
ultimate Italian pulled pork sammies, Isaboo's homemade dog food

TUESDAY/5

MONDAY/11

DINNER
Italian tabbouleh, Italian potato cake with roast sausages & crispy kale

TUESDAY/12

DINNER
carbonara Milanese-style with ramps

WEDNESDAY/13

DINNER
peperonata for grilled fish

THURSDAY/14

FRIDAY/15

DINNER
ultimate Italian pulled pork sammies, chocolate cupcakes with bacon–cream cheese frosting

THURSDAY/21

LUNCH
grilled cheese with spinach, calzone-style
DINNER
Mexican fish fry, oil and vinegar slaw, tartar sauce

FRIDAY/22

BREAKFAST
ramp and Robiola frittata
DINNER
Easter meat loaf with 8-minute eggs, feta-walnut dip, green pastitsio

SATURDAY/23

BREAKFAST
whole-grain spiced waffles, baked eggs in leek nests, baked bacon
DINNER
ramp pasta with garlic butter bread crumbs, sesame dressing

SUNDAY/24

EASTER DINNER
asparagus with shallot vinaigrette, arugula and heirloom tomato salad, caponata, arti-chokes with chile-mint dressing, saffron rice with Marcona almonds, slow-smoked chicken, bull's-eye deviled eggs

MONDAY/25

LUNCH
grilled cheese with spinach, calzone-style
DINNER
linguine puttanesca

WEDNESDAY/6

DINNER
Moroccan chicken, couscous

THURSDAY/7

FRIDAY/8

DINNER
pasta with bacon, ramps & ricotta

SATURDAY/9

DINNER
steaks with French onions, sour cream onion rings, creamed spinach

SUNDAY/10

BREAKFAST
smoky huevos rancheros

DINNER
intense mushroom-barley salad, braised artichokes, bacon-wrapped chicken

SATURDAY/16

BRUNCH
croque madame

DINNER
chicken vindaloo, hot curry spice blend

SUNDAY/17

DINNER
braised artichokes, penne alla Norma with fennel & Fresno chile

MONDAY/18

BREAKFAST
rolled omelets with cheese and asparagus

DINNER
spring risotto, Caesar salad with kale

TUESDAY/19

BREAKFAST
multigrain pecan waffles with berries

WEDNESDAY/20

BREAKFAST
BLT with eggs and Cheddar cheese on toast

DINNER
country-style chicken livers

TUESDAY/26

DINNER
Mexican-style fried chicken, saffron rice pilaf, lemon-garlic guacamole, pico de gallo, black beans with queso fresco, jalapeño poppers

WEDNESDAY/27

THURSDAY/28

DINNER
chicken saltimbocca with tagliatelle

FRIDAY/29

DEVILED EGGS
Caesar-stuffed eggs
deviled ham & eggs
green olive deviled eggs
bull's-eye deviled eggs

SATURDAY/30

I made a **Sicilian Sauce** and served it over **Homemade Spinach Garganelli**. This sauce can also be made way ahead and frozen. Freeze flat in a gallon-size plastic food storage bag or small sandwich-size bags for smaller servings.

Sicilian Sauce

¼ cup **EVOO**
6 to 8 **anchovy fillets**
1 **red Fresno chile** or Italian red cherry pepper, seeded and finely chopped
6 cloves **garlic**, finely chopped
2 tablespoons chopped fresh **oregano**
2 tablespoons **tomato paste**
1 cup **red wine**
1 (28- or 32-ounce) can **San Marzano tomatoes** (look for DOP on the label)
8 to 10 torn fresh **basil leaves**

In a large skillet, heat the EVOO (4 turns of the pan) over medium heat. Add the anchovies, cover the pan with a splatter screen or lid, and shake until the anchovies begin to break up. Reduce the heat a bit, uncover, and stir until the anchovies melt into the oil. Add the chile, garlic, and oregano. Cook for 2 to 3 minutes.

Add the tomato paste and let it cook out for a minute before deglazing the pan with the red wine. Add the tomatoes and basil. Simmer until thick, about 30 minutes.

Makes about 3 cups

Homemade Spinach Garganelli

You can freeze this pasta or you can cook it fresh in salted boiling water, in which case it takes only a couple of minutes to cook through. They just float like gnocchi when they're done and they don't taste gummy anymore. They are delicious! We love them, and we make them often— sometimes with butter and cheese or a light herby pesto or, as on this night, a simple Sicilian-style tomato sauce.

1 (10-ounce) box **frozen chopped organic spinach**, thawed and wrung completely dry in a clean kitchen towel
12 ounces **ricotta**, preferably sheep's milk, drained of excess liquid
Freshly grated **nutmeg**
Salt and **pepper**
1½ tablespoons **EVOO**
1 large **egg yolk**
1½ cups all-purpose **flour**
1 cup **semolina flour**, plus more dusting

Place the spinach in a food processor and pulse-chop it even further into little itty-bitty bits. Add the ricotta to the food processer with a little dusting of nutmeg, salt, and pepper. Drizzle in the EVOO (1½ turns of the bowl) and add the egg yolk. Add the all-purpose flour and semolina flour and process until combined. Remove the dough from the processor and knead it lightly,

then cover with a kitchen towel and let it relax for about 30 minutes.

Roll the ball of dough out into a long, oval piece, a couple of feet long and ¼ to ½ inch thick. Cut into thin ropes about ¼ inch wide. Cut the ropes with a sharp paring knife into little 1¼- to 1½-inch pieces. If you have the little wooden paddle (see Tip), use it to shape the garganelli. Or you could roll the dough into a similar shape by hand—it just won't have any ridges.

Dust a big baking sheet with a little semolina flour. Once the pasta is rolled, you throw it onto the semolina-dusted baking sheet. Then it's ready to cook (or freeze for later).

Serves 4

To make garganelli, you need a little wooden paddle with grooves cut into it. You can roll them by hand, but they won't have the little ridges. Garganelli are similar in shape to cavatelli, which you could substitute here.

🔵 APRIL 2/LUNCH

We (me and my friends Charlie, Kim, and Spike) went to Maison Premiere, an oyster bar in Williamsburg, Brooklyn, where I had a delicious cocktail with gin and sea salt and vanilla. John tried to re-create that cocktail for me; it's called the Undertow (check it out on *Cocktails* page 48).

🔵 APRIL 2/DINNER

We went to Motorino and had ramp pizza.

🔵 APRIL 3/BREAKFAST

Dandelion Greens with Eggs & Potatoes

John and I do this dish a ton. It's a Sunday brunch kind of a thing.

3 tablespoons **EVOO**
8 flat **anchovy fillets**
4 baby **Yukon Gold potatoes**, very thinly sliced (like potato chips)
¼ cup chopped **flat-leaf parsley**
4 cloves **garlic**, finely chopped
¼ teaspoon crushed **red pepper flakes**
Black pepper
1 bunch **dandelion greens**, stems discarded and leaves chopped
Freshly grated **nutmeg**
2 tablespoons **butter**
8 large **eggs**

In a medium skillet, heat the EVOO (3 turns of the pan) over medium-low heat until hot. Add the anchovies, cover the pan with a splatter screen or lid, and shake until the anchovies begin to break up. Reduce the heat a bit, uncover, and stir until the anchovies melt into the oil, about 2 minutes.

Add the potatoes, parsley, garlic, and red pepper flakes and spread evenly in the pan; season with black pepper. Cook, turning, until the potatoes are golden, about 10 minutes. Fold in the dandelion greens, season with nutmeg, and cook over low heat, turning a few times, until softened, 7 to 8 minutes.

In a large nonstick skillet, melt 1 tablespoon of the butter over medium-low heat. Crack in 4 of the eggs, season with black pepper, flip, and cook to desired doneness, 3 to 7 minutes. Repeat with the remaining 1 tablespoon butter and 4 eggs. Serve with the potatoes and greens.

Serves 4

We made **Ultimate Italian Pulled Pork Sammies** for dinner. While I was up, I also made a batch of **homemade dog food** for Isaboo.

Ultimate Italian Pulled Pork Sammies

The pulled pork makes enough for 8 sandwiches plus great leftovers.

13 fresh **long red chiles**
6 **frying peppers** (cubanelles) or red bell peppers or a mix of both
6 pounds boneless **pork butt** (shoulder)
Juice of 1 **lemon**
¼ cup **EVOO**, plus some for drizzling
1 head **garlic**, cloves cracked from skins
6 fresh **bay leaves**
4 sprigs fresh **rosemary**, leaves stripped
2 tablespoons **thyme leaves**
A handful of **flat-leaf parsley**
Salt and **pepper**
1 large **onion**, very thinly sliced
1 cup **dry white wine**
2 cups **chicken stock**
1 (28-ounce) can **San Marzano tomatoe**s (look for DOP on the label)
2 bundles **broccoli rabe**, trimmed
8 large Italian **sub-style rolls** or ciabatta bread cut for 8 sub-size sandwiches
4 cups shredded **sharp provolone cheese** or 24 deli-cut slices provolone

Preheat the broiler to high.

Arrange 12 of the chiles and all of the frying peppers on a baking sheet and char evenly all over—keep the oven door slightly ajar to allow steam to escape. Place the charred peppers in a bowl and cover. When cool enough to handle, peel, seed, and slice.

Turn off the broiler and preheat the oven to 325°F.

Butterfly the pork shoulder open and flatten it out. Place the lemon juice and about ¼ cup EVOO in a food processor. Coarsely chop the remaining red chile and add it to the processor with the garlic, bay leaves, rosemary, thyme, and parsley. Pulse-chop into a thick, pesto-like sauce.

Season the meat with salt and pepper and slather with the sauce. Roll the meat up and secure it tightly with kitchen twine. Drizzle the meat with EVOO to coat and season liberally with salt and pepper. Heat a large Dutch oven over medium-high heat and brown the meat all over.

Remove the roast; add the onion and wine to the pot and stir to deglaze. Add the stock and set the meat back in the pan. Pour the tomatoes over the top of the meat and lightly crush them with your hands, arranging the tomatoes over the meat. Cover the pan and roast for 2 hours.

Switch on the broiler, uncover the pan, and broil to brown the tomatoes a bit. Remove from the oven and let rest for 30 minutes.

Shred the pork, place it in a dish, then strain or mill the braising liquid and pour it over the top.

While the meat rests, bring a few inches of water to a boil. Salt the water and parboil the broccoli rabe 3 to 4 minutes. Plunge into ice-cold water to stop the cooking and drain well.

When ready to make the sammies, warm the pulled pork through. Split the rolls and cover with cheese; broil to melt. Top the cheese with the rabe and peppers, then cover that with hot juicy pork and serve.

Serves 8

APRIL 6, 2011/ DINNER

Dinner was **Moroccan Chicken**, a stew that I served with **Couscous.**

Moroccan Chicken

I always use skin-on, bone-in chicken here: thighs, drummers, and breasts. I cut the breasts into quarters so all the pieces are the same shape and size as the thighs and the drumsticks.

12 to 16 pieces **chicken**
Salt and **pepper**
3 tablespoons **EVOO**
4 tablespoons (½ stick) **butter**
2 large **onions**, cut into wedges
3 Meyer **lemons** or small organic lemons, un-peeled, cut into ¼- to ½-inch-thick slices
A handful of fresh **bay leaves**
A couple of handfuls of buttery **green olives**
1 tablespoon ground **coriander**
1 tablespoon ground **cumin**
1 tablespoon ground **ginger**
2 teaspoons **turmeric**
1 teaspoon **smoked black pepper** or smoked paprika
½ teaspoon ground **cinnamon**
Pinch of **saffron threads**
Pinch of ground **cardamom**
¼ cup **flour**
4 cups **chicken stock**

Season the chicken with salt and pepper to taste. In a large Dutch oven or heavy-bottomed skillet, heat the EVOO (3 turns of the pan) over medium-high heat. Working in batches, add the chicken and brown all over, transferring to a plate as it's cooked.

Add the butter to the pan and when the butter foams, add the onions, lemons, bay leaves, and olives; stir and season with salt and pepper. Sprinkle in the coriander, cumin, ginger, turmeric, smoked black pepper, cinnamon, saffron, and cardamom. Stir that until it's very fragrant. Sprinkle in the flour and stir to cook out the flour. Whisk in the stock, slide the chicken back in, and simmer until the chicken is cooked through, 8 to 10 minutes.

Serves 4

Couscous

1½ cups **chicken stock**
2 tablespoons **butter**
1½ cups **couscous**
1 cup mixed chopped **fresh mint** and **flat-leaf parsley**
1 cup **Marcona almonds** (see Tip), toasted and coarsely chopped

In a medium saucepan, bring the stock and butter to a boil. Stir in the couscous, cover, turn off the heat, and let stand for 5 minutes. Fluff the couscous with a fork and stir in the mint, parsley, and almonds.

Serves 4

You could use ½ cup toasted slivered almonds instead of the Marcona almonds.

APRIL 8, DINNER

Pasta with bacon, ramps & ricotta: Cook 1/2 pound bacon in a drizzle of EVOO. Pour off all but 2 tablespoons of the fat. Reduce the heat; add ramp whites and/or garlic and a little finely chopped Fresno chile; stir 2 minutes. Meanwhile, cook some pasta. Add a little starchy pasta cooking water to the sauce; toss with the ramp tops, about 1 cup fresh sheep's milk ricotta cheese, freshly grated pecorino, and chopped parsley. Mix that together and serve.

🕐 APRIL 9/DINNER

We had **Steaks with French Onions** (garnished with **Sour Cream Onion Rings**), sliced tomatoes, and **Creamed Spinach.**

Steaks with French Onions

4 tablespoons (½ stick) **butter**
2 large **onions**, very thinly sliced
1 fresh **bay leaf**
⅛ teaspoon ground **thyme**
Salt and **pepper**
2 tablespoons **flour**
¼ cup **dry sherry** or white wine
1 (10.5-ounce) can **beef consommé**
4 **steaks** (hanger, strip, or flat iron—your choice) brought to room temp
EVOO
4 slices **white bread**, lightly toasted and cut in half diagonally

In a large skillet, heat the butter over medium-low heat. Add the onions, bay leaf, thyme, and salt and pepper to taste. Cook, stirring occasionally, to caramel in color and very soft, 40 to 45 minutes.

Sprinkle the caramelized onions with the flour and cook 1 minute, then stir in the sherry and deglaze the pan. Add the beef consommé and simmer gently 5 minutes until a very thick sauce forms.

Meanwhile, heat a cast-iron skillet or griddle over medium-high heat. Pat the steaks very dry, drizzle the pan with EVOO, and rub over the surface of the pan with a paper towel. Add the steaks and cook 4 minutes on each side (for 1-inch-thick meat) for a pink center. Season the steaks with salt and pepper.

Place 2 toast points on each dinner plate. Top the steaks with the onion sauce.

Serves 4

Sour Cream Onion Rings

Vegetable oil or canola oil, for deep-frying
½ cup sour cream
1½ cups buttermilk
¼ cup finely chopped chives
Salt and pepper
1½ cups flour, for dredging
1 medium-large yellow onion, cut into ¾- to
   1-inch-thick rings

Fill a countertop fryer with oil or pour 2 inches of oil into a large Dutch oven. Heat the oil to 350°F. (The oil is ready when a 1-inch cube of white bread cooks to golden brown in 40 seconds.)

Whisk together the sour cream and buttermilk. Stir in the chives and salt and pepper to taste. Pour the flour into a shallow dish and season it with salt and pepper as well. Double-coat the onion rings: first in buttermilk, then flour, then repeat.

Frying a few rings at a time, fry the rings to crispy and golden.

Serves 4

Creamed Spinach

2 tablespoons butter
1 tablespoon EVOO
1 large shallot, finely chopped
3 or 4 cloves garlic, finely chopped
1 or 2 scallions, finely chopped
¼ cup dry sherry
1 cup heavy cream
Freshly grated nutmeg
Salt and pepper
1 (6.5-ounce) package Boursin cheese,
   4 ounces soft goat cheese, or 4 to 5 ounces
   Gorgonzola dolce cheese
3 large bunches spinach, stemmed and
   chopped (see Tip)

In a large skillet, melt the butter in the EVOO. Add the shallot, garlic, and scallions and stir for a couple of minutes. Add the sherry and stir another minute. Add the cream and nutmeg, salt, and pepper to taste. Cook at a low bubble until reduced by about one-third, about 5 minutes.

Stir in the cheese until melted. Add the spinach and wilt. Cover and let cook over medium-low heat, stirring occasionally, about 5 minutes.

Serves 4

If you want to substitute frozen spinach, buy 2 boxes (10 ounces each) organic chopped spinach. Defrost them completely, wring out the spinach in a kitchen towel, then separate it with your fingers when you add it to the cheese sauce.

🕐 **APRIL 10/BREAKFAST**

Smoky Huevos Rancheros

4 **corn tortillas**
EVOO for brushing and drizzling
Salt and **pepper**
½ small **onion**, finely chopped
2 cloves **garlic**, finely chopped
1 tablespoon pureed **chipotle in adobo**
1 (14.5-ounce) can petite **diced tomatoes with chiles**
1 (8-ounce) can **tomato sauce**
1 **bay leaf**
1 small **cinnamon stick**
⅓ pound fresh **chorizo**
1 (15-ounce) can **black beans**, rinsed and drained
½ teaspoon ground **cumin**
4 extra-large **eggs**
Juice of 1 **lime**
1 **avocado**, sliced
1 cup shredded **Chihuahua cheese**
1 cup crumbled **queso fresco** or shredded mild cheese of your choice
A small handful of **cilantro leaves**

Preheat the oven to 400°F. Brush the tortillas with EVOO and season with a pinch of salt. Arrange the tortillas on a rack over a baking sheet. Bake to crispy and golden, 10 to 12 minutes.

Meanwhile, in a food processor, combine the onion, garlic, chipotle, diced tomatoes, and tomato sauce and process until smooth. Pour the pureed sauce into a medium saucepan and add the bay leaf, cinnamon stick, salt, and pepper. Bring to a bubble, then reduce to a simmer and cook about 20 minutes. Remove the bay leaf and cinnamon stick.

Add a drizzle of EVOO to a medium skillet and heat over medium-high heat. Add the chorizo and brown. Add the beans and cumin and reduce the heat to low.

Add a drizzle of EVOO to a nonstick skillet. Add 4 eggs and cook to order (sunny side up, over easy, or fried).

Squeeze the lime juice over the avocado.

To serve, place a tortilla on a plate and top with some Chihuahua cheese and black beans. Pour the red sauce over the beans in a thin, even layer and top with some crumbled queso fresco. Top that with an egg. Arrange the avocado around the dish, sprinkle with cilantro and more queso fresco, and serve.

Serves 4

🕐 **APRIL 10/DINNER**

We had **Bacon-Wrapped Chicken, Intense Mushroom-Barley Salad,** and **braised artichokes.**

Bacon-Wrapped Chicken

1 **chicken**, cut into 8 pieces (reserve the wings
for other use such as stock) and skinned
4 cloves **garlic**, minced
1 fresh **chile**, such as Fresno chile, finely
chopped
About 2 tablespoons very finely chopped **rosemary**
About 2 tablespoons finely chopped **thyme**
Sea salt and coarsely ground **pepper**
About ¼ cup **EVOO**
8 fresh **bay leaves**
6 thin slices good-quality **bacon**

Place the chicken in a dish with the garlic, chile,
rosemary, and thyme. Season lightly with sea salt
and more heavily with pepper. Drizzle the EVOO
over the chicken, then toss to evenly coat the chicken
pieces with the herbs and garlic. Use right away or
cover and marinate in the fridge up to overnight.

Preheat the oven to 375°F. Arrange a wire rack
over a baking sheet.

Place a bay leaf on top of each piece of chicken,
using small leaves for the legs. Wrap a bacon slice
around each piece of chicken so that the flesh is
partially exposed and the bay leaves peek out
from under the bacon.

Arrange the chicken on the rack. Bake until the
bacon is crisp and the chicken cooked through,
about 45 minutes.

Serves 4

Intense Mushroom-Barley Salad

3 cups chicken or vegetable **stock**
A handful of **dried porcini mushrooms** (about
1 ounce)
1 cup **pearled barley**
3 tablespoons **EVOO**, plus more for drizzling
¾ pound mixed fresh **mushrooms**, sliced
2 cloves **garlic**, chopped
1 to 2 tablespoons thinly sliced or chopped
fresh **sage**
Salt and **pepper**
A splash of **dry sherry** or Marsala
½ cup chopped **flat-leaf parsley**
¼ cup finely chopped **chives**
¼ cup **pine nuts**, toasted
Juice of 1 **lemon**

In a small saucepan, bring 1 cup of the stock
to a boil. Place the porcini in a heatproof bowl,
pour the boiling stock over them, and steep for 20
minutes to soften. Reserving the soaking liquid,
drain and chop the porcini.

Transfer the strained porcini soaking liquid to
a saucepan, add the remaining 2 cups stock, and
bring to a simmer. Add the barley, bring to a boil,
reduce the heat to medium-low, and simmer until
tender and the liquid is absorbed, 30 to 40 minutes. Transfer the barley to a serving dish.

In a large skillet, heat the 3 tablespoons EVOO.
Add the fresh mushrooms and cook until lightly
browned. Add the garlic, sage, and salt and pepper to taste. Add the sherry to deglaze the pan.
Then dump the mushrooms onto the barley.

Add the parsley, chives, pine nuts, lemon juice,
a drizzle of EVOO, and salt and pepper to taste.
Toss everything together.

Serves 4

I braised artichokes with fresh bay leaf, lemon, and fennel seed. I chilled them and then dressed them with more lemon juice, mint, and parsley or basil.

⏰ **APRIL 11/ DINNER**

Dinner was **Italian Potato Cake with Roast Sausages & Crispy Kale,** and a grain side that was sort of an Italian version of **tabbouleh**. John poured a Tenuta delle Terre Nere Etna Rosso, 2007.

Italian Potato Cake with Roast Sausages & Crispy Kale

⅓ cup **EVOO**, plus more for drizzling
2 large cloves **garlic**, smashed
1 **red Fresno chile** or Italian red cherry pepper, halved
2½ pounds **Yukon Gold potatoes**, cut into ⅛-inch-thick slices
Sea salt and **pepper**
3 tablespoons chopped fresh **rosemary**
2 teaspoons **fennel seeds**
½ cup freshly grated **Parmigiano-Reggiano** cheese

2 pounds fresh **spicy lamb**, **pork**, or **chicken sausages**
1 large bunch or 2 small bunches **lacinato kale** (also called black, Tuscan, or dinosaur kale), stemmed and coarsely chopped
Freshly grated **nutmeg**

Preheat the oven to 425°F.

In a small saucepan, heat the EVOO, garlic, and chile over medium heat for 2 to 3 minutes to infuse the oil.

Place the potatoes in a bowl and season with sea salt. Add the infused oil (discarding the garlic and chile), rosemary, fennel, and Parm and toss to coat evenly. Arrange the potatoes in a layered pattern from the center of a 10-inch skillet outward and up the sides; gently pile in the remaining potatoes and press down.

Place the skillet over medium-high heat and cook for 10 minutes to get the potatoes on the bottom layer, as well as the pan itself, nice and hot. Cover with parchment paper, set a pie plate on top, fill with beans or pie weights, transfer to oven, and bake 20 minutes.

Remove the weights and parchment and return to the oven and bake until deep golden on top, 15 to 20 minutes. Remove from the oven (but leave the oven on). Set the potatoes aside to cool to room temp.

When the potatoes are just about ready to come out of the oven, bring a skillet full of water to a boil, add the sausages, and cook to heat through. Drain, coat the sausages with a drizzle of EVOO

and arrange on a wire rack set over a baking sheet.

In a large bowl, toss the kale with a light drizzle of EVOO and season with sea salt, pepper, and a hint of nutmeg. Place the sausages and kale in the oven and roast until both are crispy, 10 to 12 minutes.

Place a plate over the top of the cooled potato cake, flip, and unmold. Cut the potato cake into wedges and serve with sausages and kale.

Serves 4

Italian Tabbouleh

You can also make this with farro, which you should cook according to package directions.

> 1 cup **bulgur** (or cracked wheat)
> 1 cup **boiling water**
> ½ cup chopped fresh **basil**
> ½ cup chopped fresh **mint**
> ½ cup chopped **flat-leaf parsley**
> Juice of 2 **lemons**
> ¼ cup **EVOO**
> 3 **plum tomatoes**, seeded and chopped
> ½ **red onion**, chopped
> 1 large clove **garlic**, grated or pasted
> **Salt** and **pepper**

In a large heatproof bowl, douse the bulgur with the boiling water. Cover and let stand for 20 minutes.

Add the basil, mint, parsley, lemon juice, EVOO, tomatoes, onion, garlic, and salt and pepper to taste. Stir, stir, stir and let that refrigerate for 30 minutes to chill.

Serves 4

APRIL 12, DINNER

Carbonara Milanese-style with ramps: Take 1 bundle of ramps, soak them, and separate the whites from the greens. Finely chop the whites, 4 cloves of garlic, and 1 chile pepper. Sauté them in 3 tablespoons EVOO with ¼ pound pancetta, diced. (If the pancetta you get is thick-sliced, pound it a little bit first before dicing.) Add some coarse black pepper. Stir, stir, stir for a couple of minutes and add in the greens from the ramps, then add ½ cup white wine. Stir about 1 cup warm saffron stock into 3 Araucana egg yolks. Toss the ramps-pancetta mixture and tempered egg yolks with egg tagliatelle that has been cooked to al dente. Toss in a couple of handfuls of pecorino cheese. There's your carbonara Milanese. We had an Il Sasso Carmignano 2007 to go with it.

When we make simple fish—broiled cod or haddock or halibut or grilled fish—we often top it with **peperonata**, as we did this night with snapper.

Peperonata for Grilled Fish

This makes enough peperonata for four entrée servings of any mild fish, halibut to snapper, broiled or grilled or sautéed. You can use regular sugar in this but I use superfine; we always have it around because John makes cocktails with it.

2 to 3 tablespoons **EVOO**
2 **cubanelle peppers**, sliced
2 small **red Fresno chiles**, sliced
1 **red bell pepper** (see Tip), thinly sliced
1 **red onion**, quartered and thinly sliced
A few cloves of **garlic**, very thinly sliced
Salt and **pepper**
1 teaspoon **sugar**
2 tablespoons **white balsamic vinegar**
A handful of chopped **flat-leaf parsley**

In a large skillet, heat the EVOO (2 to 3 turns of the pan) over medium-high heat. Add the cubanelles, Fresno chiles, bell pepper, onion, and garlic. Season with salt and pepper to taste and stir until they soften, 7 to 8 minutes.

Sprinkle with the sugar. Douse it with the vinegar (2 quick turns of the pan) and add the parsley. Give the pan a little shake. That's it. That's peperonata sauce. You can serve it on any grilled fish, but it's also tasty on chicken and even with sausages or on bread.

Serves 4

I like the rectangular-shaped field bell peppers.

APRIL 15

Once a year I go back to my old stomping grounds at Lake George High School to do a fund-raiser. This particular year when I was there a young lady named McKenna made me a recipe book. There was also a young gentleman (who looked strangely a little like Ashton Kutcher as a kid) who brought me flowers. We had over five hundred people there watching me do a cooking class, and we handed out ten scholarships to students, plus the school got some funds for whatever they'd like to put them toward. It's always nice to go back, and give back, in this sort of way.

My good friend Andrew Kaplan (aka Kappy) was here and we celebrated his birthday. I made him **Ultimate Italian Pulled Pork Sammies** (see April 4, page 4) on ciabatta. We drank Clio, one of our fave wines, and we chatted about doing this book—*My Year in Meals*—because Kappy is the person who inspired me to keep this photographic food journal. Instead of birthday cake, we had **Chocolate Cupcakes with Bacon–Cream Cheese Frosting.**

Chocolate Cupcakes with Bacon–Cream Cheese Frosting

CUPCAKES
½ cup unsweetened **cocoa powder**
½ cup **buttermilk**
1 cup **flour**
1 teaspoon **baking soda**
½ teaspoon **baking powder**
½ teaspoon **salt**
Pinch of **ground cloves**
2 **eggs**
1 cup **granulated sugar**
½ cup packed **light brown sugar**

FROSTING
4 tablespoons (½ stick) **butter**, softened
8 ounces **cream cheese**, softened
2 cups **confectioners' sugar**
1 teaspoon **vanilla extract**
2 tablespoons **milk**
6 slices **bacon**, cooked until crisp and finely chopped (reserve 15 pieces for garnish)

Preheat the oven to 350°F. Line 15 cupcake cups with paper liners. In a small bowl, stir together the cocoa powder and 3 to 4 tablespoons warm water; it should be a little looser than a thick paste. Stir in the buttermilk.

In a medium bowl, combine the flour, baking soda, baking powder, salt, ground cloves, and both sugars and mix with a fork to combine.

In a separate bowl, beat the eggs for 30 seconds to a minute. Add half the cocoa powder mixture and stir, then half the flour mixture and stir. Add the remaining cocoa powder mixture and then flour and stir until just combined.

Fill the cups halfway with the batter and bake until a wooden skewer inserted into the center comes out clean, 18 to 20 minutes. Let cool completely.

Beat the butter and cream cheese together. Add the sugar, vanilla, and the milk (by tablespoons). Stir in the bacon. Frost the cooled cupcakes and garnish with a piece of bacon.

Makes 15 cupcakes

I made **Croque Madame.** We washed that down with Billecart-Salmon Rosé Champagne.

Croque Madame

Salt and **pepper**
1 bundle thin **asparagus**, trimmed into 4-inch tips (reserve stems for another use)
3 tablespoons **butter**, plus more for cooking the eggs
3 tablespoons **flour**
2 cups **whole milk**
Freshly grated **nutmeg**
1 tablespoon chopped fresh **tarragon**
2 tablespoons **Dijon mustard**
8 slices **brioche bread**
¾ pound **ham**, thinly sliced
2 cups grated **Gruyère** cheese
4 large Araucana **eggs**

Preheat the oven to 375°F.

In a saucepan, bring a few inches of water to a boil. Add salt and the asparagus, and cook a couple of minutes to tender-crisp. Cold-shock in a bowl of ice water and dry in a kitchen towel.

In a small saucepan, melt the butter over medium heat. Add the flour and cook a minute, then whisk in the milk. Season with salt and pepper and cook the sauce at a low bubble until very thick, 7 to 8 minutes. Season with a little nutmeg and the tarragon. Remove from the heat and stir in the mustard.

Line a baking sheet with parchment paper and arrange 4 slices of bread on it. Top them with half of the béchamel sauce, all of the asparagus tips, the ham, and half of the cheese. Set another slice of bread on each sandwich and cover with the remaining sauce and cheese. Transfer to the oven and bake 15 minutes, until the bread is toasted on the bottom and the cheese is deep golden on top.

When the sandwiches are almost done, heat a medium nonstick skillet over medium heat with a pat of butter. Add the eggs, season with salt and pepper, and cook according to preference. Top each sandwich with an egg.

Serves 4

John must have been out of town or something; it was just me and Mommy. I made my **Chicken Vindaloo** and served it up with some jasmine rice. Washed it down with a little Syrah.

Chicken Vindaloo

This is my usual vindaloo, which is skin-on, bone-in chicken, but I made it for us with the skin off. Also, I left off the cilantro for my mom, who doesn't like cilantro.

8 pieces **chicken**, a combination of legs, thighs, and/or breasts
Hot Curry Spice Blend (recipe follows) or
    2 tablespoons curry powder blended with
    1 tablespoon hot paprika
6 cloves **garlic**, finely chopped
Salt and **pepper**
Juice of 2 **limes**
2 tablespoons **vegetable** or **peanut oil**
1 **onion**, chopped
2 inches fresh **ginger**, grated or minced
2 fresh **bay leaves**
1 Fresno or other medium-hot **fresh red chile**, seeded and finely chopped
1 (14.5-ounce) can **petite diced tomatoes**
1 cup **chicken stock**
3 to 4 cups cooked **jasmine rice**

GARNISHES
Chopped toasted **peanuts** or sliced **almonds**
Finely chopped **mint** and **cilantro**
Lime wedges

Place the chicken in a shallow dish and dress with half of the spice blend (or curry powder mixture), 2 cloves' worth of the garlic, salt and pepper, and the lime juice. Cover and let marinate 45 minutes to 1 hour.

In large deep skillet or Dutch oven, heat the oil over medium-high heat. Add the onion, ginger, the rest of the garlic, the bay leaves, chile, remaining spice blend (or curry powder mixture),

and salt to taste. Cook, stirring frequently, 7 to 8 minutes to soften.

Add the tomatoes and stock and bring to a boil. Slide in the chicken and partially cover the pan with a lid or foil, to allow some steam to escape. Reduce the heat to a simmer and braise the chicken in the sauce about 20 minutes. Serve over the jasmine rice, topped with the garnishes.

Serves 4

HOT CURRY SPICE BLEND

1 tablespoon **turmeric**
2 teaspoons ground **cumin**
2 teaspoons ground **coriander**
2 teaspoons hot **paprika**
1 teaspoon **dry mustard**
¼ teaspoon ground **cardamom**
¼ teaspoon ground **cinnamon**

Combine all together.

Makes 3 generous tablespoons

We had **braised artichokes** (see April 10, page 10) for an appetizer, followed by **Penne alla Norma with Fennel & Fresno Chile.**

Penne alla Norma with Fennel & Fresno Chile

2 medium firm **eggplants**, peeled and diced
Sea salt and **pepper**
¼ cup **EVOO**
1 **red Fresno chile**, thinly sliced or finely chopped
4 to 5 cloves **garlic**, thinly sliced or chopped
1 teaspoon **fennel seeds**
1 (28- or 32-ounce) can **San Marzano tomatoes** (look for DOP on the label)
A few leaves of torn fresh **basil**, plus more for garnish
A small handful of chopped **flat-leaf parsley**
1 pound **penne pasta**
Grated ricotta salata cheese, for serving

Place the eggplants in a strainer set over a sink and season well with salt. Let that drain for 20 to 30 minutes.

Bring a large pot of water to a boil.

Meanwhile, in a large skillet, heat the EVOO over medium to medium-high heat. Add the chile, garlic, and fennel seeds and stir that around for a minute or two. Add the eggplant and cook until very light brown. Add the tomatoes, lightly crushing them up, the basil, parsley, and salt and pepper to taste.

Salt the boiling water and cook the penne to al dente. Before draining, ladle out about a cup of the starchy pasta cooking water and add it to the sauce. Drain the pasta and toss with the sauce.

Serve topped with the grated cheese and garnished with a little more basil.

Serves 4

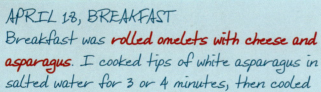

APRIL 13, BREAKFAST
Breakfast was **rolled omelets with cheese and asparagus**. I cooked tips of white asparagus in salted water for 3 or 4 minutes, then cooled them and set aside. I made each person a 2-egg omelet. Cooking one omelet at a time, you heat butter over medium to medium-low and pour in the eggs. When the eggs are almost set completely through, add a little bit of cheese to each omelet, a couple of ounces total (in this case I used a ripe aged goat cheese that was nice and gooey; Taleggio, which is my husband's favorite cheese, also works beautifully). Then put a few sprigs of tarragon, finely chopped chives, and salt and pepper into the center of the omelet. Add some of the blanched white asparagus. Then you roll the omelet and serve.

We had **Spring Risotto** and **Caesar Salad with Kale.**

Spring Risotto

I used asparagus that were kind of tough and thick, so I used a vegetable peeler to trim the ends.

4 cups **chicken stock**
1 large pinch of **saffron** (about 30 threads)
A few handfuls of **ramps** (wild leeks) or
    1 bunch spring onions (4 or 5)
3 tablespoons **EVOO**
3 or 4 cloves **spring garlic**, thinly sliced, or
    2 large cloves purple garlic, finely chopped
Salt and **pepper**
1½ cups **arborio rice**
½ cup **dry white wine**
½ cup shelled fresh **peas** (optional; I add them
    in when they are in season)
1 bunch **asparagus** (larger stalks are fine),
    thinly sliced on an angle
Juice of ½ **lemon**
3 tablespoons **butter**
A couple of handfuls of freshly grated
    Parmigiano-Reggiano cheese

In a saucepot, combine the stock, 2 cups water, and the saffron. Bring to a low boil, then reduce the heat to medium-low.

Wash the ramps or spring onions and trim up. Finely chop the whites of the ramps or spring onions. Cut the green ramp tops into 1-inch pieces and set aside.

In a round-bottomed pan, heat 2 tablespoons EVOO (2 turns of the pan) over medium-high heat. Add the ramp or onion whites, the garlic, and salt and pepper to taste, and stir 2 to 3 minutes.

Add the rice and stir a minute or 2 more; add the wine and stir until absorbed into the rice fully. Begin adding warm stock, a few ladlefuls at a time. With each addition of stock, stir the rice vigorously to build up the starch; do not add more liquid until most of the last addition has been absorbed. The rice will be al dente after 18 minutes. If you are using peas, stir into the rice halfway through the cooking time. If you have stock left at the end, don't sweat it. The dish will take about 5 cups of liquid, more or less, but never exactly the same amount twice.

Begin preparing the asparagus in a separate skillet 2 to 3 minutes before the risotto is done cooking. Heat the remaining 1 tablespoon EVOO in a skillet (1 turn of the pan) over medium-high heat. Add the asparagus and lightly brown, 2 to 3 minutes. Season with salt and pepper, and douse the pan with the lemon juice.

Finish the risotto by stirring in the butter, Parm, the ramp greens, and half the asparagus. Serve the risotto in shallow bowls and top with remaining asparagus to garnish.

Serves 4

Caesar Salad with Kale

We use tender kale straight from our garden. And I always use farmers' market eggs in a Caesar salad to lower the risk of salmonella. If you use very fresh eggs from a reliable source, you can make Caesar salad or anything with a soft yolk.

4 cloves **garlic**
6 tablespoons **EVOO**
1 packed cup cubed **Pullman bread** (1- to
  1½-inch cubes)
Coarse **black pepper**
2 teaspoons **anchovy paste** (optional for strict
  vegetarians)
6 to 8 drops **Worcestershire sauce** (about
  1 teaspoon) (optional for strict vegetarians)
1 large organic **egg yolk** or ¼ cup pasteurized
  egg product
Juice of 1 large **lemon**
5 to 6 cups stemmed and chopped **kale**, or a
  combination of kale and romaine lettuce
2 handfuls of freshly grated **Pecorino Romano**
  or **Parmigiano-Reggiano cheese**
Coarse salt

Crack the garlic away from its skin with a good whack of your hand against the flat of your knife, centered on top of each clove. Rub the inside of your salad bowl (I use a wooden bowl) with a clove of cracked garlic. Place that clove and a second clove aside. Mince the remaining 2 cloves and place them in a small bowl.

Heat a small skillet over medium heat. Add 2 tablespoons EVOO (2 turns of the pan) and the 2 cracked garlic cloves. When the garlic "speaks" by sizzling in the EVOO, add the bread cubes and toast until golden, tossing occasionally, 6 to 8 minutes. Sprinkle the cubed bread with a little pepper and remove from the heat.

Combine the minced garlic and the remaining 4 tablespoons EVOO (3 glugs) in a small bowl or in a small skillet. Heat the garlic and EVOO, either in a microwave oven for 1 minute, or over low heat on a stovetop for 2 to 3 minutes. Stir the anchovy paste into the warm EVOO with a fork and let stand until the EVOO returns to room temperature. (I go a little heavier on the anchovy paste for my family. We use up to a good solid tablespoon; we like a lot of anchovy in the dressing.)

Add the Worcestershire sauce and egg yolk to a salad bowl and stir with a fork. Add the lemon juice and stir into the egg. Add the EVOO-garlic-anchovy mixture in a slow stream and continue to beat with a fork.

Add the kale to the bowl and toss to coat. Add a generous amount of cheese and the croutons and toss again to coat. Season with salt and pepper to taste (I use a ton of black pepper).

Serves 4

🕐 APRIL 19/BREAKFAST

Multigrain Pecan Waffles with Berries

I always brush the waffles with melted butter when they come off the iron.

  2 cups **multigrain pancake mix**
  1½ to 2 cups **milk**
  2 tablespoons **butter**, melted, plus more for
    brushing
  2 organic **eggs**
  1 teaspoon **vanilla extract**
  Freshly grated **nutmeg**
  1 cup chopped toasted **pecans**
  Blackberries and **red raspberries**, for serving

Heat a waffle iron.

In a bowl, blend together the pancake mix, milk, melted butter, eggs, and vanilla. Season with a little nutmeg. Stir in the nuts. Cook in the waffle iron. Brush with melted butter. Top with berries.

Serves 4

APRIL 20, BREAKFAST

BLT with eggs and Cheddar on toast: I baked pepper bacon in the oven until crisp. I then mixed watercress leaves, torn basil, flat-leaf parsley, and scallions with about a teaspoon of lemon juice, a drizzle of EVOO, and salt and pepper. I sliced up some nice ripe tomatoes and I made BLT sandwiches on white toast with sliced XXX Cheddar (that's the sharp white Cheddar that I get from Oscar's Smokehouse in Warrensburg, New York) and over-easy or over-medium or fried eggs.

🕐 APRIL 20/DINNER

We spent Passover with our friend Lenny Fox and his family. All I brought was Mommy's **Country-Style Chicken Livers** (when I make the livers and I know I'll be serving my friend Jane, I add a splash of sherry, because I know she likes that). Ivona is the name of the woman who made dinner. She made short ribs, root vegetable puree, and kale. Jane made tuna crudo with hot peppers on dandelions and we also had matzo ball soup.

Country-Style Chicken Livers

I serve the chicken livers with sprouted wheat toasts that I cut into small squares (or the Rubschlager rye or pumpernickel that you can buy in party loaves, although our favorite is sprouted wheat). I lightly toast the sprouted wheat bread in a 325°F oven on a wire rack set over a baking sheet (so the heat can circulate all the way around the toast). You're not looking for it to be brown, just nice and toasty, lightly crisp. I also serve very thinly sliced shallot (use a truffle shaver—see page 154—or a mandoline) and cornichons and a grainy Dijon or cassis-flavored Dijon—a pink Dijon mustard that has cassis liqueur mixed into a grainy Dijon. Really pretty and delicious. My mom loves tarragon Dijon with the livers. Plain old Dijon is cool, too.

8 tablespoons **butter** (1 stick), cut into small pieces
2 large **onions**, thinly sliced
1 fresh or dried **bay leaf**
1 pound **chicken livers**, cleaned, trimmed, and patted dry
½ teaspoon ground **thyme**
Salt and **pepper**
3 ounces (6 tablespoons) **dry sherry** or cognac

In a large skillet, melt the butter over medium heat. Add the onions and bay leaf and cook, stirring occasionally, until tender and browned, 20 to 25 minutes.

Push the onions to the side of the pan and increase the heat to high. Add the chicken livers to the center of the pan and cook until browned, then stir in the onions and season with the thyme and salt and pepper to taste. Then deglaze the pan with a little dry sherry or cognac. Discard the bay leaf.

In a food processor, puree the livers and onions until smooth. Pack into a crock and serve warm or cool (press a piece of plastic wrap directly onto the surface of the spread if not serving immediately).

Makes 1 pound

🔵 **APRIL 21/GOOD FRIDAY LUNCH**

Grilled Cheese with Spinach, Calzone-Style

1 box (10 ounces) **organic chopped frozen spinach**, thawed and wrung dry in a clean towel
2 tablespoons **EVOO**
2 cloves **garlic**, finely chopped
Salt and **pepper**
Freshly grated **nutmeg**
1 cup sheep or cow's milk **ricotta**
⅓ to ½ cup freshly grated **Parmigiano-Reggiano cheese**

2 tablespoons chopped fresh **thyme**
Good-quality salted **butter**, melted
8 hand-cut slices (½ inch thick) good-quality **white bread**
Deli-sliced **provolone cheese**
Deli-sliced Wisconsin **mozzarella cheese**

Separate the spinach to loosen the leaves after drying. In a medium skillet, heat the EVOO (2 turns of the pan) over medium heat. Add the garlic and stir 2 minutes, then stir in the spinach. Season with salt, pepper, and nutmeg. Remove from the heat.

In a bowl, stir together the ricotta, Parm, thyme, and salt and pepper to taste.

Liberally butter one side of all the bread slices.

Build the sandwiches: a slice of bread (buttered side down), provolone, spinach, ricotta-Parm, mozzarella, bread (buttered side up).

Heat a griddle over medium heat. Grill the sandwiches until deeply golden and the cheese has melted.

Serves 4

We had **Mexican Fish Fry** and **oil and vinegar slaw** on the side. We also had fresh peas and pea shoots dressed with lemon, lots of chopped mint, salt and pepper, and melted butter.

Mexican Fish Fry

Frying oil, such as safflower oil or vegetable oil with omega-3s
1 cup **Mexican beer**
1 cup **flour**
1 teaspoon ground **coriander**
1 teaspoon ground **cumin**
1 teaspoon **paprika**
½ teaspoon **cayenne pepper**
Salt and **black pepper**
4 thick 6-ounce pieces sustainable **white fish**, such as cod, haddock, or pollack
Lemon wedges, **malt vinegar**, and **Tartar Sauce** (recipe follows), for serving

Preheat the oven to 275°F. Place a rack over a baking sheet. Fill a countertop fryer with oil or pour a few inches of oil into a large Dutch oven. Heat the oil to 365°F.

In a bowl whisk together the beer, flour, coriander, cumin, paprika, and cayenne; season with salt.

Coat the fish in the beer batter and fry to deep golden, 6 to 7 minutes. Drain on a wire rack and season with a pinch more salt. Keep warm in the oven on the rack set into the baking sheet.

Serve it up with lemon wedges, malt vinegar, and tartar sauce.

Serves 4

TARTAR SAUCE

The base mayonnaise for the tartar sauce is really easy, easy, easy. It's from Mark Bittman. When I first read his description, it sounded like something that would take a long time to come together, but it really doesn't.

1 **egg yolk**
2 teaspoons **Dijon mustard**
1 cup **grapeseed oil**
Salt
Juice of ½ **lemon**
1 teaspoon **hot sauce**
½ teaspoon **Worcestershire sauce**
2 to 3 tablespoons finely chopped **baby gherkins**, sweet pickle relish, or dill relish
About 2 tablespoons grated **onion** or grated shallot
2 tablespoons small **capers**
1 tablespoon chopped fresh **dill**
1 tablespoon chopped **flat-leaf parsley**

In a bowl, whisk together the egg yolk and mustard. In a slow stream, whisk in the oil. Season with salt. Stir in the lemon juice, hot sauce, Worcestershire sauce, pickles, onion, capers, dill, and parsley.

Makes 1 cup

The **oil and vinegar slaw** was cabbage and carrot in an oil and vinegar dressing. Combine ¼ cup vinegar, a tablespoon of superfine sugar, about 1½ teaspoons fine sea salt, 1 teaspoon celery seed, about ¼ cup vegetable oil or olive oil. Whisk, whisk, whisk. Combine minced or grated shallot with that, a grated carrot, and a small head (about 1 pound) of white cabbage, shredded. Toss that all together and let it hang out.

April 22, BREAKFAST
Ramp and Robiola frittata: Take a handful of ramps, finely chop the whites, reserve the greens. Sauté the ramp whites in 3 tablespoons butter. Add 9 eggs, salt, and pepper. Fold in the ramp greens. I cooked it in my frittata pan and when the frittata was just about done I put thinly sliced Robiola up on top and let that melt down over.

🕐 APRIL 22/DINNER

Baked peppers stuffed with **Feta-Walnut Dip** to start, then **Easter Meat Loaf with 8-Minute Eggs** and **Green Pastitsio.**

I took my Feta-Walnut Dip (recipe follows) and made **baked stuffed peppers**. I split some mild red peppers, seeded them, and stuffed them with the cheese mixture. Then I chilled them, topped them with a little sprinkle of Parm (or kasseri) cheese, and baked them in a 400°F oven until they were golden on top.

Feta-Walnut Dip

12 ounces **feta cheese**, crumbled
¼ cup **Greek yogurt**
1 cup ground toasted **walnuts**
2 tablespoons **EVOO**
2 **egg yolks**
Small handful of **flat-leaf parsley**, chopped
Leaves from 1 or 2 sprigs **oregano**, finely
   chopped

Stir together the feta, yogurt, ground walnuts,
EVOO, egg yolks, parsley, and oregano.

Makes about 4 cups

Easter Meat Loaf with Eggs

10 extra-large organic **eggs**
3 cups coarsely chopped or torn **peasant
   bread** or stale Italian bread
1 cup **milk**
2 tablespoons **EVOO**, plus more for drizzling
1 **onion**, finely chopped
1 large **shallot**, finely chopped
4 cloves **garlic**, finely chopped
½ cup **dry white wine**
2 pounds **ground lamb**
1 tablespoon grated **lemon zest**
1 teaspoon **dried oregano** or 1 tablespoon
   fresh oregano, chopped
Sea salt (go easy) and **coarse black pepper**
   (go heavier)
1 package (10 ounces) **frozen chopped organic
   spinach**, thawed, drained, squeezed dry,
   and separated
Freshly grated **nutmeg**
½ cup finely crumbled **feta cheese**
½ cup **mint leaves**, finely chopped, plus more
   for garnish
½ cup **flat-leaf parsley leaves**, finely chopped,
   plus more for garnish
Lemon wedges, for serving

Preheat the oven to 400°F.

Place 8 of the eggs in a pot and cover with
cold water. Bring to full boil, turn off the heat,
cover, and let stand 10 minutes. Crack the shells
and run under cold water to quick-cool. Peel the
eggs and trim ½ inch off of the top and bottom
of each egg. (The eggs run down the center of the
meat loaf as it cooks, and when you slice it, each
person will get some yolk and white if the whites
have been trimmed a bit.)

Soak the bread in the milk for 5 minutes.

In a skillet, heat the 2 tablespoons EVOO
(2 turns of the pan). Add the onion, shallot, and
garlic and cook to tender. Deglaze with the wine
and set aside to cool.

Place the lamb in large bowl, then wring out
the bread and crumble it into the bowl with your
fingertips. Add the lemon zest and oregano, and
season with sea salt and pepper. Add the spinach
and season it with a hint of freshly grated nutmeg.
In a small bowl, beat the remaining 2 eggs and
add to the lamb. Add the cooled onion mixture,
the feta, mint, and parsley. Mix well to combine.

Form a 10-inch-long layer of meat loaf about
2 inches thick on a baking sheet. Top with a line
of the hard-boiled eggs running down the center.
Use the remaining meat loaf mixture to encase
the eggs in the center of the loaf. Drizzle the loaf
with EVOO. Bake 1 hour.

Switch on the broiler to crisp up the top. Let
stand for 10 minutes before serving. Garnish with
more chopped herbs and serve with lemon wedges
alongside.

Serves 8

Green Pastitsio

For this dish I like Greek macaroni #2 or ziti.

Salt and pepper
1 pound ziti or long, hollow pasta tubes
¼ cup EVOO
6 cloves garlic, sliced or chopped
1 large or 2 medium onions, chopped
1 large or 2 medium bunches Swiss chard, stemmed, leaves chopped
1 bunch scallions, chopped
¼ cup fresh dill
¼ cup fresh mint leaves
¼ cup flat-leaf parsley leaves
4 tablespoons (½ stick) butter
¼ cup flour
3 cups milk
Freshly grated nutmeg
1 cup shredded kasseri cheese (see Tip)
1 cup crumbled Greek feta
1 cup freshly shredded or grated Parmigiano-Reggiano cheese

Preheat the oven to 375°F.

Bring a large pot of water to a boil. Salt the water and undercook the pasta by about 2 minutes.

While the water is coming to a boil, in a large skillet, heat the EVOO (4 turns of the pan) over medium to medium-high heat. Add the garlic and onions, soften a few minutes, then stir in the chard to wilt. Add the scallions, dill, mint, parsley, and pepper to taste. Reduce the heat to a simmer and keep the greens warm.

Meanwhile, in a saucepan, heat the butter over medium to medium-high heat. As soon as the butter melts, add the flour and stir 1 minute. Whisk in the milk and season with salt, pepper, and nutmeg to taste. Cook until the sauce is thickened, 4 to 5 minutes.

Drain the pasta and return to the cooking pot. Add the cooked greens, kasseri, feta, and Parm and toss to combine; taste and adjust seasoning.

Place half of the pasta mixture in a 9 by 13-inch casserole dish and top with half of the sauce. Top with the remaining pasta mixture and the remaining sauce. Bake until deeply golden up on top and bubbling, about 20 minutes. Let cool slightly and serve.

Serves 4 to 6

Kasseri is a medium-hard cheese usually made from sheep's milk. It is traditionally used in Greek dishes as well as Turkish dishes.

We had **Whole-Grain Spiced Waffles, baked bacon,** and **baked eggs in leek nests.** We often make the baked eggs in the pizza oven the morning after we've made pizza for dinner. Believe it or not, the oven is still hot 8 to 10 hours later.

Baked bacon: Preheat the oven to 375°F. Arrange a pound of bacon in a single layer on a slotted broiler pan. Bake until crispy, 15 to 18 minutes.

Whole-Grain Spiced Waffles

Serve with crispy bacon, blackberries, and warm dark amber maple syrup.

½ teaspoon ground **ginger**
½ teaspoon ground **cinnamon**
¼ teaspoon freshly grated **nutmeg**
A pinch of ground **cloves**
2 cups **whole-grain waffle mix**
2 tablespoons melted **butter**, plus some for
  brushing the waffle iron
1 **egg**, beaten
1½ to 2 cups **2% milk**
1 teaspoon **vanilla extract**
½ to ¾ cup chopped toasted **pecans**

Heat a waffle iron. (I use mine at the highest setting.)

Mix the spices into the waffle mix. Add the butter, egg, and enough milk to get a consistency that is just pourable—start with 1½ cups milk; if the mixture is too thick to pour, add more milk. Stir in the vanilla and pecans.

Liberally brush the hot waffle iron with melted butter. Fill with enough waffle mix to just cover the nubs. Cook the waffles until crisp.

Serves 4

Baked eggs in leek nests: Bring a few inches of salted water to a boil; blanch halved leeks or ramps for no more than 1 minute. Drain on a kitchen towel. Brush a muffin tin with EVOO. Line the muffin cups with leeks or ramps, overlapping layers, to create small green onion nests. Fill each nest with an egg and top each egg with a dab of butter, a sprinkle of shredded sharp Cheddar, 2 dashes of hot sauce, salt and pepper, and a sprinkle of finely chopped fresh thyme. Bake at 425°F for 12 to 15 minutes, depending on how done you like your eggs—at 12 minutes the eggs with be runny at the center; at 15 minutes, they will be hard.

After an experiment with a pasta dish using nettles (see below), we ended up with a favorite spring standby: **Ramp Pasta with Garlic Butter Bread Crumbs**. We also had a tricolor greens salad with a sesame seed dressing.

We tried to have pasta with nettles for dinner. The recipe was well balanced, but this was our first outing with nettles. They looked great at the farmers' market, so then I read up on how to cook with nettles. I drew up a blueprint for our meal. I gotta say—I don't get it. The color of the nettles was unappealing; the flavor, I don't know. We didn't dig it. And so we had Ramp Pasta instead (see recipe below).

Ramp Pasta with Garlic Butter Bread Crumbs

Salt and pepper
1 pound tagliatelle noodles (I like Delverde brand)
2 bunches ramps, white and greens separated
¼ cup EVOO
2 to 3 cloves garlic, thinly sliced
¼ to ⅓ cup white wine
2 tablespoons butter
Juice of ½ lemon or lime
¼ cup finely chopped toasted pistachios
1 cup grated Parmigiano-Reggiano cheese, plus more for serving
A handful of finely chopped flat-leaf parsley
2 tablespoons finely chopped fresh mint
Grated zest of 1 lemon or lime
Garlic Butter Bread Crumbs (recipe follows)

Bring a large pot of water to a boil. Salt the water and cook the pasta to al dente. Before draining, reserve a ladle of the starchy pasta cooking water. Drain the pasta.

Finely chop the ramp whites and coarsely chop the greens. In a large skillet, heat the EVOO (4 turns of the pan). Add the garlic and ramp whites. Stir 2 to 3 minutes. Deglaze the pan with the wine. Melt the butter. Add the lemon juice and transfer to a large serving bowl with the ramp greens. Add the ladle of reserved pasta cooking water to the ramps. Add the pasta and toss.

Garnish with pistachios, Parm, parsley, mint, and lemon or lime zest. Mix the garlic butter bread crumbs with a little grated Parm and pass the mixture at the table.

Serves 4

Choosing seasonal ingredients.

GARLIC BUTTER BREAD CRUMBS

4 tablespoons (½ stick) butter
2 large cloves garlic, finely chopped or grated
1 cup panko or coarsely ground homemade bread crumbs
A small handful of flat-leaf parsley, finely chopped

In a large skillet, melt the butter over medium heat. When the butter foams, add the garlic and stir for 1 minute. Add the bread crumbs and stir until deeply golden, nutty, and fragrant. Remove from the heat. Let cool and combine with the parsley.

Makes about 1 cup

This sesame dressing is good with escarole or tricolor greens: radicchio, romaine, and endive. For the dressing, toast a couple of tablespoons sesame seeds. Grate 1 small shallot into a bowl; add about 2 tablespoons aged balsamic vinegar and about ½ teaspoon ground fennel. Add the toasted sesame seeds in a slow stream. Whisk in about ⅓ cup EVOO, season with salt and pepper to taste. Toss with lettuces of choice.

EASTER DINNER

APRIL 24, EASTER WEEKEND (it was a late Easter)

We had Tuscan Galia melon with prosciutto di Parma, **artichokes with a chile-mint dressing, asparagus with shallot vinaigrette, Bull's-Eye Deviled Eggs,** and **Caponata.** For the main, we had **Slow-Smoked Chicken, Saffron Rice with Marcona Almonds,** and an arugula and heirloom tomato salad with spring onions and spring garlic.

Asparagus with shallot vinaigrette: Boil up ¼ cup red wine vinegar with 2 teaspoons of sugar and pour it over a couple of finely chopped shallots. Whisk in ⅓ cup EVOO and salt and pepper. Pour the dressing over 2 bundles of asparagus tips. I parboiled them 2 minutes in salted water, drained them, cold-shocked them, arranged them on a large platter. I made disks of oranges by peeling and slicing a seedless orange. Arrange the orange slices over the asparagus and pour the shallot vinaigrette down over the top of that.

Artichokes with chile-mint dressing: Boil up halved small artichokes in acidulated water—that's water with a lot of lemon in it—until they're tender. Cool them and drain well, then toss with chile and mint, garlic, lemon juice, olive oil, salt, pepper, and fennel salt.

Caponata

We eat caponata at room temperature or cold with toast, or just as a cold salad. My mom also likes caponata with a little bit of pasta or polenta as a supper, or even just on bread as a sandwich.

¼ cup **EVOO**
1 medium **eggplant**, diced
1 **red onion**, chopped
1 or 2 ribs **celery**, from the heart, chopped
1 **red bell pepper**, diced
2 **cubanelle peppers** (long green Italian frying peppers), diced
1 **red Fresno chile**, thinly sliced or finely chopped
3 or 4 cloves **spring garlic**, thinly sliced
A handful of **Sicilian olives**, pitted and chopped
A small handful of **golden raisins**
1 (28- or 32-ounce) can **San Marzano tomatoes** (look for DOP on the label)
A few leaves torn **basil**
¼ cup **flat-leaf parsley**, chopped
2 to 3 tablespoons **pistachios**, toasted and coarsely chopped
2 to 3 tablespoons **pine nuts**, toasted

In a large Dutch oven, heat the EVOO (4 turns of the pan) over medium-high heat. Add the eggplant, onion, celery, bell pepper, cubanelles, chile, garlic, olives, and raisins. Drain off half the juice from the tomatoes and crush the tomatoes by hand as you add them to the pot. Cook partially covered, stirring occasionally, until the caponata comes together and the vegetables are tender. Stir in the basil and parsley. Garnish with the toasted pistachios and pine nuts.

Makes about 4 cups

Saffron Rice with Marcona Almonds

Marcona almonds are super delicious Spanish-style almonds. They have a really deep flavor, but you could use regular slivered almonds here instead.

4 cups **chicken stock**
A generous pinch of **saffron threads**, 24 to 30 threads
3 tablespoons **butter**
½ cup broken **lemon spaghetti** (available at some Italian markets)
1½ cups **long-grain white rice**
1 bunch **spring onions**, chopped, whites and greens kept separate
1 to 2 tablespoons fresh **thyme leaves**
Grated zest and juice of 1 **lemon**
A handful of chopped **flat-leaf parsley**
Salt and **pepper**
1 cup **Marcona almonds**, dry-roasted, chopped

In a saucepan, combine the stock and saffron and simmer until reduced to 3 cups.

Meanwhile, in a medium saucepan, heat the butter, add the spaghetti, and toast to deep golden, 2 to 3 minutes. Add the rice and stir that around a minute. Stir in the onion whites, saffron stock, thyme, lemon zest, parsley, salt, and pepper. Bring to a boil, then reduce the heat to low, cover, and cook to tender, 17 to 18 minutes. Check on the rice after 12 to 13 minutes and if it is dry, stir in a little extra stock.

Fluff the rice and stir in the lemon juice, onion greens, and almonds.

Serves 4

Slow-Smoked Chicken

After brining the chicken overnight, we spatch-cocked it, which means we split the chicken by cutting along the backbone and then opening it up. This is so it can sit flat as it cooks. And if you don't have a smoker, use the glaze on a broiled or grilled chicken.

For Easter dinner, I garnished the chicken with lots of chopped spring onions, spring garlic, fresh thyme and rosemary, and lots of Cerignola olives (big green Italian olives). We use this basic recipe all the time, but I almost always change up the glaze that we use. For example: Lemon Pepper Glaze (see May 29, page 48) or Orange-Rosemary Glaze (see May 31, page 51) or Thai-style (see Tip). You can also make the glaze below with Meyer lemon zest instead of lemon and lime zest, and use Meyer lemon juice to squeeze over the chicken after it comes out of the smoker.

THE BRINE

3 tablespoons **kosher salt**
1 **lime**, sliced
A handful of coarsely chopped **fresh herbs** (rosemary, thyme, cilantro)
2 or 3 cloves **garlic**, smashed
1 whole **chicken** (4 to 5 pounds)

THE GLAZE

½ cup **chicken stock**

⅓ cup **honey**
⅓ cup **cider vinegar**
¼ cup **tequila**
Strips of zest from 1 **lemon**
Strips of zest from 1 **lime**

FOR SERVING

Juice of 2 **limes**
3 **scallions**, very thinly sliced

Brine the chicken: In a glass or plastic container big enough to hold the chicken and the liquid, combine 1 gallon water with the salt, lime slices, herbs, and garlic. Mix to dissolve the salt. Add the chicken and brine overnight in the fridge.

Pat the chicken dry and spatchcock it. Discard the brine. Slow-smoke the chicken at 300°F for about 1½ hours.

Meanwhile, after the chicken has been cooking for 45 minutes, make the glaze: In a small sauce-pan, combine the chicken stock, honey, vinegar, tequila, lemon zest, and lime zest. Cook until the glaze is reduced to ½ cup.

When the chicken has 30 to 45 minutes to go, baste with the glaze and continue smoking.

To serve, slice the chicken up on a huge carving board, douse it with a little lime juice, and top it with some very thinly sliced scallions or green onions sliced on an angle.

Serves 4

We also make a Thai-style smoked chicken. For the brine, we add fresh ginger and remove the thyme and rosemary. Then for the glaze, we add garlic and ginger and use kecap manis (a thick, sweet soy sauce) instead of the honey. We garnish the dish with cilantro leaves and a little shredded basil or Thai basil.

Bull's-Eye Deviled Eggs

This is my traditional deviled egg mixture, but I put a very thin ring of Fresno chile on the top of each deviled egg to look like a bull's-eye. For other varieties, see pages 34–35.

1 dozen organic **eggs**
3 to 4 tablespoons **mayonnaise**
2 tablespoons grated **onion**
2 tablespoons **pickle relish** (I like Heinz)
1 clove **garlic**, grated
1 tablespoon **mustard**, yellow or Dijon
2 to 3 teaspoons **hot sauce**
1 teaspoon **Worcestershire sauce**
1 teaspoon **sweet paprika**
Salt and **pepper**
Thinly sliced fresh **red chile**, such as a small Fresno, for garnish

Place the eggs in a saucepan, cover with cold water, and bring to a full boil. Turn off the heat, cover the pot, and let the eggs stand for 10 minutes; drain.

Crack the eggs by shaking the pot and running them under cold water until cool enough to handle. Peel the eggs, then halve them lengthwise, or trim the ends to present the eggs upright. You should have 12 upright eggs or 24 egg halves.

Remove the yolks and transfer to a bowl. Add the mayo (start with 3 tablespoons), the grated onion (grating directly over the bowl to catch the onion juice), the relish, garlic, mustard, hot sauce, Worcestershire, paprika, salt, and pepper. Mash until very smooth, adding the final tablespoon of mayo if too dry.

Spoon the egg mixture into a resealable bag. Snip off a corner of the bag and squeeze the filling into the egg whites, overstuffing them a little, and garnish with a bull's-eye of thinly sliced red chile.

Makes 12 to 24

● APRIL 25 / LUNCH

We had **Grilled Cheese with Spinach, Calzone-Style** (see April 21, page 19).

● APRIL 25 / DINNER

Linguine Puttanesca

We like to use pepperoncini spaghetti from Buon Italia, located in the Chelsea Market.

About ¼ cup **EVOO**
7 or 8 good-quality **anchovy fillets**
5 or 6 cloves **garlic**, chopped
1 **red Fresno chile** or **Italian red cherry pepper**, seeded and finely chopped
¼ to ⅓ cup **dry vermouth**
1 (28- or 32-ounce) can **San Marzano tomatoes** (look for DOP on the label)
A few leaves of basil, torn
About ½ cup **oil-cured black olives**, pitted and coarsely chopped
3 to 4 tablespoons **capers**
Salt and a few grinds of **black pepper**
¼ cup chopped **flat-leaf parsley**
1 pound **linguine** or other pasta of choice.

Bring a large pot of water to a boil.

Meanwhile, in a deep skillet, heat the EVOO (4 turns of the pan) over medium heat. Add the anchovies, stirring and breaking them up until they melt into the oil. Reduce the heat a bit, add the garlic and chile, and stir 2 to 3 minutes. Deglaze the pan with the vermouth. Increase the heat a little, add the tomatoes, and break them up into coarse pieces. Stir in the basil, olives, capers, and pepper. Bring the sauce to a bubble, then reduce the heat and simmer for about 20 minutes. Stir in the parsley.

Salt the boiling water and cook the pasta to al dente. Before draining, ladle out about a cup of the starchy cooking water and add to the sauce. Drain the pasta and add to the sauce, tossing with tongs for 1 or 2 minutes for the flavors to absorb.

Serves 4

To make this with fresh tomatoes, use a couple of pints of cherry or grape tomatoes, put a lid on the pan, and cook until they burst. Then mash them up a little. You can serve this sauce with short- or long-cut pasta—linguine, spaghetti, penne, it all works.

● APRIL 26 / DINNER

Jalapeño Poppers to start. Then we had my **Mexican-Style Fried Chicken.** I served it up with **Saffron Rice Pilaf, Lemon-Garlic Guacamole, Pico de Gallo,** and black beans with queso fresco.

Jalapeño Poppers

16 fat **jalapeño chiles**
1 **red Fresno chile**, seeded and finely chopped
8 ounces **cream cheese**, softened
3 tablespoons grated **onion**
2 cloves **garlic**, grated or pasted
1 teaspoon ground **cumin**
¾ cup shredded **sharp Cheddar cheese**
¾ cup shredded **Monterey Jack cheese**
Kosher salt and **pepper**
¾ cup **panko bread crumbs**
½ cup grated **Parmigiano-Reggiano cheese**
All-natural **cooking spray**

Preheat the oven to 425°F.

Slice off one-third of the chiles lengthwise. Seed the chiles to make "boats" for the filling. Finely chop enough of the trimmings to measure 3 to 4 tablespoons. (I usually use about half of the total amount, reserving any remaining jalapeño for other recipes, such as salsas.)

In a bowl, combine the chopped jalapeño and Fresno chiles, the cream cheese, onion, garlic, cumin, and shredded cheeses. Stir until blended and season with salt and pepper. Spoon the filling into the hollowed-out chiles.

Stir the panko and Parm together on a plate and roll the stuffed tops of the poppers in the panko-Parm mixture. Arrange the poppers on a baking sheet and coat with a little cooking spray. Roast until the peppers are tender-crisp and the filling is browned and bubbling, 15 to 18 minutes. Let stand 10 minutes and serve.

Makes 16 poppers

Mexican-Style Fried Chicken

Serve with assorted hot sauces and honey for drizzling.

- ¾ cup **honey**, plus more for drizzling
- 3 tablespoons **cider vinegar**
- 4 skin-on, bone-in **chicken thighs**
- 4 skin-on, bone-in **drumsticks**
- 2 large skin-on, bone-in **chicken breasts**, halved crosswise into pieces similar in shape and size to the thighs
- **Salt** and **pepper**
- **Oil** for frying, such as soy or canola
- 4 extra-large **egg whites**
- 1 cup **flour**
- ¾ cup **cornmeal** or fine bread crumbs
- 1 teaspoon **baking powder**
- 1 tablespoon ancho or medium-heat **chile powder**
- 1½ teaspoons smoked **sweet paprika**
- 1 teaspoon **garlic powder**
- 1 teaspoon **granulated onion**
- 1 teaspoon ground **cumin**
- 1 teaspoon ground **coriander**
- 1 **lime**, cut into wedges, for serving

In a large bowl, combine the honey and vinegar. Add the chicken and toss to coat. Marinate 4 hours in the fridge.

Drain the chicken pieces on paper towels and season with salt and pepper.

Fill a countertop fryer with oil or pour 3 inches of oil into a large Dutch oven. Heat the oil to between 350° and 375°F for frying.

Line up 2 shallow bowls on the counter: Beat the egg whites in one; mix together the flour, cornmeal, baking powder, and spices in the second. Coat the chicken in the egg whites, then toss in the flour mixture. Fry in small batches until deep golden and juices run clear, 12 to 14 minutes per batch. Season the hot chicken with a little extra salt as it comes out.

Serve with lime wedges.

Serves 4 to 6

Lemon-Garlic Guacamole

- ½ small **red onion**, finely chopped
- Juice of 1 **lemon**
- Juice of 1 **lime**
- **Salt**
- 2 **avocados**
- 1 large **jalapeño chile**, seeded and finely chopped
- Small handful of **cilantro leaves**, finely chopped
- 1 large or 2 medium cloves **garlic**, pasted or grated

In a medium bowl, douse the onion with the citrus juices. Salt liberally and let stand 10 minutes.

Scoop the avocado flesh into the bowl (see Tip). Add the jalapeño, cilantro, and garlic and mash with a fork until fairly smooth. Adjust the salt.

Makes 1½ cups

Here's a neat trick. Halve the avocados and remove the pits, but leave them in their skins. Place a metal cooling rack over the bowl you are making the guacamole in. Working with one half at a time, place the avocado cut side down on the rack and press down, pushing it through the rack. The rack will dice it as it's being added to the bowl. My friend George taught me this trick. The spoon is overrated.

Saffron Rice Pilaf

2 tablespoons **butter**
½ cup broken **thin spaghetti**
1¾ cups **chicken stock**
1 cup **long-grain white rice**
¼ cup **golden raisins**, chopped
1 **red Fresno chile**, halved
1 large **bay leaf**
1 **cinnamon stick**
A generous pinch of **saffron** threads
Salt

In a saucepan, melt the butter over medium-high heat. Add the pasta and toast until golden, about 5 minutes. Stir in the chicken stock, rice, raisins, chile, bay leaf, cinnamon stick, and saffron and season with salt. Bring to a boil, then reduce the heat, cover, and simmer until tender, about 18 minutes.

Serves 4

Pico de Gallo

I like to make this with a combination of red and green heirloom tomatoes.

3 **plum tomatoes**, seeded and diced
1 small **jalapeño chile**, seeded and finely chopped
½ small **onion**, finely chopped
A few sprigs of **cilantro** (see Tip), finely chopped
A few fresh **mint leaves**, finely chopped
Juice of 1 **lime**
Coarse salt

Combine all the ingredients in a small bowl and set aside until ready to serve.

Makes about 2 cups

Cutting cilantro with some mint helps if you find cilantro a little soapy in flavor or too strong. Mincing it with a little mint can dial it back.

Black beans with queso fresco: Rinse and drain canned black beans; reheat with beer and cumin, diced onion, minced garlic, and chopped fresh jalapeño. I topped the black beans with pickled jalapeño and crumbled queso fresco.

APRIL 28/DINNER

Chicken Saltimbocca with Tagliatelle

Note that you will need 12 toothpicks to prepare this dish. And if you don't want the pasta, the chicken is a great stand-alone, too.

6 **chicken breast cutlets** (about 2 ounces each), pounded ⅛ inch thick
Salt and **pepper**
12 very thin slices **prosciutto di Parma**
12 fresh **sage leaves**
Flour, for dredging
4 tablespoons **EVOO**
6 tablespoons (¾ stick) **butter**
½ pound **egg tagliatelle** or egg noodles
2 cloves **garlic**, sliced
½ cup **Marsala** wine
1 cup **chicken stock**
A small handful of finely chopped **flat-leaf parsley**
Grated **Pecorino Romano cheese**

Bring a large pot of water to a boil for the pasta. Warm a platter in a low oven (250°F).

Season the chicken cutlets very lightly with salt and evenly with finely ground pepper on both sides. Cover the chicken carefully with prosciutto

and set 2 leaves of sage on each piece of chicken. Stitch the sage leaves in place with the toothpicks.

Lightly dredge the cutlets in flour. Then in a large skillet, heat 2 tablespoons EVOO (2 turns of the pan) over medium heat. Once the EVOO is hot, add 1 tablespoon butter and cook 3 of the cutlets a couple of minutes on each side to light golden. Place the cutlets on the warm platter and cover loosely with foil. Wipe the skillet, add the remaining 2 tablespoons EVOO (2 turns of the pan) and another tablespoon of butter, and cook the remaining chicken.

After the first batch of chicken is removed, drop the pasta into the pot and cook to al dente.

Transfer the second batch of chicken to the platter and remove all the toothpicks. Wipe the excess EVOO from the skillet and return it to the stove with the garlic and Marsala. Reduce by half over medium-high heat and add the chicken stock. Heat to a bubble, then whisk in the remaining 4 tablespoons butter and the parsley.

Drain the pasta, reserving $\frac{1}{2}$ cup of the starchy cooking water.

Spoon half of the sauce over the chicken and add the starchy cooking water to the remaining sauce. Add the pasta to the pan and toss for 1 to 2 minutes, allowing the flavors to absorb. Garnish with cheese.

Serve 2 or 3 pieces of chicken on each plate with pasta alongside.

Serves 2 generously

Deviled Eggs

I love deviled eggs so much. My mom usually likes them plain, so I usually just make the plain recipe—that's the one we make at home the most—but not to be missed are my Caesar-Stuffed Eggs, Deviled Ham & Eggs, and Green Olive Deviled Eggs. Those are all favorites of ours.

CAESAR-STUFFED EGGS

12 large organic **eggs**
1 to 2 teaspoons **anchovy paste**
1½ teaspoons **Worcestershire sauce**
3 tablespoons **mayonnaise**
1 clove **garlic**, grated
½ small **onion**, grated
¼ cup grated **Parmigiano-Reggiano cheese**
Juice of ½ **lemon**
Salt and **pepper**
2 cups shredded **romaine lettuce**

Put the eggs in a saucepan and fill it halfway with cold water. Set over high heat. When the water boils, turn off the heat and place the lid over the pot of eggs and let sit for 10 minutes.

Place the pot of cooked eggs in the sink and run some cold water over the eggs until both the water and the pan feel cool. When the eggs are cool enough to handle, roll each egg on a work surface to crack the shell. Carefully peel off the eggshells and discard.

Place the eggs on a cutting board and cut a quarter off the egg from the fat rounded end to expose the yolk. Next, cut just a sliver off the opposite end, the pointed end, so that the egg is able to sit upright without rolling over. Once all the eggs have been cut, scoop out their yolks into a medium mixing bowl. Place the egg whites back in the egg container for easy transport and filling, making sure the holes are pointing up so that you are able to fill them with the Caesar mixture.

To the bowl with the yolks, add the anchovy paste, Worcestershire sauce, mayonnaise, garlic, onion, Parm, lemon juice, salt, and pepper. Mash up the yolks with a fork until the mixture is paste-like. Mix in half of the shredded romaine, reserving the rest for garnish.

Spoon the egg mixture into a resealable plastic bag and squish it all into one of the bottom corners. Snip off the corner and squeeze out a bit of the filling into each of the egg whites. Once all the eggs are filled, place a little bit of shredded romaine on top of each for garnish.

Serves 6 to 8

DEVILED HAM & EGGS

12 large organic **eggs**
6 to 8 slices **deli ham**, chopped finely
2 tablespoons **mayonnaise** (use just enough to bind)
3 tablespoons **yellow mustard**
2 tablespoons **pickle relish**
½ small **onion**, grated
A few dashes **hot sauce** (add more if you like it spicy!)
¼ cup chopped **flat-leaf parsley**
¼ cup chopped fresh **dill**
Salt and **pepper**

Put the eggs in a saucepan and fill it halfway with cold water. Set over high heat. When the water boils, turn off the heat and place a lid over the pot. Let sit 10 minutes.

Place the pot of cooked eggs in the sink and run some cold water over the eggs until both the water and the pan feel cool. When the eggs are cool enough to handle, roll each egg on a work surface to crack the shell, then carefully peel off the eggshells.

Place the eggs on a cutting board and cut a quarter off the egg from the fat rounded end to expose the yolk. Next, cut a sliver off the opposite end, the pointed end, so the egg is able to sit

upright without rolling over. Once all the eggs have been cut, scoop out their yolks into a medium mixing bowl. Place the egg whites back in the egg container for easy transport and filling, making sure the holes are pointing up so that you are able to fill them.

Break the egg yolks up a little bit using a fork. Add in the ham, mayo, mustard, relish, onion, hot sauce, parsley, and dill. Give it a good stir and add salt and freshly ground black pepper to taste.

Make yourself a fancy instant pastry bag by spooning the egg yolk mixture into a resealable plastic bag and squishing it all into one of the bottom corners. Snip off a small triangle from the bottom of the bag and squeeze out a bit of the filling into each of the egg whites.

Serves 6 to 8

GREEN OLIVE DEVILED EGGS

12 large organic **eggs**
1 cup **green olives with pimientos**, finely chopped (save some for garnish)
2 tablespoons **mayonnaise** (use just enough to bind)
3 tablespoons **yellow mustard**
2 tablespoons **pickle relish** (eyeball it)
¼ small **onion**, grated
A few dashes **hot sauce** (add more if you like it spicy!)
¼ cup chopped **flat-leaf parsley**
¼ cup chopped fresh **dill**
Salt and **pepper**

Put the eggs in a saucepan and fill it halfway with cold water. Set over high heat. When the water boils, turn off the heat and place a lid over the pot. Let sit 10 minutes.

Place the pot of cooked eggs in the sink and run some cold water over the eggs until both the water and the pan feel cool. When the eggs are cool enough to handle, take them out of the water. Roll each egg on a work surface to crack the shell, then carefully peel off the eggshells.

Place the eggs on a cutting board and cut a quarter off the egg from the fat rounded end to expose the yolk. Next, cut just a sliver off the opposite end, the pointed end, so the egg is able to sit upright without rolling over. Once all the eggs have been cut, scoop out their yolks into a medium mixing bowl. Place the egg whites back in the egg container for easy transport and filling, making sure the holes are pointing up so that you are able to fill them.

Break the egg yolks up a little bit using a fork. Add in the olives, mayo, mustard, relish, grated onion, hot sauce, parsley, and dill. Give it a good stir and add salt and freshly ground black pepper to taste.

Make yourself a pastry bag by spooning the egg yolk mixture into a resealable plastic bag and squishing it all into one of the bottom corners. Snip off a small triangle from the bottom of the bag and squeeze out a bit of the filling into each of the egg whites.

Serves 6 to 8

MAY

SUNDAY/1	MONDAY/2	TUESDAY/3	WEDNESDAY/4	THURSDAY/5

DINNER

pancetta-wrapped shrimp with sage, spring risotto

WEDNESDAY/11	THURSDAY/12	FRIDAY/13	SATURDAY/14	SUNDAY/15

SATURDAY/21	MONDAY/23	WEDNESDAY/25	THURSDAY/26	FRIDAY/27

THURSDAY/26

DINNER

bagna cauda dip, asparagus with lemon vinaigrette, fava bean spread, crab cakes, fried dandelion greens with fried eggs

FRIDAY/27

DINNER

pico de gallo, bean dip, lemon-garlic guacamole, flat iron steaks with tre colore pesto & quick-roasted tomatoes, grilled corn with chipotle cream & cotija

SUNDAY/22	TUESDAY/24

FRIDAY/6

DINNER
grilled steaks with spring garlic and rosemary; grilled portobellos; onion, tomato, and arugula salad

SATURDAY/7

DINNER
chicken francese with pasta, Galia melon with prosciutto, limoncello sorbet with fresh berries

SUNDAY/8

BREAKFAST
stacked BLT egg cake

MONDAY/9

LUNCH
piadinas with bresaola
DINNER
Caesar salad with kale, pasta all'arrabbiata

TUESDAY/10

May 10 through May 25 vacation in Morocco

MONDAY/16

TUESDAY/17

WEDNESDAY/18

THURSDAY/19

FRIDAY/20

SATURDAY/28

DINNER
chicken & veal saltimbocca with tagliatelle, berries with lemon curd and meringue

SUNDAY/29

BRUNCH
deviled ham, BLTs with fried green tomatoes and eggs, ricotta ranch
DINNER
slow-smoked chicken, lemon-pepper glaze, buffed-up baked beans, prosciutto with large figs, fennel and cabbage slaw

MONDAY/30

BREAKFAST
sausage and waffles with cherries
DINNER
two kinds of burgers, oil and vinegar slaw, bull's-eye deviled eggs, corn on the cob with herb butter, double-baked crazy-

MONDAY/30

crisp oven fries, dogs Chicago style, sour cream onion rings

TUESDAY/31

DINNER
slow-smoked chicken, orange-rosemary glaze

MAY 1/DINNER

We had our friend Carice van Houten over (she had just won a Tribeca Film Festival award for best actress in a narrative feature film). As an appetizer, we had **Pancetta-Wrapped Shrimp with Sage**. Then **Spring Risotto** (see April 18, page 16) with peas, spring onions, and asparagus.

Pancetta-Wrapped Shrimp with Sage

- 12 (6- to 8-count) **shrimp** or prawns, tail-on and deveined
- 1 **lemon**, halved
- 1 tablespoon **EVOO**, plus more for liberal drizzling
- **Sea salt** and **pepper**
- 12 large fresh **sage leaves**
- 12 slices **pancetta** or thinly sliced prosciutto

Rinse and dry the shrimp. Dress the shrimp with the juice of ½ lemon; cut the remainder of the lemon into small wedges. Drizzle the shrimp liberally with EVOO and season with a little sea salt and some pepper. Place a sage leaf down the back of each shrimp where it has been deveined and then wrap carefully and snugly with pancetta or prosciutto. Repeat with remaining shrimp.

In a large skillet, heat 1 tablespoon EVOO (1 turn of the pan) over medium to medium-high heat. Add the shrimp and cook to pink and firm and until the pancetta or prosciutto is crisp, 6 to 8 minutes, turning occasionally. Serve with the lemon wedges alongside.

Serves 4

MAY 2/DINNER

We ate out at Motorino Pizza.

MAY 5/DINNER

It was Cinco de Mayo and John and I went out to dinner. We ate at El Parador Cafe. We love it there. We like their chicken, their Parador chicken. It's just a really nice family-owned place that's been around forever in New York. One of our favorite date night places.

MAY 6/DINNER

We had **grilled steaks** with spring garlic and rosemary and marinated **grilled portobellos**. Served that up with a simple **tomato and wild arugula salad**.

Grilled steaks: I coated loin steaks with EVOO, spring garlic, rosemary, sliced chile, cracked black pepper, and sea salt. I let the steaks hang out for an hour to come to room temperature in the seasonings. We grilled them up (medium-high grill, about 8 minutes total for medium-rare) and then we sliced them. I doused them with lemon juice, seasoned with a little extra sea salt, and dressed them with a little chopped parsley.

Grilled portobellos: I sliced 3 large, trimmed portobello mushrooms in half and marinated them in a mixture of 3 to 4 tablespoons Worcestershire sauce, ½ cup dry sherry, ⅓ cup EVOO, porcini salt, and black pepper for about 45 minutes (while the steaks were marinating). We put those on the grill after the steaks; they took only 5 or 6 minutes.

We also made an **onion-tomato-arugula salad:** sliced tomatoes mixed with red onion, parsley, and wild arugula, seasoned with celery salt and pepper and a drizzle of EVOO.

🕐 **MAY 7/MOTHER'S DAY EVE DINNER**

I made my mom **Chicken Francese with Pasta**, but first we had Galia melon with prosciutto (which I put out with lime wedges and black pepper) and a selection of nuts, olives, and cheese. To go with the chicken there was a tomato-asparagus salad with basil, lemon, and wild arugula. For dessert, we had limoncello sorbet with fresh berries.

Chicken Francese with Pasta

Salt and **pepper**
1 pound **linguine** or thin spaghetti
4 skinless, boneless **chicken breast** halves, butterflied (see Tip)
Flour, for dredging
3 **eggs**, lightly beaten
4 tablespoons **EVOO**, plus more for drizzling
6 tablespoons (¾ stick) **butter**
A handful of fresh **mint leaves**, chopped
A handful of **flat-leaf parsley leaves**, chopped
1 or 2 chopped **ramp whites** (or scallions or a small leek when ramps aren't in season)
1 **anchovy fillet**, chopped
½ cup **white wine**
½ cup **chicken stock**
Lemon wedges, for serving

Preheat the oven to 275°F. Place a cooling rack on a baking sheet (for keeping the chicken warm

after sautéing). Bring a large pot of water to a boil. Salt the water. Cook the linguine to al dente and drain.

Meanwhile, put a piece of wax or parchment paper over the chicken and pound each out a bit to make very large cutlets. Season the chicken well with salt and pepper.

Place the flour in a shallow bowl and the beaten eggs in another bowl. Heat 2 tablespoons EVOO and 2 tablespoons butter in a large skillet over medium to medium-high heat. Dip 2 pieces of the chicken in the flour, shaking off the excess, and then in the egg to coat, then sauté until golden, about 2 minutes per side. Transfer to the rack on the baking sheet. Repeat with another 2 tablespoons each EVOO and butter, and the remaining chicken cutlets. Transfer to the oven.

Drizzle a little more EVOO into the pan. Add the mint, parsley, ramp whites, and anchovy, cook for a minute or two, then douse the pan with the wine. Add the chicken stock and the remaining 2 tablespoons butter. Mix that all together and toss with the drained pasta.

Serve the chicken with the pasta alongside.

Serves 4

Lay a skinless, boneless half chicken breast flat on a cutting board. One side is thicker than the other (the thicker side would have been nearest the breastbone). Take a very sharp knife and begin cutting horizontally into the thicker part of the breast; cut into and across the breast but not all the way through. Pull back the top half as you cut. Then you open the breast up and it's butterflied. It looks like a butterfly or a big heart-shaped object.

MAY 8, MOTHER'S DAY BREAKFAST

Stacked BLT egg cake: First I dressed fairly small vine-ripened tomatoes with thyme, salt, pepper, and olive oil and roasted them in a 325°F oven on baking sheets for 35 to 40 minutes. I sautéed 6 chopped slices of bacon. I beat 6 eggs with a splash of milk; a little hot sauce, salt, and pepper; a couple of cloves of green garlic (finely chopped); and a handful of finely chopped parsley. I cooked 3 small omelets (6 inches each, 2 eggs each). I browned them on both sides, using a plate to flip the omelet, and then I set them aside to cool. I mixed sheep's milk ricotta with salt and pepper. To make the stacked egg cake, I put 1 omelet on the plate and topped it with tomatoes, a few leaves of torn basil, and the bacon. Then another omelet, which I topped with a layer of the fresh ricotta. Then the last omelet—so you're 3 omelets high—that I topped with arugula and shaved Parm.

Mother's Day celebration at the Ridge Terrace Restaurant, near Lake George.

🕐 **MAY 9/LUNCH**

We made **piadinas**, which are sandwiches made on superthin Italian bread that comes in packages that I buy at the Buon Italia Market. It's very, very thin. It's thinner than a pita and you fold it in half and you put it on a panini press with assorted fillings.

We made the **piadinas with bresaola**, which is cured beef. It's sort of like prosciutto but it's made out of beef loin instead of pork. So the piadina was thinly sliced bresaola with arugula and thinly sliced Robiola cheese.

⏱ **MAY 9/DINNER**

We made a giant **Caesar Salad** (see April 18, page 16), but this one we made with a mixture of romaine and kale instead of just kale. We also had **Pasta all'Arrabbiata**.

Pasta all'Arrabbiata

You could substitute 12 plum, Roma, or vine-ripened tomatoes from your garden for the canned. Peel them first: score an X into the skin at the bottom of each tomato, drop into boiling water until the skin curls back at the X (30 seconds to 1 minute depending on freshness), cold-shock in a bowl of ice water, peel, cut in half, seed, and chop.

¼ cup **EVOO**
3 **red Fresno chiles**, very thinly sliced
4 large cloves **garlic**, very thinly sliced
1 (28- or 32-ounce) can **San Marzano tomatoes** (look for DOP on the label)
10 to 12 **basil leaves**, torn
A small handful of chopped **flat-leaf parsley**
1 pound **red pepper spaghetti** or chittara spaghetti
1 cup grated **pecorino cheese**

In a large skillet, heat the EVOO (4 turns of the pan) and sauté the chiles and garlic. Add the tomatoes, basil, and parsley. Cook down for 20 to 30 minutes.

Bring a large pot of water to a boil. Salt the water and cook the spaghetti to al dente. Before draining, ladle out about a cup of the starchy pasta cooking water and add to the sauce. Drain the pasta and add to the sauce along with the pecorino, tossing with tongs for 1 to 2 minutes for the flavors to absorb.

Serves 4

MAY 10 THROUGH MAY 25

Vacation in Morocco.

⏱ MAY 26/DINNER

I served steamed artichokes with **Bagna Cauda Dip, Fava Bean Spread** on semolina toasts, **Crab Cakes** in a pool of "bloody gazpacho," **asparagus with lemon vinaigrette**, and **fried dandelion greens** with fried eggs.

Bagna Cauda Dip

This warm dip is enough for 1 large or 2 medium globe artichokes that have been steamed.

    1 head **garlic**
    Sea salt
    3 tablespoons **EVOO**
    10 to 12 **anchovy fillets**
    3 tablespoons **butter**
    1 cup **heavy cream**
    A few grinds of **pepper**

Bring a small saucepan of water to a low boil. Add the garlic and simmer for 20 minutes. Let cool, then drain, peel, and mash into a paste. Season with sea salt.

Meanwhile, in another small saucepan, heat the EVOO (3 turns of the pan) over medium heat. Add the anchovies and stir to melt them into the olive oil. Add the butter, heavy cream, and pepper. Reduce for 20 minutes over a low simmer.

Whisk the garlic paste into the anchovy-cream mixture and serve that as a warm dip.

Makes about 1 cup

Fava Bean Spread

I parboiled about 2½ pounds fava bean pods for 4 to 5 minutes in salted water. I shocked them in ice water. When they were cool enough to handle I shelled and peeled them. I serve the fava bean puree as crostini on toasted semolina-polenta bread. The bread has a little corn going through it. The puree is delicious just with crusty white toast as well. Or you could put the fava over burrata mozzarella (the one with the cream in the center). You break up the burrata, drizzle EVOO over it, and then put a pile of the fava puree in the center of it and everyone mops it up with charred bread or warm bread.

    1½ cups shelled, peeled **fava beans**
    Juice of 1 **lemon**
    ¼ cup fresh **mint leaves**
    ¼ cup **flat-leaf parsley leaves**
    ½ cup grated **pecorino cheese**
    2 cloves **garlic** (see Tip), grated
    1 teaspoon **fennel seeds**
    A handful of **golden raisins**
    Salt and **pepper**
    ¼ to ⅓ cup **EVOO**

In a food processor, puree the fava beans, lemon juice, mint, parsley, cheese, garlic, fennel seeds, raisins, and salt and pepper to taste. As the mixture comes together, start streaming in the EVOO until the puree is a spreadable consistency.

Makes about 2 cups

> The garlic I use is rocambole, which is a hardneck garlic. I get it from Keith's at the Union Square Greenmarket in Manhattan.

Crab Cakes

If you'd prefer not to shallow-fry the crab cakes, you can bake them instead. Coat both sides of the crab cakes with cooking spray and place on a rack set over a baking sheet. Bake at 375°F until golden brown. Serve the crab cakes as is, with Cocktail Sauce (see September 1, page 134) or Tartar Sauce (see April 21, page 21). On this day I served them in a pool of "Bloody Gazpacho": I took my Gazpacho Italiano (see July 18, page 95) and added a shot of vodka to it. I put some of that in a shallow bowl and topped it with the crab cakes.

5 tablespoons **butter**
2 large **shallots**, finely chopped
3 cloves **garlic**, grated or finely chopped
1 **red Fresno chile**, minced
3 ribs **celery**, finely chopped
½ cup **dry vermouth**
2 cups **panko bread crumbs**
3 **eggs**
1 teaspoon **hot sauce**
1 tablespoon **grainy mustard**
2 teaspoons **Old Bay seasoning**
2 tablespoons chopped **fresh thyme**
2 tablespoons finely chopped **chives**
1 pound **crabmeat**, picked through for any
  bits of shell
1 cup **Wondra flour**
2 tablespoons chopped **flat-leaf parsley**
½ cup **EVOO**

In a medium skillet, melt the butter over medium heat. Add the shallots, garlic, chile, and celery and cook until tender, 4 to 5 minutes. Add the vermouth to the pan to deglaze and reduce the liquid by half. Add 1 cup of the panko, turn the heat off, and let the mixture cool in the pan.

While the mixture is cooling, in a bowl, beat 1 of the eggs together with the hot sauce, mustard, 1 teaspoon of the Old Bay, the thyme, and chives. Add the cooled shallot mixture to the bowl along with the crab, and gently combine, trying not to break up the crab too much. Form the crab cakes into disks about 3 inches across and ¾ to 1 inch thick.

Line up 3 shallow bowls on the counter: Spread the flour out in one; beat the remaining 2 eggs with 2 tablespoons water in the second; and mix together the remaining 1 cup panko, remaining 1 teaspoon Old Bay, and the parsley in the third. Coat the crab cakes in the flour, then in egg, and finally in the panko mixture, pressing to make sure the coating sticks.

In a large skillet, heat the EVOO over medium-high heat. When the oil shimmers, add the crab cakes to the pan and shallow-fry them until deeply golden brown on both sides.

Serves 4

Asparagus with lemon vinaigrette: I parboiled asparagus in a little boiling salted water for just 2 minutes because it was so thin and tender. I combine a grated shallot, a little sea salt, ½ teaspoon superfine sugar, finely ground black pepper, the juice of a lemon, and ¼ to ⅓ cup of EVOO. Whisk, whisk, whisk, and pour it over the asparagus.

We also had *fried dandelion greens* cooked in olive oil with a little anchovy and a touch of lemon juice. We topped the dandelion greens with fried eggs.

Mexican Night: Mexican Fiesta pico de gallo, **Bean Dip, Lemon-Garlic Guacamole** (see April 26, page 31), **Flat Iron Steaks with Tre Colore Pesto & Quick-Roasted Tomatoes, Grilled Corn with Chipotle Cream & Cotija**. I also cooked up some rice to go on the side.

I made my Pico de Gallo (see April 26, page 32), but to make it a colorful "Mexican Fiesta" pico, I used a combination of yellow and red tomatoes, and green jalapeño and red Fresno chiles.

Bean Dip

2 tablespoons **corn oil**
1 small **onion**, finely chopped
2 or 3 cloves **garlic**, sliced
1 **jalapeño chile**, chopped
1 teaspoon ground **coriander**
1 teaspoon ground **cumin**
Salt and **pepper**
1 (15-ounce) can **refried beans**
Tortilla chips, for serving

In a medium skillet, heat the oil over medium to medium-high heat. Add the onion, garlic, jalapeño, coriander, cumin, and salt and pepper to taste. Cook until the onion is tender, 6 to 7 minutes.

Add 1 cup water and bring to a boil. Cook 2 to 3 minutes to reduce. Transfer to a food processor, add the refried beans, and process until smooth. Transfer to serving dish. Serve with tortilla chips.

Makes about 2 cups

Flat Iron Steaks with Tre Colore Pesto & Quick-Roasted Tomatoes

4 (7- to 8-ounce) **flat iron steaks**
12 **plum** or **Roma tomatoes**
1 head **garlic** (I used hardneck), separated into
   cloves; peel 1 clove and grate or paste
¾ cup **EVOO**, plus more for drizzling
Salt and **pepper**
½ head **radicchio**, chopped
1 **endive**, sliced
1 cup **flat-leaf parsley leaves**
½ cup **basil leaves**
About 3 tablespoons **pine nuts**, lightly toasted
Juice of 1 **lemon**
2 small handfuls of grated **Parmigiano-
   Reggiano cheese**
Charred or warm split **ciabatta**

Heat a grill pan or griddle to medium-high heat or prepare an outdoor grill. Position a rack in the center of the oven and preheat to 500°F or the highest setting. Remove the steaks from the fridge and let come to room temperature.

Halve the tomatoes and pile on a baking sheet with the unpeeled garlic. Dress with about ¼ cup EVOO and salt and pepper. Arrange the tomatoes cut-side down. Roast until charred and slumped, 20 to 25 minutes.

Place the radicchio, endive, parsley, basil, pine nuts, the pasted or grated garlic, lemon juice, Parm, and salt and pepper in a food processor. Pulse-chop, then stream in about ½ cup EVOO to form a pesto sauce. Transfer to a serving dish.

Dress the meat with a scant drizzle of EVOO and season with salt and pepper. Grill or griddle 3 to 4 minutes on the first side, then turn and cook 3 minutes more for a pink center. Remove and let rest.

Serve the steaks with pesto on top and tomatoes and garlic alongside with warm bread for slathering. Push the garlic from their skins and rub into the bread and top with charred tomatoes, skinned or left intact.

Serves 4

Grilled Corn with Chipotle Cream & Cotija

1 cup **heavy cream**
1 to 2 tablespoons **pureed chipotle chile in adobo**
4 ears **corn**, husked
Vegetable oil or all-natural cooking spray
Grated zest and juice of 1 **lime**
Grated **cotija** or crumbled queso fresco
Finely chopped **cilantro**, for garnish

In a small saucepan, cook the cream at a low simmer until reduced by one-third to one-half. Stir in the pureed chipotle.

Prepare an outdoor grill. If the corn is not sugary sweet, I parboil it before grilling. If it's very sweet I throw it directly onto the grill. Before grilling, brush the corn with a little vegetable oil or coat with all-natural cooking spray to char it up. To serve, squeeze the lime over the corn, drizzle with chipotle cream, add a little grate of lime zest, then add some cheese. Garnish with a little cilantro.

Serves 4

We had **Chicken & Veal Saltimbocca with Tagliatelle** (see April 28, page 32 for the chicken saltimbocca recipe; but substitute 3 veal cutlets for 3 of the chicken cutlets). For dessert I made **berries with lemon curd and meringue**.

*For the **berries with lemon curd and meringue,** I macerated a pint of berries with a little sprinkle of superfine sugar, the juice of ½ lemon, and a few mint and basil leaves muddled in a splash of liqueur. You can use Grand Marnier, Cointreau, Frangelico, or amaretto. I served the berries with warmed lemon curd over meringue. Or you could serve the berries over ice cream or sorbet.*

We had **Deviled Ham** on crackers to start and then **BLTs with fried green tomatoes** and eggs.

Deviled Ham

Deviled ham is delicious as a spread on saltines or crackers. It's delicious spread on toast as a snack or a light lunch with a salad on the side. It's also a really nice brunch item. Sometimes I also use steamed asparagus tips and I'll do a layer of deviled ham, a layer of steamed asparagus tips, and a layer of cheese. Sometimes I've even used it to make a Croque Monsieur (see February 4, page 252) or Croque Madame (see April 16, page 13). I'll take a little thin layer of deviled ham on white toast, top it with béchamel and Gruyère, and bake that and serve topped with an egg. It's all good. You could substitute ½ pound of leftover white meat chicken or deli-sliced chicken breast as well to make deviled chicken.

½ pound **prosciutto cotto**, coarsely chopped
2 small ribs **celery**, with leafy tops, from the heart, coarsely chopped
1 **red Fresno chile**, coarsely chopped (Seed it if you don't want it to be too spicy. I leave the seeds in)
½ small **red onion**, coarsely chopped
A small handful **flat-leaf parsley leaves**
2 small cloves **garlic**, grated or pasted
3 tablespoons **yellow mustard**
2 rounded tablespoons **pickle relish**
2 teaspoons **hot sauce** (I like Frank's RedHot)
2 teaspoons **Worcestershire sauce** (I like Lady Jayne, which I get online)
Pinch of my **Rachael Ray 24/7 Seasoning** or black pepper

Combine everything in a food processor and pulse until it's very, very finely chopped and well combined, almost smooth.

Makes about 1½ cups

I made **BLTs with fried green tomatoes**: First I made the Fried Green Tomatoes (see July 12, page 85). Then I baked off some bacon (artisanal bacon or black pepper bacon or Oscar's bacon: www.oscarssmokedmeats.com). I also made a **ricotta ranch** (fresh ricotta cheese flavored like ranch dressing): I took sheep's milk ricotta cheese and flavored it with a little grated red onion, salt and pepper, finely chopped chives, parsley, dill, a little splash of half-and-half to thin it out, a dash of hot sauce, and a dash of lemon. You pile the fried green tomatoes up with a little ricotta ranch. Top them with lettuce (and red tomato if you like) and the bacon and an over-easy egg, with salt and pepper on it. Nice little brunch item.

🕐 MAY 29/DINNER

We started with grilled prosciutto-wrapped figs (see page 48). Then we had John's **Slow-Smoked Chicken** (see April 24, page 28, for the recipe), which has to be brined a day before. The idea for this version of our smoked chicken came from the brilliant chef Adam Perry Lang's book *BBQ 25*, which is a must-have for any hard-core BBQ aficionado. For the brine, we used several bay leaves, some rosemary, thyme, crushed garlic, a rounded tablespoon of chili flakes, about 2 tablespoons of peppercorns, a few shakes of Worcestershire, and a big pinch of salt. You can paste that all in a food processor or just throw it into a container; it doesn't really matter. Add enough water to cover. We used fruitwood to smoke this chicken, and the baster that we used was **Lemon-Pepper Glaze**. We also had **buffed-up baked beans** and **fennel and cabbage slaw**.

We wrapped **large fresh figs with 18-month prosciutto,** brushed them lightly with a little olive oil, and grilled them over low to medium heat, turning occasionally, until the ham was crispy. We served them with wedges of lime.

Buffed-up baked beans: I took a traditional 3-pound, 7-ounce can of baked beans that I jazzed up with garlic (spring garlic), scallions, Fresno chiles, thick Worcestershire (a heavy steak sauce) or homemade steak sauce, and 2 teaspoons coarse black pepper. All that is mixed into the baked beans along with 6 to

8 slices of partially cooked bacon (you cook it or bake it halfway) that you chop up and scatter on top. Bake it off in the oven until the beans are browned and bubbling.

We also did **fennel and cabbage slaw,** which was ½ head of shredded cabbage and 1 bulb (thinly sliced) fennel tossed with lemon juice, vinegar, a little superfine sugar, salt, pepper, and olive oil.

Lemon-Pepper Glaze

Use this glaze instead of the glaze in the Slow-Smoked Chicken recipe (see April 24, page 28). Save the lemon that you're taking the zest off (for the glaze) for squeezing on the chicken after it comes out of the smoker.

¼ cup white balsamic or cider **vinegar**
⅓ cup **honey**
½ cup **stock**
1 tablespoon **coarse pepper**
Strips of zest from 1 **lemon**
¼ cup **EVOO**

Combine all the ingredients in a saucepan and let it reduce at a low simmer while the chicken cooks up, then start basting during the last half hour.

Makes 1 cup

Memorial Day

MAY 30, 2011

BREAKFAST
We had sausage and **Multigrain Pecan Waffles** (see April 19, page 17), but I used walnuts instead of pecans and I served fresh cherries on top instead of berries. Delicious.

DINNER
I made two kinds of burgers (a plain beef burger topped with an **oil and vinegar slaw**, and then a **Swiss Mushroom Burger**) and **dogs, Chicago style**. We also had my **Bull's-Eye Deviled Eggs** (see April 24, page 29), corn on the cob with herb butter, **Sour Cream Onion Rings** (see April 9, page 7) and my **Double-Baked Crazy-Crisp Oven Fries**.

We made **dogs, Chicago style**, with cucumbers seasoned with celery salt and fresh dill, sliced ripe tomatoes, and all of the Chicago fixin's. I put all of the fixin's out in my mini tabletop Vienna Beef Hot Dog cart that sits on the countertop. It's very cute. Kappy is from Chicago, so he sends me all my Chicago toppings when I need them replenished.

I cooked up **beef burgers** flavored with Worcestershire, a little grated onion, salt, and pepper. I basted the grilled burgers with BBQ sauce when they were about to come off the grill and topped them with a little **oil and vinegar slaw**: oil, vinegar, salt, pepper, a little sprinkle of superfine sugar, shredded white cabbage, and a little bit of grated carrot. We served the burgers with or without Cheddar cheese. We made them to order on brioche rolls that had black pepper on them.

Swiss Mushroom Burgers

RANCH DRESSING

1 cup **sour cream**
¼ to ⅓ cup **buttermilk**
¼ cup finely chopped **mixed fresh herbs** (dill, parsley, chives, and thyme)
1 tablespoon fresh **lemon juice**
1 tablespoon **hot sauce**
1 clove **garlic**, grated
Salt and **pepper**

BURGERS

1½ pounds **ground beef chuck**
About ¼ cup **Worcestershire sauce**
3 tablespoons grated **onion**
Coarse salt and **pepper**
4 deli slices (not too thin) **Swiss cheese**
3 tablespoons **butter**
1 pound **white mushrooms**, sliced
1 **shallot**, finely chopped
⅓ cup **dry sherry**
4 **brioche** or other soft rolls, split

Make the ranch dressing: In a bowl, stir together the sour cream, buttermilk, herbs, lemon juice, hot sauce, and garlic; season with salt and pepper.

Make the burgers: Combine the beef, Worcestershire, onion, salt, and lots of pepper. Form into 4 patties (thinner at the center and thicker at the edges for even cooking). Cook the burgers on the grill. Top the patties with the cheese, folded to fit the burgers, during the last 2 minutes of cooking.

Meanwhile, in a skillet, melt the butter over medium heat. Add the mushrooms and cook until browned, about 12 minutes. Add the shallot, season with salt and pepper, and cook for 2 to 3 minutes more. Deglaze the pan with the sherry and remove from the heat.

Put the cheeseburgers on the roll bottoms and top with the mushrooms. Slather the roll tops with the ranch dressing and set into place.

Serves 4

Double-Baked Crazy-Crisp Oven Fries

6 **medium-starchy potatoes**, such as Idaho
EVOO, for drizzling
Kosher salt and **pepper**

Preheat the oven to 350°F. Set a cooling rack over each of 2 baking sheets.

Peel the potatoes, leaving a patch of the skin at both ends. Cut each potato lengthwise into very thin (⅛- to ¼-inch) slices—the thinner they are, the crispier the end product will be. Cut those slices into strips that are just as thin.

In a large bowl, drizzle the fries very lightly with EVOO—a couple of turns of the bowl should do the trick. Season with salt and pepper.

Arrange the fries on the racks in a single layer without crowding either rack.

Roast 30 minutes. Remove the fries and increase the oven temperature to 425°F. Return the fries to the oven and bake until very crispy and brown, 15 to 20 minutes.

Serves 6

🕐 **MAY 31/DINNER**

We made **Slow-Smoked Chicken** (see April 24, page 28), but we made the brine a little differently (don't forget, you have to brine the day before).

Orange-Rosemary Brine & Glaze

Follow the Slow-Smoked Chicken recipe, but use this brine and glaze instead.

THE BRINE
2 quarts **water**
3 to 4 tablespoons **superfine sugar**
3 tablespoons kosher or fine sea **salt**
3 tablespoons white balsamic or white wine **vinegar**
About ½ cup grated **onion**
1 **lemon**, sliced
1 **orange**, sliced
A few sprigs of **rosemary**, chopped

THE GLAZE
A few tablespoons **butter**
2 medium or 1 large **shallot**, finely chopped or grated
1 or 2 cloves **garlic**, finely chopped
¼ cup **Marsala**
Grated zest and juice of 1 **orange**
½ cup **chicken stock**
⅓ cup **honey**
1 to 2 tablespoons finely chopped **rosemary**
1 teaspoon **fennel pollen**
1 teaspoon dried **thyme**
1 teaspoon dried **oregano**
Salt and **pepper**

Make the brine: Combine all the ingredients.

Make the glaze: In a saucepan, heat the butter. Add the shallot and garlic and sauté. Deglaze with the Marsala. Add the orange zest and juice, stock, honey, rosemary, fennel pollen, thyme, oregano, salt, and pepper. Cook until the glaze is reduced to ½ cup.

JUNE

WEDNESDAY/1

BREAKFAST
brioche toast, omelet with sautéed shallots

THURSDAY/2

BRUNCH
tuna melts
DINNER
swordfish cutlets, fresh tomato relish, aglio e olio, Sicilian-style orange salad

FRIDAY/3

BREAKFAST
popper hash
DINNER
Bolognese with pappardelle

SATURDAY/4

LUNCH
potato & lentil dish, Italian sliced chicken & pork hoagies
DINNER
mixed herb pesto penne

SUNDAY/5

BREAKFAST
mushroom frittata

SATURDAY/11

SUNDAY/12

DINNER
pork & ancho chile stew, pico de gallo

MONDAY/13

DINNER
lentil soup with sherry mushrooms

TUESDAY/14

WEDNESDAY/15

DINNER
green rice with beans; leg of lamb; pepper; onion, and tomato salad

TUESDAY/21

WEDNESDAY/22

DINNER
carbonara with spring herb gremolata, bistecca, porcini steak sauce

THURSDAY/23

BREAKFAST
scape frittata
DINNER
branzino with crispy kale, thyme rice, carrots and asparagus with mint and tarragon

FRIDAY/24

BREAKFAST
almond custard brioche French toast
DINNER
grilled ribs, bourbon BBQ sauce

SATURDAY/25

DINNER
spaghetti with red pepper pesto

MONDAY/6

BREAKFAST
rise and shine super sliders

DINNER
sloppy dawgs, chicken & biscuit sliders

TUESDAY/7

DINNER
zucchini-mint pesto with shallots & cream with penne

WEDNESDAY/8

DINNER
chicken vindaloo

THURSDAY/9

FRIDAY/10

DINNER
roast pork shoulder sandwiches with fennel slaw

THURSDAY/16

DINNER
Caesar tagliatelle

FRIDAY/17

SATURDAY/18

SUNDAY/19

DINNER
homemade beef jerky (Father's Day)

MONDAY/20

DINNER
chicken spiedies with sesame sauce

SUNDAY/26

MONDAY/27

TUESDAY/28

DINNER
roasted eggplant appetizer, tzatziki, ajvar, surf & turf, ricotta-stuffed zucchini flowers, fresh spinach with chile and garlic

WEDNESDAY/29

DINNER
swordfish cutlets, fresh tomato relish, Sicilian-style orange salad, aglio e olio, semifreddo

THURSDAY/30

JUNE 1, BREAKFAST

*I made **brioche toast:** thick-cut slices of brioche grilled in melted butter and topped with sliced fresh berries and a drizzle of good Italian honey. I also made an **omelet**. Sautéed some shallots and added beaten eggs with little bits of cold butter mixed in. Added Swiss cheese. Served that with baked artisanal herbes de Provence bacon.*

JUNE 2/BRUNCH

Tuna Melts

Sometimes I make an extra-wide tuna melt: I take 2 hand-cut slices of toast and trim off the crust on one side. Then I halve a third slice of toast and marry the trimmed piece of toast with the half-slice so each person actually gets 1½ slices of toast. It looks like a super-fat, wide piece of toast. Top it with your tuna and toppings; when the cheese melts it just looks like one giant slice of bread underneath. You don't know it's actually two pieces. Serve it with or without an egg on top.

TUNA SALAD
1 (6-ounce) can line-caught **tuna**
½ small **red onion**, finely chopped
A couple of small ribs **celery**, minced
1 **red Fresno chile**, minced
2 cloves **garlic**, pasted
3 tablespoons **capers**
3 to 4 tablespoons coarsely chopped pitted **niçoise olives** (or whichever olives you have on hand)
¼ cup chopped **mixed fresh herbs**: rosemary, thyme, parsley, chive
Juice of 1 **lemon**
3 tablespoons **EVOO**
Black pepper

ASSEMBLY
3 hand-cut slices **white bread**, toasted
Tomato slices
1 cup shredded **Fontina cheese**
2 fried eggs (optional)
Chopped **green spring onions**, for garnish

Preheat the oven to 375°F.

Mix all the tuna salad ingredients together. Spread on top of the bread; top with the tomato and then the cheese. Bake until the cheese melts. Garnish with chopped green spring onion or garnish with any of the herbs that you included in the tuna salad, or just serve it straight up. Tuna melt is a beautiful thing.

Makes 2 double-wides

JUNE 2/DINNER

For dinner we had one of our favorites, **Swordfish Cutlets**. I always serve that with a **fresh tomato relish**, and for this dinner I added a little bit of spring garlic and some garlic scapes to that. We also had my **Sicilian-style orange salad** and **Aglio e Olio** for a side pasta.

Swordfish Cutlets

For each cutlet, I use a very thin slice of swordfish that I pound between two sheets of parchment paper until it's paper thin, so you can almost read the newspaper through it. To bread them you don't need flour and egg; the breading is fine bread crumbs (they're Italian bread crumbs that look like dust; I get them from Buon Italia in the Chelsea Market in Manhattan) mixed half-and-half with panko. Or instead of panko you can use homemade bread crumbs and make them nice and coarse.

- 8 thinly sliced **swordfish steaks** (about ½ inch), cut from one side of the bloodline
- 2 cups fine **dry bread crumbs**
- 2 cups **panko bread crumbs**
- 3 **lemons**, 2 zested and 1 cut into wedges for serving
- ½ cup **flat-leaf parsley**, finely chopped
- 2 or 3 cloves **garlic**, chopped
- 1 **anchovy fillet**, very finely chopped (optional)
- **Sea salt** and **pepper**
- **EVOO**, for frying and drizzling

Preheat the oven to 275°F. Set up a cooling rack over a rimmed baking sheet. (This will be for keeping the swordfish warm. The rack allows the heat to circulate all the way around the cutlets so they'll stay nice and crispy on both sides. If you put them directly on a baking sheet they'll tend to get a little sweaty on the bottom and stay crisp only on top.)

Trim the skin from the edges of the fish. Place the fish between two pieces of parchment paper and pound gently to ¼-inch thickness.

Combine the fine bread crumbs and panko in a shallow dish. Stir in the lemon zest, parsley, garlic, and anchovy (if using). Work the ingredients through the bread crumbs with your fingers. Season the swordfish cutlets on both sides with salt and pepper. Press the cutlets firmly into the bread crumbs so that they are evenly coated on both sides.

In a large skillet, heat a layer of EVOO (about ⅛ inch) over medium to medium-high heat.

Working in batches, add the swordfish cutlets and cook until they're deeply golden brown, about 12 minutes per side. Keep them warm in the oven until you're ready to serve. Serve with lemon wedges for squeezing.

Serves 4

I top my swordfish cutlets with a **fresh tomato relish**, sort of a tomato raw sauce: Chop plum or vine-ripened tomatoes that have been gently seeded into small dice (about ¼ inch). I mix that together with minced or finely chopped red onion and some combination of chopped basil leaves and flat-leaf parsley leaves. I toss that together lightly, using my fingertips. I do not add oil, and just season it to taste with sea salt.

Aglio e Olio

You can use regular spaghetti, but for this meal I used lemon-flavored spaghetti.

⅓ cup **EVOO**
8 to 10 **anchovy fillets**
5 or 6 cloves **garlic**, thinly sliced or chopped
2 **red Fresno chiles**, seeded and finely chopped
⅓ cup **dry vermouth**
Salt
1 pound **spaghetti**
½ cup **flat-leaf parsley**, chopped
Black pepper

Bring a large pot of water to a boil.

Meanwhile, in a skillet, heat the EVOO over medium heat. Melt the anchovy fillets into the oil, stirring the anchovies until they break up and dissolve completely into the oil. Add the garlic and chiles; reduce the heat to low. Stir that a few minutes, then add the vermouth.

Salt the boiling water and cook the pasta to al dente. Before draining, ladle out about a cup of the starchy pasta cooking water and add to the sauce. Drain the pasta and add to the sauce along with the parsley, tossing with tongs for 1 to 2 minutes for the flavors to absorb. John and I usually add a little black pepper as well because we like things ridiculously spicy.

Serves 4

For the **Sicilian-style orange salad**, I started with seedless oranges (or you can do blood oranges when they're in season) that I peeled and then sliced into ¼-inch-thick rounds. I topped them with a little bit of thinly sliced red onion, finely chopped garlic scapes, and fresh oregano or marjoram (a couple of sprigs per platter of oranges). Then you can drizzle them with EVOO, season with salt and pepper, and, if you like, put a little shaved young pecorino cheese with it. That's also delicious. (See photo, page 250.)

🕐 **JUNE 3/BREAKFAST**

Popper Hash

Serve the hash topped with over-easy eggs. Cook them in a separate skillet while you make the hash.

¼ to ⅓ pound **bacon**, chopped
EVOO
1 large **russet (baking) potato**, peeled and chopped
2 teaspoons **Old Bay seasoning**
1 tablespoon ground **coriander**
1 tablespoon ground **cumin**
Black pepper
1 **red onion**, diced
1 or 2 cloves **garlic**, chopped
2 **jalapeño chiles**, sliced
2 or 3 **scallions**, chopped, whites and greens separate
2 cups shredded **extra-sharp Cheddar cheese**
4 **eggs**, cooked over-easy
Chopped **cilantro**, for garnish

In a large broilerproof skillet, cook the bacon in a little EVOO until browned. Transfer the bacon to paper towels to drain. Add the potato to the pan and season with Old Bay, coriander, cumin, and black pepper. Partially cover the pan and cook for a few minutes to sweat it out and get it going to tender. Add the onion, garlic, jalapeños, and scallion whites; partially cover; and let that cook out a couple of minutes.

Preheat the broiler.

Save a little bacon for garnish and stir the rest into the hash. Cover the hash with Cheddar and broil to melt the cheese.

To serve, slide the eggs on top of the hash and then garnish with the scallion greens, cilantro, and reserved bacon bits. Serve it right out of the skillet.

Serves 2

🕐 **JUNE 3/DINNER**

I made **Bolognese with Pappardelle** because it was 36 degrees out (in June!) so it was certainly cold enough that we wanted a hearty dinner.

Bolognese with Pappardelle

2 tablespoons **EVOO**
¼ pound **pancetta**, cut into small dice or ground
1 pound **ground beef sirloin**
1 pound **ground pork**
1 **onion**, cut into small dice
1 **carrot**, cut into small dice
2 ribs **celery**, cut into small dice
3 or 4 cloves **garlic**, minced or grated
Salt and **pepper**
¼ teaspoon freshly grated **nutmeg**
2 **bay leaves**
1 tablespoon **thyme leaves**, chopped
1 teaspoon dried **marjoram** or oregano
¼ cup **tomato paste**
2 cups **dry white wine**
3 cups **beef stock**
½ teaspoon crushed **red pepper flakes**
1 cup **whole milk** or cream
1 pound **pappardelle** or fettuccine pasta
At least 1 cup grated **Parmigiano-Reggiano**
 cheese, plus more to pass at the table
½ cup **flat-leaf parsley**, chopped

In a large pot, heat the EVOO (2 turns of the pan) over medium-high heat. Add the pancetta and cook, stirring occasionally, until browned and the fat is rendered, 3 to 4 minutes. Add the sirloin and pork to the pot and brown 12 to 15 minutes. Add the onion, carrot, celery, and garlic and cook, stirring, until softened, 8 to 10 minutes more.

Season with salt, pepper, nutmeg, bay leaves,

thyme, and marjoram or oregano. Stir in the tomato paste, cook for a minute or so, then add the wine and scrape up all the drippings.

Reduce the wine by half, 3 to 5 minutes, then stir in the stock and bring to a boil. Reduce the heat to a simmer and let the sauce thicken, 1 to 1½ hours, stirring occasionally to keep the sauce from sticking to the bottom of the pan.

Add the milk or cream and let simmer as the water for the pasta comes up to a boil and the pasta cooks.

When the pot of water is boiling, salt the water and cook the pasta to al dente. Just before draining reserve 1 cup of starchy cooking water.

Drain the pasta and toss it back into the pot it was cooked in, along with the reserved cooking water, about a cup of Parm, and a couple of handfuls of chopped parsley. Add half the pasta sauce and toss well to coat.

Serve the pasta in shallow bowls, topped with additional sauce. Pass the remaining Parm at the table.

Serves 4 to 6

⬤ JUNE 4/LUNCH

For lunch we had **Italian Sliced Chicken & Pork Hoagies** and a warm **lentil-potato dish with ham and mushrooms.**

Italian Sliced Chicken & Pork Hoagies

1 (¾- to 1-pound) **pork tenderloin**, well trimmed
1¼ to 1⅓ pounds **skinless, boneless chicken breasts**
EVOO, for drizzling
Montreal Steak Seasoning or salt and pepper

HOAGIE DRESSING
½ small **red Fresno chile pepper**, finely chopped
1 large clove **garlic**, grated
1 **shallot**, minced, or 3 tablespoons grated red onion

1 rounded teaspoon **superfine sugar**
Juice of ½ **lemon**
3 tablespoons **red wine vinegar**
2 teaspoons finely chopped **thyme leaves**
1 tablespoon finely chopped **fresh basil**
1 tablespoon finely chopped **flat-leaf parsley**
½ cup **EVOO**
1 rounded tablespoon **Dijon mustard**
Salt and **pepper**

1 cup drained **giardiniera** (hot pickled vegetable), store-bought or homemade (page 168)
4 Italian **hoagie** or **sub rolls** (10- to 12-inch)
Deli-sliced **provolone cheese**
Chopped **romaine lettuce**
Sliced ripe **tomato**
Thinly sliced **red onion**

Preheat the oven to 500°F. Set a cooling rack over a baking sheet.

Dress the pork and chicken in a drizzle of EVOO and season. Place the pork on the rack and roast 10 to 12 minutes. Reduce the heat to 425°F and roast 15 minutes more. *Do not open the oven.* Remove the meat (the internal temp should be 145° to 155°F). Let the meat rest 5 to 10 minutes before very thinly slicing on an angle.

Meanwhile, heat a cast-iron pan or griddle on medium-high heat. Cook the chicken, turning occasionally, until firm and the juices run clear, 12 to 15 minutes. Let the meat rest 5 to 10 minutes before very thinly slicing on an angle.

Make the dressing: In a bowl, combine the chile, garlic, shallot or onion, and superfine sugar. Add the lemon juice, vinegar, and herbs. Whisk in the EVOO in a slow stream. Add the mustard and salt and pepper to taste and whisk to emulsify.

Pulse-chop the giardiniera to a fine relish in a food processor.

Arrange the pork and chicken on the rolls and top with cheese, lettuce, tomato, onion, and giardiniera. Pour the dressing over the relish, and set hoagie tops in place.

Serves 4

Lentils and potatoes with mushrooms and ham: I cooked 1 cup Puy lentils in a pot of water for 20 minutes, and about 15 minutes in I added a potato (peeled and diced) for the last 5 minutes of cook time. I diced ¼ to ⅓ pound thick-cut hot ham and rendered that out a bit in a skillet. I added ⅓ to ½ pound sliced cremini mushrooms to the skillet and browned them. Then I added a diced red chile, a diced onion, and 1 or 2 minced cloves of garlic and sautéed. I added the drained lentil-potato mixture and doused the pan with sherry (or sherry vinegar). You can serve this warm or turn it into a cold salad: Make the mixture the same way and then combine with chopped celery, parsley, sherry vinegar, and olive oil. That's a great cold salad.

JUNE 4/DINNER

Mixed Herb Pesto Penne

¼ cup **pine nuts**
1 cup **basil leaves**
½ cup **flat-leaf parsley leaves**
¼ cup **mint leaves**
About 2 tablespoons fresh **thyme leaves**
2 cloves **garlic**, grated or pasted
⅓ cup grated **Parmigiano-Reggiano cheese**
Juice of ½ **lemon**
Salt and **pepper**
About ½ cup **EVOO**
1 pound **penne rigate pasta**
1 small **russet (baking) potato**, peeled and cut into ¼-inch dice
A couple of handfuls of **haricots verts** (about ⅓ pound), trimmed and cut into thirds

In a food processor, combine the pine nuts, herbs, garlic, Parm, lemon juice, and salt and pepper to taste. Pulse-chop, then with the machine running stream in the EVOO to form a thick sauce. Transfer to a large bowl.

Bring a large pot of water to a boil and salt the water. Add the pasta and cook 6 minutes. Add the potato and cook 1 minute. Add the beans and cook until the pasta is cooked to al dente, 2 to 3 minutes. Ladle out 1 cup of the starchy cooking water and stir into the pesto. Drain the pasta and toss with the sauce.

Serves 4 to 6

JUNE 5, BREAKFAST. **Mushroom frittata:** I sautéed a couple of handfuls of sliced cremini mushrooms, ½ diced onion, and 2 minced cloves of garlic in a little olive oil. When they were tender, I added ¼ cup chopped mixed herbs, eggs beaten with milk and little pieces of cold butter (which is a trick my grandpa used to do), and salt and pepper. When the eggs set, I transferred the skillet to the oven and baked until lightly browned, then topped with Fontina and Parm and popped it under the broiler just to brown the cheese.

JUNE 6, BREAKFAST. **Rise and shine super sliders:** I used a little egg ring (or you could use a round cookie cutter) to cook perfectly round fried eggs. You could also pour beaten eggs onto a griddle and let them cook until the top starts to dry, then fold the eggs into quarters and you have a folded scrambled egg. If you make scrambled eggs, you can add cooked chopped bacon and parsley to the beaten eggs (John's style of scrambled eggs); you could put hot sauce into the scramblers as well. If you make fried eggs, you could put crispy bacon and hot sauce directly on the fried eggs. Then I take melted butter and I mix in hot sauce and chives and I brush that all over toasted English muffins. You put your fried egg or your folded scrambled egg on the English muffin. That gets topped off with a beef or pork sausage patty (I made mine from Oscar's Smokehouse breakfast sausage).

🕐 JUNE 6/DINNER

We did **Sloppy Dawgs** and **Chicken & Biscuit Sliders**.

Sloppy Dawgs

- 1 tablespoon **EVOO**
- 1½ pounds **hot dogs** (beef, pork, turkey, or tofu), chopped or thinly sliced
- 1 medium **onion**, finely chopped
- 2 cloves **garlic**, finely chopped or grated
- 1 **red bell pepper**, finely chopped
- 1 cup canned **baked beans**
- 2 tablespoons **light brown sugar**
- 2 tablespoons **red wine vinegar**
- 2 tablespoons **Worcestershire sauce**
- 1 cup or 1 (8-ounce) can **tomato sauce**
- **Kosher salt** and **black pepper**
- 6 crusty **split-top hot dog rolls**, 6 burger rolls, or 12 slider rolls, toasted and lightly buttered

Heat the EVOO, 1 turn of the pan, in a large skillet over medium-high heat. Add the hot dogs and cook until golden brown, 4 to 5 minutes. Add the onion, garlic, and bell pepper, and cook 3 to 5 minutes to soften. Stir in the beans.

In a medium bowl, stir together the brown sugar, vinegar, Worcestershire sauce, and tomato sauce. Stir the sauce mixture into the pan, season with salt and pepper, and simmer over low heat until thickened, about 5 minutes.

Spoon the filling into the hot dog rolls or over

the roll bottoms and top with onion, pickles or relish, and mustard. If serving on burger or slider rolls, set the tops in place.

Serves 4

Chicken & Biscuit Sliders

8 **buttermilk biscuits**, homemade (from scratch or from a mix) or good-quality store-bought, warmed and split

OIL-AND-VINEGAR SLAW
½ pound **coleslaw mix** or ¼ head green cabbage, shredded
½ small **red onion**, very thinly sliced
3 tablespoons **cider vinegar**
2 tablespoons **vegetable oil**
1 teaspoon **celery salt**
Kosher salt and **pepper**

FRIED CHICKEN
1½ to 2 pounds **skinless, boneless chicken thighs** or **breasts**, trimmed into 8 (3- to 4-ounce) pieces to fit the biscuits
2 cups **buttermilk**
1½ cups **flour**
1 tablespoon **dry mustard**
1 tablespoon **poultry seasoning**
Vegetable oil, for frying

ORANGE-MAPLE DRIZZLE
½ cup **dark amber maple syrup**
Grated zest of 1 **orange** or a curl of zest
1 tablespoon **sriracha sauce**

If you're making your own biscuits, bake them now. You'll need eight 3-inch biscuits.

Make the slaw: In a small bowl, combine the coleslaw mix and red onion. Add the vinegar, oil, and celery salt; season with salt and pepper and toss to coat the veggies with dressing.

Make the chicken: Season the chicken with salt and pepper. Stir the chicken and buttermilk together in a small bowl and let sit for 30 minutes.

Place the flour, mustard, and poultry seasoning in a paper sack, and shake to combine.

Fill a countertop fryer with oil, or pour a few inches of oil into a large Dutch oven. Heat the oil to 350° to 375°F. The oil is ready for frying when bubbles stream out rapidly from the handle of a wooden spoon inserted into the oil.

While the frying oil is heating, make the drizzle: Stir the maple syrup, orange zest, and sriracha together in a small saucepan. Warm over low heat.

When the frying oil is ready, add the chicken pieces to the sack of seasoned flour. Fold the top closed and shake the bag. Shake any excess flour off the chicken pieces and add them to the hot frying oil. Fry the chicken 7 to 8 minutes for thighs, a minute or two less for breasts, until deeply golden and the juices run clear when the chicken is poked. Remove from the oil with a skimmer or tongs and cool on a cooling rack.

Place the chicken on the biscuit bottoms and top with a spoonful of the spicy orange-maple drizzle and some slaw. Set the biscuit tops in place.

Makes 8 sliders

🕐 JUNE 7/DINNER

Zucchini-Mint Pesto with Shallots & Cream with Penne

1 or 2 tablespoons **EVOO**
1 pound small **zucchini**, seeded and sliced into half-moons
1 or 2 large cloves **garlic**, grated or pasted
½ cup fresh **mint leaves**
¼ cup fresh **tarragon**
½ cup packed **basil leaves**
2 to 3 tablespoons **butter**
1 large or 2 small **shallots**, thinly sliced
⅓ to ½ cup **dry white wine** or champagne
½ cup **heavy cream**
Salt
1 pound **penne pasta**
¾ cup grated **pecorino** or **Parmigiano-Reggiano cheese**, or a mixture

In a large skillet, heat the EVOO (1 or 2 turns of the pan) over medium-high heat. Add the zucchini and garlic and cook until lightly golden, 6 to 7 minutes. Transfer ⅓ to ½ cup of the zucchini mixture to a food processor. Let it cool a bit, then add the mint, tarragon, and basil. Pulse that into a pesto-like substance.

Bring a large pot of water to a boil. Meanwhile, in a separate skillet, melt the butter and sauté the shallots. Deglaze the pan with the wine and let that cook down by about half. Stir in the cream and the reserved sautéed zucchini and heat that back through. Stir in the pesto.

Salt the boiling water and cook the penne to al dente. Before draining, ladle out about 1 cup of the starchy pasta cooking water and add to the sauce. Drain the pasta, add to the sauce along with the cheese, and toss with tongs 1 or 2 minutes for the flavors to absorb.

Serves 4

🕐 JUNE 8/DINNER

We had **Chicken Vindaloo** (see April 16, page 14) with store-bought naan bread and jasmine rice scented with lime zest.

🕐 JUNE 10/DINNER

Roast Pork Shoulder Sandwiches with Fennel Slaw

You can roast the pork for the sandwiches ahead of time. Let the roast cool to room temp, cover, and store. To serve, slice 1-inch-thick pieces and reheat in a shallow pan of warm chicken stock to heat through.

3½ to 4 pounds boneless **pork shoulder**
Sea salt and **coarse black pepper**

1 head **garlic**, separated and chopped
Leaves from 5 or 6 sprigs of **rosemary**, finely chopped
2 tablespoons **fennel seeds**
¼ cup **EVOO**, plus more for liberal drizzling
4 **onions**, cut into thin wedges
1 cup **dry white wine**
1 rounded tablespoon **superfine sugar**
Juice of ½ **lemon**
2 tablespoons white balsamic or **white wine vinegar**
½ pound **cabbage**, very thinly sliced or mandoline-sliced
1 bulb **fennel**, very thinly sliced or mandoline-shredded, plus a handful of fronds
4 **ciabatta** or other crusty sandwich/sub rolls

Preheat the oven to 375°F.

Have the butcher butterfly the meat for you or take a very sharp knife and split the shoulder open and across the meat, opening the shoulder like a book, about 1 to 1½ inches thick. Heavily season the meat with lots of pepper and sea salt, the garlic, rosemary, and fennel seeds. Roll the meat up and tie with kitchen twine. Drizzle liberally with EVOO; season with salt and pepper. Drizzle the onions with EVOO and season with salt and pepper. Scatter across a baking pan, set the meat on top, and roast for 1 hour.

Douse the pan with the wine and roast until the internal temperature reaches 145° to 150°F. Let stand 15 minutes, then slice.

Make the fennel slaw: In a large bowl, combine the sugar, lemon juice, vinegar, ¼ cup EVOO, and salt and pepper to taste. Add the cabbage, fennel, and the fronds to the dressing.

To serve, pile the sliced meat on rolls and top with the warm onions and cold fennel slaw.

Serves 4, with plenty of leftovers

I shot a video with Mario Batali for a piece he did for the Web in conjunction with *Vanity Fair*. We hung out on a boat on a beautiful warm day and then that night John and I had **Pork & Ancho Chile Stew** and I made my usual **Pico de Gallo** (see April 26, page 32), but I added slices of an underripe avocado.

Pork & Ancho Chile Stew

1 **red onion**, sliced
Juice of 2 **limes**
Salt and **pepper**
5 or 6 **ancho chiles**, stemmed and seeded
4 cups **chicken stock**
½ cup blanched **almonds**
½ cup unsalted **peanuts**
A handful of **raisins**
3 or 4 cloves **garlic**, grated or pasted
1 small **yellow onion**, chopped
1 tablespoon unsweetened **cocoa powder**
½ teaspoon **ground cloves**
2 pounds **pork shoulder**, cut into bite-size cubes
2 tablespoons **vegetable oil** or peanut oil
1 **cinnamon stick**
2 large **bay leaves**
12 flour or corn **tortillas**, charred or warmed
Queso fresco or cotija cheese, crumbled

Separate the red onion into rings and place in a small plastic food storage container; dress with the lime juice and salt and pepper to taste. Cover and refrigerate until serving time.

Place the ancho chiles in a pot and cover with the stock. Heat the stock to soften the chiles, about 10 minutes.

In a large Dutch oven, brown the nuts over medium heat. Transfer the nuts to a food processor. Working in batches if necessary, add the reconstituted chiles and stock, the raisins, garlic, onion, cocoa, cloves, and salt and pepper and puree.

Pat the meat dry. Heat the oil in the Dutch oven over medium-high heat. Season the meat

with salt and pepper and brown in 2 batches. Pour the sauce over the meat and bring to a boil. Add the cinnamon stick and bay leaves, reduce the heat to a simmer, and cook to very tender, 1¼ to 1½ hours, depending on how large you cubed the meat. Remove the cinnamon and bay leaves and serve the stew with the tortillas, lime-pickled onions, and crumbled cheese.

Serves 4 to 6

Lentil Soup with Sherry Mushrooms

2 tablespoons **EVOO**
3 tablespoons **butter**, plus more for brushing
1 pound **cremini mushrooms**, chopped
4 **shallots**, chopped
2 large cloves **garlic**, chopped
Salt and **pepper**
½ cup **dry sherry**
1 fresh **bay leaf**
4 cups **chicken stock**
1½ cups **Puy green lentils**
1 bunch **spinach** (from the farmers' market), cleaned, tough stems removed
Grated zest of 1 **lemon**
Freshly grated **nutmeg**
Naan or **pita bread**, for serving
Greek yogurt, crème fraîche, or sour cream, for serving (optional)

In a soup pot or Dutch oven, heat the EVOO over medium-high heat. Melt the butter into the oil. Add the mushrooms and cook until browned, 12 to 15 minutes. Add the shallots and garlic and season with salt and pepper. Add the sherry and bay leaf and cook for a few more minutes. Stir in the chicken stock, lentils, and 3 cups water. Bring to a boil, then reduce the heat to a simmer and cook for 20 minutes.

Stir in the spinach to wilt it, and add the lemon zest, 5 to 10 grates of nutmeg, and salt and pepper to taste.

Warm the bread on a griddle and brush with melted butter. Ladle the soup into bowls and top with a dollop of yogurt, if desired. Serve with the bread.

Serves 4

🕐 JUNE 15/DINNER

I made a beautiful summer **Green Rice with Beans**, which I served with a **leg of lamb** (see July 30, page 104, for how to roast a leg of lamb) cooked up with chiles, garlic, and lots of mint and rosemary. When the roast was done, I topped it with lemon juice. We also had a **pepper, onion, and tomato salad.**

Green Rice with Beans

About two dozen very large **fava pods**
⅓ pound very thin **green beans**, trimmed
7 tablespoons **EVOO**
8 to 10 **garlic scapes** (preferably from rocambole garlic), thinly sliced
Salt and **pepper**
1½ cups **long-grain white rice**
2¾ cups **chicken stock**
½ cup **vegetable stock**
¼ pound **arugula**
1 cup **basil leaves**
Juice of 1 **lemon**

Shell the favas and parboil them in a pot of boiling water for 2 to 3 minutes; rinse under cold water, peel, and split (I ended up with a couple of handfuls of peeled, split favas). In the same boiling water, parboil the green beans for about 2 minutes, then cold-shock in ice water and drain them. Cut them into thirds and set aside with the favas.

In a saucepan, heat 3 tablespoons EVOO (3 turns of the pan) and cook the garlic scapes for 2 or 3 minutes. Season with salt and pepper. Add the rice and chicken stock and cook until just tender, 17 to 18 minutes. Spread the rice out on a baking sheet to quick-cool it.

In a food processor, combine the vegetable stock, arugula, basil, lemon juice, about ¼ cup EVOO (just eyeball it), and salt and pepper. Pulse it into a pesto-like sauce.

Stir the pesto and sautéed scapes into the cooled rice. Stir in the green beans and fava beans. Adjust the salt and pepper to taste.

Serves 4

Pepper, onion, and tomato salad: Sliced peppers and onions dressed with olive oil, salt, and pepper; and seeded Roma tomatoes dressed with garlic, thyme, olive oil, salt, and pepper.

🕐 **JUNE 16/DINNER**

Caesar Tagliatelle

Salt and **pepper**
1 pound **egg tagliatelle** noodles (I like Delverde brand)
¼ cup **EVOO**, plus some for drizzling
6 **anchovy fillets**
4 large cloves **garlic**, grated or finely chopped
2 teaspoons to 1 tablespoon **Worcestershire sauce**
2 medium heads **escarole**, shredded
¼ teaspoon freshly grated **nutmeg**, or to taste
1 **lemon**, halved
2 large **egg yolks**
1 cup grated **Pecorino Romano cheese**

Bring a large pot of water to a boil.

Meanwhile, in a large skillet, heat the ¼ cup EVOO (4 turns of the pan) over medium-high heat. Add the anchovies, cover the pan with a splatter screen or lid, and shake until the anchovies begin to break up. Reduce the heat a bit, uncover, and stir until anchovies melt into the oil, about 2 minutes. Reduce the heat to medium-low and add the garlic. Stir 1 minute, then add the Worcestershire.

Add the escarole several handfuls at a time, wilting the greens in the garlic oil. Season the greens with lots of pepper and a little nutmeg, then squeeze the juice of the lemon over the pan.

Salt the water and cook the pasta to just shy of al dente. Before draining, ladle out 1 cup of the starchy pasta cooking water and beat into the egg yolks to warm them. Drain the pasta. Remove the escarole from the heat and add the drained pasta and the warmed yolks. Stir to combine. Add half of the cheese and toss vigorously for 1 minute. Dress the pasta with a drizzle of EVOO and transfer to a serving dish. Pass the remaining cheese at the table.

Serves 4

🕐 **JUNE 19/FATHER'S DAY**

Homemade Beef Jerky

This is a recipe that I make every year, and it makes enough to feed all the men in my family: my husband, who is the father of our pit bull; my father-in-law; my dad; and my brother. You could also take this in a more Asian direction; see the Tip.

¼ cup **Worcestershire sauce**
2 tablespoons **black peppercorns**
2 to 3 large fresh **bay leaves**
4 large cloves **garlic**
1 **red Fresno chile** (including seeds)
1 **jalapeño** or **serrano chile** (including seeds)
2 bottles Negra Modelo **beer**
2 cups bottled **teriyaki sauce**
2 pounds **beef round**, very thinly sliced (less than ¼ inch thick)
Cracked black pepper

Combine everything but the beef and cracked pepper in a heavy-duty blender or strong food processor and process to a paste.

Pat the meat completely dry. Place it in a container, cover with the paste, and let it soak for a few hours. Don't brine it for more than half a day or it will be too salty.

Preheat the oven to 200°F.

Arrange wire racks on baking sheets and spread the beef slices over them. Top the beef with some

cracked pepper. Put the beef in the oven and bake until it's dry but not brittle; you want it to have a little chew left to it. It can be in the oven anywhere from 4 to 6 hours, depending on how thin you cut the beef and how long you brined it. I rotate the pans every hour or so.

To store, wrap tightly in plastic wrap, and keep in the refrigerator for 1 to 2 months.

For a different kind of jerky, use soy sauce or tamari instead of teriyaki. Add grated ginger and a small handful each of cilantro and mint to the paste. Use a Japanese or Asian-style beer such as Sapporo instead of the Negra Modelo.

🕐 JUNE 20/DINNER

Chicken Spiedies with Sesame Sauce

About ½ cup **EVOO**
4 large cloves **garlic**, minced or grated
A handful of **flat-leaf parsley**, finely chopped
A handful of **basil leaves**, thinly sliced
1 to 2 tablespoons fresh **thyme leaves**, chopped
Grated zest and juice of 2 **lemons**
1 teaspoon crushed **red pepper flakes**
Salt and **pepper**
¼ cup **tahini paste**
1 tablespoon **white balsamic** or **white wine vinegar**
4 **skinless, boneless chicken breast halves**, cut into bite-size pieces
4 **crusty sub rolls**, split
1 heart of **romaine lettuce**, shredded

1 cup drained **giardiniera** (Italian hot pickled vegetables), store-bought or homemade (page 168), chopped

In a large bowl, whisk together the EVOO, garlic, parsley, basil, thyme, all the lemon zest, half the juice from 1 lemon, the red pepper flakes, and salt and black pepper to taste. Take a couple of spoonfuls of the dressing, transfer to a small bowl, and stir in the tahini, vinegar, and the remaining lemon juice. Set the sesame sauce aside.

Add the chicken to the mixture in the large bowl, and marinate in the fridge for at least 1 hour or up to several hours.

Preheat a grill pan or grill to medium-high.

Skewer the chicken on metal skewers and grill until cooked through, 12 to 15 minutes.

Char or toast the sub rolls, then fill them with the shredded lettuce, giardiniera, and the chicken chunks. Drizzle with the sesame sauce and serve hot.

Serves 4

🕐 JUNE 22/ BELATED FATHER'S DAY DINNER

The first course was **Carbonara with Spring Herb Gremolata.** We then had **Bistecca**, huge Florentine-style steaks, which we served with **Porcini Steak Sauce.**

Bistecca

In Italian, *bistecca* means beefsteak. We cooked the steak the way they do in Florence. You cook it outside over an open wood fire. I have an Italian grill grate that just sits over an open fire and you just throw the meat on it. Serve the bistecca with the Porcini Steak Sauce (recipe follows).

3 tablespoons ground **black pepper**
2 tablespoons kosher or sea **salt**
2 tablespoons **fennel seeds**
2½ to 3 pounds **porterhouse steaks**
1 **red Fresno chile**, minced
2 tablespoons minced fresh **rosemary**
EVOO, for drizzling

With a mortar and pestle, crush the pepper, salt, and fennel seeds together. Rub the mixture over the steaks and sprinkle with the chile and rosemary. Drizzle with EVOO, slather all that around, and marinate in the fridge for 4 hours.

If cooking over a charcoal or gas grill, get a nice char on both sides and move to a cooler part of the grill if it is a really thick cut of meat. For medium, cook to an internal temperature of 140°F. Serve with the sauce.

Serves 6

PORCINI STEAK SAUCE

A handful of **dried porcini mushrooms**
1 cup **beef stock**
EVOO
1 **shallot**, finely chopped
2 cloves **garlic**, finely chopped
2 tablespoons aged **balsamic vinegar**
¼ cup **Worcestershire sauce**
2 tablespoons **dark brown sugar**
2 teaspoons **coarse black pepper**
1 cup good-quality **ketchup** (I like Heinz organic)

In a small saucepan, simmer the porcini in the beef stock to soften the mushrooms and reduce the liquid, 15 to 20 minutes. Process to a puree.

In a small saucepan, heat a drizzle of EVOO over medium heat. Add the shallot and garlic and cook to soften. Add the pureed porcini, balsamic vinegar, Worcestershire, brown sugar, pepper, and ketchup, and simmer over low heat to thicken, about 20 minutes.

Makes about 2 cups

Carbonara with Spring Herb Gremolata

½ cup **mixed fresh herbs**: parsley, chives, thyme
Grated zest of 1 **lemon**
¼ cup **EVOO**
¼ pound **pancetta** or guanciale, finely diced
Salt and **coarsely ground pepper**
4 large cloves **garlic**, finely chopped
½ cup **dry white wine**
1 pound **egg tagliatelle** (I like Delverde brand) or spaghetti
3 large **egg yolks**
½ cup grated **Pecorino Romano cheese**

Finely chop the herbs and combine with the lemon zest (this is the gremolata).

Bring a large pot of water to a boil for the pasta.

Meanwhile, in a large skillet, heat the EVOO (4 turns of the pan) over medium heat. Add the pancetta or guanciale, season with pepper, and cook until browned, 2 to 3 minutes. Stir in the garlic, reduce the heat a bit, and stir another 2 to 3 minutes. Add the wine.

Salt the boiling water and cook the pasta to al dente. Ladle out 1 cup of the starchy pasta cooking water and beat into the egg yolks to warm them.

Drain the pasta and toss with the garlic and pancetta and the warmed egg yolks. Sprinkle in half the cheese and continue tossing to coat, 1 minute more. Serve in shallow bowls with the remaining cheese and the herb gremolata sprinkled over the top.

Serves 4

🕐 JUNE 23/BREAKFAST

We had a **Scape Frittata**, which I served with herbes de Provence artisanal bacon from Aux Délices des Bois. (I always bake bacon in the oven on a slotted broiler pan at 375°F until crisp.)

Scape Frittata

3 tablespoons **EVOO**
1 tablespoon **butter**
6 garlic **scapes**, finely chopped
6 spears **asparagus**, thinly sliced
Salt and **pepper**
8 **eggs**, lightly beaten
¼ cup chopped **fresh herbs**, including tarragon and parsley
1 cup shredded **Cheddar cheese**

Preheat the oven to 400°F.

In a large skillet, heat the EVOO (3 turns of the pan). Melt in the butter. Add the garlic scapes and asparagus and sauté until just tender, about 3 to 4 minutes; season with salt and pepper. Pour the eggs over the vegetables, stir in the herbs, and let the eggs set. Using a spatula, lift the eggs off

the bottom of the skillet, allowing more of the liquid to run underneath.

When the frittata has set, transfer to the oven and bake until the top is deep golden brown, 10 to 12 minutes. Remove the frittata from the oven, top with cheese, and let the cheese melt. Cut into wedges and serve.

Serves 3 or 4

🕐 **JUNE 23/DINNER**

We had sautéed **Branzino with Crispy Kale**, thyme-scented rice, and **carrots and asparagus with mint and tarragon.**

Branzino with Crispy Kale

1 bunch **lacinato kale** (also called black, Tuscan, or dinosaur kale), stemmed
1 tablespoon **EVOO**, plus more for drizzling
Kosher salt and **pepper**
Freshly grated **nutmeg**
4 (5-ounce) **branzino fillets**
Wondra flour, for dredging
Splash of **dry vermouth**
3 tablespoons **butter**
1 **lemon**
2 tablespoons finely chopped **flat-leaf parsley**
½ cup sliced **almonds**, toasted and chopped

Position a rack in the center of the oven and preheat the broiler.

Drizzle the kale with a little EVOO and season with salt, pepper, and nutmeg. Arrange on a rack set over a rimmed baking sheet and broil until crisp, about 5 minutes.

Turn the oven to 250°F and place a serving platter in to warm.

In a large skillet, heat 1 tablespoon EVOO (1 turn of the pan) over medium-high heat. Sprinkle the fish with salt and pepper, then dredge in a little bit of flour. Add the fish to the pan and sauté until just cooked through, about

3 minutes on each side. Douse the fish with the vermouth, then transfer to the platter and cover to keep warm.

Return the skillet to the heat. Add the butter and cook until browned, about 3 minutes. Grate the zest of the lemon and add it to the browned butter, then squeeze in the juice from half the lemon. Stir in the parsley.

Arrange the fish on a bed of crispy kale. Slice the remaining lemon half into 4 thin rounds and place one on each piece of fish. Spoon the brown butter sauce and the almonds on top.

Serves 4

Carrots and asparagus with mint and tarragon: I sautéed thinly sliced baby carrots and ½ pound thinly sliced asparagus in a combination of EVOO and butter. I added 4 finely chopped garlic scapes and seasoned with salt and pepper. I added in chopped mint and tarragon just before serving.

Almond Custard Brioche French Toast

3 large **eggs**, lightly beaten
½ cup **heavy cream** or half-and-half
1 cup **milk**
1 teaspoon **almond extract**
Pinch of ground **cinnamon**
Pinch of freshly grated **nutmeg**
6 (1¾-inch-thick) slices day-old **brioche**
Sliced **almonds**
4 tablespoons (½ stick) **butter**
2 tablespoons **canola oil**

Preheat the oven to 250°F.

In a baking dish, whisk together the eggs, cream, milk, almond extract, cinnamon, and nutmeg until combined. Soak the bread slices in the egg mixture until completely soaked through. On wax paper, scatter sliced almonds and turn the bread slices to coat with the almonds.

On a large griddle, heat 2 tablespoons butter and 1 tablespoon oil over medium-high heat until it begins to sizzle. Add 3 slices of bread at a time and cook, turning once, until golden and crisp on both sides, about 2 minutes per side. Repeat with the remaining butter, oil, and bread. You can keep each batch warm in the oven while you're making the next batch.

Serves 4

🕐 **JUNE 24/DINNER**

We had baby back ribs with **Rib Rub**, served with my **Bourbon BBQ Sauce.**

Baby back ribs: We took 6 to 8 racks of baby back ribs, and rubbed them with our own rub (see below). I first seasoned the ribs with salt and pepper, then rubbed them with the spice rub and let them hang out several hours (or you can even do it the night before). Then we wrapped them and grilled them over indirect heat at 300°F for 1 hour 15 minutes to 1 hour 30 minutes. We unwrapped them and added some grated onion and doused the ribs with a little beer or apple juice, wrapped them back up, and cooked for another 45 minutes. Then we unwrapped the whole shebang and let them finish grilling 15 more minutes.

Rib Rub

½ cup **Montreal Steak Seasoning** or my **Rachael Ray 24/7 Seasoning**
⅓ cup **dark brown sugar**
3 tablespoons **smoked sweet paprika**
1 tablespoon ground **red pepper powder** (which I get at the Italian market) or crushed red pepper flakes
1 tablespoon **celery seeds**
1 tablespoon ground **coriander**
1 tablespoon ground **cumin**
1 tablespoon ground **fennel** or fennel pollen

Combine all ingredients. Store in an airtight container.

Makes about 1 cup

Bourbon BBQ Sauce

1 cup good-quality **ketchup** (I like Heinz Organic)
2 shots good-quality **bourbon**
2 large cloves **garlic**, finely chopped
2 tablespoons **Dijon mustard**
2 tablespoons **dark brown sugar**
2 tablespoons **dark amber maple syrup**
2 tablespoons **Worcestershire sauce**
2 tablespoons **cider vinegar**
1 teaspoon ground **ginger**
1 teaspoon **coarsely ground pepper**
1/8 teaspoon freshly grated **nutmeg**

Combine all the sauce ingredients in a medium skillet and bring to a low bubble. Simmer gently 20 minutes to reduce.

Makes a little over 1 cup

🕐 **JUNE 25/DINNER**

Spaghetti with Red Pepper Pesto

For this I like to use a spaghetti that actually tastes like red peppers. It's peperoncino spaghetti, a dried pasta that I get at Buon Italia market in New York. The sauce is also delicious with just straight-up regular semolina spaghetti.

3 **red bell peppers**
3 Fresno or other **medium-hot fresh red chile peppers**, seeded
3 tablespoons **pine nuts** or sliced almonds, toasted
A small handful of **basil leaves**
Leaves from 2 sprigs **oregano** (about 1 tablespoon) or 1 teaspoon dried
2 or 3 cloves **garlic**, finely chopped or grated
Salt and **pepper**
1/3 cup grated **pecorino cheese**, plus more for serving
1/3 cup **EVOO**
1 pound **spaghetti**
Additional torn **basil**, chopped **mint**, and **parsley**, for garnish (optional)

Bring a pot of water to a boil for the pasta.

Roast the bell peppers and chiles directly over a flame on the stovetop or under the broiler to blacken the skins all over. Place the peppers in a bowl and cover with plastic wrap until cool. Peel and seed the peppers.

Place the peppers and chiles in a food processor and add the nuts, basil, oregano, garlic, and salt and pepper to taste. Add the cheese, turn the processor on, and stream in the EVOO to form a thick pesto-like sauce.

Salt the boiling water and cook the spaghetti to al dente. Before draining, ladle out and reserve 1 cup of the starchy pasta cooking water. Drain the pasta and return to the pot. Toss the pasta with the pesto and half the starchy water for a minute or two to combine thoroughly, adding a little more starchy water if necessary. Serve with more cheese and some torn basil leaves or finely chopped mint and parsley, if desired.

Serves 4

🕐 **JUNE 28/DINNER**

We started with my dippers (John calls them Dips and Dats): **Roasted Eggplant Appetizer, Tzatziki,** and **Ajvar.** For the next course, **Surf & Turf** (flat iron steaks and skewered scallops and shrimp). On the side, I served fresh spinach with a little chile and garlic and zucchini flowers stuffed with ricotta (see July 12, page 85).

Roasted Eggplant Appetizer

2 small firm **eggplants**
A handful of fresh **mint**
A handful of **flat-leaf parsley**
Small handful of fresh **dill**
¼ cup **EVOO**
Sea salt and **black pepper**

Preheat the oven to 400°F. Pierce the skin of the eggplants with a sharp knife in several places and place the eggplants right on the oven rack. Roast until they look like flat tires. They shouldn't take more than about 30 minutes.

Once the eggplant is cool enough to handle, scrape the flesh away from the eggplant skin (discard the skin). Put the flesh into a food processor with the mint, parsley, and dill. Drizzle in the EVOO and add salt and pepper to taste. Puree to a smooth paste. That's a great dipper spread.

Makes about 2 cups

Tzatziki

⅓ seedless **cucumber**, peeled and grated
Salt and **pepper**
1 cup **Greek yogurt** (whole milk or 2%)
Pinch of ground **cumin**
1 large clove **garlic**, grated or minced
Juice of ½ **lemon**
1 tablespoon finely chopped fresh **dill**

Place the grated cucumber in a small strainer and sprinkle with salt. Let sit for 20 minutes, and then press out the liquid.

In a food processor, combine the drained cucumber, yogurt, cumin, garlic, lemon juice, dill, salt, and pepper and pulse to combine.

Makes about 1½ cups

Ajvar

Since this calls for a roasted eggplant, I just threw it in when I was roasting the other eggplants.

3 large **red bell peppers**
1 small **eggplant**, roasted and peeled
2 or 3 **small red chiles** (see Tip), coarsely chopped
Vinegar (sherry, balsamic, or red wine)
Salt and **pepper**
3 to 4 tablespoons **EVOO**

Char the bell peppers all over on the stovetop over a gas flame or under the broiler. Place the blackened peppers in a bowl and cover tightly. When cool enough to handle, wipe off the charred skins with a paper towel, seed the peppers, and put them into a food processor. Add the eggplant, chiles, a little splash of vinegar, and salt and pepper to taste. Turn the processor on and stream in enough EVOO to turn that into a smooth thick dip.

Makes about 1½ cups

Fresno chiles are a good choice because they're not too spicy. . . . To seed or not to seed is up to you. If you want it spicy, leave the seeds and the ribs in; if not, strip them out.

Surf & Turf

8 to 12 large **scallops**
8 to 12 large **shrimp**
4 to 6 **flat iron steaks**
6 to 8 **garlic scapes**, coarsely chopped
1 cup **flat-leaf parsley leaves**
3 or 4 small sprigs fresh **oregano or marjoram**
1 **chile pepper**
Juice of 2 **lemons**, 1 zested
1½ cups **EVOO**
Salt and **pepper**

On skewers, thread the scallops and shrimp together so the scallops are nested in the curls of the shrimp. Place the skewers and steaks in a container large enough to hold them for marinating.

Combine the garlic scapes, parsley, oregano, chile pepper, lemon zest, lemon juice, EVOO, and salt and pepper to taste. Reserve about one-third of the marinade for drizzling when the food comes off the grill. Pour the rest over the steaks and seafood skewers. Let it hang out for a bit while you're heating up your grill.

Grill the steaks and the seafood until the seafood is pink and opaque and firm and until the steaks are browned and evenly marked on both sides. A thin flat iron steak about 1 inch thick shouldn't take more than 3 to 4 minutes on each side.

Served up the sliced steak with the seafood on top with a little extra drizzle of the reserved marinade.

Serves 4 to 6

🕐 JUNE 29/DINNER

We had **Swordfish Cutlets** topped with a fresh tomato relish. I also made a **Sicilian-style orange salad** and a pasta side of **Aglio e Olio** (see June 2, page 56). For dessert we made a **Semifreddo** from a recipe I got from Caterina, my Italian teacher.

Semifreddo

My Italian teacher, Caterina, gave me this delicious recipe. You need to make this days ahead of time.

> 3 **egg yolks**
> 3 tablespoons **sugar**
> 2 cups **heavy cream**
> 3 tablespoons strong brewed **espresso** (see Tip), chilled
> **Semisweet chocolate**, for grating (optional)

Amaretti, strawberries, raspberries, or **tube ice cream cookies** (like pirolines) to decorate

Line the bottom and sides of an 8 by 4-inch or 9 by 5-inch loaf pan with parchment paper or wax paper. Do this by fitting a sheet of the paper into the pan and then cutting at the corners and folding the extra in. Leave a little overhang all around to make it easier to remove the semifreddo.

In a medium bowl, with an electric mixer, beat the egg yolks and sugar for 15 minutes.

In another bowl, beat the cream until stiff peaks form (chilling the beaters and the bowl in the freezer makes it easier to whip the cream).

Fold the whipped cream into the beaten yolk mixture. Divide the mixture between 2 bowls. To one, slowly add the cold espresso and gently combine.

Layer in the plain mixture and then the espresso mixture. If desired, grate some chocolate between layers for a pretty "dark line" that will show up when you slice the semifreddo. Cover with foil and put in the freezer until frozen, 3 to 4 hours.

Take it out of the freezer, uncover, turn upside down, peel off the paper, and decorate with amaretti, strawberries, raspberries, or ice cream cookies.

Slice at the table. If you wait 5 minutes, it gets softer.

Serves 6 to 8

To get the strongest espresso, brew the coffee and take the first coffee that comes out.

Note from Caterina: You can also add another flavor like chocolate or Nutella and work with three mixtures when you layer.

JULY

FRIDAY/1

BREAKFAST
Provence frittata
DINNER
batter-dipped zucchini flowers, porcini steak sauce, cheesy ciabatta bread, Caesar salad with kale

SATURDAY/2

DINNER
cherry tomato fusilli, slow-smoked chicken

SUNDAY/3

MONDAY/4

BREAKFAST
whole-grain pancakes with mixed berries, baked bacon
DINNER
pulled pork with bourbon BBQ sauce, oil & vinegar slaw, sweet & spicy pickles, sliders, deviled eggs, corn on the cob with chile-herb butter, Yukon Gold potato salad

TUESDAY/5

DINNER
risotto Milanese with garlic scapes, garlic scape pesto

MONDAY/11

DINNER
pico de gallo, lemon-garlic guacamole, crabby guacamole, apple & almond guacamole, bean dip, salsa verde, Margarita BBQ sauce, slow-smoked chicken, baked black beans, savoy-fennel slaw, grilled corn with chipotle cream & cotija

TUESDAY/12

DINNER
Caesar spaghetti, ricotta-stuffed zucchini flowers, fried green tomatoes

WEDNESDAY/13

DINNER
grilled shrimp sandwiches, raita, fried green tomatoes

THURSDAY/14

BRUNCH
ham & eggs crêpes
DINNER
slow-smoked sea bass, herbed orzo, tomato salad, lentil salad

FRIDAY/15

DINNER
7-hour brisket, red corn on the cob, red cabbage slaw, smoky BBQ sauce

THURSDAY/21

DINNER
porcini steak sauce, Swiss chard au gratin, celery salad, tomato and arugula salad, grilled steaks

FRIDAY/22

BREAKFAST
baked polenta with eggs, braised Italian sausages

SATURDAY/23

SUNDAY/24

DINNER
creamy saffron sausage cauliflower pasta

MONDAY/25

| WEDNESDAY/6 | THURSDAY/7 | FRIDAY/8 | SATURDAY/9 | SUNDAY/10 |

WEDNESDAY/6

July 6 to July 10 in Sun Valley

SUNDAY/10

DINNER
BLT pasta

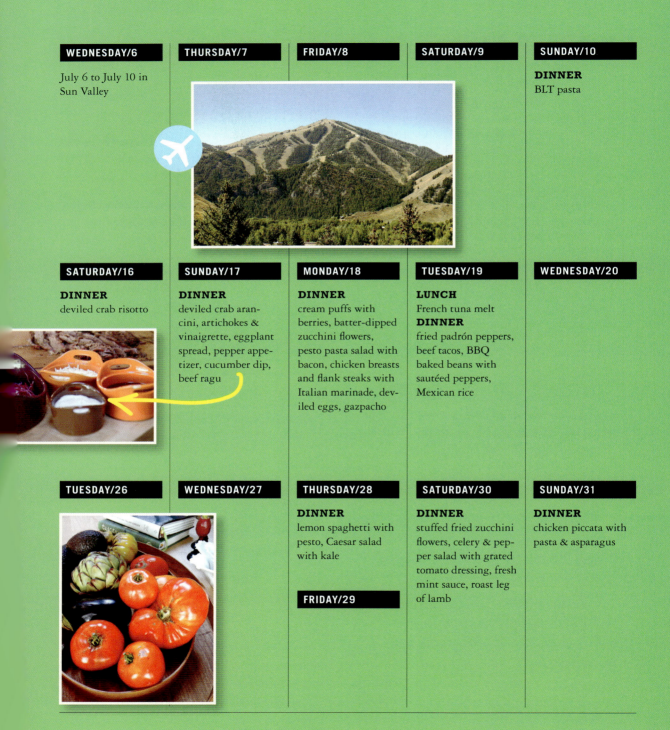

SATURDAY/16

DINNER
deviled crab risotto

SUNDAY/17

DINNER
deviled crab arancini, artichokes & vinaigrette, eggplant spread, pepper appetizer, cucumber dip, beef ragu

MONDAY/18

DINNER
cream puffs with berries, batter-dipped zucchini flowers, pesto pasta salad with bacon, chicken breasts and flank steaks with Italian marinade, deviled eggs, gazpacho

TUESDAY/19

LUNCH
French tuna melt
DINNER
fried padrón peppers, beef tacos, BBQ baked beans with sautéed peppers, Mexican rice

WEDNESDAY/20

TUESDAY/26

WEDNESDAY/27

THURSDAY/28

DINNER
lemon spaghetti with pesto, Caesar salad with kale

FRIDAY/29

SATURDAY/30

DINNER
stuffed fried zucchini flowers, celery & pepper salad with grated tomato dressing, fresh mint sauce, roast leg of lamb

SUNDAY/31

DINNER
chicken piccata with pasta & asparagus

Provence Frittata

I like to use my frittata pan to make this: It's just two skillets, one skillet inverted on top of the other. They lock together and you can just flip the frittata right over and cook it on the stovetop all the way through. If it's just for me and John I would use 6 eggs; if we were feeding 3 or 4 people I would use 8.

1 tablespoon **EVOO**
3 tablespoons **butter**
1 large **shallot**, finely chopped
1 or 2 cloves **garlic**, chopped
1 **plum tomato**, seeded and diced
5 or 6 thin spears **asparagus**, sliced on an angle
6 to 8 large **eggs**, lightly beaten
¼ cup chopped **mixed fresh herbs** (parsley, tarragon, thyme, rosemary, basil) and a pinch of dried lavender (see Tip)

Preheat the oven to 375° to 400°F.

In a medium skillet, heat the EVOO and butter. Once the butter foams, add the shallot, garlic, tomato, and asparagus. You sauté that out a little bit. Then pour in the eggs. Once the eggs go in, stir in the herbs. Let the eggs start to set, then transfer it to the oven. Let it cook until browned and puffed.

Serves 3 or 4

Instead, you could use store-bought dried herbes de Provence. Take a tablespoon of that and throw it on top of a small pile of flat-leaf parsley and chop it together. The parsley will give it a fresh herb taste and the herbes de Provence will already have the blend of the rosemary and the thyme and the lavender.

We started with **Batter-Dipped Zucchini Flowers** for an appetizer, followed by **grilled flank steaks** (and sautéed peppers and onions) topped with **Porcini Steak Sauce** (see June 22, page 67). We also had a **Caesar Salad with Kale** (see April 18, page 16), and I made some **Cheesy Ciabatta Bread** to pass alongside. (It was delicious.)

Batter-Dipped Zucchini Flowers

Light-bodied **vegetable oil**, for frying
2 cups **flour**
1 teaspoon **fennel salt** or kosher salt
1 teaspoon **fennel pollen** or ground fennel
2 cups chilled **pilsner** or other lager-style beer, or club soda
4 **egg whites**, beaten to soft peaks
24 **zucchini blossoms** (stamens removed)
Sea salt
Lemon wedges, for serving

In a large pot, heat about 2 inches of oil over medium heat to 350°F. Combine the flour, fennel salt or kosher salt, and fennel pollen or ground-fennel in a medium bowl, then mix in the beer. Fold in the egg whites. Dredge the blossoms in the batter, shaking off the excess; place in the oil, without crowding the pan. Cook, turning once, 2 to 3 minutes total. Transfer to paper towels to drain. Sprinkle with a little sea salt and serve with lemon wedges.

Makes 24 pieces

Throw your **flank steak** onto a hot grill. Timing will depend on how large your piece of flank steak is. We usually cook ours 5 to 7 minutes on each side, then let it rest, and then thinly slice it. Drizzle the sliced steak with a little EVOO, a little sea salt—you can sprinkle with finely chopped fresh herbs—just plain old parsley is terrific. Serve it up with Porcini Steak Sauce (page 67) on the side. I also sautéed some peppers, onions, and garlic (or garlic scapes) to throw on top.

Cheesy Ciabatta Bread

1 head **garlic**, cloves separated
8 tablespoons (1 stick) **butter**, softened
1 loaf **ciabatta bread**, split
1/2 cup grated **pecorino cheese**
1/2 cup grated **Parmigiano-Reggiano cheese**
2 tablespoons chopped **flat-leaf parsley**
2 tablespoons fresh **thyme leaves**, chopped
1 teaspoon dried **oregano** or marjoram

Position a rack in the center of the oven and preheat to 350°F.

In a small saucepan, simmer the garlic cloves in water over medium heat for about 20 minutes. Drain, then squeeze the garlic from the skins and mash into a paste with a fork. Mix the garlic into the softened butter.

Meanwhile, toast the bread in the oven. Slather with the garlic butter and top with the cheeses and herbs. Turn on the broiler and place the bread back in the oven to brown the cheese.

Serves 4 to 6

John made a **Slow-Smoked Chicken** (see April 24, page 28) that he had first brined (you have to do that the day before so it can brine overnight). With that, we had a side pasta of **Cherry Tomato Fusilli**.

Cherry Tomato Fusilli

Fusilli lunghi is long curly spaghetti. Fun to eat.

1/4 to 1/3 pound **pancetta**, finely diced
1/4 cup **EVOO**
1 **chile pepper**, finely chopped
2 medium **onions** (1 red, 1 white), chopped
3 or 4 cloves **spring garlic**, chopped
2 fresh **bay leaves**
2 pints **cherry tomatoes**
1/2 cup **white wine**
Salt
1 pound **fusilli lunghi pasta**
A generous handful of chopped **flat-leaf parsley**
18 to 20 fresh **basil leaves**, torn
Grated **pecorino** or **Parmigiano-Reggiano cheese** (see Tip)

Bring a large pot of water to a boil.

Meanwhile, in a large skillet, cook the pancetta in the EVOO until it starts to look a little crispy. Add the chile, onions, garlic, and bay leaves. Sauté that out until the onions are nice and sweet. Add the tomatoes and wine. Put a lid on it and let the cherry tomatoes cook until they burst, shaking the pan every once in a while.

Salt the boiling water and cook the pasta to al dente. Before draining, ladle out 1 cup of the starchy pasta cooking water and add to the tomatoes in the skillet.

Drain the pasta. Take the bay leaves out of the sauce; add the parsley, basil, and the drained pasta and toss.

Serve topped with cheese.

Serves 4

HAPPY 4th of JULY

July 4, BREAKFAST

In the morning I made whole-grain pancakes with mixed berries. I thought the mixture of black, blue, and red berries was nice for 4th of July. When I make berry pancakes I usually put some berries in the pancake batter, but sometimes I also mix the berries with a little booze or just a sprinkle of sugar, and I usually add a little finely chopped mint. I serve the pancakes with warm syrup and the slumped berries (and the pancakes also have a couple of berries running through them). They are very berry-licious.

We also had baked bacon. My favorite bacon comes from Oscar's Smokehouse in Warrensburg, New York. They ship! We never panfry bacon; we always bake our bacon on a slotted broiler pan. Preheat the oven to 375°F. Arrange 1 pound of bacon in a single layer on a slotted broiler pan. Bake until crispy, 15 to 18 minutes.

July 4, DINNER

We made a 7-pound pulled pork with my Bourbon BBQ Sauce (see June 24, page 71) served on rolls. We also had Bull's-Eye Deviled Eggs (see April 24, page 29), Yukon Gold Potato Salad, oil & vinegar slaw, corn on the cob with chile-herb butter, and My Sweet & Spicy Pickles. We also had grilled sliders with provolone and fixin's, including my balsamic ketchup.

For the pulled pork, we got a 7-pound pork butt (shoulder). We soaked wood chips for 30 minutes. Build your charcoal for indirect cooking on the grill. Oil up and spice the meat with a seasoning rub. When the grill comes to 325°F, put the pork fat side up on the grill. Cook it for 4 hours without turning. John added a couple of extra coals every

hour and a half. You try and keep the heat constant at 325°F. While the pork was cooking, I made a batch of my Bourbon BBQ Sauce (page 71) that I gussied up by adding a caramelized onion or two and a little palmful of ground fennel or fennel pollen, since it was going with pork and I like those flavors together. When the pork is done you let it rest and then you shred it up and add it to the BBQ sauce. Serve with rolls.

I also made **sliders** with my burger blend (which is half beef chuck, one-quarter sirloin, and one-quarter brisket). Then for every pound of ground beef mixture, I added 2 small cloves of grated garlic, 3 tablespoons or so of grated onion (grate it right over the meat so the juice falls into the bowl). I seasoned with kosher salt and lots of coarse black pepper. I added a little bit of grassy flat-leaf parsley very finely chopped, a few tablespoons of Worcestershire sauce, and a drizzle of EVOO. We formed the sliders into 3-ounce portions and grilled them up. Then we topped them with provolone cheese (still on the grill, so the cheese melts). We put them on slider rolls that had chopped giardiniera (store-bought or homemade, page 168), lettuce, tomato, onion, and balsamic ketchup (see below).

To make **balsamic ketchup** for the sliders, for every ½ cup of good-quality ketchup, add 3 tablespoons of my Balsamic Drizzle (already reduced balsamic that you can buy). You can also make your own "drizzle" by reducing balsamic vinegar with a little brown sugar.

I made **corn on the cob with chile-herb butter**. Stir a handful of chopped fresh herbs such as parsley, thyme, and chives plus minced chiles into melted butter. Grill or boil the corn and when it's cooked, slather it with the chile-herb butter.

The **oil and vinegar slaw** was made with shredded white cabbage dressed with olive oil, lemon juice, and vinegar (white vinegar, white wine vinegar, or cider vinegar). Then celery seed, salt, and pepper, and to sweeten it up, a little pinch of superfine sugar or honey.

Yukon Gold Potato Salad

I love this potato salad. It is so tasty.

8 medium **Yukon Gold potatoes** (2½ to 3 pounds), quartered
1 large **shallot**, grated
3 tablespoons **white balsamic vinegar**
Salt and **pepper**
EVOO
3 tablespoons **honey**
3 tablespoons **Dijon mustard**
1 cup **fresh peas**, blanched, or 1 cup thawed frozen organic peas
¼ **red bell pepper**, finely chopped
3 or 4 **scallions**, thinly sliced on an angle
3 **gherkins**, finely chopped
1 or 2 tablespoons **dill pickle relish**
A handful of **fresh tarragon leaves**, chopped

Place the potatoes in a pot and cover with cold water by an inch or so. Bring to a boil over high heat, reduce the heat to medium-low, and cook the potatoes until fork-tender, about 10 minutes.

Place the shallot in the bottom of a salad bowl and stir in the vinegar and a couple of pinches of salt. Let that bleed out for a couple of minutes. Then whisk in about ½ cup EVOO (just eyeball it). Then whisk in the honey and mustard.

Add the warm potatoes to the bowl so they can absorb the dressing. Add the peas, bell pepper, scallions, gherkins, relish, tarragon, and salt and pepper to taste. Mix all that together.

Serves 4

My Sweet & Spicy Pickles

2 cups white balsamic or cider **vinegar**
½ cup **sugar**
2 teaspoons **sea salt**
1 large clove **garlic**, halved
½ small **red onion**, thinly sliced
4 **kirby cucumbers**, cut into ⅛- to ¼-inch slices
1 small **fresh red chile**, such as Fresno, sliced
2 **bay leaves**
A few sprigs of **fresh dill**
1 teaspoon **coriander seeds**
1 teaspoon **mustard seeds**
1 teaspoon **black peppercorns**

In a small saucepan, combine ⅔ cup water, the vinegar, sugar, salt, and garlic and bring to a low boil to dissolve the sugar and salt. Reduce the heat to low.

Layer the onion, cucumbers, chile, bay leaves, dill, coriander seeds, mustard seeds, and peppercorns into a tight-fitting plastic or glass container.

Pour the hot brine over the cucumber mixture, cover the container tightly, and chill 24 hours or several days, turning occasionally. The pickles will keep in the refrigerator for up to 1 month.

Makes about 1 pint (80 to 100 slices)

🕐 **JULY 5/DINNER**

I made **Risotto Milanese with Garlic Scapes** for dinner, but since I had lots of scapes to use up, I made **Garlic Scape Pesto** for later.

Risotto Milanese with Garlic Scapes

4 cups **chicken stock**
A big pinch of **saffron threads**
4 tablespoons **EVOO**
⅓ pound **pancetta** or thick-cut slab bacon, diced
8 to 10 **garlic scapes**, finely chopped
Salt and freshly ground **pepper**
1½ cups **arborio rice**
½ cup **dry white wine**
2 tablespoons **butter**
¾ cup grated **Parmigiano-Reggiano cheese**
½ pint **cherry tomatoes**, quartered
2 **shallots**, finely chopped
1 small bunch thin **asparagus**, very thinly
   sliced on an angle
A small handful of finely chopped **flat-leaf parsley** and sliced or torn **basil**, for garnish

Bring the chicken stock, 1 cup water, and the saffron to a boil in a saucepan, then reduce the heat to a low simmer.

In a pot with a rounded bottom, heat 2 table-spoons EVOO (2 turns of the pan) over medium-high heat. Add the pancetta or bacon and cook until some of the fat has rendered, about 5 minutes. Add the garlic scapes and stir until softened, 2 to 3 minutes. Season with salt and pepper and cook, stirring, about 1 more minute. Add the rice and stir. Add the wine and cook, stirring, until the liquid has been absorbed. Begin adding the hot chicken stock, a few ladles at a time, stirring constantly and cooking until the liquid has been absorbed before adding more. Continue adding stock and cooking until the rice is al dente, about 18 minutes total.

When the risotto is about done, cut the butter into small pieces and add it to the risotto, stirring until melted. Stir in the cheese and the tomatoes, then remove from the heat.

In a medium skillet, heat the remaining 2 tablespoons EVOO (2 turns of the pan) over medium-high heat. Add the shallots and aspara-gus, season with salt and pepper, and sauté until the asparagus is tender-crisp, about 5 minutes.

Serve the risotto in shallow bowls topped with the asparagus and shallot mixture and garnish with parsley and basil.

Serves 4

Garlic Scape Pesto

I made a batch of scape pesto and threw it into the freezer. When I serve that I usually serve it over lemon spaghetti, which is lemon-flavored spaghetti imported from Italy. Pesto is one of those things that work with both short-cut pasta and long-cut pasta. It doesn't really matter.

1 cup **garlic scapes**
1 cup fresh **basil** or **mixed herbs** (basil, tarragon,
   and parsley; or just basil and parsley)
2 to 3 tablespoons toasted **pistachios** or **pine nuts**
A couple of handfuls of grated **pecorino**
   or **Parmigiano-Reggiano cheese** (or a
   combination of the two)
¼ to ⅓ cup **EVOO**
Salt and **pepper**
Juice of 1 small **lemon** (optional)

Combine the garlic scapes, herbs, nuts, and cheese in a food processor. Add enough EVOO to make a thick sauce. Season with salt and pepper. Sometimes for brightness I add a little lemon juice.

Makes about 1 cup

JULY 6 TO JULY 10

We were in Sun Valley.

BLT Pasta

2 tablespoons **EVOO**, plus extra for drizzling
12 slices good-quality **smoky bacon**, cut into
   ½-inch pieces
1½ cups **panko bread crumbs**
A handful of **flat-leaf parsley**, chopped
A couple of generous handfuls of grated
   Parmigiano-Reggiano cheese
1 small **red onion**, finely chopped
4 cloves **garlic**, chopped or grated
⅛ teaspoon crushed **red pepper flakes**
2 pints **cherry tomatoes**
Salt and **pepper**
1 pound **bow-tie pasta**
4 cups **arugula** (a couple of bunches), coarsely
   chopped
1 cup fresh **basil** (about 20 leaves), torn or
   coarsely chopped

Heat a drizzle of EVOO in a skillet over medium to medium-high heat. Add the bacon and brown until crisp. Remove and drain on paper towels. Add the panko to the bacon drippings and toast until golden brown. Add the parsley and Parm. Toss to combine, turn off the heat, and reserve the crumbs.

Bring a large pot of water to a boil.

Meanwhile, heat 2 tablespoons EVOO (2 turns of the pan) in a large skillet with a tight-fitting lid over medium heat. Add the onion and garlic and cook, stirring frequently, until softened, 3 to 4 minutes. Add the red pepper flakes and cherry tomatoes. Season with salt and pepper, then cover the pan tightly with the lid. Cook, shaking occasionally, until the tomatoes begin to burst, about 8 minutes. Remove the lid and gently mash up the tomatoes a bit with a wooden spoon.

Salt the boiling water and cook the bow-ties to al dente. Before draining, ladle out about a cup of the starchy pasta cooking water and add to the cherry tomato sauce. Drain the pasta and add to the sauce along with the arugula, basil, and reserved bacon. Season with salt and pepper and toss to combine. Garnish the bowls of pasta with the seasoned bread crumbs and serve.

Serves 4

🕐 **JULY 11/DINNER**

July 11th was a real whopper! It was Mexican Night. I made a **Pico de Gallo** (see April 26, page 32). We had **Guacamole 3 Ways: Lemon-Garlic Guacamole** (my basic recipe; see April 26, page 31), **Crabby Guacamole**, and **Apple & Almond Guacamole**; **Bean Dip** (see May 27, page 44); **Salsa Verde**; John's **Slow-Smoked Chicken** (see April 24, page 28), which I served with **Margarita BBQ Sauce**, **baked black beans**, **savoy-fennel slaw**, and **Grilled Corn with Chipotle Cream & Cotija** (see May 27, page 45). For dessert: sorbets and fresh fruits. Nice and refreshing.

Guacamole 3 Ways

Big shout-out to La Condesa in Austin, Texas. They make an amazing guacamole sampler. Because I visit Austin only once or twice a year, I had to come up with my own knockoffs for the other 363 nights of the year.

CRABBY GUACAMOLE

Lemon-Garlic Guacamole (page 31)
8 ounces **lump crabmeat**
Old Bay Seasoning
1 small rib **celery** with leafy top, from the
   heart, finely chopped
1 small **red Fresno chile**, seeded and finely
   chopped
A few dashes of **hot sauce** (I like Frank's RedHot)

Prepare the basic guacamole. In a separate bowl, run your fingers through the crab to check for bits of cartilage and shell. Season the crab to taste with Old Bay. Add half of the crab to the guacamole, along with the celery and chile. Gently combine, transfer to a serving bowl, and cover the top of the mound of guacamole with the remaining crab. Garnish with a little hot sauce.

Makes 2 to 2½ cups

APPLE & ALMOND GUACAMOLE

Lemon-Garlic Guacamole (page 31)
½ Honeycrisp, Fuji, or Gala **apple**, peeled and
   finely chopped
1 tablespoon **lemon juice**
1 rounded tablespoon **pureed chipotle in adobo**
   (see Tip)
A handful of sliced **almonds**

Prepare the basic guacamole. Dress the apple
with about 1 tablespoon of lemon juice. Set
aside 1 rounded tablespoon of apple and stir the
rest into the guacamole along with the pureed
chipotle in adobo. Mound into a serving dish and
chill until you are ready to serve. When ready to
serve, toast the almonds until very fragrant and
deeply golden. Top the guacamole liberally and
entirely with the toasted nuts, and garnish with
the reserved apple.

Makes about 2½ cups

To dial back the heat level, I seed
the chipotle peppers. I also puree a
whole can at a time and throw it into
the freezer. The next time you need
some, break off a 1-inch chunk per
tablespoon for your recipe.

Salsa Verde

When I can find them, I make this recipe with fresh tomatillos, as you will see on other nights in this book. This night, I made it with canned tomatillos, as fresh were not available, and it was equally delicious. If you can get fresh tomatillos, use the recipe from December 11 (page 209).

1 large **poblano pepper**
2 tablespoons **corn oil**
1 medium **onion**, chopped
2 to 3 cloves **garlic**, finely chopped
1 teaspoon ground **cumin**
Salt and **pepper**
1 (14-ounce) can **tomatillos**
1 tablespoon good-quality **honey**
Juice of 1 **lime**
Small handful **cilantro leaves**
1/2 **avocado** (optional)

Char the poblano directly over a gas flame or under the broiler. Blacken the skin evenly, all over. Place in a bowl and cover. When cool enough to handle, rub the charred skin off with a paper towel. Halve and seed the pepper, coarsely chop, and put in a food processor.

Meanwhile, in a skillet, heat the oil (2 turns of the pan) over medium to medium-high heat. Add the onion and garlic; sprinkle with the cumin and salt and pepper to taste. Cook until softened, 6 to 7 minutes.

Add the sautéed onion and garlic, the tomatillos, honey, lime juice, and cilantro to the food processor. (If you want a creamy salsa, add the avocado.) Puree into a fairly smooth sauce. Adjust the salt and pepper to your taste.

Makes about 2 cups

Margarita BBQ Sauce

1 **ancho chile**, stemmed and seeded
1 cup **chicken stock**
1 cup good-quality **ketchup** (I like Heinz Organic)
2 large cloves **garlic**, finely chopped
2 tablespoons **dark brown sugar**
2 tablespoons **dark amber maple syrup**
2 tablespoons **Worcestershire sauce**
1 1/2 tablespoons **cider vinegar**
1/2 cup **beef stock**
Juice of 2 **limes**
2 shots good-quality **tequila**
1 teaspoon smoked **paprika**
Coarse black pepper

In a small saucepan, combine the ancho chile and stock. Simmer for about 20 minutes to

*I baked canned **black beans** with bacon, brown sugar, cumin, Worcestershire, salt, pepper, and grated red onion running through them.*

*We also had a shredded **savoy-fennel slaw**. To 1 small head of shredded savoy cabbage I added 1 bulb of fennel, shredded or very thinly sliced. I dressed it with lime juice, cider vinegar, honey, and vegetable oil and seasoned it with fennel, salt, and black pepper.*

soften. Transfer the chile and the cooking liquid to a food processor and puree.

Combine the ancho puree and the rest of the sauce ingredients in a small saucepan and bring to a simmer. Cook at a low bubble until it's nice and thick, 15 to 20 minutes.

Makes about 1½ cups

🕐 JULY 12/DINNER

Ricotta-stuffed zucchini flowers to start, then **Fried Green Tomatoes** and a family favorite, **Caesar Spaghetti.**

Ricotta-stuffed zucchini flowers: I usually use sheep's milk ricotta that I mix with EVOO, salt, pepper, and thyme. The filling also had a little shaved summer truffle in it. I loosely stuffed the flowers and left them raw. When you're serving raw zucchini flowers, you just gently remove the stamens, fill the blossoms with a little of the ricotta filling, and let the pretty orange tips of the flowers just hang open. Then I garnish with a little drizzle of good-quality oil.

Fried Green Tomatoes

Fried green tomatoes are delicious as is, but they're also great with a dollop of fresh ricotta on top. Or use them instead of red tomatoes in a caprese, layered with fresh mozzarella, basil, and EVOO. Or in a BLT sandwich instead of the sliced tomato, and on and on and on.

2 firm green or very underripe **tomatoes**
Salt and **pepper**
Flour, for dredging
Fennel pollen or ground fennel
2 **eggs** or egg whites, beaten
⅓ cup fine **dry bread crumbs**
⅓ cup **cornmeal**
⅓ cup **panko bread crumbs**
⅓ cup grated **Parmigiano-Reggiano cheese**
A handful of **flat-leaf parsley,** finely chopped
Canola oil or light olive oil, for shallow-frying, plus a drizzle

Trim the tops and bottoms of the tomatoes and cut crosswise into about 4 slices each, no more than ½ inch thick. Salt the sliced tomatoes on each side and drain on a doubled paper towel for a few minutes, then season with a little pepper.

Line up 3 shallow bowls on the counter: Spread the flour out in one and season with some fennel pollen; beat the eggs (or whites) in the second; and mix together the fine bread crumbs, cornmeal, panko, Parm, and parsley in the third. Coat the tomatoes in the flour, then in egg, and finally in the panko mix, pressing to make sure the coating sticks.

Heat ⅛ inch of oil in a skillet over medium to medium-high heat. Add the tomatoes and cook to golden and crisp, a few minutes on each side. Cool on cooling rack.

Makes 8 to 10 slices

We made sandwiches on brioche rolls with **Grilled Shrimp**, a little chopped lettuce, and **Raita**. The brioche rolls I get from Amy's Bread, and they're like hot dog rolls. They're made out of brioche and they're designed for making lobster rolls, but we use them for crab salad and grilled shrimp. We also had more **Fried Green Tomatoes** (see July 12, page 85, for the recipe). My husband cannot get enough of the fried green tomatoes. Delicious!

Grilled Shrimp

Eyeball the spices using the palm of your hand. You could of course substitute some prepared curry powder for all the spices; I'd say a rounded tablespoon of a curry powder blend of your choice.

½ cup **Greek yogurt**
1 large clove **garlic**, grated
1 inch fresh **ginger**, grated
Juice of 1 small **lemon**
1 teaspoon **fine sea salt**
1 teaspoon ground **fenugreek**
1 teaspoon **turmeric**
¾ teaspoon ground **coriander**
¾ teaspoon ground **cumin**
1 pound (20–24 count) **shrimp**

In a bowl, combine the yogurt, garlic, ginger, lemon juice, salt, and spices. Add the shrimp, toss to coat, and marinate for at least 30 minutes and up to several hours in the fridge.

Preheat the grill. Grill the shrimp in a fine-mesh wire grilling basket for seafood so the shrimp don't fall through the grate. We grill the shrimp until opaque and cooked through.

Serves 4

Raita

1 **green apple**, peeled and grated
1 cup **Greek yogurt**
¼ cup **cilantro leaves**, plus a few more for garnish
¼ cup fresh **mint leaves**
Juice of 1 **lime**
1 or 2 thin **scallions**, finely chopped
¼ teaspoon ground **cardamom**
Salt and **pepper**

Put the apple in a food processor with the yogurt, cilantro, and mint. Pulse to combine. Add the lime juice, scallions, cardamom, and salt and pepper to taste. Whizz to combine. Refrigerate until ready to serve.

Makes about 1½ cups

Ham & Eggs Crêpes

I made 2 crêpes apiece for the two of us. I had a few extra crêpes that I wrapped and put in the fridge. You can stuff them with whatever you like later. We serve the crêpes with a salad of garden greens lightly tossed with a lemon or Dijon vinaigrette.

⅔ cup **farro flour** or buckwheat flour
½ cup **all-purpose flour**
Salt and **pepper**
1 cup **milk**

3 tablespoons extra-light **olive oil** or vegetable oil
3 tablespoons **butter**, plus more for the crêpe pan
6 large **eggs**
1 or 2 tablespoons finely chopped **chives**
1 or 2 tablespoons finely chopped **tarragon**
¼ pound good-quality **ham**, diced
Grated **Gruyère** or **Fontina cheese**

Whisk together the flours, a pinch of salt, the milk, and oil. Add about ⅓ cup water (to get the consistency of thin pancake batter). Let the batter rest for about 2 hours.

Heat a crêpe pan over medium to medium-high heat. Melt 1 tablespoon butter and swirl in ¼ cup of batter. Cook about 1 minute on the first side and about 30 seconds on the second side. Cook the rest of the crêpes, adding more butter to the pan if you need to. Pile your crêpes up.

In a medium bowl, beat together the eggs, chives, tarragon, and salt and pepper to taste.

In a large skillet, melt 3 tablespoons butter over medium heat. Add the ham to the butter when the butter foams. When the ham starts to brown up at the edges, add the eggs and stir that until soft scrambled.

Spoon some ham and eggs onto a crêpe and sprinkle in a little grated cheese. Wrap and roll.

Serves 2 (with leftover crêpes)

🕐 JULY 14/DINNER

We had a very thick, beautiful piece of **sea bass** that we slow-smoked. We served that up with **Garden Tomato Salad**, **Lentil Salad**, and a side of **herbed orzo**.

Slow-smoked sea bass: We had a 2- or 3-inch-thick piece of sea bass (about 2 pounds, to feed 3 to 4 people). It was dressed with EVOO, French sea salt, and pepper. We put it on a foil tray and smoked it at 325°F until opaque and cooked through, about 1 hour to 75 minutes. Then we just doused it with a ton of lemon. It was delicious.

Herbed orzo: I cooked orzo to al dente and mixed in chopped mint and parsley, 2 tablespoons chopped oregano, 1 chopped chile, a couple of cloves of garlic (pasted), the juice of a lemon, and ⅓ cup EVOO—and I just eyeballed all that.

Garden Tomato Salad

Sometimes we use ricotta salata grated over the top of the salad as well.

- 4 large **tomatoes**, chopped
- ¼ medium **seedless watermelon**, chopped
- 5 or 6 **mini sweet peppers** (see Tip), thinly sliced
- ½ **seedless cucumber**, chopped
- 1 small **red onion**, quartered and sliced
- ¾ to 1 cup **flat-leaf parsley** tops, chopped
- **EVOO**
- **Salt** and **pepper**
- 8 ounces **Greek feta cheese**, crumbled

Combine all the salad ingredients and dress with EVOO, salt, and pepper. Top with the feta.

Serves 4

Mini sweet peppers look like jalapeños or Fresno chiles, but they're sweet, not hot. If you can't find them, chop up 1 small bell pepper.

Lentil Salad

- ¾ cup **green (Puy) lentils**
- ½ cup finely chopped **mixed sweet and hot peppers**
- 1 small **onion**, finely chopped
- ½ **green apple**, finely chopped
- ⅓ cup **pine nuts** or pistachios (or a combination), toasted
- ¼ cup **mint**, finely chopped
- Juice of 1 **lemon**
- Juice of 1 **lime**
- 2 to 3 teaspoons **honey**
- **EVOO** or vegetable oil
- **Salt** and **pepper**

In a saucepan of boiling salted water, cook the lentils until tender, 20 to 25 minutes. Drain them and transfer to a bowl. Add the peppers, onion, apple, nuts, mint, lemon juice, lime juice, and honey; dress with EVOO, salt, and pepper to taste.

Serves 4

I made a bunch of different **Dips and Dats** (see June 28, page 72), and we made a **7-Hour Brisket** with **Smoky BBQ Sauce**. I served the brisket on seeded sourdough rolls from Amy's Bread (I just warmed them, I didn't toast) with **Red Cabbage Slaw** and **Horseradish Sauce**. We also served **red corn on the cob**.

7-Hour Brisket

Be sure to soak the wood chips first.

1 (8-pound) **brisket**, fat trimmed to ⅛ inch on top
Pepper
Spice Rub (recipe follows)
1 **red onion**, grated
½ cup **apple juice** or cider
½ cup **lager beer**, at room temperature
Smoky BBQ Sauce (recipe follows)
8 **seeded sourdough rolls**, split
Coarsely grated extra-sharp **Cheddar cheese**
Red Cabbage Slaw (recipe follows)
Horseradish Sauce (recipe follows)

Generously coat the brisket with lots of black pepper on all sides, then the spice rub, massaging the spices into the meat. Cover with plastic wrap and let sit overnight in the fridge.

Preheat a smoker to 250°F and set up for cooking over indirect heat by placing coals and a couple of handfuls of wood chips (apple or cherry chips are nice) to one side.

Place the brisket fat side up on the grate on the opposite side from the coals and cook for 4 hours.

Remove the brisket from the smoker and slather with the grated onion. Using a double layer of foil, create a pouch/packet around the brisket. Add the apple juice and beer and tightly seal the foil pouch. Place the brisket back in the smoker for 2 hours, adding a handful of chips and 12 or so coals.

After 2 hours, open the lid and let the brisket sit in the packet for another hour.

While the brisket finishes cooking, make

the Smoky BBQ Sauce, Red Cabbage Slaw, and Horseradish Sauce.

Thinly slice the brisket against the grain on a large cutting board. Add some BBQ sauce to the brisket slices and give everything a rough chop to combine.

Pile the roll bottoms with brisket and top with a sprinkle of Cheddar and some slaw. Slather the roll tops with horseradish sauce and set the tops in place.

Serves 8 (with leftovers)

SPICE RUB

3 tablespoons **smoked sea salt**
2 tablespoons **light brown sugar**
3 tablespoons **sweet paprika**
1 tablespoon **mustard seeds**
1 tablespoon **garlic powder**
2 teaspoons ground **coriander**
2 teaspoons ground **cumin**
2 teaspoons ground **ginger**
1½ teaspoons ground **red pepper** (see Tip)

In a small bowl, combine the rub ingredients.

Makes about ¾ cup

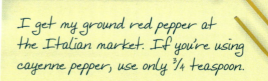

I get my ground red pepper at the Italian market. If you're using cayenne pepper, use only ¾ teaspoon.

SMOKY BBQ SAUCE

1 cup good-quality **ketchup** (I like Heinz Organic)
2 large cloves **garlic**, finely chopped
2 tablespoons **dark brown sugar**
2 tablespoons **dark amber maple syrup**
2 tablespoons **Worcestershire sauce**
1½ tablespoons **cider vinegar**
½ cup **beef stock**
1 teaspoon **smoked sweet paprika**
Coarsely ground pepper

Combine all the ingredients in a small sauce-pan. Bring to a simmer and cook at a low bubble for 15 to 20 minutes.

Makes about 2 cups

RED CABBAGE SLAW

2 packed cups **shredded red cabbage**
½ cup grated **red onion** (1 small or ½ medium)
1 **Granny Smith apple**, peeled and grated
3 tablespoons **vegetable oil**
2 tablespoons **cider vinegar**
1 teaspoon **superfine sugar**
Kosher salt and **pepper**

Mix all ingredients together in a medium bowl until the cabbage is coated with dressing. Refrigerate until needed.

Makes about 3 cups

HORSERADISH SAUCE

1 cup **sour cream**
1 tablespoon **heavy cream**
1 tablespoon chopped **chives**
1 to 2 tablespoons prepared **horseradish** (to taste)
Kosher salt and **pepper**

In a small bowl, stir together all the ingredients. Refrigerate until needed.

Makes about 1 cup

We also served **red corn on the cob**. The kernels are deep ruby red in color. If the corn is fresh and sweet, throw it straight onto the grill. If not, parboil it first, then throw onto the grill. When it comes off, brush with butter that was melted with salt and pepper, a chile pepper, chopped garlic scapes, and some fresh thyme.

Deviled Crab Risotto

Whenever you make risotto, use a round-bottomed pot so you can get to all the rice as you're stirring. You should also invest in a risotto spoon: it's flat on one side and round on the other with a hole in the middle so that you develop a lot of starch. It doesn't cost much, just a couple of bucks. But if you don't have one, at least make sure you're using a spoon that fits into the corners of the pan as snugly as possible.

4 cups **chicken stock**
A generous pinch of **saffron threads**
2 tablespoons **EVOO**
3 slices good-quality **bacon**, finely chopped
1 small-to-medium **onion**, finely chopped
1 rib **celery** with leafy top, from the heart, finely chopped
1 **red Fresno chile**, seeded and very finely chopped
2 or 3 large cloves **garlic**, finely chopped
1 tablespoon fresh **thyme**, finely chopped
1½ cups arborio or carnaroli **rice**
Salt and **pepper**
½ cup **dry white wine**
8 ounces **crabmeat** (from a plastic tub, not a can), picked over
Old Bay seasoning
Hot pepper sauce
½ cup freshly grated **Parmigiano-Reggiano cheese**
3 tablespoons **butter**

In a small saucepan, bring the stock, saffron, and 1 to 2 cups water to a low boil. Reduce the heat to low and just let it steep and stay warm.

In a heavy skillet, heat the EVOO (2 turns of the pan) over medium heat. Add the bacon and cook until crisp, 2 to 3 minutes. Stir in the onion, celery, chile, garlic, and thyme. Stir that around a minute or two to sweat it out.

Add the rice and stir for 1 minute; season with salt and pepper. Add the wine and cook to evaporate. Begin adding the warm saffron stock a few

ladlefuls at a time, allowing it to absorb almost completely before adding more, stirring rapidly and frequently to develop the starch, until the risotto is creamy. From the time you begin adding the liquids it takes exactly 18 minutes.

Near the end, when the rice is almost done to al dente, after about 16 minutes, run your fingers through the crabmeat to make sure you've removed all the pieces of shell. Season with a little sprinkle of Old Bay and a couple of dashes of hot sauce.

Stir the cheese and butter into the risotto. Remove the risotto from the heat and gently stir in the crab. Serve immediately in shallow bowls.

Serves 4

I made **Deviled Crab Arancini,** from the leftovers of Deviled Crab Risotto from the night before (this page). We started with **Eggplant Spread, Pepper Appetizer, Cucumber Dip,** and **Artichokes & Vinaigrette,** and the main was **Smoked Beef Ragu with Pappardelle.**

Eggplant Spread

Serve the spread on crostini.

1½ pounds (2 to 3 small) firm **eggplant**, halved lengthwise
2 tablespoons **EVOO**
Salt and **pepper**
2 cloves **garlic**, minced
3 tablespoons **tahini paste**
Juice of 1 **lemon**
A generous handful of **flat-leaf parsley**

Preheat the broiler to high.

Brush the cut sides of the eggplant with the EVOO and drizzle over the skin side. Season with salt and pepper. Place cut side down on a nonstick baking sheet and broil 4 to 5 inches from the heat until the skin is charred and the flesh is very tender, 15 to 20 minutes. Cool for 5 minutes.

Scoop the eggplant flesh off the skin into a food processor. Paste garlic with some salt, mashing it with the side of your knife. Add the garlic, tahini, lemon juice, and parsley to the processor and process until smooth. Adjust the salt.

Makes 2 to 3 cups

Pepper Appetizer

1 medium **eggplant**, halved lengthwise
2 tablespoons **EVOO**
Salt and **pepper**
3 **red bell peppers**
2 **red Fresno chiles** or 1 Italian red cherry pepper
1 head **garlic**, roasted (see page 114) and squeezed out, or a couple of cloves of raw garlic, grated or pasted
Juice of 1 **lemon**

Preheat the oven to 400°F.

Place the eggplant on a baking sheet, drizzle with the EVOO, and season with salt and pepper. Place in the oven and roast until soft and starting to collapse, about 40 minutes. Halfway through the cooking, add the bell peppers and chiles to the pan.

Remove from the oven, let the eggplant cool, and place the peppers in a bowl. Cover the bowl with plastic wrap and let steam for about 15 minutes.

Peel and seed the peppers and place in a food processor along with the flesh of the eggplant, the garlic, and lemon juice. Season with salt and pepper and puree.

Makes about 2 cups

Cucumber Dip

You can also add a nice drizzle of EVOO to this, but it's gilding the lily and not necessary.

Salt and **pepper**
⅓ to ½ **seedless cucumber**, peeled and grated
1 to 1½ cups **Greek yogurt**

Juice of ½ **lemon**
1 or 2 large cloves **garlic**, grated
A scant teaspoon ground **cumin**
Fresh dill or dill pollen (optional)
Flat-leaf parsley (optional)

Salt the cucumber and let it sit in a strainer for 20 to 30 minutes to completely drain.

Squeeze out all the liquid and throw the cucumber into a food processor with the yogurt, lemon juice, garlic, cumin, and salt and pepper to taste. Add in some dill or parsley if you like. Puree.

Makes about 1½ cups

Deviled Crab Arancini

Arancini are little fried rice balls. The word *arancini* means little oranges and this dish is named that because they look like little oranges. I served these delicious little fried crab rice balls up with lemon wedges on a bed of arugula leaves dressed with lemon, olive oil, and sea salt. If you want a really cheesy crust for the arancini, you could add Parm to the coating mixture: an equal mixture of bread crumbs, cornmeal, and cheese. I used leftover crab risotto for this, but you might want to make the whole recipe so you can get a lot of arancini.

Vegetable oil, for frying
Flour, for coating
2 large **eggs**
1 cup **fine dry bread crumbs**
1 cup **fine cornmeal**
1 tablespoon **Old Bay seasoning**
Leftover **Deviled Crab Risotto** (page 91)

In a deep, heavy pot, heat 3 inches of oil over medium heat until it reaches 350° to 375°F on a deep-fry thermometer. (To test: At this temperature the tip of the handle of a wooden kitchen spoon will bubble when inserted in the oil.)

Line up 3 bowls on the counter: Put the flour in one, beat the eggs with a splash of water in the second, and mix together the bread crumbs, cornmeal, and Old Bay in the third.

Using a scoop, make 2-inch balls of the risotto, then roll them with your hands (wetting your palms in warm water now and then). Coat the balls in the flour, then in the beaten egg, then in the seasoned bread crumbs.

Working in batches, add the risotto balls to the hot oil and cook until deep golden, about 3 minutes per batch. Transfer to a paper towel–lined rack to cool briefly, then serve hot.

The number of servings will depend on how much risotto you use.

Artichokes & Vinaigrette

You can either steam the artichokes (as I do) or boil them. If you boil them, put a lot of lemon in the water and salt the water; I also put a dish towel up on top to keep the artichokes from bobbing around and to keep them submerged in the water.

4 large or 6 medium **artichokes**, trimmed (see Tip)
Juice of 1 or 2 **lemons**, plus ½ lemon
2 **shallots**
Kosher or **sea salt**
3 tablespoons **vinegar** (white balsamic, sherry, or white wine, or a combo of all three)
1 rounded teaspoon **Dijon mustard**
⅓ to ½ cup **EVOO**
Pepper

Set up a steamer. Rub the artichokes with the ½ lemon. Steam the artichokes until they're nice and tender, until the leaves can be easily pulled off, about 30 minutes. Then cool them upside down so they can drain while they're cooling.

I then pull out the centerpieces and scrape out the choke material (all the little fibers at the center). I don't remove the chokes before I boil them because it's too much of a pain.

Grate the shallots into a small bowl and season with some kosher or sea salt. Stir in the lemon juice, vinegar, and mustard. Whisk in the EVOO and season with salt and pepper. Put the vinaigrette out with the cooled artichokes for dipping.

Serves 4 to 6

Pull off a few of the dark outer leaves from the artichokes, then trim the stems up but leave them intact. Cut about ½ inch off the top of the artichokes, and with scissors, cut off any pointy leaves.

Smoked Beef Ragu with Pappardelle

I made a ragu with leftover beef from my 7-Hour Smoked Brisket and tossed it with pappardelle.

2 tablespoons **EVOO**
2 **carrots**, chopped
2 ribs **celery**, chopped
3 cloves **garlic**, chopped
1 **onion**, chopped
1 fresh **bay leaf**
3 tablespoons **tomato paste**
1 cup **dry red wine**
2 to 3 cups **beef stock**
1 to 2 cups coarsely chopped **leftover brisket**
    or **other cooked meat**
Salt
1 pound **pappardelle** pasta
½ cup **flat-leaf parsley**, chopped
Grated **pecorino Romano cheese**, for serving

Bring a large pot of water to a boil.

While the pasta water is coming up to a boil, start the sauce: In a large skillet, heat the EVOO (2 turns of the pan) over medium-high heat. Add the carrots, celery, garlic, onion, bay leaf, and tomato paste. Stir until fragrant. Add in the wine, stock, and leftover brisket. Bring up to a simmer and cook for 5 minutes.

Salt the boiling water and cook the pappardelle to al dente. Drain the pasta and toss with the sauce. Add the parsley and serve, passing grated cheese at the table.

Serves 4

Today is my mom's birthday. We had **Grilled Chicken & Steak with Italian Marinade**, **Bull's-Eye Deviled Eggs** (see April 24, page 29) and an Italian spin on **Gazpacho**. I made **Batter-Dipped Zucchini Flowers** (see July 1, page 76) and a **Pesto Pasta Salad** with lots of chunky vegetables and bacon at my mother's request. She said "I want a pasta salad with lots of vegetables and bacon," so that's what she got. Dessert was **Cream Puffs with Berries**.

Mom looked really, really pretty. She wore a brown Alicia Mugetti outfit with her crab medallion (her birth sign is Cancer so she had a really cool crab medallion necklace) and her little ruby bell necklace and her father's ring with rubies. My Aunt Cheech came and my cousin Charlie. My brother, Manny; his baby; my sister, Maria; and John—it was a nice family occasion.

Grilled Chicken & Steak with Italian Marinade

Italian Marinade (recipe follows)
6 **skinless, boneless chicken breast halves**
2½ to 3 pounds **flank** or **flat iron steaks**

Set aside one-third of the marinade. Divide the remaining marinade between 2 large sturdy resealable plastic bags. Add the chicken to one and the steak to the other. Marinate for at least 30 minutes, up to several hours.

Preheat the grill. The chicken breasts usually cook in 10 to 12 minutes, depending on the size of the breast. We usually cook them toward the center of the grill and then move them off to the side for the last few minutes of cook time. A large piece of steak will take 10 to 15 minutes if you want it pink in the center (the longer time if the steak is more than an inch thick at the center). The smaller flat iron steaks will take less time.

Take the steak and chicken off and let them rest a little bit. Thinly slice the steaks against the grain and thinly slice the chicken on an angle; dress with the reserved marinade.

Serves 6 to 8

ITALIAN MARINADE

This marinade is like an Italian dressing

About 1 cup **EVOO**
Juice of 1 **lemon**
3 to 4 tablespoons **red wine vinegar**
1 tablespoon **superfine sugar**
2 rounded tablespoons **Dijon mustard**
3 tablespoons grated **red onion**
2 cloves **garlic**, grated or pasted
2 tablespoons chopped **flat-leaf parsley**
2 tablespoons chopped fresh **basil**
2 tablespoons chopped fresh **thyme**

Combine all the ingredients.

Makes about 1½ cups

Gazpacho Italiano

I serve the gazpacho in little chilled glasses—demitasse cups are cute, or shooter glasses.

1 **Italian red pepper** (see Tip)
1½ **fresh red chiles**, seeds and all, chopped
½ **seedless cucumber**, peeled and chopped
1 slice good-quality **white bread**, crust removed, torn
1 small **red onion**, coarsely chopped
2 cloves **garlic**, grated
2 to 3 small ribs **celery** with leafy tops, from the heart, chopped
A small handful of **flat-leaf parsley**
A few leaves of fresh **basil**, torn
1 (28-ounce) can Italian **San Marzano tomatoes** (look for DOP on the label) or 12 plum tomatoes
EVOO, for drizzling
Juice of 1 **lemon**
Kosher salt and **pepper**

Char the red pepper directly over a gas flame or under the broiler. Place in a bowl and cover. When cool enough to handle, peel, seed, and coarsely chop the pepper and put in a food processor.

Add to the processor the chiles, cucumber, bread, onion, garlic, celery, parsley, basil, tomatoes, a drizzle of EVOO, lemon juice, and salt and pepper to taste. Process until fairly smooth. Chill.

Serves 6

If you can't get an Italian red pepper, buy a large red bell pepper (usually marked red field pepper) that looks like a giant rectangle, not a little square bell pepper.

Pesto Pasta Salad with Bacon

It's like BLT pasta salad. I used Italian Florentine pasta twists.

3 tablespoons **pistachios**, toasted
3 tablespoons **pine nuts**, toasted
1 cup **basil leaves**
1 packed cup **flat-leaf parsley**
Juice of 1 **lemon**
½ cup grated **Parmigiano-Reggiano cheese**
Salt and **pepper**
½ cup **EVOO**
1 pound **pasta twists** or bow-tie pasta
¾ pound **bacon**
3 or 4 plum or vine-ripened **tomatoes**, seeded and chopped, or 1 pint cherry tomatoes, halved
A couple of handfuls of **arugula**, coarsely chopped

Preheat the oven to 375°F.

Bring a large pot of water to a boil.

Meanwhile, combine the pistachios, pine nuts, basil, parsley, lemon juice, Parm, salt, and pepper in a food processor. Pulse until finely chopped. Stream in the EVOO and pulse until combined. Transfer the pesto to a large bowl.

Salt the water and cook the pasta to al dente. Before draining, ladle out 1 cup of the starchy cooking water and stir into the pesto. Drain the pasta and let cool completely.

Arrange the bacon slices on a slotted broiler pan and bake in the oven until crispy and cooked, about 8 minutes. Chop the bacon.

Add the bacon, tomatoes, and arugula to the pesto bowl along with the cooled pasta. Toss together and serve.

Serves 4

Cream Puffs with Berries

Mom wanted éclairs with berries. We had strawberries and blackberries with a little superfine sugar and a little bit of chopped mint, and we doused it with some limoncello, my mom's favorite liqueur. You can also use Frangelico, amaretto, Grand Marnier, etc.

PASTRY CREAM
¾ cup **sugar**
A pinch of **salt**
3¼ cups **milk**
¼ cup **cornstarch**
3 **egg yolks**
1½ teaspoons **vanilla extract**

CREAM PUFF DOUGH
6 tablespoons (¾ stick) **butter**
½ teaspoon **salt**
1 cup **flour**
4 **eggs**

Make the pastry cream: In a medium saucepan, combine the sugar, salt, and 3 cups of the milk. Bring up to a bubble over medium heat.

While the milk is heating up, combine the remaining ¼ cup milk with the cornstarch in a bowl and stir until completely dissolved. In another large bowl, break up the egg yolks and whisk them together.

Using a whisk, add the cornstarch mixture into the simmering milk and stir constantly until thickened, about 2 minutes (it's OK if the mixture boils lightly).

When the mixture has thickened up, slowly add a couple of ladlefuls of the hot liquid into the bowl with the egg yolks while whisking constantly. Add the egg yolk mixture back to the pan, return it to medium heat, and simmer until thickened, about 2 minutes. Remove the pot from the heat and stir in the vanilla extract.

Transfer the mixture to a bowl and cover with plastic wrap, pushing the plastic down so that it covers the surface of the cream. Refrigerate until chilled, at least 2 hours and up to overnight.

Make the cream puffs: Preheat the oven to 400°F. Line a baking sheet with parchment paper.

In a medium saucepan, combine 1 cup water, the butter, and salt. Heat over medium-high heat until the butter has melted and the water is boiling. Add the flour and cook, stirring constantly with a wooden spoon. Stir until the mixture begins to create a dough ball in the center of the pot and the dough is completely pulling away from the sides of the pan, about 2 minutes.

Transfer the mixture to the bowl of a stand mixer fitted with a paddle attachment. On low speed, add the eggs to the mixture one at a time, scraping the sides of the bowl well after each addition and beating until the bowl feels cool (the mixture should be very smooth and silky).

Transfer the mixture to a resealable plastic bag and cut ½ inch off of one corner to create a pastry bag. Squeeze the mixture into desired shapes (I do mine in round dollops, about the size of a

Ping-Pong ball) onto the baking sheet and bake until golden brown and puffed with little sweat beads on top of them, about 40 minutes.

The pastries can be made a day or two ahead of time and kept in an airtight container at room temperature. If they feel soggy when you take them out, pop them into a 400°F oven for a couple of minutes until they crisp up again. Allow them to cool before filling.

Assemble the cream puffs (they should be assembled the day of serving): Give the pastry cream a stir to break it up and smooth it out, then transfer it to a resealable plastic bag. Cut off about ¼ inch from one corner to make a pastry bag.

Slice the top third off each cream puff. Squeeze the pastry cream onto the bottoms and replace the tops.

Makes 24 to 30 cream puffs

JULY 19/LUNCH

French Tuna Melt

1 large clove **garlic**
¼ to ⅓ cup minced **red onion**
Juice of 1 **lemon**
Sea salt
1 or 2 small ribs **celery**, finely chopped
1 **fresh chile**, seeded and minced
2 tablespoons chopped fresh **tarragon**
2 tablespoons chopped **flat-leaf parsley**
1 tablespoon fresh **thyme**, chopped
Old Bay seasoning
1 (6-ounce) can line-caught no-salt-added albacore **tuna**, drained
¼ cup **EVOO**
Pepper
2 **brioche lobster rolls** (hot dog–style buns, split on top)
¼ cup shredded **Cheddar** or **Gruyère cheese**
1 **tomato**, diced

Grate the garlic into the bottom of a small bowl. Add the onion, lemon juice, and a little salt. Let that sit a few minutes so that the onion bleeds

out into the lemon juice. Add the celery, chile, tarragon, parsley, thyme, and a little Old Bay.

Preheat the broiler.

Flake the tuna into the bowl with the seasonings and dress it with the EVOO and some black pepper. Put the tuna mixture on the rolls. Top with the shredded cheese. Run under the broiler to melt and serve topped with diced tomato.

Makes 2 sandwiches

🕐 **JULY 19/DINNER**

We had fried **padrón peppers** for an appetizer, then **Beef Tacos**, **Mexican Rice**, and **BBQ baked beans** with sautéed peppers.

I took a dozen padrón peppers (fairly mild little green chiles from the farmers' market) and browned them up in oil and seasoned them with a little sea salt. You eat those just as is, as an appetizer. Mostly the peppers are mild, but one out of every handful of them is very spicy, so it's kind of fun.

Beef Tacos

This taco mixture is mildish; if you want more spice, use 2 scant tablespoons of chipotle powder instead of the ancho.

1 tablespoon **EVOO**
1½ pounds **ground beef**
1 small **onion**, finely chopped
2 cloves **garlic**, finely chopped
1 **jalapeño chile**, finely chopped
2 tablespoons **ancho chile powder** or a mild chili blend, such as Gebhardt's
1 tablespoon ground **coriander**
1 tablespoon ground **cumin**
1 tablespoon **tomato paste**
Salt
1 cup **beef** or **chicken stock**
1 cup room-temperature **lager beer**
Soft flour or corn **tortillas**, or taco shells
Toppings: **lettuce, tomato, onion, shredded cheese**

Preheat a medium skillet over medium-high heat. Add the EVOO (1 turn of the pan) and the meat. Brown the meat for 2 or 3 minutes. Add the onion and garlic and cook another 3 to 5 minutes. Stir in the jalapeño, chile powder, coriander,

cumin, and tomato paste. Cook for 1 minute more. Season with salt to taste. Stir in the stock and beer. Reduce the heat to medium-low and simmer until ready to serve.

Serve the meat with the tortillas and top with lettuce, tomato, onion, and shredded cheese.

*I served the tacos with good-quality store-bought **baked beans** that I dressed up: I sautéed hot and sweet peppers with onions and I just stirred in the beans.*

Mexican Rice

1 tablespoon **EVOO**
2 tablespoons **butter**
¼ cup **orzo** or broken spaghetti
1 cup **long-grain white rice**
2 plum or vine-ripened **tomatoes**, finely chopped
3 cloves **garlic**, chopped
1 small **onion**, chopped
2 cups **chicken stock**
Salt

Heat a medium-size saucepan over medium heat; add the EVOO and butter. When the butter has melted into the EVOO, add the pasta and cook until browned and fragrant. Stir in the rice. Stir in the tomatoes, garlic, and onion. Add the stock, bring to a boil, and cover. Reduce the heat and cook until the rice is tender, about 16 to 18 minutes. Season with salt and serve.

Serves 4

🕐 **JULY 20/DINNER**

We went to the Harvest Restaurant and I had my favorite pizza, which is green peppers, onions, and hot peppers. It's called the Rachael Ray.

🕐 **JULY 21/DINNER**

We had **grilled steaks** with **Porcini Steak Sauce** (see June 22, page 67), **tomato and arugula salad**, and a **Celery Salad** made with celery that we grew from seeds from Italy. And I made a **Swiss Chard au Gratin** inspired by a gardening book, a gift from my husband.

*When **grilling steaks**, I usually like a nice flat iron or strip. This night we rubbed the steaks with a little cut garlic, dressed with some EVOO, salt, and pepper. Brought them to room temperature for an hour and then we grilled them. Let them rest, thinly slice, and then serve them up with Porcini Steak Sauce.*

Swiss Chard au Gratin

John gave me a beautiful book on Italian gardens and how to cook up the vegetables from them. This is my version of one of those recipes.

1 head **garlic**, top cut off to expose the cloves
EVOO
Salt and **pepper**
2¼ to 2½ pounds **Swiss chard** or rainbow chard (3 or 4 large bunches)
4 tablespoons (½ stick) **butter**
¼ cup **flour**
2½ cups **whole milk**
Freshly grated **nutmeg**
2 cups freshly shredded **Parmigiano-Reggiano cheese**

Position a rack in the center of the oven and preheat to 425°F.

Drizzle the bulb of garlic with EVOO and season with salt and pepper. Wrap in foil and bake until tender, about 45 minutes. Remove from the oven and turn the oven down to 400°F. Let the garlic cool, then squeeze out of the skins and mash to a paste.

Bring a large pot of water to a boil. Add salt to the water.

Discard the chard stems, but keep the leaves whole. Add the chard leaves to the boiling water—the pot will be packed at first—and cook 10 minutes. Place in a colander and run under cool water; drain well. Transfer the leaves to a clean kitchen towel and twist the towel to squeeze out excess liquid. Chop the greens.

Meanwhile, in a saucepan, melt the butter over medium heat. Whisk in the flour and cook 1 minute. Whisk in the milk; season with salt and pepper and a little nutmeg. Stir in the roasted garlic paste and cook the sauce until thick enough to coat the back of a spoon. Adjust seasonings to taste.

Layer half the greens in a medium baking dish (8 to 10 inches long); top with half the sauce and half the cheese; repeat layers, ending with cheese.

Bake the gratin for 15 minutes.

Serves 4

I made a **tomato and arugula salad topped with bacon.** I baked off some bacon, cut it into large pieces, arranged tomato, red onion, and arugula on a platter, and scattered the bacon over it. I dressed the salad with EVOO, salt, and pepper.

Celery Salad

We grew beautiful celery from seeds from Italy.

1 or 2 teaspoons **anchovy paste**
Juice of 1 large **lemon**
¼ to ⅓ cup **EVOO**
1 **red Fresno chile**, chopped
A couple of handfuls of finely chopped **flat-leaf parsley**
1 small head **celery** (or ½ a normal supermarket head), thinly sliced on an angle
1 to 2 tablespoons **capers**
½ small **red onion**, thinly sliced

In a salad bowl, whisk the anchovy paste into the lemon juice. Whisk in the EVOO. Add the chile, parsley, celery, capers, and red onion.

Serves 4

🕐 **JULY 22/BREAKFAST**

Baked Polenta with Eggs

Softened **butter**, for greasing the pan
¾ cup **milk**
¾ cup **chicken stock**
½ cup quick-cooking **polenta**
½ teaspoon **fennel pollen**
1 teaspoon ground **sage**
½ to ¾ cup grated **Parmigiano-Reggiano cheese**
Salt and **pepper**
4 **eggs**

Preheat the oven to 375°F. Butter a medium baking dish or 4 individual gratin dishes.

In a medium saucepan, bring the milk and stock to a boil over medium heat. To the bubbling milk and stock, slowly whisk in the polenta and continue whisking until it begins to thicken and resemble hot oatmeal, about 3 minutes. Turn off the heat and stir in the fennel pollen and sage. Stir in the cheese and season with salt and pepper.

Pour the polenta into the baking dish, make 4 cup-like depressions in the polenta, and put an egg in each indent. Bake until the eggs are soft to medium set, about 15 minutes.

Serves 4

You could serve the polenta and eggs with **braised Italian sausages.** To braise sausages, put them in a skillet with about ¼ inch of water; bring them to a boil. Drizzle in a little olive oil and cook the sausages through; as the water evaporates, the oil will crisp up the casings.

🕐 JULY 24/DINNER

Creamy Saffron Sausage Cauliflower Pasta

You could also make this without the cauliflower. It still would be delicious. I use a mixture of pecorino and Parm a lot because I always have both of them on hand. Pecorino is tangy, Parmigiano is nutty, so the flavors actually balance.

2½ cups **chicken stock**
A generous pinch of **saffron threads**
Kosher salt and **pepper**
1 head **cauliflower**, whole but cored
1 tablespoon **EVOO**
1 pound bulk **Italian sweet sausage**
3 or 4 cloves **garlic**, finely chopped
1 yellow **onion**, finely chopped
½ cup **dry white wine**
1 **bay leaf**
1 thin **cinnamon stick** (2 to 3 inches long)
1 (28- or 32-ounce) can **San Marzano tomatoes**
   (look for DOP on the label)
1 cup **heavy cream**
1 pound **penne rigate** pasta
½ cup grated **Parmigiano-Reggiano cheese**
½ cup grated **pecorino cheese**
Chopped **flat-leaf parsley**, for serving

Preheat the oven to 400°F. Heat the stock with the saffron in a small saucepan over medium heat.

Meanwhile, in a medium pot, bring 1½ cups water to a boil. Add salt, then add the cauliflower. Cover and steam until tender, about 12 minutes. Drain and break into florets.

In a Dutch oven, heat the EVOO (1 turn of the pan) over medium-high heat. Add the sausage and, as it cooks, crumble it into very small pieces. Add the garlic and onion and cook for 5 minutes. Deglaze with the wine. Add the bay leaf, cinnamon stick, tomatoes, saffron stock, and heavy cream and stir to break up the tomatoes. Simmer until thickened, about 30 minutes. Discard the bay leaf and cinnamon stick and season with salt and pepper.

Meanwhile, bring a large pot of water to a boil. Add salt and cook the pasta to just shy of al dente. Before draining, reserve a ladle of the starchy cooking liquid. Drain the pasta and return to the pot.

Add the cauliflower, sausage sauce, and a little of the reserved cooking liquid to the pasta and stir to combine. Mix in the Parm and pecorino and garnish with the parsley.

Serves 4

🕐 JULY 28/DINNER

Dinner was **Lemon Spaghetti with Pesto** (I use lemon-infused spaghetti imported from Italy) made with a garlic-scape pesto and a **Caesar Salad with Kale** (see April 18, page 16) from our garden.

Lemon Spaghetti with Pesto

Garlic scapes are the curly-topped bright-green stem of the garlic flower that forms before the bulb matures. I buy my lemon spaghetti from Buon Italia.

5 to 6 **garlic scapes**, chopped
½ cup fresh **tarragon leaves**
1 cup **parsley or basil leaves**, or a combination
  of the two
Grated zest and juice of 1 **lemon**
½ cup **EVOO**
3 tablespoons **pistachios**, toasted
3 tablespoons **pine nuts**, toasted
½ cup grated **Parmigiano-Reggiano cheese**
½ cup grated **Pecorino Romano cheese**
Salt
1 pound **lemon spaghetti** (available at some
  Italian markets)

Bring a large pot of water to a boil.

Meanwhile, combine the scapes, tarragon, and parsley or basil in a food processor. Pulse. Add the lemon zest and juice, the EVOO, pistachios, pine nuts, and cheeses. Pulse until combined. Transfer the pesto to a large bowl (see Tip).

Salt the boiling water and cook the spaghetti to al dente. Before draining, ladle out 1 cup of the starchy cooking water and add it to the pesto. Drain the spaghetti and toss it with the pesto for a minute or two until the pasta is evenly coated.

Serves 4

If you don't want your serving dish to look messy, you can toss the pesto, pasta, and pasta cooking water in the pasta cooking pot instead. Return the pasta to the hot pot after you drain it, then add the starchy cooking water and the pesto, and toss it all in there. Then transfer it to the serving dish.

⏱ **JULY 30/DINNER**

Trying to keep up with zucchini flowers from the garden, I made **stuffed fried zucchini flowers**. Then we had **Roast Leg of Lamb** (with a **Fresh Mint Sauce**) and a **Celery & Pepper Salad with Grated Tomato Dressing**.

For the **stuffed fried zucchini flowers**: Season sheep's milk ricotta with fresh thyme, a drizzle of good EVOO, salt, and pepper. Pull the stamens out of the zucchini flowers and add enough filling to fill the bottom of the flower. Twist the ends of the flower together. Make a mixture of bread crumbs and cheese (I used a mixture of panko, fine Italian bread crumbs, and cornmeal with a handful of pecorino) and season it up with fennel salt and fennel pollen as well. Roll the stuffed flowers in flour, then in beaten egg, then in the bread-crumb mixture. Shallow-fry the stuffed flowers in olive oil in a skillet until they're deeply golden all over. Drain them on a wire rack and season them with a little more salt.

Roast Leg of Lamb

We top the lamb with shaved fennel and red onions, roasted red peppers, and some of the fresh mint sauce.

> 6-pound **boneless leg of lamb**
> **EVOO**
> **Kosher salt** and **black pepper**
> 2 to 3 large **bay leaves**
> 1 bunch of **mint**
> 1 bunch of **rosemary**
> 1 head **garlic**, separated into cloves and peeled
> 1 cup **white wine**
> **Fresh Mint Sauce** (recipe follows)

Bring the lamb to room temp, pat it dry, and rub with EVOO on both sides. Season the inside (where the bone was) heavily with salt and pepper. Place the bay leaves and mint at the center, then roll the leg of lamb into the shape of a roast.

Cut several shallow slits into the lamb and stuff with sprigs of rosemary and cloves of garlic until the roast is studded evenly all over. Rub the fatty side of the lamb with lots of salt and pepper and tie with kitchen twine.

Position a rack in the center of the oven and preheat to 425°F.

Arrange the lamb on a roasting rack in a roasting pan or set a wire rack over a rimmed baking sheet. Roast the lamb for 20 to 25 minutes. Add the wine to the pan and reduce the oven temperature to 325°F. Roast 12 minutes per pound, until the internal temperature reads 135° to 140°F on a meat thermometer. Let the meat rest before slicing and serving with the mint sauce.

Serves 6 to 8

FRESH MINT SAUCE

> 1 cup **white balsamic vinegar**
> 1/3 cup **sugar**
> 1 tablespoon **sea salt**
> 3 large **shallots**, coarsely chopped
> 1 loosely packed cup **mint leaves**
> 1/2 cup **flat-leaf parsley**

In a small saucepan, combine the vinegar, 1/2 cup water, and the sugar. Bring to a boil over medium heat. Add the salt and stir until the sugar and salt are dissolved. Reduce the heat to low.

Put the shallots, mint, and parsley in a food processor and pulse to finely chop, then transfer the mixture to a small storage container. Pour the hot brine over the shallot mixture. Cover the container with a lid and refrigerate until ready to serve or let stand at room temperature until ready to serve.

Makes about 1 to 1½ cups

Celery & Pepper Salad with Grated Tomato Dressing

> 1 head **cauliflower**, broken into florets, steamed, and cooled
> 1 small head **celery**, 6 to 8 ribs, thinly sliced on an angle
> 1 **bell pepper**, chopped
> 2 **red Fresno chiles**, thinly sliced
> 1/2 cup **Titan parsley leaves** (similar to Italian flat-leaf parsley)
> 1 or 2 cloves **garlic**, thinly sliced
> 6 **anchovy fillets**, chopped
> 1 very ripe **tomato**
> 1 to 2 tablespoons **blood orange vinegar** (or you could use white wine or red wine vinegar)
> About 1/3 cup **EVOO**
> **Salt** and **pepper**
> Torn **basil leaves**

In a salad bowl, combine the cauliflower, celery, bell pepper, chiles, parsley, garlic, and anchovies.

Grate the tomato with a box grater into a small bowl. Add the vinegar, then stream in and whisk the EVOO. Season with salt and pepper to taste. Add that to the salad bowl and toss everything together. Garnish with basil.

Serves 4 to 6

🕐 JULY 31/DINNER

Chicken Piccata with Pasta & Asparagus

Salt and **pepper**
½ pound **asparagus**, cut into 2½-inch pieces
¼ pound thin **green beans**, halved on an angle
1½ pounds **chicken breast cutlets** (halve chicken breasts horizontally and pound out to ⅛-inch thickness), or 4 thin pieces firm, white-fleshed sustainable fish, such as tilapia fillets
Flour, for dredging
A sprinkle of **poultry seasoning** or ground thyme (for chicken) or Old Bay seasoning (for fish)
2 tablespoons **EVOO**
4 tablespoons (½ stick) **butter**
½ pound **thin spaghetti** or angel hair pasta
4 cloves **garlic**, finely chopped
1 **shallot**, finely chopped
4 **Meyer lemons** or 3 small lemons
3 tablespoons **capers**
1 cup **dry, crisp white wine**, such as sauvignon blanc
1 cup **chicken stock**
½ cup **flat-leaf parsley leaves**, finely chopped
½ cup **green peas**
Torn **basil** or **tarragon**, for garnish

Preheat the oven to 200°F.

In a pot of boiling salted water, blanch the asparagus and green beans for 2 to 3 minutes, then cold-shock and drain. Reserve.

Bring a large pot of water to a boil for the pasta. Place a serving platter in the oven to warm.

Season the chicken cutlets or fish fillets with salt and pepper and dredge in flour seasoned with poultry seasoning or Old Bay. In a large skillet, heat the EVOO (2 turns of the pan) and 1 tablespoon butter over medium heat. Add the chicken or fish and sauté until lightly golden on each side, 8 minutes. Transfer to the warm platter.

Salt the boiling water and cook the pasta to al dente. Drain.

Add the remaining 3 tablespoons butter to the skillet and melt. Add the garlic and shallot and cook for 2 to 3 minutes. Slice one lemon and add it to the skillet along with the juice of a second lemon. Add the capers and stir for a minute more; add the wine and reduce for a minute, then add the stock and parsley. Simmer to thicken a bit, then spoon half of the sauce over the chicken or fish and cover with foil. Add the peas to the remaining sauce in the skillet, along with the juice of the remaining lemons and the asparagus, beans, and drained pasta. Toss to combine and season with salt and pepper to taste.

Serve the cutlets with the pasta alongside, garnished with a few leaves of basil or tarragon.

Serves 4

AUGUST

MONDAY/1
DINNER
easy pesto with trofie or saffron gnocchetti sardi

TUESDAY/2

WEDNESDAY/3
DINNER
Greek meatballs & tzatziki subs

THURSDAY/4

FRIDAY/5

THURSDAY/11
DINNER
light zucchini pasta, Thai basil drizzle, eggplant stacks with raw tomato sauce

FRIDAY/12

SATURDAY/13
DINNER
swordfish cutlets, tomato relish, roasted eggplant pasta

SUNDAY/14
BRUNCH
piadinas with bresaola and Robiola
DINNER
artichokes stuffed with tomato salad, lemon vinaigrette, fava bean spread, porcini pasta, veal chops with gorgonzola

MONDAY/15
DINNER
truffle garganelli

SUNDAY/21
DINNER
pulled pork, slow-smoked chicken, jalapeño poppers, pickled onions & chiles, red pork posole, Mexican rice, mushroom fundido

MONDAY/22
BREAKFAST
BLTs over eggs
DINNER
poached tarragon creamed chicken, bull's-eye deviled eggs

TUESDAY/23
DINNER
drunken lamb ragu with spaghetti, Caesar salad, batter-dipped zucchini flowers

WEDNESDAY/24
DINNER
porcini pappardelle

THURSDAY/25

SATURDAY/6	SUNDAY/7	MONDAY/8	TUESDAY/9	WEDNESDAY/10
DINNER Thai-style chicken with basil	**LUNCH** onion-Gruyère frittata **DINNER** pork chops smothered with peppers & onions, buttery tomato spaghetti	**DINNER** red pepper minestrone soup	**DINNER** Tuscan pesto penne, broiled tomato crostini	

TUESDAY/16	WEDNESDAY/17	THURSDAY/18	FRIDAY/19	SATURDAY/20
	DINNER cherry tomato pasta	**LUNCH** French onion French bread pizza, garden salad with Meyer lemon vinaigrette **DINNER** 7-hour smoked brisket, corn on the cob brushed with chili powder, my sweet & spicy pickles, fancied-up baked beans	**BREAKFAST** tagliatelle carbonara Milanese style	**BREAKFAST** frittata with chanterelles and zucchini flowers **LUNCH** niçoise salad, Meyer lemon vinaigrette

FRIDAY/26	SATURDAY/27	SUNDAY/28	MONDAY/29	TUESDAY/30
DINNER stuffed mushrooms, swordfish cutlets, tomato relish, roasted eggplant pasta	**DINNER** Sicilian-style orange salad, fava bean spread, fried green tomatoes, garden salad, egg tagliatelle with truffle butter, grilled snapper with pesto	**BREAKFAST** multigrain nutty waffles **DINNER** chicken curry, spice mix for curry, homemade rice pilaf	**DINNER** roast pork sandwiches with giardiniera	

WEDNESDAY/31

DINNER
Mexican pesto with whole wheat penne

Easy Pesto with Trofie or Saffron Gnocchetti Sardi

Trofie are very tiny little twisty-shaped pasta. Gnocchetti sardi are little teeny-tiny, baby gnocchi-shaped pasta that you can get saffron flavored. I get them at the Buon Italia market. Any short-cut pasta will do here.

3 tablespoons **pistachios**, toasted
3 tablespoons **pine nuts**, toasted
1 or 2 large cloves **garlic**, pasted
½ cup fresh **tarragon**
1 cup **basil leaves**
A small handful of **mint leaves**
⅓ cup grated **Parmigiano-Reggiano cheese**
1 teaspoon **ground fennel** or fennel pollen
Grated zest and juice of 1 **lemon**
Salt and **pepper**
⅓ cup **EVOO**
1 pound **trofie**, saffron-flavored gnocchetti sardi, or other short-cut pasta

In a food processor, combine the pistachios, pine nuts, garlic, tarragon, basil, mint, Parm, fennel, lemon zest, lemon juice, and salt and pepper to taste. Pulse until finely chopped. Stream in the EVOO and process to a pesto.

Bring a large pot of water to a boil. Salt the water and cook the pasta to al dente. Before draining, ladle out and reserve 1 cup of the starchy pasta cooking water. Drain the pasta.

Toss the pasta with the pesto and some starchy cooking water. Serve that hot or cold or at room temperature.

Serves 4

Greek Meatball & Tzatziki Subs

Salt and **pepper**
½ **seedless cucumber**, peeled and grated
3 tablespoons **EVOO**
1½ pounds **ground lamb** or **beef**
1 slice **white bread** (1 inch thick, crust trimmed) soaked in ½ cup **milk**
2 pinches of ground **cinnamon**
3 tablespoons grated **red onion**
3 cloves **garlic**, grated or pasted
¼ cup **mint leaves**, finely chopped
Juice of 1 **lemon**
1 tablespoon finely chopped fresh **oregano**
1 large **egg**
4 **pitas**, sliced open
1½ cups **Greek yogurt**
¼ cup chopped fresh **dill**
1 teaspoon ground **cumin**
Toppings: sliced **cucumbers**, **hot peppers**, **sweet peppers**, **onion**, **tomato**, shredded **lettuce**

Salt the cucumber and let drain in a strainer for 20 minutes.

Preheat the oven to 450°F. Place a cooling rack over each of 2 baking sheets.

Pour the EVOO into a bowl, add the meat, and season with salt and pepper. Squeeze out the bread and crumble into the bowl. Add the cinnamon, onion, 2 of the garlic cloves, the mint, half the lemon juice, the oregano, and egg, and mix to combine. Scrape into 24 balls and place on the baking sheet. Roast to golden brown, 15 to 18 minutes. Remove from the oven and set the broiler to high. Char the pitas under the broiler, 30 seconds to 1 minute on each side.

Press the cucumber to get out excess water; transfer to a food processor. Add the yogurt, dill, cumin, the remaining lemon juice, remaining garlic, and salt to taste. Process into a smooth sauce.

Fold the meatballs in the warm pitas and top with yogurt sauce and toppings.

Serves 4

Thai-Style Chicken with Basil

I made this with Bhutanese red rice, which has a great mahogany color. But jasmine rice is fine, too.

2 tablespoons **butter**
2¾ cups **chicken stock** or broth
1½ cups **red rice** or jasmine rice
Peanut or vegetable oil, for stir-frying
1½ pounds **skinless, boneless chicken breasts**
   or **thighs**, chopped into bite-size pieces
White or **black pepper**
1 **red Fresno chile** (milder) or Thai chile (hotter),
   seeded and thinly sliced or finely chopped
1½ inches **fresh ginger**, grated or minced
3 or 4 large cloves **garlic**, chopped
1 red or yellow **bell pepper**, thinly sliced
About 2 tablespoons **kecap manis** (sweet soy
   sauce) or 2 tablespoons tamari mixed with
   1 teaspoon sugar
1½ to 2 tablespoons **fish sauce**
1 cup Thai or regular **basil leaves**, torn
1 **lime**

In a saucepan, bring the butter and stock to a boil, stir in the rice, and return to a boil. Then reduce the heat to low, cover, and simmer until tender, 16 to 18 minutes. Fluff with a fork.

When the rice is about ready, in a large skillet, heat a thin layer of oil, about 1½ tablespoons, over high heat. Pat the chicken dry and season with a little pepper, add to the pan in a single layer and do not touch for 2 minutes, then stir-fry until golden, 5 to 6 minutes. Transfer to a plate.

Add a little more oil to the skillet and then add the chile, ginger, garlic, and bell pepper and stir-fry to tender-crisp, about 3 minutes. Add the kecap manis (or soy and sugar), fish sauce, and chicken and toss to coat.

Remove from the heat and wilt in half of the basil leaves. Grate a little lime zest into the pan and squeeze in the juice of ½ lime. Toss again to combine, and serve with the rice. Garnish with the remaining basil.

Serves 4

AUGUST 7, LUNCH. Onion-Gruyère frittata: In a pan, I caramelized onions in melted butter and when the onions were nice and caramel in color, I added ½ cup of beef stock. In a separate pan, I browned some chopped bacon and removed it, leaving a few tablespoons of fat. I added some sliced mushrooms to the bacon pan and browned them. Then I added a small bundle of spinach, wilted that in, and added a little grated garlic. Bacon back in the pan. I beat 8 eggs with ½ cup cream and I poured that into the skillet. I let the bottom of the frittata set, then I baked it in a 400°F oven for 20 minutes. I topped it with the onions and some shredded Gruyère and I put it back in the oven to brown on top.

We had **Pork Chops Smothered with Peppers & Onions** and a side pasta of **Buttery Tomato Spaghetti**.

Pork Chops Smothered with Peppers & Onions

4 bone-in **pork chops**, 1½ inches thick
Kosher salt and **pepper**
3 tablespoons **EVOO**
1 teaspoon **fennel seed**
1 **red bell pepper**, very thinly sliced
1 **cubanelle pepper**, thinly sliced
1 **red Fresno chile**, thinly sliced
1 large **onion**, thinly sliced
4 cloves **garlic**, thinly sliced
2 tablespoons **tomato paste**
½ cup **dry white** or **red wine**
1½ cups **chicken stock**

Preheat the oven to 400°F. Bring the chops to room temperature.

Season the chops with a liberal amount of salt and pepper.

In a large ovenproof skillet, heat 2 tablespoons of the EVOO (2 turns of the pan) over medium-high to high heat. When the oil begins to smoke, add the chops and brown on both sides, 3 or 4 minutes per side. Transfer to a plate.

Add the remaining 1 tablespoon EVOO (1 turn of the pan) to the skillet, add the fennel seed, peppers, chile, onion, and garlic and cook to soften, about 5 minutes. Add the tomato paste and stir 1 minute. Deglaze the pan with the wine and stir in the stock. Nestle the pork into the pan and move the peppers and onion on top of the chops. Place in the oven and roast until the pork is cooked through but still juicy, about 10 minutes.

Serves 4

Buttery Tomato Spaghetti

Using crushed tomatoes rather than breaking down whole tomatoes cuts the cook time of this sauce in half.

6 tablespoons **butter**
1 small **onion**, peeled and halved
1 large clove **garlic**, grated or pasted (optional)
1 (28- or 32-ounce) can **crushed San Marzano tomatoes** (look for DOP on the label)
A few leaves of torn **basil**
Salt
1 pound **spaghetti**
Freshly grated **Parmigiano-Reggiano cheese**

Heat a large pot of water to a boil.

In a saucepan, melt the butter over medium heat. Add the onion and garlic (if using), crushed tomatoes, basil, and salt to taste and cook for 20 minutes, stirring occasionally, to reduce.

After 12 to 13 minutes of sauce cooking time, salt the boiling water and cook the spaghetti to al dente. Before draining, ladle out about a cup of starchy pasta cooking water and add to the sauce.

Remove the onion halves from the sauce. Drain the pasta, add to the sauce, and toss to combine. Serve topped with Parm.

Serves 4 to 6

Red Pepper Minestrone Soup

4 large **red bell peppers**
1 head **garlic**, top sliced off to expose the cloves
¼ cup **EVOO**, plus more for drizzling
¼ pound **smoky bacon** or pancetta, chopped
2 tablespoons fresh **rosemary**, finely chopped
2 tablespoons fresh **thyme**, finely chopped
1 tablespoon fresh **oregano**, chopped
3 or 4 cloves **garlic**, sliced

2 **carrots**, chopped
2 ribs **celery**, chopped
1 large fresh **bay leaf**
1 fresh **red chile**, seeded and finely chopped
1 **onion**, chopped
1 **russet (baking) potato**, peeled and chopped
Kosher salt and **pepper**
¼ cup **tomato paste**
½ cup **dry white wine**
1 small bunch **Tuscan kale**, stemmed and chopped
8 cups **chicken stock**
1 can (14 ounces) **red beans** or **chickpeas**, rinsed and drained
Freshly grated **nutmeg**
¾ cup **ditalini** (or other small pasta) or broken thin spaghetti
4 tablespoons (½ stick) **butter**, softened
Crusty Italian bread, for serving
Grated **pecorino cheese**, for serving

Preheat the broiler. Arrange the bell peppers on a baking sheet and broil, turning occasionally, until the skins are blackened. Transfer the peppers to a bowl and cover. When cool enough to handle, peel and seed the peppers. Puree the peppers in a food processor with any juices that collected in the bowl.

Preheat the oven to 400°F. Drizzle the garlic with EVOO and wrap in foil. Roast until tender, about 45 minutes.

In a Dutch oven or other heavy pot, heat the ¼ cup EVOO over medium-high heat. Add the bacon and cook until crisp. Add the rosemary, thyme, oregano, sliced garlic, carrots, celery, bay leaf, chile, onion, and potato and season with salt and pepper. Partially cover the pot and cook, stirring, until the vegetables are soft, 7 to 8 minutes. Stir in the tomato paste and cook for 1 minute. Deglaze with the wine, stirring and scraping up any browned bits from the bottom of the pot with a wooden spoon. Add the kale and cook until wilted. Add the stock, beans, and a few gratings of nutmeg and bring to a boil. Stir in the roasted pepper puree.

Bring the soup to a low boil. Add the pasta and cook until al dente. (Or cook the pasta separately in salted boiling water.)

Meanwhile, squeeze the roasted garlic into a bowl and mash with the butter. Slice the bread, then broil or grill until charred.

Divide the soup among shallow bowls. Top with pecorino and a drizzle of EVOO. Slather the bread with the garlic butter and serve with the soup.

Serves 4 to 6

🕐 **AUGUST 9/DINNER**

Started with **Broiled Tomato Crostini** followed by **Tuscan Pesto Penne.**

Broiled Tomato Crostini

2 pints **grape tomatoes**
¼ cup **EVOO**
Salt and **pepper**
1 loaf **sesame semolina bread**
2 cloves **garlic**, halved
4 **scallions**, finely chopped
½ cup **basil leaves**, thinly sliced

Preheat the oven to 400°F.

Coat the tomatoes in the EVOO and season with salt and pepper. Roast 20 minutes to concentrate the flavor and burst the tomatoes.

Slice the loaf of bread horizontally to get 2 large "planks," each 1 inch thick.

When you remove the tomatoes from the oven, switch on the broiler. Char the bread on both sides, then rub the hot bread with the cut garlic.

In a bowl, lightly mash the roasted tomatoes and combine with the scallions and basil. Top the large planks with the tomato mixture, then cut each giant crostino into 4 pieces, to get 8 pieces total.

Makes 8 crostini

Tuscan Pesto Penne

1 cup fresh **basil leaves**
½ cup flat-leaf **parsley leaves**
⅓ cup grated **Parmigiano-Reggiano cheese**
¼ cup fresh **mint leaves**
¼ cup **pine nuts**
About 2 tablespoons fresh **thyme leaves**
2 cloves **garlic**, grated or pasted
Juice of ½ **lemon**
Salt and **pepper**
About ½ cup **EVOO**
1 pound **penne pasta**
1 small **russet (baking) potato**, peeled and cut
　 into ¼-inch dice
⅓ pound **haricots verts**, trimmed and cut
　 crosswise into thirds

Combine the basil, parsley, cheese, mint, pine nuts, thyme, garlic, and lemon juice in a food processor and season with salt and pepper. Turn the processor on and add the EVOO in a slow stream, blending until a thick sauce forms. Transfer to a large bowl.

Bring a large pot of water to a boil. Salt the water, add the pasta, and cook for 6 minutes. Add the potato and cook for 1 more minute. Add the haricots verts and cook until the pasta is al dente, 2 to 3 minutes more. Before draining, ladle out 1 cup of the starchy cooking water and add it to the pesto. Drain the pasta, then add it to the bowl with the pesto and toss to coat.

Serves 4 to 6

🕐 **AUGUST 11/DINNER**

I made **Eggplant Stacks** with a **Raw Tomato Sauce** and we had a **Light Zucchini Pasta with Thai Drizzle**.

Eggplant Stacks

Salt and **pepper**
1 **eggplant**, cut crosswise into ½-inch-thick
　 slices
¼ to ⅓ cup **EVOO**
1 or 2 cloves **garlic**, smashed
1 **red Fresno chile**, sliced, or ⅛ teaspoon
　 crushed red pepper flakes
12 slices fresh **mozzarella cheese**
15 **basil leaves**, torn
Raw Tomato Sauce (recipe follows)

Salt the eggplant and place on a kitchen towel or folded-up paper towels for 20 minutes so that it can sweat out a little. (The salt draws out the liquid and the bitterness, although most bitterness has been bred out of eggplant at this point.)

Meanwhile, in a small saucepan, combine the EVOO, garlic, and chile. Heat to infuse the oil with flavor.

Preheat the oven to 425°F. Set a wire rack over a baking sheet.

Place the eggplant on the rack. Brush it with some of the chile-garlic oil and season with pepper. Roast until golden, 15 to 20 minutes.

Take the eggplant out of the oven and make stacks with the mozzarella and basil. I make stacks that are 3 or 4 layers high and then pour the raw sauce over the top and serve.

Serves 2

RAW TOMATO SAUCE

2 or 3 sweet red **tomatoes**
3 tablespoons grated **onion** (red or yellow)
1 clove **garlic**
EVOO
Salt and **pepper**

Grate the tomatoes on the large side of a box grater: you need about 1 cup of grated tomato total. Grate in the onion and garlic. Add a healthy drizzle of EVOO and add salt and pepper to taste. Stir that together.

Makes 1 generous cup

Light Zucchini Pasta

You can also make this with penne rigate if you want a short-cut pasta. Also, the Thai Basil Drizzle makes a little more than you need. Hold on to it for other dishes; store in the refrigerator.

¼ cup **EVOO**
2 medium-large or 4 small **zucchini**, sliced
Fennel salt or **fennel pollen**
Salt and **pepper**
⅓ cup **mint leaves**, chopped
3 or 4 cloves **garlic**, finely chopped or grated
Grated zest and juice of ½ **lemon**
1 pound **egg tagliatelle** (I like Delverde brand)
Zucchini flowers, torn up, for garnish (optional)
Grated **pecorino cheese**
Thai Basil Drizzle (recipe follows)
½ cup fresh **sheep's milk ricotta cheese**

Bring a large pot of water to a boil.

Meanwhile, in a large skillet, heat the EVOO (4 turns of the pan) over medium-low heat. Toss the zucchini with the fennel salt or pollen and salt and pepper. Brown the zucchini in the oil. Add the mint and garlic and cook until golden, about 1 minute. Add the lemon zest to the pan and continue cooking another 30 seconds. Season with salt and pepper.

Salt the boiling water and cook the tagliatelle to al dente. Before draining, ladle out 1 cup of the

starchy cooking water and add it to the zucchini. Drain the pasta and add it to the zucchini along with the lemon juice. Toss with the zucchini flowers (if using) and lots of grated pecorino.

Spoon the pasta into shallow bowls and drizzle it back and forth with the basil drizzle. Top with a dollop of ricotta cheese for mixing in.

Serves 4

THAI BASIL DRIZZLE

Thai basil tastes like sweet basil with a hint of anise or fennel flavor to it.

1 packed cup **Thai basil leaves**
Juice of 1 **lemon**
½ cup **EVOO**
Sea salt

Blend the basil, lemon juice, EVOO, and salt until it's very, very smooth. I put it in a little squirt bottle.

Makes about 1 cup

One of our favorites for dinner: **Swordfish Cutlets** (see June 2, page 55) with a **fresh tomato relish**. The side pasta this night was a **Roasted Eggplant Pasta**.

Roasted Eggplant Pasta

This eggplant sauce is delicious just on crostini by itself. It makes a sort of poor man's caviar (the eggplant seeds make it look like caviar). I used a pasta that looks like the curls from a person with very, very curly hair. It's not fusilli, but it's little pasta curls.

1 medium **eggplant**, halved lengthwise
EVOO for drizzling
Salt and **pepper**
½ cup **flat-leaf parsley leaves**
Leaves from a sprig of **rosemary**, finely chopped
Leaves from 1 or 2 sprigs of fresh **thyme**, finely chopped
Zest of 1 **lemon**
2 cloves **garlic**, chopped or grated, or roasted garlic (see Tip)
1 pound **capricci pasta curls** (I get mine from Buon Italia) or other short-cut pasta
1 cup grated **pecorino cheese**

Preheat the oven to 400°F.

On the cut sides of the eggplant, use a sharp paring knife to crosshatch the flesh ½ inch apart on an angle and all around the edge. Drizzle a baking sheet with some EVOO and season the eggplant with salt and pepper. Place the eggplant cut side down and roast until very tender, about 20 minutes.

Meanwhile, finely chop the herbs, lemon zest, and garlic together and transfer to a pasta bowl.

Bring a large pot of water to a boil. Salt the water. Once the eggplant is done, add the pasta to the boiling water and cook to al dente. Before draining, ladle out 1 cup starchy cooking water. Drain the pasta.

Scoop the eggplant out of the skin into the pasta bowl with the herbs and add the pecorino. Mix in the starchy cooking water and the pasta and toss to combine.

Serves 4

I roast a whole head of garlic while I'm roasting the eggplant. Separate 2 heads garlic into cloves, but leave the skins on. Put them in the middle of a sheet of foil, drizzle with 1 tablespoon EVOO, and season with salt and pepper. Close the foil to make a little pouch. Place in the oven until the cloves soften and you smell the aroma of garlic, 30 to 40 minutes. Remove from the oven, let cool for 5 to 10 minutes so it is easy to handle, and squeeze the garlic out from the skin.

AUGUST 14, BRUNCH

We had **piadinas** for brunch. That's very, very, very thin flatbread that you put into your panini press. I get mine at the Buon Italia market and I build a sandwich of bresaola, which is air-dried beef, leftover basil oil, sliced Robiola cheese, a few leaves of arugula, and a few thin slices of hot chile. You just build them on half of the piadina, fold it over, and then put it into the panini press until it's melty and the outside is marked.

AUGUST 14/DINNER

For antipasto we had **artichokes stuffed with tomato salad** with a **Lemon Vinaigrette** for dipping, and **Fava Bean Spread** (see May 26, page 42) with little toasts. The main course was **Veal Chops with Gorgonzola** with a side dish of **Porcini Pasta**.

Artichokes stuffed with tomato salad: This is my version of the salad that's served at The Ivy restaurant in Los Angeles. I'm more of a New York girl than an LA girl, but I do love the Ivy and I love the artichokes that they serve there filled with grape or cherry tomato salad. I was just sort of daydreaming about it and the artichokes looked so great at the market I decided to try my hand at making them. In a steamer, I steamed the artichokes until very tender. Cool them upside down to let them drain. Remove the fibrous choke and all the inner leaves. I made my **tomato salad** with little teeny tiny tomatoes called 100-count tomatoes. (That refers to their size—they are so tiny that you would need 100 of the tomatoes to make a pound.) I halved them and I tossed them with very thinly sliced baby fennel from our garden, a few tablespoons of fresh tarragon, some flat-leaf parsley, a little bit of minced red onion, EVOO—just enough to coat—and I seasoned with salt and pepper. Then you fill the artichokes at the center with the salad and you serve Lemon Vinaigrette (see below) in little ramekins alongside for dipping. This is a delicious lunch or starter course for a cold summer dinner. Don't forget to put out an extra dish for discarded leaves.

LEMON VINAIGRETTE

Juice of 1 **lemon**
3 tablespoons **white balsamic vinegar**
1 tablespoon **Dijon mustard**
1 teaspoon **fennel salt** or **fennel pollen**
Sea salt and **pepper**
⅓ to ½ cup of **EVOO**

Whisk together the lemon juice, vinegar, mustard, fennel salt, and salt and pepper. Stream in the EVOO as you whisk.

Makes about ¾ cup

Porcini Pasta

You could use a mixture of any thinly sliced fresh mushrooms in place of the porcini. For the pasta, I used mafalde, which is a long, curly-edged pasta, like a narrow lasagna.

2 tablespoons **EVOO**
2 tablespoons **butter**
1 pound fresh **porcini**, thinly sliced
2 cloves **garlic**, finely chopped
2 tablespoons chopped fresh **rosemary**
2 tablespoons chopped **flat-leaf parsley**
2 tablespoons chopped fresh **thyme leaves**
1 cup **dry white wine** (see Tip)
1 (28-ounce) can **San Marzano tomatoes** (look for DOP on the label)
Chicken or **vegetable stock** (optional)
Salt
1 pound **mafalde pasta**
Grated **Parmigiano-Reggiano cheese**, for serving

In a large skillet, heat the EVOO (2 turns of the pan) and butter over medium-high heat. When the butter foams, add the mushrooms and let them lightly brown, 15 minutes or so. Add the garlic and herbs and stir. Add the wine and cook until reduced by half.

Add the tomatoes, breaking them up gently with a potato masher. Reduce the heat to a simmer and let that cook until it's as thick as you like, 30 to 40 minutes. If the sauce becomes a little too thick, add a little chicken or vegetable stock.

Bring a large pot of water to a boil. Salt the water and cook the pasta to al dente. Drain and add the pasta to the skillet with the mushrooms. Toss together and serve topped with Parm.

Serves 4

You could substitute ½ cup dry sherry or Marsala for the wine and let that reduce down by half to ¼ cup.

Veal Chops with Gorgonzola

8 ounces **Gorgonzola dolce cheese**
4 tablespoons (½ stick) **butter**, softened
4 bone-in **veal chops**, 1 inch thick, at room temperature
Kosher salt or sea salt and **pepper**
¼ cup chopped fresh **sage** (about 6 sprigs)
1 tablespoon **EVOO**
½ cup **dry vermouth**

Preheat the oven to 350°F. In a small bowl, blend the Gorgonzola and butter. Set aside.

Heat a cast-iron skillet over medium-high heat. Season the chops with salt and pepper. Rub about 1 tablespoon of sage onto both sides of each chop. Add the EVOO (1 turn of the pan) to the hot skillet. Add the chops and brown on both sides,

then transfer the skillet to the oven and bake for 5 to 6 minutes if you want them a little on the pink side, or 7 to 8 minutes if you want them medium. Take them out of the oven and douse the pan with the vermouth to finish.

Dividing evenly, top the hot chops with the Gorgonzola-butter mixture and then let that melt down a little bit until it becomes this nice slather.

Serves 4

🕐 AUGUST 15/DINNER

Truffle Garganelli

I cooked garganelli, which is a fresh egg pasta that they sell in the freezer section at Buon Italia.

1 tablespoon **EVOO**
4 tablespoons (½ stick) **butter**
1 large **shallot**, chopped
2 cloves **garlic**, minced
1 tablespoon **white truffle paste**
½ cup **white wine**
3 to 4 tablespoons finely chopped **chives**
Sea salt and **pepper**
1 pound **garganelli pasta**
1 cup freshly grated **Grana Padano cheese**

Bring a large pot of water to a boil.

Meanwhile, in a medium saucepan, heat the EVOO (1 turn of the pan) over medium-high heat. Add the butter and when it begins to foam, add the shallot, garlic, and truffle paste. Stir that around for a few minutes. Then add the wine, chives, and salt and pepper.

Salt the boiling water and cook the garganelli to al dente. Before draining, ladle out ½ cup of the starchy cooking water and stir it into the truffle sauce. Drain the pasta and add it to the sauce along with the cheese, tossing 1 or 2 minutes to absorb the flavors. Season with sea salt and toss.

Serves 4

AUGUST 16, DINNER. We ate at The Ridge Terrace in Lake George, New York. That's a restaurant where I used to be a waitress. It's owned by the Rios family and I go there every summer, especially around our birthdays. When I go to The Ridge Terrace, I love to get their beef brochette, which is filet mignon with bordelaise sauce and peppers and onions on skewers over rice pilaf. We always get the eggplant appetizer: fried eggplant layered with a spicy red sauce and mozzarella cheese up on top. (The chef is from Mexico, so he adds a little bit of cinnamon to the tomato sauce.) It's delicious. It's just unbelievable. Mommy usually gets salmon and John usually gets Veal à la Raymond. Chef Rios (whose name is Raymond) and his two sons, Michael and Raymond, all work at the restaurant. I don't know if the Veal à la Raymond is named after Chef or his son, but it's delicious. It has white asparagus, and the veal cutlets are stuffed with crabmeat—and I think there was a hollandaise sauce over it.

Cherry Tomato Pasta

We don't usually put cheese on anchovy pasta, but we can't be the boss of you, so if you want to put cheese on it, go for it. This is sort of like a puttanesca minus the black olives and capers.

- ¼ cup **EVOO**
- 6 to 8 **anchovy fillets**
- 1 **fresh red chile** (see Tip), seeded and finely chopped
- 6 cloves **garlic**, finely chopped
- 2 pints **cherry tomatoes**
- **Salt**
- 1 pound **spaghetti**
- ½ cup chopped **flat-leaf parsley**
- 1 tablespoon fresh **thyme leaves**, finely chopped
- ¼ cup fresh **basil leaves**, chopped

Bring a large pot of water to a boil for the pasta.

Meanwhile, in a large skillet, heat the EVOO (4 turns of the pan) over medium heat. Add the anchovies and cover the pan with a splatter screen or lid, shaking until the anchovies begin to break up. Reduce the heat a bit, uncover, and stir until the anchovies melt into the oil. Add the chile and garlic; stir a couple of minutes more. Add the tomatoes, cover, and cook over medium-high heat to burst the tomatoes, 7 to 8 minutes. Gently mash up with a wooden spoon.

Salt the pasta water and cook the spaghetti to al dente. Before draining, ladle out 1 cup of starchy pasta cooking water and add to the sauce along with the parsley, thyme, and basil. Drain the pasta and toss to combine and for the sauce to absorb, 1 minute.

Serves 4

We grow little red hot peppers in our garden, so I use those. You could use Fresno or Italian red cherry peppers. And if you can't find a good-looking fresh hot chile in the market, substitute 1 teaspoon crushed red pepper flakes.

I made a **Meyer Lemon Vinaigrette** that went on an enormous garden salad to serve with **French Onion French Bread Pizzas.**

French Onion French Bread Pizzas

- 8 tablespoons (1 stick) **butter**
- 1 teaspoon **dried thyme**
- 6 large **yellow onions**, very thinly sliced
- 2 fresh **bay leaves**
- **Kosher salt** and **pepper**
- ⅓ cup **dry sherry**
- 2 (10.5-ounce) cans **beef consommé**
- 1 large or 2 medium loaves **French bread**, split horizontally and then halved crosswise to make 4 pieces
- 2 cups shredded **Gruyère cheese**
- 12 ounces ripe **Camembert cheese**, sliced

In a large high-sided skillet, heat the butter over medium heat. Add the thyme, onions, and bay leaves and season with salt and pepper. Cook low and slow until deep caramel in color and very sweet, 35 to 40 minutes. Deglaze with the sherry, stirring and scraping up any browned bits from the bottom of the skillet with a wooden spoon. Stir in the consommé and cook down for 5 minutes.

Preheat the oven to 400°F. Toast the bread in the oven. Remove the bay leaves and top with the onion mixture and the cheeses. Return to the oven and bake until the cheese is melted and lightly browned.

Serves 4

Meyer Lemon Vinaigrette

1 medium **shallot**
Sea salt and **pepper**
Juice of 2 **Meyer lemons**
2 scant tablespoons **Dijon mustard**
1 rounded tablespoon **honey**
A little **fennel salt** or **fennel pollen**
½ to ¾ cup **EVOO**

Grate the shallot into a salad bowl. Sprinkle with a little salt and add the lemon juice. Let the shallot sit in the lemon juice for a few minutes. Add the mustard, honey, fennel salt, and pepper to taste. Whisk in the EVOO.

Makes about 1 cup

AUGUST 18/DINNER

For dinner we had sammies made with **7-Hour Smoked Brisket** along with **My Sweet & Spicy Pickles** (see July 15, page 89, and July 4, page 80) for those two recipes), and **fancied-up baked beans** and **chili-brushed corn on the cob.**

With the 7-Hour Brisket, I served **chili-brushed corn on the cob.** Season melted butter with some chili power, salt, and pepper and brush that over corn on the cob (we cook our corn on the grill).

I made **fancied-up baked beans** by adding a lot of extra baked then chopped Oscar's Smokehouse bacon to canned baked beans. I put in some chiles and scallions and lots of black pepper and I just popped it into the oven to brown.

**AUGUST 19/
JOHN'S BIRTHDAY BREAKFAST**

John wanted carbonara for breakfast so he's the boss of that. I don't think I've ever served anybody egg tagliatelle for breakfast but there ya go. I did. He wanted it Milanese-style.

Tagliatelle Carbonara Milanese-Style

Sometimes I use a mixture of Parmigiano and pecorino instead of just pecorino.

¼ teaspoon **saffron threads** (2 pinches)
3 tablespoons **EVOO**
⅓ pound **pancetta**, cut like thick bacon at the deli counter, then diced
4 cloves **garlic**, grated or finely chopped
½ cup **dry white wine**
1 teaspoon **turmeric**
Salt and **black pepper**
1 pound **egg tagliatelle** (I like Delverde brand)
2 yolks from **Araucana eggs** (see Tip)
1 cup grated **pecorino cheese**
A generous handful of **flat-leaf parsley**, finely chopped

Place the saffron in a small saucepan with 1 cup cold water. Bring to a boil, reduce to a simmer, and let it steep 6 to 8 minutes, while the pasta water comes to a boil.

Bring a large pot of water to a boil.

Meanwhile, in a large skillet, heat the EVOO (3 turns of the pan) over medium heat. Add the pancetta and cook until just about crisp, 4 to 5 minutes. Add the garlic after 2 to 3 minutes and stir another 2 to 3 minutes until fragrant. Stir in the wine and turmeric.

Salt the boiling water and cook the tagliatelle to al dente. Before draining, ladle out ½ cup starchy pasta cooking water and beat into the egg yolks to warm them. Drain the pasta and add to the skillet. Pour the saffron water over the pasta and toss to combine. Season with pepper. Add in half the cheese and all of the parsley, pour in the egg mixture, and turn off the heat. Toss the pasta to coat evenly in golden sauce. Top with additional cheese and serve immediately.

Serves 4

Araucana eggs are from the crazy chickens that look like Billy Idol with the funny stick-up feathers on top of their heads. The shells are a bluish-green color. They sell these eggs at some supermarkets, too.

AUGUST 19/DINNER

John had his carbonara for breakfast and we went back to The Ridge Terrace Restaurant for dinner. Then he had cannoli from Bruno Bakery in Manhattan for dessert when we got home. John doesn't like cake. It's a real pain to try to write Happy Birthday on a cannoli shell, that's all I'm saying.

ANNUAL BIRTHDAY PORK FEST

John loves pork, so one year for his birthday I made him his own **porchetta**, which is when you wrap an entire pork roast in pork belly—it's like a pig wrapped in pig. They sell them in all of the big open markets in Italy. They're gigantic and they roast for many hours. I made John a **mini porchetta** that took me 4 days to cure.

Then another year I made him a **wild boar sausage hash**. I took a pound of wild boar sausage (you can order it online) and browned it with some diced Yukon Golds. Then I added some chiles and mild frying peppers. I threw in some pimiento peppers, red onion, and garlic and seasoned with lots of fresh rosemary and black pepper. Top the hash with over-easy eggs.

AUGUST 20, BREAKFAST. John's bandmates were staying with us for the weekend, so I started prepping. I made an enormous amount of food for the next day. I was feeding 6 men and me. **Frittata with chanterelles and zucchini flowers:** Just sautéed up some chanterelle mushrooms. I added in some zucchini flowers that were torn from the garden and I made a frittata for John and me, probably 6 eggs, started on the stove, transferred it to the oven, let it cook through, yum, yum, yum.

LUNCH. **Niçoise salad:** This is olive oil-poached tuna over salad. You cover the tuna with olive oil, add a little bundle of tarragon, bay, thyme, zest of 1 lemon, and sliced garlic. Turn the heat to medium-high, and when it starts to bubble, you turn it off and let the tuna cool in the olive oil. I use a 1-inch-thick piece of tuna (about 1 pound). You then break it up into pieces. I made a niçoise salad with an assortment of lettuces from our garden. I topped it with anchovy fillets, niçoise olives, tomatoes from our garden, blanched asparagus tips, quartered hard-boiled eggs, dill, parsley, chives, and tarragon. I topped it with the poached tuna and I served it with the Meyer Lemon Vinaigrette (see August 13, page 119). Or you can use the Lemon Vinaigrette that I often serve with artichokes (see August 14, page 116).

Here's what I made for the band: **Jalapeño Poppers** (see April 26, page 30) and **Mushroom Fundido** to start, then **Red Pork Posole** (made with **Pulled Pork**) with **Pickled Onions & Chiles, Mexican Rice** (see July 19, page 99). John also made his **Slow-Smoked Chicken** (see April 24, page 28; remember the chicken has to be brined overnight).

Mushroom Fundido

You fill the tortillas with the fundido and you eat it immediately. I serve it right out of the hot skillet, cast-iron or whatever kind of sturdy skillet you think would present well at your dinner table. That's a great starter for people to watch you make. It's very exciting.

3 tablespoons **EVOO**
1 pound **mushrooms**, quartered
Salt and **pepper**
1 medium **onion**, chopped
2 cloves **garlic**, chopped
1 **jalapeño chile**, thinly sliced
1 **red Fresno chile**, thinly sliced
½ cup **dry sherry**
1 to 2 tablespoons finely chopped **fresh thyme**
3 cups shredded cheese (I used a combination of **sharp Cheddar and Manchego**)
Warm, charred **tortillas**, for serving

In a large, heavy skillet (like cast-iron), heat the EVOO (3 turns of the pan) over medium-high heat. Add the mushrooms and brown them. Season with salt and pepper. When the mushrooms are browned, add the onion, garlic, and chiles and cook for a few minutes. Deglaze the pan with the sherry. When the sherry almost evaporates out of the pan, add the thyme and cheese. Stir until it melts, take it off the heat, and serve it with the tortillas.

Serves 4 to 6

Red Pork Posole

This is a good make-ahead stew. Just let cool and refrigerate, then reheat gently to serve.

4 **ancho chiles**, stemmed and seeded
3 cups **chicken** or **vegetable stock**
2 tablespoons **EVOO**
1 large **onion**, chopped
4 cloves **garlic**, chopped
1 tablespoon **smoked sweet paprika**
1 tablespoon **chili powder**
1½ teaspoons ground **cumin**
Kosher salt and **black pepper**
2 (14-ounce) cans **hominy**, rinsed and drained (about 3 cups)
A handful of **cilantro leaves**, chopped
1 generous tablespoon **agave syrup** or honey
2 **limes**
½ recipe **Pulled Pork** (recipe follows)

Pickled Onions & Chiles (recipe follows)
Queso fresco or other mild cheese, for topping
Warm, charred flour or corn **tortillas**, for serving

Place the ancho chiles and 1 cup of the stock in a saucepan. Add a little water, if necessary, so the liquid covers the chiles. Bring to a low boil, then reduce the heat to a simmer, and cook until the chiles are soft. Carefully transfer the chiles and the cooking liquid to a food processor and process until smooth.

Meanwhile, in a large soup pot, heat the EVOO (2 turns of the pan) over medium heat. Add the onion, garlic, smoked paprika, chili powder, cumin, and salt and pepper to taste. Cook until the vegetables are very soft, 10 to 12 minutes.

Stir in the chile puree, hominy, cilantro, the remaining 2 cups stock, the agave syrup, juice of 1 lime, and the pulled pork. Add just enough water, 1 to 2 cups, to form a stew as loose or thick as you like. Bring to a simmer, then spoon the stew into shallow bowls and top with pickled onions and chiles and queso fresco. Serve with warm charred tortillas for dipping and wrapping and the second lime cut into wedges.

Serves 4 to 6

PULLED PORK

You need only half of this pork to make the Red Pork Posole, but the leftovers make really, really good sandwiches.

4 pounds **boneless pork butt** (shoulder)
Kosher salt and **pepper**
2 tablespoons **vegetable oil**
1 **onion**, root end attached, sliced into thin wedges
1 large **carrot**, sliced on an angle
2 to 3 small ribs **celery**, with leafy tops, from the heart, sliced on an angle
1 small bulb **fennel**, sliced
4 large cloves **garlic**, sliced
Leaves from a small handful of fresh **thyme sprigs**
2 **fresh bay leaves**
1½ cups **dry white wine**
4 cups **chicken stock**

Preheat the oven to 350°F.

Pat the pork dry of any juices and generously season with salt and pepper. In a large Dutch oven or heavy-bottomed pot, heat the oil (2 turns of the pan) over medium-high heat. Place the pork in the pot and brown well on all sides.

Remove the pork and reduce the heat to medium. Add the onion, carrot, celery, fennel, garlic, thyme, bay leaves, and salt and pepper to taste. Cook to soften the vegetables, about 10 minutes; then deglaze the pot with the wine, scraping up the bits stuck to the bottom of the pot. Add the chicken stock and stir. Slide the pork back into the pot and bring to a low boil. Cover the pot and place in the oven for 2 to 2½ hours, turning the meat halfway through cooking. Keep the pork in the oven until the meat is tender and falls apart when pulled at with a fork.

Remove the pork from the pot, place on a platter, and when cool enough to handle, pull the meat apart with 2 forks. Divide the meat into two equal portions. Strain the cooking liquids and add to one half; set that half aside for use in other dishes. (The remaining half of the meat is used in the posole recipe.)

PICKLED ONIONS & CHILES

These pickled onions and peppers make powerful companions to the smoky mild pork posole.

1 cup **cider vinegar**
¼ cup **sugar**
1 teaspoon **kosher salt**
1 teaspoon **coriander seeds**
2 **red onions**, cut into ¼-inch rings
1 **jalapeño chile**, sliced into rings
2 **red Fresno chiles**, sliced into rings

In a saucepan, combine the vinegar, ½ cup water, the sugar, salt, and coriander seeds. Bring to a boil over medium-high heat, stirring until the sugar is dissolved.

Arrange the onions and chile rings in a small container with a tight-fitting lid and pour the brine over the top. Cool, cover, and store chilled for a minimum of several hours and up to several days.

Makes about 2 cups

AUGUST 22, BREAKFAST

BLTs over eggs: I buttered the toast with a Dijon herb butter: softened butter (about 2 tablespoons) with Dijon (1 rounded tablespoon). Add finely chopped fresh herbs (whatever you have on hand) and salt and pepper. I put the buttered sides of the toast on the inside, and then I build a BLT: toast, fried egg (over medium), bacon, lettuce, tomato. I always bake bacon in the oven on a slotted broiler pan at 375°F until crisp and uniform.

Bull's-Eye Deviled Eggs (see April 24, page 29, for the recipe) and melon with prosciutto, followed by **Poached Tarragon Creamed Chicken** and a **baby fennel and tomato salad**. We had Galia melon with prosciutto and I dressed the melon with lime and cracked black pepper.

Poached Tarragon Creamed Chicken

3 tablespoons **butter**, plus more softened for the toast
2 tablespoons **flour**
⅓ cup **dry white wine**
1½ cups **chicken stock** (see Tip)
Kosher salt and **white** or **black pepper**
¾ cup frozen **baby peas**
½ cup **heavy cream**
1 (4-ounce) jar chopped **pimientos**, drained
2 to 3 tablespoons chopped fresh **tarragon**
1 rounded tablespoon **Dijon mustard**
Freshly grated **nutmeg**
Shredded Poached Chicken Breasts (recipe follows)
4 slices (1½ inches thick) good-quality **white bread**

In a saucepan, heat 3 tablespoons butter over medium heat. Add the flour and cook, whisking, for 1 minute. Whisk in the wine and cook until slightly reduced, 1 minute. Whisk in the stock and simmer until thickened. Season with salt and

pepper. Add the peas, heavy cream, and pimientos and return to a low simmer. Add the tarragon, mustard, and a few grates of nutmeg, then stir in the chicken.

Toast the bread, then liberally butter and cut corner to corner. Ladle the creamed chicken over the toast points and serve.

Serves 4

Use the stock you get from poaching the chicken in Shredded Poached Chicken Breasts.

SHREDDED POACHED CHICKEN BREASTS

6 **skin-on, bone-in chicken breast halves** (or 3 full breasts)
4 cloves **garlic**, smashed
2 to 3 ribs **celery**, quartered
1 **bay leaf**
1 **carrot**, quartered
1 **lemon**, sliced
1 **onion**, quartered
Herb bundle: fresh **parsley, rosemary, sage, and thyme** tied with kitchen twine
Kosher salt

Put the chicken in a medium stockpot. Add the garlic, celery, bay leaf, carrot, lemon, onion, and herb bundle and sprinkle with salt. Add enough water to cover the chicken. Bring to a boil, then reduce the heat to a simmer and cook for 45 minutes.

Remove the chicken from the liquid and let cool. Strain the stock. Remove the skin and bones from the chicken, and shred the meat using your fingers or 2 forks.

Makes 4 to 6 cups

We made a baby fennel and tomato salad with a little bit of oil and vinegar and a sprinkle of fennel salt.

🕐 AUGUST 23/DINNER

We had **Batter-Dipped Zucchini Flowers** (see July 1, page 76), **Drunken Lamb Ragu with Spaghetti**, and **Caesar Salad** (see April 18, page 16. I often make this salad with all kale, but this day I used half romaine lettuce, half kale, both from our garden).

Drunken Lamb Ragu with Spaghetti

2 tablespoons **EVOO**
1½ teaspoons **fennel seeds**
1½ pounds **ground lamb** (or a mix of beef and pork)
2 fresh or dried small **red Fresno chiles**, seeded and finely chopped
1 **onion**, finely chopped
5 or 6 cloves **garlic**, chopped
3 tablespoons **fresh rosemary**, minced
Salt and **pepper**
2 tablespoons **tomato paste**
2 cups **dry red wine**

2 cups **chicken** or **beef stock**

1 can (32 or 28 ounces) **San Marzano tomatoes** (look for DOP on the label), or when ripe and in season use 10 to 12 fresh plum or Roma tomatoes, peeled and chopped

1 long strip of **orange zest**

1 pound **bucatini** or **pici** (fat spaghetti, not hollow)

Fresh **sheep's milk ricotta** or shaved pecorino cheese

Minced **fresh mint** and **flat-leaf parsley**, for garnish

In a large Dutch oven, heat the EVOO (2 turns of the pan) over medium-high heat. Add the fennel seeds and stir. Add the meat and brown well while crumbling. Add the chiles, onion, garlic, rosemary, and salt and pepper to taste. Cook to soften the onion, 5 minutes. Add the tomato paste and stir until fragrant. Add the wine and reduce by half. Add the stock and the tomatoes, breaking the tomatoes up with a spoon. Reduce the heat to a simmer, then throw in the orange zest to mellow the sauce. Simmer for 30 minutes to cook down the tomatoes. Discard the orange zest.

Bring a large pot of water to a boil. Salt the water and cook the pasta to al dente. Just before draining, ladle 1 cup of the starchy pasta cooking water into your sauce. Drain the pasta and toss with the sauce to combine, 1 to 2 minutes. Serve in bowls topped with the ricotta or shaved pecorino and garnished with mint and parsley.

Serves 4

⏱ AUGUST 24/DINNER

Porcini Pappardelle with a simple mixed salad.

Porcini Pappardelle

2 tablespoons **EVOO**

4 tablespoons (½ stick) **butter**

½ pound **fresh porcini mushrooms** or mixed mushrooms, thinly sliced

½ cup minced **celery** tops

1 small **carrot**, finely chopped

1 small **onion**, finely chopped; or 2 large shallots, finely chopped

3 or 4 cloves **garlic**, finely chopped or grated

About 2 tablespoons fresh **sage leaves**, very thinly sliced

2 tablespoons fresh **thyme leaves**

1 fresh **bay leaf**

½ cup **Marsala wine** (Opici is my favorite)

1 cup **chicken** or **vegetable stock**

Salt

1 pound **pappardelle pasta**

½ cup grated **Parmigiano-Reggiano cheese**

Bring a large pot of water to a boil.

Meanwhile, in a large skillet, heat the EVOO (2 turns of the pan) and melt the butter over medium heat. Add the mushrooms. Once they brown, add the celery, carrot, onion, garlic, sage, thyme, and bay leaf and increase the heat to medium-high. Cook, stirring occasionally, until the mushrooms darken, 7 to 8 minutes. Deglaze with the Marsala and then add the stock. Let cook out for a few minutes. Remove the bay leaf.

Salt the boiling water and cook the pappardelle to al dente. Before draining, ladle out about a cup of the starchy pasta cooking water and add to the sauce. Drain the pasta and add to the sauce along with the Parm, tossing with tongs for 1 or 2 minutes for the flavors to absorb.

Serves 4

🕐 AUGUST 25/MY BIRTHDAY!

We went out to The Ridge Terrace restaurant.

🕐 AUGUST 26/DINNER

I made the family favorite, **Swordfish Cutlets** (see June 2, page 55) with **tomato relish**, and a side of capricci pasta with the sauce for **Roasted Eggplant Pasta** (see August 13, page 114). We started with **Stuffed Mushrooms**.

Stuffed Mushrooms

When I'm making stuffed mushrooms, I buy cremini a little on the larger side and I usually handpick them. Then I parbake them—cook them about halfway—so that the mushrooms don't taste raw once they're stuffed.

MUSHROOMS & STUFFING
12 large **cremini mushrooms**
EVOO
Porcini salt or sea salt and **pepper**
4 tablespoons (½ stick) **butter**
1 **portobello mushroom cap**, chopped
2 tablespoons fresh **thyme leaves**
1 or 2 **garlic cloves**, grated
⅓ cup **dry sherry**
1 bunch **fresh spinach** (see Tip)
1 cup **panko bread crumbs**
1 **egg**, beaten
¾ cup loosely packed grated **Parmigiano-Reggiano cheese**

BÉCHAMEL SAUCE
2 tablespoons **butter**
2 tablespoons **flour**
1 cup **milk**
Salt and **pepper**
1 **egg yolk**

Preheat the oven to 400°F.

Stem the cremini mushrooms. Chop the stems and set aside. Dress the cremini caps lightly in EVOO and season with porcini salt or sea salt and pepper. Set the caps stemmed side down (so that the liquids drain away from the mushroom as the mushrooms start to shrink up) on a baking sheet and bake 10 to 12 minutes. Take the mushroom caps out but leave the oven on.

To make the stuffing: In a skillet, melt the butter in 2 tablespoons EVOO. Add the chopped stems and portobello caps and cook that about 12 minutes or so until it's tender. Add in the thyme and a couple of cloves of garlic. Deglaze the pan with sherry and spin that around.

Add in the spinach and wilt it into the mush-

rooms. Transfer the mixture to a bowl and cool it. Stir in the panko so it can absorb the liquids from the spinach and the mushrooms. Stir in the egg and Parm.

Stuff the mushrooms using a small eyeball-size scoop (I overfill them). Arrange them tightly together in a small baking dish.

Before they go into the oven, make a little sauce: Melt the butter in a saucepan. Whisk in the flour, then the milk, and cook, whisking, until the sauce thickens. Season with salt and pepper. Whisk a little of the hot sauce into the egg yolk to temper it, then stir the warmed egg yolk back into the sauce.

Spoon the sauce down over the top of each mushroom cap, then bake until the sauce is bubbling and browned on top.

Makes 12 mushrooms

I buy the bundles of fresh farm spinach that have flat-looking leaves, not the stuff in the sack that's like dark, dark, dark green.

AUGUST 27/DINNER

Our friends Kim and Charlie were up this weekend for dinner. Kim is a pescatarian: she just eats

fish (although she will eat chicken stock). And she will eat pasta at my house, although the rest of the time she's gluten free. She actually has a T-shirt that says "I will eat your wheat" that Kappy made for her. We had **Fava Bean Spread** (see May 26, page 42), **Sicilian-style orange salad** (see June 2, page 56), **Grilled Snapper with Pesto**, **Fried Green Tomatoes** (see July 12, page 85), **Egg Tagliatelle with Truffle Butter**, and **garden salad with peppers, onions, and celery**.

Grilled Snapper with Pesto

This should be enough pesto to top fish for 4 people, but it will depend on the size of the snapper. The snapper is simply prepared: I sprinkle it with a little sea salt and I arrange it on planks (see Tip) and grill.

3 tablespoons **pistachios**, toasted
3 tablespoons **pine nuts**, toasted
½ cup fresh **thyme leaves**
½ cup fresh **oregano leaves**
½ cup **arugula leaves**
½ cup **basil leaves**
½ packed cup **flat-leaf parsley leaves**
½ cup grated **Parmigiano-Reggiano cheese**
Grated zest and juice of 1 **lemon**
Salt and **pepper**
½ cup **EVOO**
1½ pounds **snapper fillets**

Preheat the grill to medium–medium high.

In a food processor, combine the pistachios, pine nuts, thyme, oregano, arugula, basil, parsley, Parm, lemon zest, lemon juice, and salt and pepper to taste. Pulse until finely chopped. Stream in the EVOO; pulse until combined.

Slather the pesto over the snapper fillets. Put on planks and grill until the fish is opaque, 15 to 20 minutes.

Serves 4

I use untreated cedar planks, but there are all different kinds of wooden grilling planks out there. They say you can get three or four uses out of them, but I never get more than one or two.

I made a garden salad with peppers, onions, and celery. I dressed it very simply with oil and vinegar, salt and pepper.

Egg Tagliatelle with Truffle Butter

1 pound **egg tagliatelle** (I like Delverde brand)
Salt and **pepper**
2 tablespoons **EVOO**
4 tablespoons (½ stick) **butter**
1 large **shallot**, minced
2 to 3 cloves rocambole or other **hardneck garlic**, minced
1 cup **champagne** or dry white wine
1 cup **heavy cream**
White truffle
¾ cup grated **Parmigiano-Reggiano cheese**

Bring a large pot of water to a boil. Salt the water and cook the tagliatelle to al dente. Drain and return to the pot.

Meanwhile, in a skillet, heat the EVOO (2 turns of the pan) over medium heat. Melt the butter into the oil. Add the shallot and garlic. Stir that a few minutes, then add the champagne or white wine. Let that bubble and reduce by half, then add the cream. Let that thicken, then shave in lots of white truffle. Toss the sauce with the pasta.

Serve topped with Parm and fine black pepper to taste and a little extra truffle up on top at the table. Wow!!

Serves 4

● AUGUST 28/BREAKFAST

Multigrain Nutty Waffles

I always brush the waffles with melted butter when they come off the iron.

2 cups **multigrain pancake mix**
1½ to 2 cups **milk**
2 tablespoons **butter**, melted, plus more for brushing
2 organic **eggs**
Freshly grated **nutmeg**
1 cup chopped **toasted nuts** (I usually use pecans, walnuts, or hazelnuts)
Mixed berries and **maple syrup**, for serving

Heat a waffle iron.

In a bowl, blend together the pancake mix, milk, melted butter, and eggs. Season with a little nutmeg. Stir in the nuts. Cook in a waffle iron. Brush with melted butter. Serve with berries and maple syrup.

Serves 4

We had **Chicken Curry** (with my own **Spice Mix for Curry**), which I served with **Home-made Rice Pilaf**.

Chicken Curry

My mom also likes her curry sprinkled with toasted unsweetened coconut.

- 4 **skin-on, bone-in chicken breast halves**
- 2 **carrots**, coarsely chopped
- 2 ribs **celery**, coarsely chopped
- 2 medium **onions**, 1 quartered (leaving the root end attached) and 1 chopped
- 4 cloves **garlic**, 2 cracked from skin and 2 grated or finely chopped
- 2-inch piece fresh **ginger**, peeled, half sliced and half grated
- 1 fresh **bay leaf**
- 1 **lime**, sliced
- 2 **cardamom pods**
- **Salt**
- 2 tablespoons **EVOO**
- 2 tablespoons **butter**
- 1 **McIntosh apple**, peeled and chopped
- 1 **red Fresno chile**, seeded and finely chopped
- 3 tablespoons **Spice Mix for Curry** (recipe follows) or store-bought curry powder
- 3 tablespoons **flour**
- ½ cup **mango chutney**, such as Major Grey

Place the chicken in a medium soup pot. Add the carrots, celery, quartered onion, whole peeled garlic, sliced ginger, bay leaf, lime slices, and cardamom pods and cover with cold water. Bring it to a boil, add a couple of pinches of salt, and reduce the heat to a low simmer. Gently poach the chicken for about 40 minutes or until cooked through.

When the chicken is cooked, strain and separate it from the stock, reserving the stock. You should have about 1 quart of strained stock. When the chicken is cool enough to handle, skin it, remove it from the bone, and pull or slice or chop the meat into bite-size pieces. Set aside.

Place a deep skillet over medium-high heat and add the EVOO (2 turns of the pan) and the butter. Add the chopped onion, grated garlic, grated ginger, apple, chile, and spice mix or curry powder. Once the onion and apple are just tender, sprinkle in the flour, stir, and whisk in the reserved 1 quart stock. Bring the mixture to a light simmer to thicken. Once the sauce thickens, add in the reserved chicken and mango chutney to sweeten a bit.

Serves 4

SPICE MIX FOR CURRY

Double or triple this recipe and keep on hand for whenever you want to make curry.

- 1 tablespoon **turmeric**
- 1½ teaspoons ground **cumin**
- 1½ teaspoons ground **coriander**
- 1½ teaspoons ground **fenugreek**
- 1 teaspoon **dry mustard**
- 1 teaspoon **sweet paprika** (see Tip)
- ⅛ teaspoon ground **cinnamon**
- 1 pinch of ground **cardamom**

Mix everything together.

Makes about 3 tablespoons

If you want a hot curry, you can substitute hot paprika or ground black pepper for the sweet paprika.

Homemade Rice Pilaf

2 to 3 tablespoons **butter**
½ cup orzo or broken **thin spaghetti**
1 cup **long-grain white rice**
2¼ to 2½ cups **chicken stock**

In a saucepan (whatever you cook rice in), melt the butter. Add the pasta and toast until very nutty and fragrant. Add the rice and stock, and bring to a boil. Cover, reduce the heat to a simmer, and cook until the rice is just tender, 17 to 18 minutes. If the rice dries out too quickly before it's tender, you could add another splash of stock.

Serves 4

AUGUST 29, DINNER

Roast pork sandwiches with giardiniera: I started with a pork tenderloin, which I drizzled with some EVOO and sprinkled with Montreal Steak Seasoning, then roasted (on a rack over a baking sheet) for 10 to 12 minutes at 500°F. Then I reduced that to 425°F and roasted until the thickest part of the pork registered 145° to 155°F, about 15 minutes (do not open the oven when it's cooking). I let it rest, and then thinly sliced. For the sandwiches, I layered the pork on ciabatta rolls and topped with provolone, chopped romaine, tomato slices, and thinly sliced red onion. Then I took some giardiniera—you can use store-bought, but I use my own homemade (page 168)—and pulse-chopped it to a relish. I scattered that on top and then closed up the sandwiches.

Mexican Pesto

Serve this with whole wheat or whole-grain penne pasta. If you want to do a mild version, get some fresh pimiento peppers (or other sweet peppers) and roast them as you would a bell pepper (char them over an open flame or under the broiler, and then peel). Use them instead of the jalapeños.

3 **jalapeño chiles** or other medium-hot chiles
1 cup **cilantro leaves**
1 cup **arugula leaves**
3 tablespoons fresh **marjoram leaves**
2 large cloves **garlic**, grated or pasted
1 tablespoon ground **cumin**
Grated zest and juice of 2 **limes**
¼ cup **pistachios**, toasted
Salt and **pepper**
⅓ cup **EVOO**

In a food processor, combine the chiles, cilantro, arugula, marjoram, garlic, cumin, lime zest, lime juice, and pistachios. Season with salt and pepper. Pulse-chop to combine. Turn the processor on and add the EVOO in a slow stream, blending until a thick sauce forms.

Makes about 1 cup

SEPTEMBER

THURSDAY/1

LUNCH
cocktail sauce (with crab claws), bacon crab cakes

DINNER
beer-batter fish fry, tartar sauce, slaw salad, salt & vinegar fries

FRIDAY/2

DINNER
za'atar chicken, lemon tahini, green harissa

SATURDAY/3

DINNER
grilled artichoke hearts, figs with pistachios, penne alla Norma

SUNDAY/4

BREAKFAST
deviled ham on toast
DINNER
St. Louis ribs, smoky BBQ sauce, corn salad

MONDAY/5

DINNER
chicken noodle soup, Welsh rarebit

SUNDAY/11

MONDAY/12

TUESDAY/13

WEDNESDAY/14

THURSDAY/15

DINNER
spaghetti with crab

WEDNESDAY/21

DINNER
tuna surprise, ultimate Italian pulled pork sammies

THURSDAY/22

ITALY!

FRIDAY/23

SATURDAY/24

SUNDAY/25

TUESDAY/6	**WEDNESDAY/7**	**THURSDAY/8**	**FRIDAY/9**	**SATURDAY/10**
	DINNER touchdown chili			**DINNER** puttanesca with cherry tomatoes, rainbow chard salad

FRIDAY/16	**SATURDAY/17**	**SUNDAY/18**	**MONDAY/19**	**TUESDAY/20**
DINNER sort of cioppino	**BREAKFAST** pecan waffles with maple-apple topping **DINNER** sliced steak tacos, orange-chile wild rice, shallow-fried stuffed zucchini flowers	**DINNER** porcini & vegetable soup	**DINNER** croque monsieur with mushrooms	**DINNER** chiles rellenos

MONDAY/26	**TUESDAY/27**	**WEDNESDAY/28**	**THURSDAY/29**	**FRIDAY/30**
DINNER pici with white ragu, Romanesco broccoli, roasted potatoes, veal saltimbocca	**DINNER** egg pasta with truffle butter sauce	**DINNER** Tuscan-style risotto with fresh walnuts	**LUNCH** squash soup **DINNER** artichokes with vinaigrette, spicy ground lamb ragu, Paolo Coluccio's cinghiale in umido	

PECORINO

Crab two ways: cracked crab claws with **Cocktail Sauce** and **Bacon Crab Cakes**.

Cocktail Sauce

Serve with cracked stone crab claws. This makes enough sauce for about 1 pound.

- ½ cup good-quality ketchup (I like First Field Jersey Ketchup or Heinz Organic)
- 3 tablespoons prepared horseradish (I like Gold's)
- 2 tablespoons Worcestershire sauce
- Juice of 1 lemon
- Lots of black pepper
- 1 to 2 teaspoons hot sauce, to taste (I like Frank's RedHot or good old Tabasco)

Mix all that together and that's your cocktail sauce.

Makes about ¾ cup

Bacon Crab Cakes

- 1 tablespoon plus ½ cup EVOO
- 2 slices bacon, finely chopped
- 5 tablespoons butter
- 2 large shallots, finely chopped
- 3 cloves garlic, grated or finely chopped
- 1 red Fresno chile, minced
- 3 ribs celery, finely chopped
- ½ cup dry vermouth
- 2 cups panko bread crumbs
- 3 eggs
- 1 teaspoon hot sauce
- 1 tablespoon grainy mustard
- 2 teaspoons Old Bay seasoning
- 2 tablespoons fresh thyme leaves
- 2 tablespoons finely chopped chives
- 1 pound crabmeat, picked through for any bits of shell
- 1 cup Wondra flour
- 2 tablespoons chopped flat-leaf parsley

In a medium skillet, heat 1 tablespoon of the EVOO (1 turn of the pan) over medium heat. Add the bacon and cook until crispy. Add the butter. When the butter begins to foam, add the shallots, garlic, chile, and celery and cook until tender, 4 to 5 minutes. Add the vermouth to the pan to deglaze and reduce the liquid by half. Add 1 cup of the panko, turn the heat off, and let the mixture cool in the pan.

While the mixture is cooling, in a bowl, beat 1 egg together with the hot sauce, mustard, 1 teaspoon of Old Bay, the thyme, and chives. Add the cooled shallot mixture and the crab to the bowl, and gently combine, trying not to break up the crab too much. Form the crab cakes into disks about 3 inches in diameter and ¾ to 1 inch thick.

Line up 3 shallow bowls on the counter. Spread the flour out in one; beat the remaining 2 eggs with 2 tablespoons water in the second; and mix together the parsley, remaining 1 teaspoon Old Bay, and remaining 1 cup panko in the third. Roll the crab cakes in the flour, then in the beaten egg mixture, then in the panko mixture.

In a large skillet, heat the remaining ½ cup EVOO over medium-high heat until shimmering. Add the crab cakes to the pan and shallow-fry them (see Tip) until deeply golden brown on both sides.

Serves 4

If you do not want to shallow-fry the crab cakes, coat both sides of the cakes with cooking spray and place on a rack set over a baking sheet. Bake at 375°F until golden brown, 15 to 20 minutes.

We had **Beer-Batter Fish Fry** with **Tartar Sauce** (see April 21, page 21). I also made a **Slaw Salad** to put up on the fish or serve alongside. For the potatoes we had **Salt & Vinegar Fries**.

Beer-Batter Fish Fry

I have a countertop fryer and I highly recommend them. It's a much less messy and labor-intensive process to deep-fry anything with these tabletop counter units and it keeps the oil from ever smoking up. I think they're wonderful.

- **Vegetable oil**, such as canola (we usually get one of the brands that have omega-3s), for deep-frying
- 2 cups **all-purpose flour**
- 2 tablespoons **Old Bay seasoning**
- 1 teaspoon **baking powder**
- 1 (12-ounce) bottle **beer**
- 1 **egg**, beaten
- 2 pounds **fish fillets** (cod, halibut, or haddock), cut into 3- to 4-inch-long chunks
- **Sea salt** and **pepper**
- **Wondra flour**, for dredging
- **Tartar Sauce** (page 21), for serving

Preheat the oven to 275°F. Set a wire rack over a baking sheet.

Fill your countertop deep-fryer with oil and heat to 375°F.

In a bowl, mix together the all-purpose flour,

Old Bay, baking powder, beer, and egg. Pat the fish dry and season it with salt and pepper. Dredge the fish in the flour. Coat the fish in the beer batter and add just a few pieces at a time to the fryer. Fry it until it's deeply golden brown, 4 to 5 minutes. Keep the fish warm on the baking sheet in the oven while you fry up the rest in batches.

Serves 4 to 6

Slaw Salad

It's also very refreshing to add baby fennel or shaved regular fennel to this slaw.

- About ¼ cup grated **shallot** or **onion**
- Grated zest and juice of 1 **lemon**
- 3 tablespoons **white balsamic** or **white wine vinegar**
- 2 teaspoons **kosher salt**
- 1 rounded teaspoon **superfine sugar**
- ¼ cup **EVOO** or vegetable oil
- 1½ teaspoons **celery seed**
- 1 **carrot**, shredded
- 1 pound **cabbage**, shredded

Grate the shallot or onion right into the salad bowl. Stir in the lemon zest, lemon juice, vinegar, salt, and sugar. Whisk in the EVOO. Stir in the celery seed, carrot, and cabbage.

Serves 4

Salt & Vinegar Fries

3 tablespoons **EVOO**
4 large **russet (baking) potatoes**, cut into wedges
2 teaspoons **Montreal Grill Seasoning**
Sea salt
Malt vinegar

Preheat the oven to 425°F with a baking sheet in the oven.

Pull the hot pan out of the oven, drizzle the EVOO over it, scatter the potatoes and grill seasoning on top, and return it to the oven. Roast the potatoes, turning occasionally, until golden brown and tender, about 40 minutes. When they come out, season them with salt and malt vinegar.

Serves 4

🕐 **SEPTEMBER 2/DINNER**

We had a **Za'atar Chicken** made with **Za'atar Spice Blend**. The chicken was served with flatbread, **Green Harissa**, and **Lemon Tahini**.

Za'atar Chicken

I started this dish the night before because it has to marinate overnight.

2 heads **garlic**, top thirds cut off to expose the cloves
¼ cup **EVOO**, plus more for drizzling
4 tablespoons (½ stick) **butter**, softened, plus some melted for serving
Leaves from 2 to 3 sprigs fresh **rosemary**, finely chopped
1 **fresh chile**, seeded and finely chopped
Grated zest and juice of 1 **lemon**
1 whole **chicken** (4 to 5 pounds), spatchcocked (see Tip)
Kosher salt and **pepper**
Za'atar Spice Blend (recipe follows)
Naan bread, pocketless pita, or other flatbread, for serving
Green Harissa (recipe follows)

Preheat the oven to 400°F. Drizzle the heads of garlic with EVOO. Wrap in foil and bake until tender, about 45 minutes.

Let the garlic cool, then squeeze out of the skins and mash into the 4 tablespoons butter. Combine with the ¼ cup EVOO, rosemary, chile, and lemon zest. Loosen the skin all over the chicken and rub onto the meat under the skin. Sprinkle the skin with salt and pepper. Put the chicken in a baking dish, cover, and let stand for at least 1 hour or overnight (in the fridge).

Preheat the oven to 325°F. Sprinkle the chicken with two-thirds of the za'atar spice blend and roast for 1 hour 15 minutes. Increase the oven temperature to 500°F and roast for 15 minutes more to crisp the skin. Let the chicken rest until cooled, then cut it into quarters.

Meanwhile, heat a griddle or grill pan and grill the naan until warm. Brush with melted butter and cut in pieces. Divide the chicken among plates and sprinkle with the remaining za'atar and the lemon juice. Serve with the naan and green harissa.

Serves 4

Spatchcocked means butterflied open with backbone removed; ask your butcher to do this for you.

ZA'ATAR SPICE BLEND

2 tablespoons toasted **sesame seeds**
2 tablespoons ground **sumac**
2 tablespoons fresh **thyme**, finely chopped
1 tablespoon ground **cumin**
1 tablespoon finely chopped **fresh oregano**
1 teaspoon **kosher salt**
1 teaspoon **coarse black pepper**

Combine all the ingredients. Store in an airtight container until ready to use.

Makes about ½ cup

GREEN HARISSA

- 1 cup **cilantro leaves**
- ⅓ cup **EVOO**
- 1 teaspoon ground **cumin**
- 2 **serrano** or **jalapeño chiles**, seeded and chopped
- 1 clove **garlic**, pasted
- 1 small bunch **spinach** (from the farmers' market), stemmed and chopped, or about 2 packed cups baby spinach
- Juice of ½ **lemon**
- **Kosher salt** and **pepper**

In a food processor, combine the cilantro, EVOO, cumin, chiles, garlic, spinach, and lemon juice and process until fairly smooth. Season with salt and pepper. Refrigerate or serve immediately.

Makes about 1 cup

Lemon Tahini

This sauce went with the chicken. It is also good with grilled chicken breasts.

- ½ cup **tahini paste**
- 1 clove **garlic**, pasted
- Juice of 1 **lemon**
- 1 tablespoon chopped fresh **dill**
- 1 tablespoon chopped fresh **marjoram** or **oregano**
- **Salt** and **pepper**

Stir everything together with about ⅓ cup water until smooth.

Makes about ¾ cup

🕐 SEPTEMBER 3/DINNER

Dinner began with an appetizer trio of herbed **grilled artichoke hearts**, fresh green figs sprinkled with chopped toasted pistachios, and bruschetta with melon, lime, and black pepper. The main course was **Penne alla Norma** (see April 17, page 15), which I made with spaghetti.

You can buy **grilled artichoke hearts** in a plastic sack at Whole Foods or you can parboil them and grill them yourself. Once grilled, heat some EVOO, add sliced garlic, stir that around for a couple of minutes, add your artichoke hearts, heat them through. Season them with thyme, salt, pepper. Add the juice of a lemon, douse the pan with ½ cup white wine, and cook them a minute more until the wine evaporates. Transfer them to a serving plate and serve them warm or at room temperature.

Deviled Ham on Toast

Deviled Ham (page 46)
4 hand-cut (about ¾-inch-thick) slices **brioche**
  or white bread, toasted
Shredded **supersharp Cheddar cheese**
1 **tomato**, sliced
4 **eggs**, cooked over-easy (optional)

Preheat the oven to 375°F.

Spread the deviled ham on the toast and place on a baking sheet. Top with Cheddar and bake until the cheese melts and turns brown. Serve it topped with a slice of tomato, and an over-easy egg (if you like).

Serves 4

⏺ SEPTEMBER 4/DINNER

I made **Smoky BBQ Sauce** (see July 15, page 90) to go on **St. Louis ribs**. (I made a double recipe of the sauce because we had 4 slabs of ribs.) We also had **Corn Salad**.

John parboiled 4 slabs of St. Louis ribs in 2 quarts of water and a couple of quarts of stock with parsley, thyme, rosemary, fresh bay leaves, and salt. (Strain and save the cooking liquid from the ribs; it's great for soups.) They simmered for 90 minutes, then he oiled up the ribs and smoked them at 300°F for 30 minutes, basting with the home-made Smoky BBQ Sauce.

Corn Salad

The best way to cut the kernels off a corncob is to invert a small bowl inside a large bowl. Stand the corncob up on the small bowl and scrape down with a small sharp knife. The larger bowl catches all the kernels so they don't fall all over the counter. Then you rub the cob with the dull side of the knife (not the blade) to push out all the liquids from the cob itself.

4 ears **corn**, shucked
2 tablespoons **EVOO**
2 tablespoons **butter**
Salt and **pepper**
Ancho chile powder
½ garden **tomato**, chopped
½ small **red onion**, chopped
1 **fresh chile**, chopped
½ cup shelled fresh **peas** or peeled fava beans
  (see Tip)
1 teaspoon fresh **thyme leaves**
Juice of 1 **lime**

Scrape the kernels off the corncobs.

In a cast-iron skillet, heat the EVOO (2 turns of the pan) and the butter. Add the corn and sear it until slightly charred and the sugars caramelize,

8 to 10 minutes. Season with salt and ancho chile powder to taste.

Transfer the corn to a bowl and let cool. Add the tomato, onion, chile, fresh peas or fava beans, thyme, and lime juice. Toss that all together and season with salt and black pepper.

Serves 4

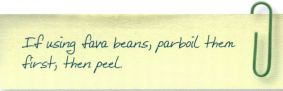
If using fava beans, parboil them first, then peel.

🕐 **SEPTEMBER 5/DINNER**

We had **Chicken Noodle Soup** that I made with the pork stock that was created when John parboiled the ribs for last night's dinner (I simmered the stock down to 2 quarts total). Then we had **Welsh Rarebit**.

Chicken Noodle Soup

Instead of the wide egg noodles, you could use a couple of handfuls of Italian dumpling noodles or any soup noodle you like.

2 tablespoons **EVOO**
2 medium **carrots**, peeled and chopped
1 **parsnip**, peeled and chopped
1 medium **onion**, chopped
2 ribs **celery**, chopped
2 **bay leaves**, fresh or dried
Salt and **pepper**
8 cups **pork stock** or good-quality chicken stock
1 pound **chicken breast tenders**, diced
½ pound **wide egg noodles**
A handful of fresh **parsley**, chopped
A handful of fresh **dill**, chopped

Place a large pot over medium heat and add the EVOO. Add the carrots, parsnip, onion, and celery as you chop them. Add the bay leaves and season with salt and pepper to taste. Add the stock to the pot, increase the heat, and bring to a boil.

Add the chicken, return the soup to a boil, and reduce the heat to medium and cook the chicken 2 minutes. Add the noodles and cook until they're tender (see Tip). Stir in the parsley and dill, remove the bay leaves, and serve.

Serves 4 to 6

If you're going to eat the soup over a couple of days, cook the noodles separately and just add them to the soup as you eat them so they don't swell up and overcook.

Welsh Rarebit

You can top the rarebit with sliced tomato and crispy bacon or you can use the hot cheese sauce to make rarebit burgers (see Tip).

2 tablespoons **butter**
2 tablespoons **flour**
2 tablespoons **Worcestershire sauce**
1 tablespoon dry or prepared **mustard**
1 teaspoon **hot sauce**
¾ to 1 cup **stout**, such as Guinness
1 pound **Cheddar cheese**, shredded
1 **egg yolk** (optional)
8 slices **pumpernickel bread**

Preheat the broiler.

In a large saucepan, melt the butter over medium heat. Whisk in the flour and cook until light brown, about 3 minutes. Stir in the Worcestershire, mustard, and hot sauce. Whisk in the stout and cook until thickened, 1 to 2 minutes. Lower the heat and stir in the cheese until smooth. Stir some of the hot cheese sauce into the egg yolk to temper it, then stir the warmed egg yolk back into the cheese sauce.

Arrange the pumpernickel slices on a rimmed baking sheet and toast both sides under the broiler. Pour the sauce over the toasts; broil until the cheese is bubbling, about 2 minutes.

Serves 4

To make rarebit burgers, toast the pumpernickel as in the rarebit recipe. Pour the sauce over the toasts (using only half the sauce if you plan to serve the burgers open-face); broil until the cheese sauce is browned and bubbly, about 2 minutes. Place a thin cooked beef burger on each of 4 slices, cover each with a handful of watercress, crisscross with 2 cooked bacon slices, and top with a slice of tomato seasoned with salt and pepper. Serve open-face with knife and fork with extra sauce on the side, or cover with the remaining toasts, cheesy side down.

I taught **Touchdown Chili** on the daytime show. It was my first chili during football season, and I made it for the first Jets game we were going to watch on the upcoming weekend.

Touchdown Chili

This is a good make-ahead. Cool and store, then bring to room temperature and add a little water to reheat over medium heat. Serve with toppings of your choice.

3 dried **ancho chiles**, stemmed and seeded
2 dried **guajillo** or **pasilla chiles**, stemmed and seeded
3 cups **beef stock**
1 tablespoon **vegetable oil** or **EVOO**
½ pound **fresh Mexican chorizo**, casings removed, or ⅓ pound good-quality bacon, finely chopped
2 pounds **ground beef chuck** (ask your butcher for a coarse grind)
Kosher salt and **coarse black pepper**
¼ cup **Worcestershire sauce**
1 large **onion**, chopped
4 cloves **garlic**, chopped
1 fresh **red Fresno** or **jalapeño chile**, seeded and chopped, or sliced with seeds for extra heat
1½ teaspoons dried **Mexican oregano**
1 tablespoon ground **cumin**
1 tablespoon ground **coriander**
¼ teaspoon ground **cloves**
A pinch of ground **cinnamon**
1 (12-ounce) bottle **Negra Modelo beer**
1 tablespoon **honey**
3 tablespoons **masa harina** or **cornmeal**
Chili Toppings (see Box)

Place the dried chiles in a pot and cover with the stock. Bring to a low boil and reduce the heat to low. Simmer gently for 10 to 15 minutes, then puree the chiles and liquid.

Meanwhile, in a Dutch oven, heat the oil over high heat. Add the chorizo or bacon and begin to render. Pat the ground beef dry with a paper towel and season with salt and pepper. Add to

the pot and develop a nice brown on the beef. Add the Worcestershire, onion, garlic, fresh chile, oregano, cumin, coriander, cloves, and cinnamon. Cook until the onion is soft; deglaze the pan with the beer. Break up the meat as it cooks.

Stir in the chile puree, the honey, and masa harina; reduce the heat and simmer 45 minutes over low heat to thicken and develop the flavors.

Serve with toppings of choice.

Serves 6

CHILI TOPPINGS
- Cilantro
- Lime wedges
- Minced onions
- Hulled pumpkin seeds (pepitas)
- Grated Manchego or Monterey Jack cheese
- Sliced pickled jalapeños or chopped giardiniera
- Sour cream
- Crushed tortilla chips or corn chips

Puttanesca with Cherry Tomatoes and **rainbow chard salad** with a blood orange vinaigrette.

Puttanesca with Cherry Tomatoes

¼ cup **EVOO**
6 to 8 **anchovy fillets**
1 fresh **red Fresno chile** or Italian red cherry pepper, seeded and finely chopped
6 cloves **garlic**, finely chopped
Splash of **dry vermouth**
2 pints **cherry tomatoes**
A handful of pitted **oil-cured black olives**
2 or 3 tablespoons chopped **capers**
Salt
1 pound **penne pasta** (see Tip)
½ cup chopped **flat-leaf parsley**

Bring a large pot of water to a boil for the pasta.

Meanwhile, in a large skillet, heat the EVOO (4 turns of the pan) over medium heat. Add the anchovies and cover the pan with a splatter screen or lid, shaking until the anchovies begin to break up. Reduce the heat a bit, uncover, and stir until the anchovies melt into the oil. Add the chile and garlic and stir a couple of minutes more. Douse with a bit of vermouth. Add the tomatoes, cover, and cook over medium-high heat to burst the tomatoes, 7 to 8 minutes. Gently mash up the tomatoes with a wooden spoon and stir in the olives and capers.

Salt the boiling water and cook the pasta to al dente. Before draining, ladle out 1 cup of starchy pasta cooking water and add to the sauce. Drain the pasta, add to the sauce, add the parsley, and toss for 1 minute to combine and for the sauce to absorb.

Serves 4

I used a spicy penne rigate flavored with pepperoncini. It's red in color because it has hot pepper in the semolina base for the pasta. I get it at Buon Italia.

I had an enormous amount of **rainbow chard** in our garden so I just stripped it, washed it, dried it, stemmed it, and shredded it like cabbage for this salad. I mixed a little grated shallot with salt and let that sit in blood orange vinegar. I added a drizzle of honey and a little fennel salt, then whisked in EVOO to emulsify. I topped it with toasted pistachios and a little grated citrus zest.

Spaghetti with Crab

I made bread crumbs from sourdough bread cubes with no crust, and toasted them with butter and garlic.

2 cups cubed **sourdough bread**
2 tablespoons plus ¼ cup **EVOO**
2 tablespoons **butter**
7 or 8 cloves **garlic**, finely chopped
Salt and **black pepper**
1 pound **spaghetti**
¼ pound **pancetta**, diced
1 **red Fresno chile**, seeded and finely chopped
1 large **shallot**, minced
½ cup chopped mixture of **celery tops**, **parsley**, **oregano**, and **thyme**
¼ cup **dry vermouth**
2 pints **100-count tomatoes** or **cherry tomatoes**
¾ pound **lump crabmeat**, picked through for any bits of shell
½ cup chopped **flat-leaf parsley** (optional)
Baby arugula (optional)

Preheat the oven to 350°F.

Spread the bread cubes on a baking sheet and bake until they are as hard as croutons, 10 to 15 minutes. Remove them but leave the oven on. Pulse-grind them in a food processor until they're like panko bread crumbs. Combine the crumbs with 2 tablespoons EVOO, the butter, and 2 cloves of the garlic. Return them to the oven to toast deeply golden. Remove from the oven.

Bring a large pot of water to a boil. Salt the water and cook the spaghetti to al dente. Before draining, ladle out 1 cup of the starchy pasta cooking water. Drain the pasta.

Meanwhile, in a large skillet, heat the ¼ cup EVOO over medium heat. Add the pancetta and render. Add the rest of the garlic, the chile, shallot, and celery top–herb mixture. Season with black pepper; cook for 2 to 3 minutes. Deglaze with vermouth. Add the tomatoes. Cover and shake the pan occasionally until the tomatoes burst.

Add the starchy cooking water to the sauce, then fold in the crabmeat. Toss together with the pasta. Serve topped with the toasted bread crumbs, and chopped parsley and baby arugula, if you'd like.

Serves 4

⏲ SEPTEMBER 16/DINNER

Sort of Cioppino

If you don't have good, ripe tomatoes, use a 32-ounce can of San Marzano tomatoes (look for DOP on the label). For a variation, wrap the pieces of cod in prosciutto so that they have a nice crispy exterior.

8 plum or vine-ripened tomatoes
6 tablespoons EVOO
3 bulbs baby fennel or 1 small bulb fennel, thinly sliced, fronds reserved
1 small onion, thinly sliced
6 cloves garlic, thinly sliced
1 rib celery with leafy tops, finely chopped
A handful of flat-leaf parsley, chopped
¼ cup chopped fresh thyme
Salt and pepper
¾ cup dry vermouth or Pernod
1 cup vegetable or chicken stock
¾ cup clam juice or seafood stock
About 10 fresh basil leaves, torn
4 (5-ounce) pieces cod, cut into 2- by 3-inch chunks
Old Bay seasoning (optional)
12 large shrimp, peeled and deveined
1 pound spaghetti
12 mussels, scrubbed
12 Manila clams

Bring a medium pot of water to a boil over high heat. Core the tomatoes and use a sharp knife to score the skin on the bottom with an "X." When the water boils, add the tomatoes and cook for 30 seconds to 1 minute, or until the skins start to loosen. Remove from the water and cold-shock in ice water. When they are cool enough to handle, remove the skins, halve, squeeze out the seeds, and coarsely chop. This can be done ahead of time.

Place a large, high-sided skillet over medium heat, add 3 tablespoons EVOO (3 turns of the pan). Add the fennel, cover, and let it sweat out for 3 to 4 minutes. Add the onion, half the garlic, the celery, half the parsley, half the thyme, and salt and pepper to taste. Let cook for a few minutes, then add ¼ cup of the vermouth. Let it evaporate out a bit, then add the tomatoes. Let the tomatoes start to cook out for a few minutes. Stir in the vegetable stock, clam juice, and half the basil. Cook over medium-low heat at a low bubble.

While the fennel-tomato sauce is cooking, heat 2 tablespoons EVOO (2 turns of the pan) in a large skillet over medium-high heat. Season the cod with Old Bay or salt and pepper and add to the skillet. Cook to golden brown on the outside and opaque in the middle, about 2 minutes per side. Transfer the cod to a plate. Add the shrimp to the pan and cook until pink and cooked through, 1 to 2 minutes per side. Transfer to the plate.

Bring a large pot of water to a boil. Salt the water and cook the spaghetti to al dente. Drain the pasta.

In the skillet the shrimp was cooked in, heat the remaining 1 tablespoon EVOO (1 turn of the pan); add the remaining garlic, parsley, thyme, and basil. Add the mussels and clams, stir to combine, and then add the remaining vermouth. Cover the pan tightly until the mussels and clams steam open, 2 to 3 minutes. Combine the mussels/clam mixture with the fennel-tomato sauce and toss all together with the cooked spaghetti.

To serve, place in bowls, dividing out the mussels and clams evenly and arranging the cod and shrimp over the top.

Serves 4

Pecan Waffles with Maple-Apple Topping

Serve these up with baked applewood-smoked bacon.

4 **McIntosh apples**, peeled and chopped
1½ cups **dark amber maple syrup**
1 **cinnamon stick**
Freshly grated **nutmeg**
1 or 2 slices **fresh ginger**
2 cups **multigrain waffle mix**
2 tablespoons **butter**, melted, plus more for the waffle iron
2 **eggs**
1½ to 2 cups **2% milk**
½ to ¾ cup chopped toasted **pecans**

In a saucepan, combine the apples, maple syrup, cinnamon stick, a few grates of nutmeg, and the ginger. Let that cook out into a nice spicy applesauce.

Meanwhile, heat the waffle iron. Mix up the waffle mix, butter, eggs, and milk. Stir in the pecans.

Cook the waffles on a buttered waffle iron on high until crisp. Serve topped with the apple-sauce.

Serves 4

SEPTEMBER 17/DINNER

We had lightly breaded, shallow-fried **zucchini flowers stuffed with corn, tomatoes, and cheese**. Also **Sliced Steak Tacos and Orange-Chile Wild Rice**.

Zucchini flowers stuffed with corn, tomato, and cheese: I took zucchini flowers and removed the stamens. I then made a filling of a little bit of charred corn, a little bit of seeded chopped tomato, fresh ricotta cheese, herbs that I used in the meal, grated Manchego cheese, and a little grated red onion. Mix all that together, fill the zucchini flowers, twist the ends of the blossom to trap the filling inside. Make a mixture of equal amounts of Italian bread crumbs, polenta, and grated pecorino cheese; season that with a little fennel salt or fennel pollen and a little sea salt, and that's the breading. Dip the blossoms in flour, then in beaten egg, then in the bread-crumb mixture and then you fry them at 375°F in a couple of inches of vegetable oil. They are delicious. You drain them on a wire rack and add a little sprinkle of sea salt before you serve.

Sliced Steak Tacos

For the best-quality tortillas, look for a small producer or the word "handmade" on the label.

¼ cup pureed **chipotle chiles in adobo** (see Tip)
Juice of 2 **limes**
2 tablespoons **honey**
2 tablespoons **Worcestershire sauce**
1½ teaspoons dried **Mexican oregano**
4 cloves **garlic**, finely chopped
¼ cup **vegetable oil**
1½ to 2 pounds **flank steak** or top round (sometimes labeled as London broil), 1 inch thick
Kosher salt and **coarse black pepper**
⅓ cup chopped **cilantro**
Sea salt
16 good-quality soft taco-size corn or flour **tortillas**, charred
Mix & Match Taco Toppings (see page 146)

Put the chipotle puree in a large resealable plastic food storage bag and add half the lime juice, the honey, Worcestershire, oregano, garlic, and vegetable oil. Close the bag and mash it up with your hands. Season the steak with salt and lots of black pepper, drop into the bag, and press out most of the air as you close up the bag. Maneuver the marinade evenly around the meat and marinate for several hours in the fridge.

Bring the beef to room temperature. Preheat the broiler and set the rack one level up from the center of the oven. Shake off the excess marinade, place the beef on a broiler pan, and broil 5 minutes on each side for rare, 6 minutes each side for pink center or medium. Let the meat rest 5 to

10 minutes, then thinly slice against the grain.

Divide the sliced steak into portions and dress each portion with the remaining lime juice, the cilantro, and sea salt. Serve with charred hot tortillas and toppings of your choice.

Serves 4 to 6

When I buy a can of chipotle chiles in adobo, I puree all of the vinegar and spices and peppers (which I seed first to make the puree not so screaming hot) in the food processor. I then take whatever I need for the recipe and put the rest in the freezer in a little plastic food storage bag clearly marked "Chipotle Paste" so that I know what it is when I look at it quizzically months later.

MIX & MATCH TACO TOPPINGS

- Corn, scraped fresh from cob, then charred in butter or oil over high heat
- Chopped hot pickled vegetables, such as chopped drained giardiniera
- Pickled jalapeño chile rings
- Crumbled queso fresco or cotija cheese
- Cilantro leaves
- Thinly sliced red onions
- Shredded cabbage
- Diced tomatoes
- Sliced avocado dressed with lemon or lime juice and salt

Orange-Chile Wild Rice

3 cups **chicken** or **vegetable stock**
1 cup **wild rice**
1 to 2 tablespoons fresh **oregano leaves**
1 to 2 tablespoons fresh **thyme leaves**
¼ cup **flat-leaf parsley leaves**
1 **orange**, sectioned and chopped
2 fresh **chiles**, such as Fresno or jalapeño, seeded and finely chopped
½ **red onion**, finely chopped
½ cup sliced **almonds**, toasted
Grated zest and juice of 1 **lime**
EVOO
Salt and **pepper**

In a medium saucepan, bring the stock to a boil. Add the wild rice, reduce to a simmer and cook until the rice blooms and is tender, about 40 minutes.

On a cutting board, finely chop the oregano, thyme, and parsley together.

When the rice is done, stir in the herb blend, orange, chiles, onion, almonds, lime zest, and lime juice. Add a drizzle of EVOO and salt and pepper.

Serve 4

🕐 **SEPTEMBER 18/DINNER**

Porcini & Vegetable Soup

This soup gave a good excuse to cook some chard because I have mountains of it in my garden. I cannot cook the stuff fast enough. For the other vegetables, you can thinly slice or chop or cut into matchsticks—just make all your shapes and sizes relatively the same.

3 to 4 tablespoons **EVOO**
½ pound **fresh porcini** (or any other mix of mushrooms you like)

1 or 2 **carrots**, sliced or chopped
1 bulb **baby fennel**, sliced or chopped
1 **onion**, sliced or chopped
2 or 3 ribs **celery**, sliced or chopped
3 cloves **garlic**, chopped
1 tablespoon fresh **thyme leaves**
1 **bay leaf**
Salt and **pepper**
½ cup **Marsala**
8 cups **vegetable stock**
Parmigiano-Reggiano rind (see Tip)
3 **tomatoes**, grated
1 bunch **rainbow chard**, ribs stripped and
    leaves coarsely chopped
Freshly grated **nutmeg**
½ pound **pasta** (whatever shape you want)
½ cup grated **pecorino cheese**

In a large saucepan, heat the EVOO (3 or
4 turns of the pan) and sauté the mushrooms.
Add the carrots, fennel, onion, celery, garlic,
thyme, bay leaf, and salt and pepper to taste.
Sweat the vegetables partially covered.

Deglaze the pan with the Marsala, then add the
stock, Parm rind, and tomatoes. Bring to a boil, then
wilt in the chard and season with a little nutmeg.

Meanwhile, in a separate pot of salted boiling
water, cook the pasta to al dente. Keep it on the side
so that the pasta doesn't get bloated in the soup.

When you're ready to serve, take a little of the
pasta, top it with a little grated pecorino, and
pour the hot soup down over it.

Serves 4

*When I make soup, I often throw
in a cheese rind. When you buy your
Parmigiano-Reggiano, always make sure
you buy a piece that has some rind on
it. It's a great flavoring for soups.*

⏱ SEPTEMBER 19
HAPPY 85TH TO TONY BENNETT

I sent him 85 of the little notebooks that he keeps
in his pocket at all times and uses for his sketch
pad when he's out and about in the world. Lovely
man, one of my favorites. I wasn't with him on his
birthday but I did go to his celebration at Lincoln
Center and he came over for a belated birthday
dinner soon thereafter.

⏱ SEPTEMBER 19/DINNER

Croque Monsieur with Mushrooms

7 tablespoons **butter**
4 scant tablespoons **flour**
2 cups whole **milk**
Salt and **white** or **black pepper**
Freshly grated **nutmeg**
1 rounded tablespoon **Dijon mustard**
1 (8-ounce) package sliced **cremini mushrooms**
6 slices **brioche bread** or white bread
½ pound thinly sliced **French-style ham** (mild,
    sweet, and buttery—not smoky)
1½ to 2 cups shredded **Comté** or **Gruyère cheese**

Preheat the oven to 375°F.

In a saucepan, melt 4 tablespoons of the butter
over medium heat. Whisk in the flour and cook
for a minute, then whisk in the milk and season
with salt, pepper, and nutmeg. Simmer at a low
bubble until thick enough to coat the back of a
spoon. Stir in the mustard.

In a large skillet, melt the remaining 3 tablespoons butter over medium-high heat. Add the
mushrooms and stir until the mushrooms are
browned, about 8 minutes. Transfer to a plate and
let cool.

Arrange the sliced bread on a baking sheet and
top with the sauce, ham, mushrooms, and cheese.
Bake to deep golden on top.

Serves 6

Chiles Rellenos

4 large **poblano peppers**
6 fresh **tomatillos**, husked
1 **yellow onion**, quartered
2 **jalapeño chiles**, 1 whole (see Tip) and
   1 seeded and finely chopped
6 cloves **garlic**, 4 whole and unpeeled,
   2 chopped
1 teaspoon ground **cumin**
A handful of **basil leaves**, plus additional for
   garnish
A handful of **cilantro leaves**, plus additional for
   garnish
Salt and **pepper**
A drizzle of **honey**
2 cups **chicken stock**
2 tablespoons **EVOO** or vegetable oil
1 large or 2 medium ears **corn**, kernels scraped
1 small **red onion**, minced
2 tablespoons **fresh thyme**
Juice of 1 **lime**
2 to 2½ cups **shredded cooked chicken**,
   rotisserie-style or poached breast meat
1 cup shredded **Cheddar, Monterey Jack**, or
   Chihuahua cheese
Frying oil, such as safflower or vegetable oil
   with omega-3s
Flour, for dredging
3 **eggs**
Panko bread crumbs, for dredging
3 to 4 tablespoons **crème fraîche**, Mexican
   crema, or sour cream
Diced heirloom **tomatoes**, for topping
Crumbled **cotija cheese**, for topping

Position an oven rack one notch above the center of the oven and preheat the broiler. Broil the poblanos until they're charred evenly all over; leave the oven door slightly ajar to allow the steam to escape. Place the charred peppers in a bowl and cover. When cool enough to handle, peel, then cut a slit in one side of each pepper and carefully remove the seeds.

Arrange the tomatillos, yellow onion quarters, whole jalapeño, and 4 unpeeled garlic cloves on the baking sheet. Broil to char the tomatillos and jalapeño all over. Turn the onion quarters once to char evenly. Let cool.

Transfer the tomatillos, onion, jalapeño, and garlic to a food processor. Add the cumin, basil, cilantro, and salt and pepper to taste. Add a drizzle of honey and about ½ cup of the chicken stock. Puree until smooth.

Transfer the puree to a saucepan, add the remaining stock, and bring to a simmer. Reduce the heat to low and simmer for 20 minutes to thicken the sauce and develop the flavors. Turn off the heat until ready to serve.

In a medium high-sided skillet, heat the EVOO (2 turns of the pan) over medium-high heat. Add the corn kernels and cook to lightly brown and caramelized at the edges, giving the pan a good shake now and then, 5 to 6 minutes. Add the red onion, thyme, finely chopped jalapeño, chopped garlic, and salt and pepper to taste. Toss together for 2 minutes more, then douse the pan with the lime juice. Transfer to a bowl to cool.

Add the chicken and shredded cheese to the cooled corn. Stuff the poblano peppers as full as possible, gently pressing to set the filling once the peppers are full. Shape them a bit, place on a plate, and chill for 1 hour to firm up.

Fill a countertop fryer with oil or pour 2 to 3 inches of oil into a large Dutch oven. Heat the oil to 350°F. (The oil is ready when a 1-inch cube of white bread cooks to golden brown in 40 seconds.)

Line up 3 shallow bowls on the counter: Spread the flour out in one, beat the eggs in the second,

and spread the panko in the third. Remove the poblanos from the fridge. Coat in the flour first, then the egg, then the panko. Fry to deep golden, 4 to 5 minutes. Drain on a cooling rack and sprinkle with salt.

Just before serving, reheat the sauce and stir in the crème fraîche, crema, or sour cream. Pour a ladle of sauce into a shallow dish or bowl. Set the fried poblanos into the sauce and garnish with tomatoes and cotija crumbles, cilantro leaves and/or torn or sliced basil.

Serves 4

For less heat in the sauce, you can seed the jalapeño that you're going to roast. Halve it lengthwise and scrape out the seeds. Leave it skin side up for the whole time it's being broiled.

🕐 **SEPTEMBER 21/DINNER**

I made **Ultimate Italian Pulled Pork Sammies** (see April 4, page 4) for John and **Tuna Surprise** for me and my friend Jane.

Tuna Surprise

1 pound **extra-wide egg noodles**
7 tablespoons **butter**
1½ cups **panko bread crumbs**
1 cup grated **Parmigiano-Reggiano cheese**
¼ cup chopped **flat-leaf parsley**
1 tablespoon **EVOO**
1 pound **button mushrooms**, very thinly sliced
1 large or 2 medium **shallots**, finely chopped
3 cloves **garlic**, finely chopped
2 tablespoons **fresh thyme**, finely chopped
Salt and **pepper**
2 tablespoons **flour**
½ cup **dry white wine**

1½ cups **half-and-half**
1 rounded tablespoon **Dijon mustard**
3 tablespoons **fresh tarragon**, chopped
2 (6-ounce) cans sustainable line-caught **tuna**, drained and flaked

Bring a large pot of water to a boil for the egg noodles. Preheat the oven to 400°F.

In a small skillet, melt 4 tablespoons of the butter. Pour into a small bowl and combine with the panko, Parm, and parsley.

In a skillet, heat the EVOO (1 turn of the pan) and the remaining 3 tablespoons butter over medium to medium-high heat. Add the mushrooms and sauté to tender, 6 to 7 minutes. Add the shallot, garlic, thyme, salt, and pepper and stir for 2 to 3 minutes more. Sprinkle in the flour and stir for a minute more; whisk in the wine, then the half-and-half. Bring the sauce to a bubble, then reduce the heat and cook until thick enough to coat the back of a spoon. Stir in the mustard and tarragon.

While the sauce thickens, salt the boiling water and cook the egg noodles to al dente.

Combine the flaked tuna with the sauce. Drain the egg noodles and return them to the cooking pot. Pour in the tuna and sauce and stir to combine. Transfer to a 9 by 13-inch baking dish and top with the bread-crumb mixture. Bake until golden, about 15 minutes.

Serves 6

Italy Trip

We went to Tuscany for our anniversary celebration at Castello di Velona. We always eat at Boccon di Vino for our first big celebration and then we have a big family night at the castle, which they cater. Boccon di Vino is extraordinary (www.boccondivinomontalcino.it). Mario Fiorani runs it and his daughter Marina is the chef . . . it's just amazing the quality food they do, and over the years they've just kept topping themselves. I think maybe the most jaw-dropping things I ever saw there were individual ravioli. Marina was feeding over seventy people and she was making individual ravioli that were as large as the dinner plate. Each one was probably 6 inches across and it was in lavender sauce and was stuffed with tuna. It was insane. Last year there was a saffron butter and poppyseed fettuccine that I tried to re-create at home and it just wasn't the same (but it was still delicious).

We had moved into our own Tuscan villa owned by our now friends Scott and Gina. Gina's dad is actually the hotel owner and she manages the property. The betrothed, her then-soon-to-be husband, is Scott. They're a very cool young couple who divide their time between Italy and America, and their property can be seen on our website, www.rachaelray.com/rach/italy.php. Here is the website for the villas: http://monteverdituscany.com.

SEPTEMBER 26, AT THE VILLA

Our little villa in Tuscany has a big beautiful kitchen and a backyard and a little garden. We served ripe pears from the local market with the pecorino that we bought that was flavored because the cheese ages under hay, so it's very grassy-tasting pecorino—salty and tangy but faintly sweet as well and just extraordinary, delicious. We put that out with some shaved fresh fennel and some assorted fennel salami from the local market.

I also made stock . . . they don't have stock in a box over there; it's not something they really sell, they just do bouillon cubes. So I had to make all of my own stocks every day kind of from scratch. I made a **porcini stock** with about 30 grams (about 1 ounce) of dried porcini, 2 cups water, some rosemary, and some root vegetables. I just threw that all into a small pot and then strained it once the flavors came together, saving the porcini to use later.

I used the porcini stock and the porcini to make a **white ragu for pici**, which is a local favorite pasta; it's like a solid bucatini. You cook a pound of pici (you could use bucatini) in a pot of salted boiling water. Before draining the pasta, ladle out about a cup of starchy cooking water and set aside for the sauce.

Meanwhile, brown a pound of ground veal in EVOO (2 turns of the pan) over high heat, then stir in ¼ pound freshly ground pork (you could use pork sausage), crumbling the meat. Add chopped vegetables: a small carrot, a small celery rib with leaves, a small onion, 3 or 4 garlic cloves, and 2 tablespoons thinly sliced sage (mine was right from our garden!) and season generously with salt and pepper. Cook the vegetables, covered, stirring occasionally, until softened, 3 to 5 minutes. Add in 3 tablespoons tomato paste and let that cook out for a couple of minutes.

Deglaze the pan with 1 cup dry white wine.

Chop the drained mushrooms from the porcini stock. Stir into the ragu and add the porcini stock (or you could use chicken or vegetable stock). Stir in 1 cup whole milk, reduce the heat to medium-high, and cook to thicken, about 45 minutes.

Stir the reserved 1 cup pasta cooking water into the ragu. Toss the pasta with the sauce and serve topped with grated pecorino cheese.

We also had some **Romanesco broccoli** (it looks like pointy cauliflower). We parboiled Romanesco broccoli florets in salted water for 4 or 5 minutes. I then took 3 to 4 tablespoons EVOO; melted in 4 or 5 flat anchovy fillets; added some chopped fresh hot chiles; added a couple of small ribs of celery, chopped; ½ red onion, chopped; a couple of cloves of thinly sliced or chopped garlic; and then I added the parboiled broccoli, a splash of vinegar, a sprinkle of sugar, and a little salt and pepper. It comes out like a sweet-and-sour flavored broccoli.

For the photographer who visited to take pictures for our magazine, I made **roasted potatoes** from the local market, barely dressed with olive oil and seasoned with sea salt and pepper and lots of rosemary from the garden and a mixture of hot and sweet locally grown peppers. You just toss it all together and throw it into the oven at 400° to 425°F until deeply golden; I flipped them once. It usually takes about 40 minutes, but of course it depends on how small or how large you cut

your potatoes. I served that up with a classic, very simple veal saltimbocca.

For a **veal saltimbocca**, the veal medallions or cutlets are pounded paper thin. You season the veal with salt and pepper, then you use a plain wooden toothpick to anchor prosciutto di Parma and a whole sage leaf on one side of the veal. You sort of sew it with the toothpick. Then you dredge that lightly in flour, shaking off the excess. The whole trick to saltimbocca is the flour dredge, not to have too much flour but to dredge it so that it gets a little crispy as you brown it in the skillet. Heat EVOO and butter (I usually use a couple of tablespoons of oil to a pat of butter) in a skillet over medium to medium-high heat. When the butter foams, working in batches, add the veal and cook it a few minutes and brown it on each side. Deglaze with dry white wine or vermouth, then add a little bit more, and another pat of butter to turn that into a nice pan sauce. You just spoon that pan sauce down over the top of the veal.

SEPTEMBER 27, AT THE VILLA

We received a fresh truffle from Paolo Coluccio, the chef who works at the Inn/Villas. He got me a white truffle and we made **egg pasta with truffle butter sauce**. It was butter with minced shallot and a little bit of garlic (1 or 2 small cloves); stir that for a couple of minutes until very

fragrant. I then added a cup of wine, a splash of whole milk or cream, and the shaved truffle, and tossed it with the pasta and lots of finely chopped parsley. Very simple, very delicious.

SEPTEMBER 28, AT THE VILLA

The next night I had risotto Tuscano: **Tuscan-style risotto with fresh walnuts**. The walnuts were just young and they were so delicious—and you could literally crack the shells with your bare hands. You put a couple of them in your hand . . . I'm not weak but I'm not an especially strong person . . . and you gave them a squeeze and they just fell apart and burst open and it was a walnut unlike any I've ever tasted. It was delicious! I made the risotto with carnaroli rice. It's one of the several types of short-grain rice you can prepare risotto with. I took a few tablespoons of EVOO (enough to cover a round-bottomed pan, so 2 to

3 turns of the pan). I added a small onion, finely chopped, and a couple of cloves of garlic, also finely chopped. Stir that until fragrant. I added 1 tablespoon each minced sage and fresh thyme, and a little salt and pepper. I then added the rice—1¼ to 1½ cups, I just sort of eyeballed it. The whole time I am preparing the risotto of course I have warm liquids ready to add to the pan. I used my own homemade vegetable stock for this but at home, back in the States, I would use a quart of chicken stock. I prefer the flavor of chicken stock, but you could use vegetable stock and thin it out with 1 to 2 cups of water. You're going to need 5 to 6 cups total for 1½ cups short-grain rice. You warm your liquids and have those ready to add as necessary.

After I add the rice to the softened onion and garlic and herb mixture, I toast the rice up for a minute or two, then add 1 cup of dry white wine and allow that to evaporate completely before I begin adding the stock. Add the stock ½ cup at a time and stir several times to develop the starches in the risotto with each addition of liquids. (From the time you begin adding liquids to your risotto it should take you 18 minutes on the nose to finish preparing the risotto to al dente; that's 18 minutes from the first addition of liquid.)

I toasted the fresh walnuts up lightly in a skillet. I put them on the cutting board, covered them with wax paper, and crushed them with a rolling pin (or you could use a meat mallet or just chop them with a knife). They were pretty finely chopped (I must have had a good cup). When the risotto was just a few minutes from being done, I added in some of the shaved white truffle, all of the walnuts, a few tablespoons of butter at the end, and a couple of handfuls of freshly grated pecorino cheese. Stir that and then add a little salt and pepper to taste and eat it immediately. *It was mind-blowingly delicious!*

I think the risotto would have been very delicious without the truffle, too. That was just a bonus, since we were here in Italy and it was

procured for us a little early for the season, so we were putting it in everything. Incidentally if you are a truffle fan, that's great. My favorite way to eat truffles is just in scrambled eggs cooked in good, good butter. Even if you never have a truffle in your whole life, you should buy a truffle shaver online or in a store next time you're out shopping for kitchen equipment. It's a wonderful instrument to shave garlic paper thin, the way Paulie did in *Goodfellas*. It's just a really useful little tool for shaving small things like baby beets and whole cloves of garlic and you just get it so thin. It's delightful. It's like a mandoline for tiny things.

SEPTEMBER 29, AT THE VILLA

For lunch, I made a **squash soup** with a big hunk of a giant, deeply orange squash that they had at the market; they would just hack off a hunk and sell it to you by the kilo. This probably weighed a pound and a half. I took a fairly small wedge. You could, of course, substitute a small butternut squash. This skin was pretty dense, so I cut the squash away from it; scooped out the seeds; cut it into irregular pieces; dressed it with EVOO, salt, pepper, and a little freshly grated nutmeg; and roasted it at 400°F for about 25 minutes or so, until the sugars of the squash started to caramelize on the baking sheet. (Skin on or skin off, it's really up to you. Once you roast it in the oven, the skin is edible on a butternut squash.)

Meanwhile, I sautéed 2 chopped carrots, 1 chopped celery rib, 1 chopped onion, and 3 or 4 cloves finely chopped garlic in a few tablespoons of EVOO. I added a couple of small pinches of saffron, a tablespoon each of grated orange and lemon zest, and 1 quart water. I cooked that until the vegetables were soft. I added the squash and I pureed the whole thing with an immersion blender. I just took it right off the stove and over to the wall, plugged the blender in, and blended

it until the soup was smooth. I adjusted the salt and pepper and served the soup in shallow bowls topped with finely chopped toasted pistachio nuts. It was delicious!

For **artichokes with vinaigrette**, I started with fairly young artichokes. I halved them and scooped out the chokes and rubbed them with lemon. I boiled them to tender in acidulated water. For the vinaigrette, I grated 1 small shallot and 1 large clove garlic into a dish, salted it, and added the juice of a lemon plus 2 tablespoons vinegar and let that sit for a few minutes. I added a teaspoon of superfine sugar and then whisked in ½ cup EVOO to emulsify. I seasoned with salt, lots of pepper, and 1 tablespoon finely chopped fresh thyme. I served it with the artichokes—the larger leaves were pulled and dipped into the dressing, the tender parts of the stem and hearts we just cut with forks and knives and dipped it in the vinaigrette.

We were given an amazing *cinghiale* sauce by Paolo. He makes his cinghiale sauce with carrots, celery, onion, garlic, a whole bottle of red wine, juniper berries, salt, pepper, and tomato (he was kind enough to share the recipe; see below). Cinghiale, of course, is wild boar and you can get it in the States. I've seen it in Italian markets. Quite frankly, it's not so wild there; it's just a pig with a couple of teeth that stick out and they're farmed like any other animal. You do see wild boars everywhere in Tuscany. I think with all the

products that use cinghiale, like *salumi* and all of the different sauces in jars and things, I'm quite sure that at this point they must also be domesticated to some extent and be raised on farms. Instead of using cinghiale, you could slow-cook pork butt (shoulder), pull that, and drop it into a sauce with root vegetables, red wine, juniper berries, salt, pepper, and tomatoes and just cook that down until you're happy with the flavor. Traditionally, that sauce is served with pappardelle (very wide thick ribbons of pasta), or any pasta that can stand up to the weight and flavor of the sauce.

I also made a **spicy ground lamb ragu** because I love ground lamb so much. I started with a pound and a half of freshly ground lamb. I browned that in a couple of tablespoons of EVOO until the lamb started to develop a nice brown crust. I then added 1½ teaspoons of fennel seed or fennel pollen and a teaspoon of crushed red pepper flakes, which I made from two very small locally grown pepperoncini (little hot peppers) and hand-chopped them to make my teaspoon. I added a couple of tablespoons of finely chopped fresh rosemary, a few finely chopped large cloves of garlic, and 1 finely chopped onion to the ground lamb and let that cook out a bit. I then added a large piece of orange zest to mellow the sauce, 2 to 3 tablespoons of tomato paste, which I stirred until fragrant, and then 2 cups dry Tuscan red wine. I let that cook out by about half. I stirred it for a minute or two and then added

in 2 cups vegetable or chicken stock. (I would have used chicken stock had I been at home, and I think pretty much the whole time I was here I just had the vegetable stock that I kept making over and over again because I had a lot of root vegetables on hand.) You then add a can of San Marzano tomatoes or 11 or 12 ripe plum or Roma tomatoes that have been peeled and cored. I used fresh San Marzano tomatoes, about 14 of them, because they were kind of small. When using fresh tomatoes, you bring the water to a low boil, score the skin of the tomato with an X, drop it into the boiling water until the skin starts to loosen—30 seconds to a minute—take them out, cold-shock them, peel, and there you go, you're all set.

I let the sauce thicken up and cook out 30 or 40 minutes. I would have added a fresh bay leaf had I been home, too. You pull out the orange zest and the fresh bay leaf at the end.

I tossed it with pici pasta again because it's one of our favorites and they have so much of it in this region. Pappardelle and bucatini would also be great choices. I topped it with fresh sheep's milk ricotta cheese and lots of finely chopped flat-leaf parsley and mint as the garnish. It was spectacular.

 Experience Rachael's Italy.

Paolo Coluccio's Cinghiale in Umido

Serve the boar over slices of grilled polenta.

2¼ pounds **wild boar**, cut into 1-inch cubes
3 tablespoons **olive oil**
3 medium **carrots**, coarsely chopped
2 ribs **celery**, coarsely chopped
2 **white onions**, coarsely chopped
Leaves from 2 sprigs **fresh rosemary**
1 tablespoon **juniper berries**
Salt
16 ounces **canned tomatoes**
1 (1-liter) bottle **red table wine**
Pink peppercorns
Chopped **parsley**

Place the meat in in a bowl of cold water (or a mixture of water and milk, which will make the meat more tender) and let sit for at least 7 hours (even better if it can sit overnight). Change the water a few times.

Heat the oil in a big pan, and stir in the carrots, celery, and onions. Drain the meat and pat it dry, then add to the pan. Stir everything for 5 minutes, then season with the rosemary, juniper, and salt to taste. Add the tomatoes and some red wine to cover. Cover the pot and cook over low heat, adding red wine as needed, until the meat is tender, about 3 hours.

Serve the meat garnished with some crushed pink peppercorns and parsley.

Serves 6

OCTOBER

SATURDAY/1

DINNER
roasted tomatillo salsa; roasted onion, chile & garlic guacamole; roasted bean dip; this week's Sunday night chili

SUNDAY/2

MONDAY/3

LUNCH
homemade Gala applesauce
DINNER
chicken curry

TUESDAY/4

DINNER
smoky mushroom & pepper ragu

WEDNESDAY/5

DINNER
tuna and pasta salad, fried green tomatoes

TUESDAY/11

DINNER
walnut risotto with white truffle & pecorino, roasted turkey breast with creamy parmigiano gravy, cranberry sauce, roast winter squash

WEDNESDAY/12

THURSDAY/13

FRIDAY/14

DINNER
Chicagoan-Italian roast beef heroes, giardiniera

SATURDAY/15

FRIDAY/21

DINNER
chicken with pumpkin seed sauce, black beans, homemade rice pilaf

SATURDAY/22

LUNCH
curried squash soup, apple & Cheddar melts
DINNER
white coq au vin, buttered herb egg noodles, country-style chicken livers

SUNDAY/23

BREAKFAST
migas
DINNER
poblano mac & Manchego with corn & mushrooms

MONDAY/24

TUESDAY/25

THURSDAY/6

DINNER
eggplant & kuri squash curry with lime red rice

FRIDAY/7

DINNER
Oktoberfest: braised sausages, German potato salad, red cabbage with apples & onions, country-style chicken livers, my sweet and spicy pickles

SATURDAY/8

SUNDAY/9

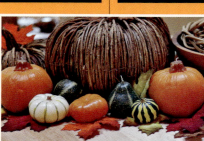

MONDAY/10

DINNER
cocktail sauce (with crab claws), porcini steak sauce, steak with garlic-sherry butter

SUNDAY/16

MONDAY/17

DINNER
hearty mac & cheese with squash & sausage

TUESDAY/18

WEDNESDAY/19

DINNER
walnut risotto with white truffle & pecorino, roasted turkey breast with creamy parmigiano gravy, cranberry pomegranate sauce, brussels sprouts with pancetta, artichokes & vinaigrette

THURSDAY/20

WEDNESDAY/26

THURSDAY/27

FRIDAY/28

DINNER
"devilish" bull's-eye cocktail sauce (with crab claws), deviled eggs (renamed Evil Eye for Halloween), cider beef, mashed potatoes & parsnips with Cheddar

SATURDAY/29

LUNCH
croque madame with white truffle
DINNER
artichokes & vinaigrette, antipasto, osso buco, polenta

SUNDAY/30

BREAKFAST
warm apples in maple syrup, whole-grain waffles with toasted walnuts
DINNER
roasted turkey breast with herb butter, mashed potatoes & parsnips with Cheddar, roasted butternut squash, green beans and cremini

MONDAY/31

DINNER
pasta e fagioli

Mexican Fiesta: **Roasted Tomatillo Salsa**; **Roasted Onion, Chile & Garlic Guacamole**; **Roasted Bean Dip**; and **This Week's Sunday Night Chili** with chili toppers.

Roasted Tomatillo Salsa

If you're making this salsa, the guac, and the bean dip, broil all the vegetables for the three recipes at the same time.

    6 **tomatillos**, husked
    ½ **onion**, cut into chunks
    2 **serrano chiles**, seeded
    2 large cloves **garlic**, unpeeled
    2 teaspoons **honey**
    ½ teaspoon ground **cumin**
    1 or 2 tablespoons **thyme leaves**
    Leaves from a sprig of fresh **oregano**
    Small handful of **cilantro**
    Small handful of **mint**
    Juice of 1 **lime**
    Salt

Position an oven rack one notch above the center of the oven and preheat the broiler. Arrange the tomatillos, onion, serranos, and garlic on a baking sheet. Broil to char the tomatillos and serranos all over. Turn the onion chunks once to char evenly. Let cool, then peel the garlic. Transfer the vegetables to a food processor; add the honey, cumin, thyme, oregano, cilantro, mint, lime juice, and salt to taste; and puree.

Makes about 1½ cups

Roasted Onion, Chile & Garlic Guacamole

    ½ **onion**
    2 large cloves **garlic**, unpeeled
    2 **jalapeño chiles**
    2 small **avocados**
    Juice of 1 **lemon**
    Small handful of **cilantro leaves**, chopped
    Salt

Preheat the broiler.

Broil the onion, garlic, and jalapeños until charred all over. Let cool, then peel and seed the jalapeño and peel the garlic. Chop that all up and combine with the avocados, lemon juice, cilantro, and salt to taste. Mash that together and serve.

Makes about 1½ cups

Roasted Bean Dip

    1 small **onion**, quartered
    2 cloves **garlic**, unpeeled
    2 **jalapeño chiles**
    1 (16-ounce) can **spicy vegetarian refried beans**
    Small handful of **cilantro**
    1 teaspoon ground **cumin**
    Salt and **pepper**

Preheat the broiler.

Broil the onion, garlic, and jalapeños until charred all over. Let cool, then peel and seed the jalapeño and peel the garlic. Transfer it all to a food processor and add the refried beans, cilantro, ground cumin, and salt and pepper to taste. Thin it out with a little water (about ⅓ cup) and puree. Keep it warm in a small saucepan over low heat until you're ready to serve.

Makes 1½ cups

This Week's Sunday Night Chili

4 fresh **red poblano chiles** (see Tip)
2 tablespoons **EVOO**, plus more for drizzling
3 dried **ancho chiles**, stemmed and seeded
3 cups **beef stock**
¼ pound **bacon**, chopped
1½ to 2 pounds **ground beef** (1 used 80% lean ground sirloin)
Salt and **pepper**
2 tablespoons **Worcestershire sauce**
1 tablespoon ground **cumin**
1 tablespoon fresh **oregano**
1 tablespoon fresh **thyme**
2 to 3 tablespoons **tomato paste**
1 (12-ounce) bottle **Negra Modelo beer**
2 teaspoons **honey**
3 tablespoons **masa harina** or **cornmeal**
Chili Toppers (see box)

Preheat the broiler to high.

Drizzle the poblanos with EVOO and place on a baking sheet. Broil, turning every 1 to 2 minutes, until charred all over. Place in a bowl and cover. Let sit for 10 to 15 minutes, then peel the poblanos and stem and seed them.

In a saucepan, combine the anchos and beef stock. Cook to reconstitute the chiles and to reduce the liquid by about a third so you end up with about 2 cups of beef stock. Puree the anchos and poblanos with the reduced stock and keep the puree warm over low heat until you need it.

Place a large Dutch oven over medium-high heat. Add 2 tablespoons EVOO (2 turns of the pan). Add the bacon and brown. Then add the beef, season with salt and pepper, and brown.

Add the Worcestershire sauce, cumin, oregano, thyme, and tomato paste and cook for 4 to 5 minutes. When the paste is fragrant, stir in the beer and honey and cook to reduce the beer by half. Add the ancho and poblano puree, and masa harina or cornmeal. Bring that to a boil, then reduce the heat to low and simmer gently for 30 minutes, stirring occasionally.

Serves 4

CHILI TOPPERS

· Grated aged Mimolette or aged Gouda cheese
· Chopped pickled vegetables (giardiniera)
· Thinly sliced serrano chiles
· Chopped pickled carrots
· Finely chopped red or white onion
· Toasted hulled pumpkin seeds (pepitas)

Red poblanos can be tough to find, but you can substitute green poblanos. The red poblanos are milder than the green, so if you're going to use green, use 2 large or 3 medium green for the 4 red. Or you could get 3 dried guajillo or pasilla chiles, which are at a mild to moderate heat level, and reconstitute them along with the anchos.

I made grilled cheese sandwiches and served them with **Homemade Gala Applesauce.**

Homemade Gala Applesauce

4 **Gala apples**, peeled and diced
3 tablespoons light or dark **brown sugar**
1 cup all-natural **apple juice** or **cider** (it should look cloudy)
Grated zest of 1 **orange**

In a medium pot, combine the apples, brown sugar, apple juice, and orange zest and cook over medium-high heat, stirring occasionally, until a chunky sauce forms, 10 to 12 minutes. If the sauce begins to spatter as it bubbles, reduce the heat. Once a sauce forms, remove the pot from the heat.

Makes about 3 cups

OCTOBER 3/DINNER

We had **Chicken Curry** (see August 28, page 130).

OCTOBER 4/DINNER

Smoky Mushroom & Pepper Ragu

2 **Italian red cherry peppers** or 2 large red Fresno chiles
1 large or 2 medium **red bell peppers**
¼ cup **EVOO**
¼ pound **pancetta** or guanciale, cut into fat matchsticks
4 or 5 **portobello mushroom caps**, gills scraped, sliced
2 tablespoons finely chopped fresh **rosemary**
1 tablespoon thinly sliced fresh **sage**
1 tablespoon finely chopped fresh **thyme**
1½ teaspoons chopped fresh **oregano**, or 1 teaspoon dried
4 large cloves **garlic**, sliced
1 large or 2 medium **onions**, chopped
Salt and **black pepper**
2 tablespoons **tomato paste**
1½ cups **dry red wine**
1 (28- or 32-ounce) can **San Marzano tomatoes** (look for DOP on the label)
1 pound **pappardelle pasta**
Grated **pecorino cheese**

Preheat the broiler and char the red cherry and bell peppers until evenly blackened. Place in a bowl and cover to cool. Peel and seed the peppers. Finely dice the cherry peppers, and chop the bell peppers into ¼-inch dice.

Meanwhile, in a large Dutch oven, heat the

EVOO (4 turns of the pan) over medium-high heat and add the pancetta to render, 2 to 3 minutes. Stir in the mushrooms and cook until dark and tender, 12 to 15 minutes.

Add the rosemary, sage, thyme, oregano, garlic, onions, and some salt and black pepper and cook 5 minutes. Stir in the tomato paste and roasted chiles and peppers. Deglaze with the wine and cook until reduced by half, scraping up the bits on the bottom of the pan, about 2 minutes. Stir in the tomatoes and simmer gently, stirring occasionally, until the tomatoes break down, 30 minutes.

Bring a large pot of water to a boil. Salt the water and cook the pappardelle to al dente. Before draining, ladle out and reserve 1 cup of the starchy pasta cooking water. Drain the pasta and toss with the sauce, the pasta cooking water, and lots of grated pecorino. Pass more cheese at the table, for topping.

Serves 4

🕐 OCTOBER 5/DINNER

I served a **tuna and pasta salad** up with **Fried Green Tomatoes** (see July 12, page 85) topped with chopped tomatoes and cooked and chopped bacon.

Tuna and pasta salad: I made a dressing with a finely chopped shallot, a couple of chopped garlic cloves, some lemon juice, white wine or white balsamic vinegar, and EVOO. I seasoned it with fennel salt (or you could use fennel pollen or ground fennel) and pepper. Then I cut up some artichoke hearts, celery, baby fennel, red onion, and parsley. Tossed all of that together with 1 pound bow-tie pasta that I cooked and let cool. I added in some good Italian tuna.

🕐 OCTOBER 6/DINNER

We had **Eggplant & Kuri Squash Curry** with **red rice** scented with Kaffir lime leaves and fresh basil.

Eggplant & Kuri Squash Curry

Dark-orange kuri squash is pretty readily available in the autumn months; it's very tasty and it's a nice size. You could substitute a small butternut squash. The curry spice blend that I made here was West Indian–style. Serve the curry over red rice, or you could use jasmine rice.

1 rounded tablespoon ground **coriander**
1 rounded tablespoon ground **cumin**
1 tablespoon **chili powder** (I like Gebhardt's) or ground ancho chile powder
1 scant tablespoon **turmeric**
½ teaspoon ground **cardamom**

Salt and pepper

Freshly grated nutmeg

3 tablespoons vegetable oil or EVOO, plus more for the squash

2 yellow onions, sliced

3 mild frying peppers (I used finger peppers, but you could substitute cubanelles), halved lengthwise and thinly sliced crosswise

4 cloves garlic, thinly sliced

1 inch fresh ginger, grated

1 small eggplant, peeled (see Tip) and cut into dice

1 kuri squash (about 1½ pounds), peeled, seeded, and cut into bite-size pieces

½ cup mango chutney

1 or 2 tomatoes, grated through the large holes of a box grater

Preheat the oven to 425°F.

In a small bowl, combine the coriander, cumin, chili powder, turmeric, cardamom, 1 teaspoon salt, a couple of pinches of black pepper, and a few grates of nutmeg.

In a large skillet, heat the oil (3 turns of the pan) over medium to medium-high heat. Add the onions, peppers, garlic, and ginger and sweat out for about 5 minutes. Add the curry spices and stir the vegetables for 2 to 3 minutes. Add the eggplant and a little more salt and pepper; give it a stir, keep it partially covered, and let the eggplant cook out with the vegetables while you roast the squash.

Toss the kuri with some oil, salt, pepper, and a little nutmeg and roast until it's golden at the edges, 20 to 25 minutes.

Stir the chutney and tomatoes into the curry to sweeten it up. Fold in the roasted squash. Serve with rice.

Serves 4

I peeled off half of the eggplant skin and left half on because I like a little texture.

Lime red rice: I made red rice according to the package directions. I cooked it in chicken stock (or you could use vegetable stock if you wanted to make this vegetarian) with Kaffir lime leaves. If you can't find lime leaves, substitute lime zest. At the very end, when the rice was done, I stirred in shredded or torn basil, thinly sliced scallions, and a little lime juice.

🕐 OCTOBER 7/OKTOBERFEST DINNER

To celebrate Oktoberfest, and because John's band was here (I usually do themed dinners for them), I served **braised sausages**, assorted mustards, chive butter (softened butter mixed with finely chopped chives), warm pumpernickel bread, venison pâté, my mom's **Country-Style Chicken Livers** (see April 20, page 18), thinly sliced radishes, my **Red Cabbage with Apples & Onions**, **German Potato Salad**, and **My Sweet & Spicy Pickles** (see July 4, page 80).

Braised sausages: I put the knockwursts, brats, and bockwursts into a skillet with a little bit of stock or water (maybe ⅛ to ¼ inch), a drizzle of vegetable oil, and a little bit of very thinly sliced onion. You shallow-braise the sausages and let the water cook away so the oil will crisp up the sausage casings.

Red Cabbage with Apples & Onions

¼ cup **vegetable oil**
1 small **red cabbage** (1¼ to 1½ pounds), cored and thinly sliced
1 tablespoon **caraway seeds**
Salt and **pepper**
1 or 2 **fresh bay leaves**
Freshly grated **nutmeg**
2 **Gala apples**, peeled and diced
1 large **red onion**, quartered and thinly sliced or chopped
1 scant tablespoon ground **cumin**
3 to 4 tablespoons **dark brown sugar**
1 (12-ounce) bottle **beer**
1 to 2 tablespoons **Montreal Steak Seasoning**

In a large, deep Dutch oven, heat the oil (4 turns of the pan). Add the cabbage and caraway seeds and season with salt and pepper. Throw in the bay leaves and start to wilt it down. Add a little sprinkle of nutmeg, the apples, and onion. Toss well (I use tongs) to combine them with the cabbage. Sprinkle in the cumin and brown sugar; add the beer. Add the steak seasoning, partially cover, and let it cook for about 1 hour.

Serves 4 to 6

German Potato Salad

3 pounds **baby red potatoes**, halved or quartered, depending on size
1½ cups canned **beef consommé**
6 slices thick-cut **bacon**, chopped
1 **red onion**, finely chopped
2 cloves **garlic**, finely chopped
1 small fresh **chile**, chopped
2 tablespoons **sugar**
½ cup **cider vinegar**
Salt and **pepper**
¼ cup **EVOO**
½ cup chopped **flat-leaf parsley**
3 tablespoons chopped **fresh dill**
Spicy brown mustard, for serving

Place the potatoes in a large pot and cover them with cold water. Bring up to a bubble over medium-high heat and cook until tender, 10 to 12 minutes. Drain thoroughly, then return them to the pot. Add the beef consommé and give them a quick stir.

While the potatoes are cooking, cook the bacon in a small skillet over medium heat until crispy. Drain on paper towels.

In the same skillet with the bacon drippings, cook the onion, garlic, and chile until the onion is soft, about 3 minutes.

In a small saucepan, dissolve the sugar in the cider vinegar over medium-high heat, about 1 minute. Season with salt and pepper, and stir in the EVOO. Pour over the cooked potatoes and toss them together with the parsley, dill, onion mixture, and the bacon.

Serves 4

🕐 OCTOBER 10/DINNER

Cracked crab claws and steamed shrimp served with **Cocktail Sauce** (see September 1, page 134), followed by **Steak with Garlic-Sherry Butter & Porcini Steak Sauce**.

oven and roast 6 minutes for medium-rare, turning once. Remove the meat and let rest.

Slather the steak with the garlic-sherry butter, slice, and top with the steak sauce.

Serves 4

London broil is not actually a single cut of meat; it's one of several cuts that are usually broiled, so grocery stores label the meat "London broil." It's usually flank steak or round steak

🕐 OCTOBER 11/DINNER

I made the **Walnut Risotto with White Truffle & Pecorino** as a first course. For the second course, we had a **Roasted Turkey Breast with Creamy Parmigiano Gravy**, which I served with **Basic Cranberry Sauce**, **steamed greens**, and **roast winter squash**. Sounds delicious—what a tasty dinner.

Steak with Garlic-Sherry Butter & Porcini Steak Sauce

1 large **rib-eye steak**, 1½ to 2 inches thick, or 2 pounds **flank steak**, or a chunk of London broil (see Tip)
2 heads **garlic**, tops cut to expose the cloves, plus 2 large cloves, finely chopped
EVOO, for drizzling
Kosher salt and **pepper**
⅓ cup **dry sherry**
4 tablespoons (½ stick) **butter**, softened
2 tablespoons finely chopped **flat-leaf parsley**
1 tablespoon finely chopped fresh **thyme**
Porcini Steak Sauce (page 67)

Bring the steak to room temperature, 30 minutes to 1 hour.

Preheat the oven to 425°F. Drizzle the garlic with EVOO and season with salt and pepper. Wrap in foil and roast until tender, 45 minutes. Leave the oven on and place a cast-iron pan in the oven to preheat.

Squeeze the garlic into a food processor and add the sherry, butter, parsley, thyme, and salt and pepper to taste. Pulse-process into a paste.

Pat the meat dry and rub with a drizzle of EVOO. Season aggressively with salt and pepper. Remove the hot cast-iron skillet from the oven and place over medium-high heat. Add the steak and brown 3 minutes on each side. Transfer to the

Walnut Risotto with White Truffle & Pecorino

5 to 6 cups **chicken stock**
2 to 3 tablespoons **EVOO**
1 small **onion**, finely chopped
1 or 2 cloves **garlic**, finely chopped
1 tablespoon minced **fresh sage**
1 tablespoon minced **fresh thyme**
Salt and **pepper**
1½ cups **carnaroli rice**
1 cup **dry white wine**
White truffle
1 cup finely chopped toasted **walnuts**
1 or 2 tablespoons **butter**
A couple of handfuls of freshly grated **pecorino cheese**

Bring the chicken stock to a boil in a saucepan, then reduce the heat to a low simmer.

Heat the EVOO (2 or 3 turns of the pan) in a pot with a rounded bottom over medium-high heat. Add the onion and garlic and stir that until fragrant. Add the sage and thyme and season with salt and pepper. Stir in the rice and toast up for a minute or two. Add the wine and allow that to evaporate completely. Begin adding the hot chicken stock, a few ladles at a time, stirring constantly and cooking until the liquid has been absorbed before adding more. Continue adding stock and cooking until the rice is al dente, 18 minutes total.

When the risotto is just a few minutes from being done, add in some shaved white truffle, the walnuts, butter, and a couple of handfuls of freshly grated pecorino. Stir that in and then add salt and pepper to taste and eat immediately.

Serve 4

Roasted Turkey Breast with Creamy Parmigiano Gravy

This recipe makes nice leftovers for sammies.

1 full or 2 half **skin-on, boneless turkey breasts**
2 cloves **garlic**, grated or pasted
8 tablespoons (1 stick) **butter**, softened
¼ cup **minced fresh herbs** (such as parsley, chives, thyme, and rosemary)
1 tablespoon **lemon juice**
Salt and **pepper**
2 tablespoons **flour**
1½ cups **chicken stock**
1 tablespoon **Worcestershire sauce**
⅓ cup **heavy cream**
¼ cup freshly grated **Parmigiano-Reggiano cheese**

Preheat the oven to 350°F. Place the turkey on a wire rack set over a baking sheet. Combine the garlic and softened butter with the herbs and lemon juice. Slather about 5 tablespoons of the garlic-herb butter over the turkey breast and sprinkle liber-

ally with salt and pepper, reserving the remaining garlic-herb butter for the gravy. Roast the turkey 45 minutes, or until 165°F on a food thermometer.

Right before serving the turkey, melt the remaining garlic-herb butter over medium heat in a saucepan. Whisk in the flour, followed by the stock, and cook to thicken. Whisk in the Worcestershire and season with salt and pepper. Stir in the cream and cheese, and keep warm until ready to serve.

Slice the turkey and serve with the gravy.

Serves 4 (with leftovers)

Basic Cranberry Sauce

1 (12-ounce) bag **fresh cranberries**
1 cup **sugar**
Pinch of **salt**
1 **cinnamon stick**
1 strip of **orange zest**
Seeds from 1 **pomegranate**, about ½ cup (optional)

Place the cranberries in a medium saucepan with the sugar, salt, cinnamon stick, orange zest, and 1 cup water. Bring to a boil and cook until all the berries pop and the sauce thickens, about 15 minutes. Cool and remove the zest and cinnamon stick. If using, peel the pomegranate in a bowl of water, separating the seeds, and drain; add the pomegranate seeds to the sauce. Serve at room temperature.

Makes 2 to 3 cups

I also served the turkey up with steamed greens—feel free to use greens of your choice such as dandelion greens, collards, chard, kale, or spinach—and roasted winter squash seasoned with olive oil or melted butter, salt, pepper, and nutmeg.

Chicagoan-Italian Roast Beef Heroes

If you make your own giardiniera, you need to start it 2 days before you use it. The recipe makes enough beef for about 10 heroes.

3 to 3½ pounds **beef chuck roast**
4 tablespoons **EVOO**
Kosher salt and **coarse black pepper**
3 **onions**, 2 chopped and 1 thinly sliced
6 cloves **garlic**, sliced
2 large fresh **bay leaves**
Small handful of fresh **thyme sprigs**
2 sprigs fresh **rosemary**
1½ teaspoons dried **oregano or marjoram**
1½ cups **dry red wine**
4 cups **beef stock**
1 (14.5-ounce) can **diced tomatoes**
4 **cubanelle** or 2 **bell peppers**, thinly sliced
Italian-style hoagie rolls (1 per person), split
    open like a book
Deli-sliced **provolone cheese** (optional)
Giardiniera (Italian hot pickled vegetables),
    store-bought or homemade (recipe follows)

Preheat the oven to 325°F. Bring the meat to room temperature.

In a large Dutch oven, heat 1 tablespoon EVOO (1 turn of the pan) over high heat. Pat the roast dry; season liberally with salt and pepper. Add the roast to the pan and brown evenly all over, then remove. Wipe the pan out and reduce the heat to medium. Add another 2 tablespoons EVOO (2 turns of the pan), the chopped onions, garlic, and herbs, and stir. Cook 5 to 6 minutes to soften. Add the wine to deglaze the pan and cook 5 minutes to reduce. Stir in the stock and tomatoes. Add the roast back to the pot, cover, and roast in the oven until tender, 3 to 3½ hours.

Remove the meat and let rest. Strain the sauce and return to the pot. Turn the heat to high and reduce the sauce by half, 10 to 15 minutes.

Meanwhile, in a skillet, heat the remaining

1 tablespoon EVOO (1 turn of the pan) over medium to medium-high heat. Add the cubanelle or bell peppers and sliced onion, and season with salt and pepper. Cook to soften, 10 to 15 minutes. Add some of the liquid from the meat to the onions and peppers to deglaze.

Thinly slice or shred the beef. Dip in some of the sauce and stuff the hoagie rolls. Top with cheese (if using), sautéed peppers, and giardiniera.

Serves 4 to 6 (with leftovers)

GIARDINIERA

¼ cup **kosher salt**
1 small **red bell pepper** or green cubanelle
    pepper, quartered, seeded, and cut into
    ½-inch slices
2 small **finger peppers**, Fresno chiles, or
    banana peppers, sliced into thin rings
2 cups **cauliflower** florets, blanched
2 **carrots**, cut into ¼-inch-thick slices
2 or 3 ribs **celery**, with leafy tops, chopped
    into 1-inch pieces
2 large cloves **garlic**, grated or minced
1 teaspoon dried **oregano** or **marjoram**
1 teaspoon **celery seeds**
¼ cup white balsamic or white wine **vinegar**
¼ cup **EVOO**
1 cup **Sicilian green olives**, pitted and chopped

Place the salt in a bowl large enough to hold all the vegetables. Add the bell or cubanelle pepper, chiles, cauliflower, carrots, and celery. Pour in enough cold water to cover. Stir to dissolve the

salt. Make sure the vegetables are covered with liquid. Cover and refrigerate for at least 2 days or up to 1 week before using.

Before serving, whisk up a dressing of garlic, oregano, celery seeds, vinegar, and EVOO. Drain the vegetables and toss with the dressing and olives.

Makes about 4 cups

⏰ OCTOBER 16/DINNER

We went to my friend Emily's for our Birthday~ Christmukkah Party.

⏰ OCTOBER 17/DINNER

Sunday Supper: **Hearty Mac & Cheese with Squash & Sausage**.

Hearty Mac & Cheese with Squash & Sausage

Cheese squash is a type of squash that you can buy at the farmers' market. It's a giant squash, orange-ish reddish in color, and you buy it by the pound. We bought a chunk that weighed a pound to a pound and a half. It tastes a little cheesy but you could substitute roasted butternut squash. Calabaza or butternut squash is what you would look for in a regular supermarket. You seed it and dice it fairly small.

Salt and **pepper**
1 pound **rigatoni pasta**
1 to 1½ pounds **cheese squash**, calabaza, or butternut squash, peeled and coarsely chopped
1 **onion**, finely chopped
3 cloves **garlic**, finely chopped
2 tablespoons finely chopped fresh **thyme**
2 tablespoons finely chopped fresh **sage**
5 or 6 **zucchini flowers**, stamens and stems removed
1½ to 2 cups **chicken stock**

1½ cups **Mammoth Cheddar** (a medium-sharp yellow Cheddar) or another sharp Cheddar
½ to ¾ cup shredded **pecorino cheese**
½ cup **heavy cream**
Freshly grated **nutmeg**
2 tablespoons **EVOO**
1 pound **merguez sausage** (spicy lamb sausage) or **Italian sweet** or **hot sausage**, casings removed

Bring a large pot of water to a boil. Salt the water and cook the rigatoni to al dente. Drain the pasta.

Meanwhile, in a large Dutch oven, combine the squash, onion, garlic, thyme, sage, zucchini flowers, and chicken stock. Partially cover and cook over medium heat until the squash and onion are tender. Puree the mixture until smooth. Pour the puree back into the pot.

Combine the two cheeses and set aside half for later. Stir the remaining cheese mixture, the cream, and a little nutmeg into the squash puree.

In a large skillet, heat the EVOO (2 turns of the pan) over medium-high heat. Add the sausage and, using the back of a wooden spoon, break it up it into little pieces as it starts to cook. Cook the sausage until browned, 4 to 5 minutes. Remove the sausage from the skillet and drain.

Position an oven rack in the center and preheat the broiler.

Add the sausage to the squash puree and toss it with the drained rigatoni. Transfer the mixture to a 9 by 13-inch baking dish. Top with the reserved cheese. Broil to brown it on top.

Serves 6

We had our friends over for dinner: amazing chef Alex Guarneschelli and her husband, Brandon Clark. I set out an antipasto of **Artichokes & Vinaigrette** (see July 17, page 93), tuna with red onion and capers on top, assorted Italian cheeses, assorted salumi, and assorted olives. The first course was the **Walnut Risotto with White Truffle & Pecorino**, followed by **Roasted Turkey Breast with Creamy Parmigiano Gravy**, **Basic Cranberry Sauce** with pomegranate seeds, and roasted squash. Apparently this is a very popular dinner (see October 11, pages 166 and 167). But this time I added **brussels sprouts**.

*I roasted parboiled **brussels sprouts** with pancetta and reduced balsamic vinegar drizzled over the top.*

● OCTOBER 21/DINNER

I served up the **Chicken with Pumpkin Seed Sauce** with a side of **black beans** and **Homemade Rice Pilaf** (see August 28, page 131).

Chicken with Pumpkin Seed Sauce

For a make-ahead meal, simmer the sauce only until not quite thick enough to serve, about 10 minutes. Return the chicken to the pot, turn off the heat, and let cool before covering and storing. Reheat over medium heat and thicken the sauce to serve.

4 to 6 **skin-on bone-in, chicken breast halves**
Kosher salt
6 to 8 **black peppercorns**
2 fresh **bay leaves**

2 small to medium **white** or **yellow onions**, 1 quartered and 1 chopped
Fresh herb bundle of cilantro, marjoram or oregano, and thyme
1¼ cups hulled **pumpkin seed** (pepitas)
2 tablespoons **EVOO**
1 teaspoon ground **cumin**
1 teaspoon dried **epazote** (optional)
Pinch of ground **cinnamon**
6 fresh **tomatillos**, husked and chopped
2 or 3 leaves **romaine** or **green leaf lettuce**, torn
2 large cloves **garlic**, grated or chopped
2 **serrano chiles** or 1 large jalapeño, seeded and chopped
Warm **corn tortillas**, for serving
Minced **red onion**, for serving

Place the chicken in a pot with just enough water to cover. Sprinkle with salt and add the peppercorns, bay leaves, quartered onion, and herb bundle. Bring to a low boil, then reduce the heat and poach the chicken until cooked through, 30 to 40 minutes.

Remove the chicken; strain and reserve the stock. Wipe the pot clean and return to the heat. Peel the skin off the chicken breasts and cover to keep warm until the sauce is ready.

Dry-toast the pumpkin seeds over medium heat until puffed and toasted, 4 to 5 minutes. Reserve ¼ cup of the toasted seeds for garnish. Puree the remaining seeds in a blender or food processor with 1 cup of the stock, the chopped onion, EVOO, cumin, epazote (if using), cinnamon, tomatillos, lettuce, garlic, and chiles.

Transfer the pumpkin seed puree to the pot

with 2½ to 3 cups of the reserved chicken stock and simmer to develop flavor and thicken, 20 minutes. Adjust the seasonings.

Pour the sauce over the chicken and garnish with the reserved toasted pumpkin seeds. Serve with warm corn tortillas, for wrapping, and minced red onions, for topping.

Serves 4 to 6

*I soak dried **black beans** overnight and then cook in stock seasoned with a little bit of cumin, salt, and pepper. Sometimes I throw in a hot pepper to simmer with the beans.*

● **OCTOBER 22/LUNCH**

Bowls of **Curried Squash Soup** with **Apple & Cheddar Melts**.

Curried Squash Soup

1 large **butternut squash** or other orange-flesh squash or pumpkin, peeled, seeded, and sliced
EVOO, for drizzling
Kosher salt and **pepper**
Freshly grated **nutmeg**
2 slightly rounded tablespoons **curry powder** (see Tip)
3 tablespoons **butter**
3 to 4 cloves **garlic**, chopped
2 **carrots**, thinly sliced
1 Gala or other crisp **apple**, peeled and chopped
1 **onion**, chopped
4 cups **chicken** or **vegetable stock**
½ cup **mango chutney**
Chopped **scallions and cilantro**, for garnish

Preheat the oven to 400°F. Dress the squash with some EVOO to coat lightly. Sprinkle with salt, pepper, and a little nutmeg. Coat with the curry powder. Roast until golden on the edges and very

tender, about 25 minutes. The spices will toast with the squash and fill the air with a terrific aroma.

Meanwhile, in a soup pot, heat a drizzle of EVOO over medium to medium-high heat. Then add the butter to melt. Stir in the garlic, carrots, apple, and onion and sprinkle with salt and pepper. Cook, partially covered, until softened, about 10 minutes.

Pour in the stock and chutney. Bring to a boil, reduce to a simmer, and cook until the vegetables are softened, about 20 minutes.

Add the roasted squash and puree with an immersion blender, thinning the soup with water if necessary. Alternatively, the soup can be pureed in batches in a food processor or high-power blender. Adjust the seasoning. Cool and store for a make-ahead meal, bringing to room temperature before reheating over a medium flame. Garnish with the scallions and cilantro.

Serves 4

For a substitute for curry powder, combine 2 teaspoons turmeric, 1½ teaspoons each ground cumin and ground coriander, ½ teaspoon each dry mustard and ground ginger, and ¼ teaspoon each ground cinnamon and cayenne pepper.

Apple & Cheddar Melts

8 slices good-quality **white bread**
Butter, softened, for spreading
Mango chutney (I like Patak's Major Grey)
¾ pound **sharp Cheddar cheese**, shredded or sliced
1 Gala or other crisp **apple**, peeled and thinly sliced

Spread each bread slice with softened butter on 1 side and chutney on the other. Fill the sandwiches, chutney sides in, with the cheese and apple in the center. Griddle the sandwiches over medium heat until deeply golden and the cheese has melted.

Makes 4 sandwiches

🕐 **OCTOBER 22/DINNER**

We began with **Country-Style Chicken Livers** (see April 20, page 18), but instead of serving them cold, I served them Tuscan-style: warm, with olive oil–drenched crostini (think sliced baguette or Italian bread toasted and drizzled with olive oil). The main was **White Coq au Vin** with **Buttered Herb Egg Noodles**.

White Coq au Vin

6 slices **bacon**, chopped
2 tablespoons **EVOO**
2¼ pounds **skinless boneless, chicken breasts and thighs**
Coarse salt and **pepper**
1 cup plus 2 tablespoons **flour**
1 large **onion**, thinly sliced
1 bulb **fennel**, thinly sliced, fronds reserved for garnish
12 **cremini mushrooms**, sliced
1 pound **baby Yukon Gold potatoes** or baby boiling potatoes, halved
2 tablespoons **butter**
1 cup dry **white wine**
2 to 3 cups **chicken stock**
2 tablespoons chopped **fresh tarragon**
A handful of flat-leaf **parsley leaves**, chopped
⅓ cup **Dijon mustard**

Preheat a large, heavy-bottomed pot over medium-high heat. Put in the bacon and cook until crispy, about 3 minutes. Drain the bacon on paper towels and set aside. Return the pot to the heat and add the EVOO (2 turns of the pan) to the bacon drippings.

Season the chicken generously with salt and pepper. Toss the chicken in 1 cup of the flour, shaking off the excess. Add the chicken to the pot in an even layer. Brown for 2 to 3 minutes on all sides. Transfer to a plate.

Add the onion, fennel, mushrooms, and potatoes to the pot and sauté until the vegetables

start to soften, 3 to 4 minutes. Add the butter and remaining 2 tablespoons flour to the veggies, stir to distribute, and cook for 1 minute. Add the wine and reduce the liquid for 2 minutes. Add only 2 cups of stock if you like a thicker consistency—or up to 3 cups if you like it a little looser—and bring it up to a bubble. Add the browned chicken. Cover the pot, reduce the heat to medium, and simmer until the chicken is cooked through, 10 to 12 minutes.

Add the chopped herbs and Dijon mustard and give it a stir to combine. Transfer to a serving platter.

Serves 4

Buttered Herb Egg Noodles

12 ounces **wide egg noodles**
Kosher salt and **pepper**
6 tablespoons (¾ stick) **unsalted butter**, cut into small pieces and chilled
3 tablespoons minced **flat-leaf parsley**
1 tablespoon chopped **fresh tarragon**
Grated zest of 1 **lemon** (optional)

Bring a large pot of water to a boil. Salt the water and cook the noodles until al dente.

Before draining the noodles, ladle ¼ cup of the noodle cooking water into a medium skillet. Set the skillet over low heat and, while whisking constantly, gradually add the butter, piece by piece (let each piece of butter melt into the sauce before adding the next bit) until a smooth sauce has formed. Stir in the parsley, tarragon, salt, and pepper. Add the lemon zest (if desired).

Drain the noodles in a colander set in the sink and leave whatever water clings to them—do not rinse. Transfer the noodles to a large bowl, add the sauce, and toss well.

Serves 4

Migas

Even though this already has jalapeño in it, you can serve it with more chopped or sliced jalapeño chile on top if you want it really spicy.

¼ cup **vegetable oil** or corn oil
6 **corn tortillas**, chopped into bite-size pieces
Salt and **pepper**
1 small **onion**, chopped
1 large **jalapeño chile**, chopped or thinly sliced
2 cloves **garlic**, finely chopped
A handful of **cilantro**, chopped
2 **tomatoes**, seeded and finely chopped
12 **eggs**
1 tablespoon **hot sauce**, or to taste
2 cups shredded **Monterey Jack cheese**
1 **avocado**, diced and sprinkled with fresh **lime juice** or lemon juice, for garnish

In a large nonstick skillet, heat the oil (4 turns of the pan) over medium-high heat. Add the tortilla pieces and brown well; season with salt. Add the onion, jalapeño, garlic, and cilantro and cook, stirring occasionally, for 5 minutes. Stir in the tomatoes.

In a bowl, whisk up the eggs, hot sauce, salt, and pepper. Pour into the skillet and scramble to desired doneness. (John likes his eggs a little runny; I like mine a little more well done.) Top with the cheese and avocado.

Serves 4

Poblano Mac & Manchego with Corn & Mushrooms

For a make-ahead meal, assemble the pasta and refrigerate. Then bring back to room temp before baking for 30 to 40 minutes.

3 tablespoons **vegetable** or **olive oil**
¾ pound **mushrooms**, thinly sliced
2 ears **corn**, kernels scraped from cobs
Salt and **pepper**
1 cup **chicken** or **vegetable stock**
2 to 3 medium **poblano chiles**, stemmed and seeded, chopped
1 small **onion**, chopped
2 cloves **garlic**, chopped
A small handful of **cilantro leaves**
3 tablespoons **butter**
2 tablespoons **flour**
1 cup **milk**
½ cup **heavy cream** or Mexican crema
2 cups shredded **Manchego cheese**
1 pound **short-cut pasta**, such as penne rigate or macaroni

In a skillet, heat the oil (3 turns of the pan). Add the mushrooms and cook until browned, 10 minutes. Add the corn kernels, season with salt and pepper to taste, and cook 5 to 6 minutes more.

In a blender or food processor, combine the stock, poblanos, onion, garlic, cilantro, salt, and pepper and puree.

In a saucepan, melt the butter over medium heat. Whisk in the flour and cook 1 minute. Whisk in the milk and cream and increase the heat a bit. Add the poblano puree and simmer to thicken and cook the sauce, 20 to 25 minutes. Stir in 1 cup of the Manchego.

Preheat the oven to 350°F.

Bring a large pot of water to a boil. Salt the water and cook the pasta to al dente. Before draining, reserve a ladleful of the starchy pasta

cooking water. Drain the pasta and toss with the sauce, mushrooms, and corn, adding a little of the starchy water if too thick.

Transfer to a 9 by 13-inch baking dish and top with the remaining Manchego. Bake until browned and bubbling, 15 to 20 minutes.

Serves 4 to 6

🕐 **OCTOBER 28/HALLOWEEN WEEKEND DINNER**

As starters, I put out cracked crab claws with **"Devilish" Cocktail Sauce** (see September 1, page 134) and **"Evil Eye" Deviled Eggs**. These were my Bull's-Eye Deviled Eggs (see April 24, page 29) that I renamed for Halloween. I used slices of pimiento-stuffed olives for the eyes, with Fresno chile eyebrows. For dinner, a fall family favorite: **Cider Beef** with **Mashed Potatoes & Parsnips with Cheddar**.

Cider Beef

I make this a lot. Everybody loves this.

2 heads **garlic**, tops cut off to expose the cloves
EVOO, for drizzling
Salt and **pepper**
¼ to ⅓ pound thick-cut **uncured bacon**, cut into fat batons
6 tablespoons (¾ stick) **butter**
2½ to 3 pounds **beef chuck**, cut into 2-inch cubes
2 tablespoons **flour**, plus more for dredging the beef
3 **carrots**, sliced in 2-inch chunks on an angle
2 **apples**, such as Honeycrisp, peeled and chopped
2 or 3 ribs **celery**, chopped
1 large **onion**, chopped
2 fresh **bay leaves**
2 to 2½ cups **organic cider** (it should look cloudy)
2 (10.5-ounce) cans **beef consommé**

Preheat the oven to 400°F.

Drizzle the garlic with EVOO, season with salt and pepper, wrap in foil, and roast to tender, 40 to 45 minutes. Take out the garlic and leave the oven on but reduce the temperature to 325°F.

Heat a large Dutch oven over medium-high heat. Add a drizzle of EVOO and the bacon. Brown and crisp the bacon, then remove with a slotted spoon and set aside. Pour some of the fat out of the pan and add 2 tablespoons of the butter.

Pat the meat dry and season liberally with salt and pepper. Dredge in flour and add to the hot pan in batches. Cook to crispy and deep brown. Add more butter as needed, 2 tablespoons at a time. Set the browned meat aside with the bacon.

Add to the pan the carrots, apples, celery, onion, bay leaves, and salt and pepper to taste and partially cover. Cook to soften the vegetables for a few minutes, then sprinkle with 2 tablespoons flour. Stir for a minute, then add the cider and consommé. Squeeze the roasted garlic into the pan and stir to combine. Add the reserved beef and bacon back to the pan, bring to a boil, then cover and transfer to the oven. Braise the meat until very tender and the sauce has thickened, about 2 hours.

Let stand for 20 minutes. Remove the bay leaves before serving.

Serves 6

Mashed Potatoes & Parsnips with Cheddar

2½ pounds **russet (baking) potatoes** (about 5 potatoes), peeled and cubed
2 or 3 large **parsnips**, peeled and cubed
Salt and **pepper**
2 tablespoons **butter**
1½ cups shredded **extra, extra, extra sharp white Cheddar** (see Tip)
1 cup **milk** (whole or 2%)
Freshly grated **nutmeg**
¼ cup finely chopped **chives**

In a large pot, cover the potatoes and parsnips with cold water. Bring to a boil, salt the water, and cook until fork-tender. Drain and return to the pot; mash with the butter, cheese, and milk. Season with salt, pepper, and nutmeg. Stir in the chives.

Serves 6

I used XXX Cheddar from Oscar's Adirondack Smokehouse in Warrensburg, New York. They ship anywhere and it is the best Cheddar cheese I have ever had.

Croque Madame with White Truffle

3 tablespoons **butter**
2 tablespoons **flour**
1¼ to 1½ cups **whole milk**
White truffle, shaved
⅛ teaspoon freshly grated **nutmeg**
Salt and **pepper**
4 large **eggs**
4 slices **white bread** (I like Amy's Bread), ½ to
   ¾ inch thick
8 slices **prosciutto cotto**
¾ pound **Fontina Val d'Aosta**, shredded
Chopped fresh **parsley, chives, or thyme** (or a
   combo), for garnish

Preheat the oven to 375°F.

In a small saucepan, melt 2 tablespoons of the butter over medium-low heat. Whisk in the flour and cook 1 minute or so. Whisk in the milk and bring to a bubble, then drop the heat to low. Stir in the truffle, nutmeg, and salt and pepper to taste. When the sauce coats the back of a spoon, remove from the heat.

In a large nonstick skillet, heat the remaining 1 tablespoon butter over medium-low heat. When the butter melts, add the eggs, keeping the whites separate from each other. Cook the eggs to order: My husband likes over-easy. I do the guests' eggs however they like.

Place the bread on a baking sheet. Top each piece of bread liberally with the sauce, 2 slices of the ham, and the cheese. Bake until deeply golden and the bread is browned on the bottom. Then top that with an egg. Garnish with the herbs.

Serves 4

I made a big antipasto with **Artichokes & Vinaigrette** (see July 17, page 93), beets with my balsamic drizzle, assorted Italian meats and cheeses, and **Giardiniera** (see October 14, page 168). Then we had the **Osso Buco** with **Polenta**.

Osso Buco

1 **orange**
3 tablespoons **EVOO**
4 to 6 **veal shank** pieces, tied with kitchen twine
Salt and **pepper**
2 tablespoons **flour**, plus more for dredging the
   veal
4 or 5 cloves **garlic**, sliced
2 or 3 small ribs **celery**, with leafy tops, chopped
1 large **carrot**, chopped
1 **onion**, chopped
1 teaspoon **fennel seeds**
3 tablespoons chopped fresh **rosemary**
2 tablespoons chopped fresh **thyme**
2 tablespoons **tomato paste**
2 large **fresh bay leaves**
1 cup **dry white wine**
2 cups **chicken stock**
A healthy pinch of **saffron threads**
1 (14.5-ounce) can **diced tomatoes in juice**
1 **red Fresno chile**, halved and seeded, or
   1 teaspoon crushed red pepper flakes
Grated zest of 1 **lemon**
¼ cup finely chopped **flat-leaf parsley leaves**
¼ cup **pistachio nuts**, toasted and processed into
   crumbs

Pull off a long strip of orange zest, then grate the rest of the zest and juice the orange. Set aside.

Preheat the oven to 325°F.

In a large Dutch oven, heat the EVOO (3 turns of the pan) over medium-high to high heat. Sprinkle the shanks with salt and pepper and dredge lightly in a little flour. Add to the pan and brown all over, turning occasionally, 12 to 15 minutes. Transfer to a large plate.

Add the garlic, celery, carrot, onion, and fennel seeds to the pan and cook, stirring, for 3 to 4 minutes. Add the rosemary, thyme, tomato paste, and bay leaves, sprinkle with salt and pepper, and stir 1 minute. Sprinkle the 2 tablespoons flour over the vegetables and stir 1 minute, then pour in the wine and deglaze the pot, scraping and stirring 1 minute. Add the chicken stock and saffron, followed by the tomatoes. Add the strip of orange zest, the orange juice, and the chile. Scrape down the pot and add back the meat. Cover and transfer to the oven. Cook for 2 hours, turning the meat once about halfway through.

When the meat is about ready to come out of the oven, combine the grated orange zest on a cutting board with the lemon zest. Chop in the parsley and pistachios, to make the gremolata topping.

Transfer the shanks to a platter and cut off the kitchen twine. Fish the bay leaves out of the sauce and place the Dutch oven back on the stove over medium-high heat. Whisk the sauce to combine and thicken, 4 to 5 minutes.

Serve the shanks in shallow bowls topped with the chunky sauce and gremolata.

Serves 4 to 6

Polenta

2 cups **chicken stock**
1 cup **whole milk**
1 cup coarse **cornmeal**
A couple of handfuls of freshly grated **Parmigiano-Reggiano cheese**
1 tablespoon **honey**
1 to 2 tablespoons **butter**
Salt and **pepper**
Freshly grated **nutmeg**

In a medium saucepan, bring the stock and milk to a boil. Reduce the heat to a simmer and gradually whisk in the cornmeal. Cook, stirring occasionally, for 15 to 20 minutes; it should be thin enough to pour, but not liquidy. Stir in the Parm, honey, butter, and salt, pepper, and nutmeg to taste.

Serves 4 to 6

OCTOBER 30/BREAKFAST

Whole-Grain Waffles with Toasted Walnuts

Serve the waffles topped with Warm Apples in Maple Syrup (recipe follows).

2 cups **multigrain pancake mix** (I like Highland Sugarworks)
2 **eggs**, lightly beaten
1 to 2 cups **milk** (whole or 2%)
2 tablespoons melted **butter**, plus more for buttering the waffle iron
1 teaspoon **vanilla extract**
⅓ cup chopped toasted **walnuts**
Freshly grated **nutmeg**

Heat the waffle iron.

In a bowl, combine the pancake mix, eggs, 1 cup of the milk, 2 tablespoons melted butter, and the vanilla. If the batter is too thick to pour, add up to 1 cup more milk. Stir in the walnuts and nutmeg to taste. I cook my waffles in a Cuisinart waffle iron, on high—I like them extra crispy.

Serves 4

WARM APPLES IN MAPLE SYRUP

2 large **Honeycrisp apples**, sliced or chopped
²⁄₃ cup **dark amber maple syrup**
¹⁄₃ cup **organic apple cider** (it should look cloudy)
1 **cinnamon stick**

Combine everything in a saucepan and bring to a low bubble. Keep warm over low heat.

Makes about 2 cups

🕐 **OCTOBER 30/DINNER**

Dinner was **Roasted Turkey Breast with Herb Butter**, **Mashed Potatoes & Parsnips with Cheddar** (see October 28, page 178), **Roasted Butternut Squash**, and **green beans and cremini**.

Roasted Turkey Breast with Herb Butter

5- to 6-pound **skin-on, boneless turkey breast**
8 tablespoons (1 stick) **butter**, softened
1 small **shallot**, chopped
1 clove **garlic**, pasted
1 teaspoon grated **lemon zest**
1 tablespoon **lemon juice**
¹⁄₄ cup **chopped fresh herbs** (I used a mix of thyme, chives, parsley, and rosemary)
Salt and **pepper**

Preheat the oven to 325°F. Place the turkey on a wire rack set over a baking sheet.

Combine the butter, shallot, garlic, lemon zest, lemon juice, herbs, and salt and pepper to taste. Slather the garlic-herb butter over the turkey breast and sprinkle liberally with salt and pepper.

Roast for 1½ to 2 hours; the internal temperature should be 165°F. Let rest for 10 minutes before carving.

Serves 6

Green beans and cremini: Sauté ³⁄₄ pound sliced mushrooms in a thin layer of EVOO with a couple of tablespoons of butter. When the mushrooms are browned, add 2 finely chopped shallots, stir for a few more minutes, season with salt and pepper, and deglaze the pan with Marsala. Toss the mushrooms with 1 pound green beans that have been blanched in salted water for 5 minutes.

Roasted Butternut Squash

You can serve each person a half or you can scoop out the flesh into a serving bowl—whatever makes you and yours happy.

3 medium **butternut** or **acorn squash**, halved and seeded
6 tablespoons (¾ stick) **butter**, cut into pieces and softened
½ cup **honey** or **maple syrup**
Freshly grated **nutmeg**
Pepper

Preheat the oven to 400°F.

Place the squash halves on a large baking sheet cut side up. Divide the butter pieces among all 6 halves, smearing it all over the cut sides.

Drizzle each half with honey and season with nutmeg and pepper. Roast the squash until the flesh is tender when poked with a fork, 40 to 60 minutes.

Serves 6

⏱ OCTOBER 31/DINNER

We had **Pasta e Fagioli**, which I amped up with leftovers from the **Osso Buco** we had recently (see October 29, page 176).

Pasta e Fagioli

Make this dish with or without meat for a hearty, slightly sweet spin on a classic.

2 heads **garlic**, tops cut off to expose the cloves
5 tablespoons **EVOO**, plus more for drizzling
Salt and **pepper**
¼ pound **guanciale** or **pancetta**, chopped
2 fresh **bay leaves**
2 sprigs fresh **rosemary** plus 2 sprigs fresh **thyme**, tied together
2 ribs **celery**, finely chopped, leaves reserved for optional garnish
1 **carrot**, finely chopped
1 **onion**, quartered lengthwise, then thinly sliced
2 tablespoons **tomato paste**
6 to 8 cups **chicken stock**
1 (15-ounce) can **cannellini beans**, rinsed and drained
1 (15-ounce) can **garbanzo beans** (chickpeas), rinsed and drained
¾ to 1 pound (1½ to 2 cups) **cooked chopped veal** or **pork** (optional)
1 small head **escarole**, chopped
Freshly grated **nutmeg**
½ pound **mezzi rigatoni** or penne rigate pasta
Grated **Grana Padano cheese**, for serving
Minced **onion**, for garnish (optional)

Preheat the oven to 425°F.

Drizzle the garlic with EVOO and sprinkle with salt and pepper. Wrap in foil and roast until soft, 40 to 45 minutes.

Meanwhile, in a soup pot, heat the 5 tablespoons EVOO (5 turns of the pan) over medium-high heat. Add the guanciale and brown, about 3 minutes. Stir in the bay leaves, rosemary and thyme, celery, carrot, and onion, and sprinkle with salt and pepper. Cook, partially covered, stirring occasionally, until the vegetables are soft, 10 to 15 minutes. Add 1 tablespoon of the tomato paste and let that cook out for a few minutes. Pour in the stock and bring to boil, then reduce the heat to a simmer.

Place 1 cup of the soup in a blender or food processor with the roasted garlic cloves (popped out of the skins), the remaining 1 tablespoon tomato paste, and half of the cannellini and garbanzo beans. Process until smooth, adding water if the soup is too thick to blend. Transfer back to the soup pot and stir to combine, adding the remaining whole beans.

Bring the soup back to a bubble. Add the veal (if using) and escarole and cook until the greens are wilted. Season with a few grates of nutmeg. Cook the pasta in the soup.

Top bowls of soup with cheese, an extra drizzle of EVOO, and celery leaves and minced onion, if using.

Serves 4

Celebrate the season with Rachael and John.

NOVEMBER

TUESDAY/1	WEDNESDAY/2	THURSDAY/3	FRIDAY/4	SATURDAY/5

THURSDAY/3

DINNER
Chicagoan-Italian roast beef heroes, giardiniera

FRIDAY/4

DINNER
homemade hot sausage, kale & lentil soup, Grandpa's stuffed artichokes

SATURDAY/5

DINNER
mushroom and burgundy stew, Bolognese with Barolo wine & black pepper

FRIDAY/11	SATURDAY/12	SUNDAY/13	MONDAY/14	TUESDAY/15

FRIDAY/11

DINNER
French onion soup with wild mushrooms

SATURDAY/12

DINNER
pizzoccheri-style supper

SUNDAY/13

DINNER
cheesy chicken in poblano sauce

TUESDAY/15

DINNER
coq au vin blanc

MONDAY/21	TUESDAY/22	WEDNESDAY/23	THURSDAY/24	FRIDAY/25

MONDAY/21

DINNER
Portuguese soup

THURSDAY/24

DINNER
roasted turkey breast and legs, apple & onion stuffing, roasted butternut squash, Elsa's poulet sauce, mashed potatoes & parsnips with Cheddar, green bean casserole, basic cranberry sauce, peas with shallots

FRIDAY/25

BREAKFAST
almond custard brioche French toast

DINNER
cider beef, turkey soup, mashed potatoes & parsnips with Cheddar

SUNDAY/6

BRUNCH
chapata with Man-chego potatoes, eggs and Serrano ham
DINNER
jalapeño poppers, Jane Fox's famous tortilla soup

MONDAY/7

TUESDAY/8

DINNER
touchdown chili

WEDNESDAY/9

THURSDAY/10

DINNER
sliced steak sliders; apple slaw; pickled onions, peppers & cucumbers; pumpkin Cheddar mac & cheese

WEDNESDAY/16

DINNER
Bolognese with Barolo wine & black pepper

THURSDAY/17

DINNER
cider beef, country-style chicken livers, mashed potatoes & parsnips with Cheddar

FRIDAY/18

SATURDAY/19

DINNER
egg tagliatelle with truffle butter

SUNDAY/20

SATURDAY/26

LUNCH
hot turkey melts with sharp Cheddar
DINNER
roasted garlic & caramelized onion sauce with homemade turkey sausage

SUNDAY/27

DINNER
homemade marinara (with a kick), pizza Margherita, blender pizza sauce, potato pizza with white truffle, pizza crust

MONDAY/28

DINNER
winter vegetable sauce

TUESDAY/29

DINNER
pasta with golden cauliflower

WEDNESDAY/30

Made **Chicagoan-Italian Roast Beef Heroes** (see October 14, page 168) for 30 people after one of John's Cringe gigs. I put them together at the TV studio because we were making the recipe for the daytime show and we had several pots of the beef working.

⏱ **NOVEMBER 4/DINNER**

I served **Grandpa's Stuffed Artichokes** and **Kale & Lentil Soup** made with **Homemade Hot Sausage**.

Grandpa's Stuffed Artichokes

Grandpa Emmanuel's stuffed artichokes appear star-like, which is what makes them so nice for the holidays. And they are delicious at room temperature, so you can make them ahead and they'll be ready whenever you are. Everyone in my family loves them so much we could all eat them as a meal, but we portion 1 large artichoke for every 4 people as a starter. Also, be sure any time you serve artichokes to place small dishes on the table to collect the leaves.

2 large or 4 medium male (tall and pointy) **artichokes**, trimmed (see Tip, page 93)
1 or 2 **lemons** (depending on if you're steaming or boiling)
⅓ cup **EVOO**, plus more for drizzling
3 tablespoons **butter**
12 flat **anchovy fillets**
6 cloves **garlic**, finely chopped
½ teaspoon crushed **red pepper flakes**
1½ to 2 cups **panko** or **homemade bread crumbs**
½ cup chopped **flat-leaf parsley**
1 cup grated **Parmigiano-Reggiano cheese**
Coarse black pepper

You can either steam or boil the artichokes. **To steam:** Set up a steamer basket over boiling water. Rub the artichokes with 1 cut lemon as you trim them. Steam the artichokes until they're nice and tender and the leaves pull away easily, about 30 minutes. **To boil:** Bring a large pot of water to a boil, then salt the water. Halve 2 lemons and juice 1 into the boiling water. Rub the artichokes with the cut lemon as you trim them. Add the lemon halves and artichokes to the water; cover with a small kitchen towel or place a plate a bit smaller than the pot lid into the pot to keep the artichokes submerged while cooking. Boil until the leaves pull away easily, about 20 minutes.

Cool the artichokes upside down so they can drain. Carefully pull out the center pieces and scrape out the choke (all the little fibers at the center), leaving the artichoke intact. Place the artichokes in a baking dish with ⅛ inch water, just enough to produce a little steam in the oven.

In a skillet, warm up the ⅓ cup EVOO over medium heat. Melt the butter into the oil. When that's warm, add the anchovies and stir until melted into the oil and butter. Add the garlic and pepper flakes and stir that for a minute or two. Add the panko a little at a time; keep adding until all of the butter-oil mixture has been absorbed evenly. Then keep cooking to toast that until deeply golden. Let cool, then stir in the parsley, Parm, and black pepper to taste.

Fill all of the leaves, leaf by leaf, of each arti-

choke until you get into the center. They should more than triple in width so you end up with a nice big casserole dish just for 2 of the large artichokes. Any leftover bread-crumb mixture can be piled onto the top of the artichokes to fill the center.

Position a rack in the middle of the oven and preheat to 400°F.

Drizzle the artichokes with a little more EVOO, cover, and roast until hot, about 20 minutes. Uncover and roast until the edges of the leaves curl up and then become a bit pointy again (you've trimmed them square at the top, but once you roast them they curl up and look like the points of a star). Serve at room temperature.

Makes 2 or 4 stuffed artichokes

Kale & Lentil Soup

You could add a cup of small-cut pasta and omit the potato, or add diced or crushed tomato and omit the tomato paste.

2 tablespoons **EVOO**, plus extra for drizzling
1½ pounds **Homemade Hot Sausage** (recipe follows)
1 **onion**, finely chopped
2 **carrots**, finely chopped
1 or 2 small ribs **celery**, finely chopped
1 **russet (baking) potato**, peeled and finely chopped
1 large **bay leaf**
Herb bundle: a few sprigs each of fresh rosemary, thyme, and parsley, tied together
Salt and **pepper**
3 tablespoons **tomato paste**
½ cup **dry white** or **red wine**
4 cups **chicken stock**
1¼ cups **brown lentils**
1 small bundle **lacinato kale** (also called black, Tuscan, or dinosaur kale), stemmed and finely chopped or shredded
Freshly grated **nutmeg**
Freshly grated **pecorino or Parmigiano-Reggiano cheese**, for serving
Warm crusty bread, for mopping

In a large soup pot, heat 2 tablespoons EVOO, 2 turns of the pan over medium heat. Crumble in the sausage and brown. Then add the onion, carrots, celery, potato, bay leaf, herb bundle, and salt and pepper to taste. Partially cover and cook 7 to 8 minutes, stirring occasionally. Stir in the tomato paste and cook until fragrant, 1 to 2 minutes. Add the wine and reduce a minute. Add the stock and 2 cups water and bring to a boil. Add the lentils and cook to tender, 25 to 30 minutes.

Wilt the kale into the soup, add a little nutmeg, and adjust the seasonings. Serve in shallow bowls and top with drizzle of EVOO and cheese. Pass bread for mopping.

Serves 4 to 6

HOMEMADE HOT SAUSAGE

1½ pounds **ground pork**, **dark meat chicken**, **turkey (dark and white meat)**, or **lamb**
4 cloves **garlic**, minced
2 teaspoons crushed **red pepper flakes**
2 teaspoons **sweet paprika**
2 teaspoons **granulated onion**
1½ teaspoons **ground sage** (if using pork or lamb) or **poultry seasoning** (if using chicken or turkey)
1 teaspoon **fennel seeds**
Salt and **pepper**

Combine all the ingredients and chill several hours or up to 2 days ahead of using.

Makes 1½ pounds sausage

I make a lot of different meat sauces. I made this **Bolognese with Barolo Wine & Black Pepper** for my mother because one of her favorite wines in the world is Barolo.

Bolognese with Barolo Wine & Black Pepper

The combo of beef and red wine is fantastic, so if you like this, you'll probably like the Mushroom & Burgundy Stew that follows.

2 tablespoons **EVOO**
¼ pound **pancetta** or guanciale, cut into small dice
1½ pounds **coarse-ground beef chuck**
2 tablespoons **butter**
Kosher or **sea salt** and **coarse black pepper**
Herb bundle: a couple of sprigs each of fresh rosemary, sage, and thyme tied together
1 fresh **bay leaf**
1 **carrot**, finely chopped
1 or 2 small ribs **celery**, finely chopped
1 **onion**, finely chopped
4 cloves **garlic**, finely chopped
3 tablespoons **tomato paste**
1½ cups Barolo or other **dry red wine**
1 (28- or 32-ounce) can **San Marzano tomatoes** (look for DOP on the label)
2 (10.5-ounce) cans **beef consommé**
1 cup **whole milk**
1 pound **pappardelle** or bucatini pasta
Freshly grated **Parmigiano-Reggiano** or pecorino cheese, for serving

In a large Dutch oven, heat the EVOO (2 turns of the pan) over medium-high heat. Add the pancetta or guanciale and brown to crisp, remove and drain. Pat the chuck dry. Add the butter to the pan; add the beef and brown well, seasoning liberally with pepper and a little salt. Break up the meat as it browns. Add the herb bundle, bay leaf, carrot, celery, onion, and garlic and cook, stirring, a few minutes to soften. Add the tomato paste and stir until fragrant, 1 to 2 minutes, then add the wine and reduce by half. Add the tomatoes and consommé. Break up the tomatoes a bit, then reduce the heat to a simmer and cook about 30 minutes to break down the tomatoes.

Stir in the milk and simmer 20 to 30 minutes more over low heat while you cook the pasta.

Bring a large pot of water to a boil. Salt the water and cook the pasta to al dente. Before draining, ladle out and reserve 1 cup of the starchy pasta cooking water. Drain the pasta.

Toss the drained pasta and sauce with the starchy cooking water. Serve in shallow bowls and top with cheese.

Serves 4 to 6

Mushroom & Burgundy Stew

For a make-ahead meal, cool the stew completely and reheat over medium heat to bubbling. Don't make the egg noodles until you're ready to serve.

¼ cup **EVOO**
4 ounces **pancetta** or 4 slices bacon, chopped (optional)
2 pounds **cremini mushrooms**, halved
2 **onions**, chopped
2 **carrots**, chopped
2 ribs **celery**, chopped
4 large cloves **garlic**, sliced
2 **bay leaves**

A sprig of fresh **marjoram**, finely chopped, or 1 teaspoon dried

Leaves from a few sprigs of fresh **thyme**, finely chopped

Salt and **pepper**

3 tablespoons **flour**

2 tablespoons **tomato paste**

2 tablespoons **Worcestershire sauce**

2½ cups **red burgundy wine**

4 cups **beef** or **mushroom stock**

1 pound **egg noodles**

2 tablespoons **butter**

A handful of **flat-leaf parsley**, finely chopped

In a large Dutch oven, heat the EVOO (4 turns of the pan) over medium-high heat. Add the pancetta or bacon (if using) and cook until crispy. Add the mushrooms and cook until browned and tender, about 15 minutes.

Add the onions, carrots, celery, garlic, bay leaves, marjoram, thyme, salt, and pepper. Cover and cook, stirring occasionally, for 10 minutes to soften the vegetables.

Stir in the flour and cook for 1 minute. Stir in the tomato paste and Worcestershire sauce. Add the wine, stir, and reduce by half, a couple of minutes, then add the stock and simmer to thicken a bit.

While the stew simmers, bring a pot of water to a boil, salt it, and cook off the egg noodles just before you're ready to serve. Drain them when they have a little bite to them and add back to the hot pot. Stir in the butter, parsley, and salt to taste. Serve the noodles in shallow bowls topped with stew.

Serves 4

⏺ **NOVEMBER 6/BRUNCH**

We had **Chapata with Manchego Potatoes, Eggs & Serrano Ham,** which is based on a lovely meal, a little appetizer, that I had with a poached egg and Serrano ham at Seamus Mullen's restaurant, Tertulia. It's a riff on his thing. Chapata is a simple and delicious tapa, an alternative to garlic bread. I just added more stuff to the potato for the chapata.

I was daydreaming about it and it was so good and I was just in the mood for it. That was my at-home version when I can't get to Seamus's place.

Chapata with Manchego Potatoes, Eggs & Serrano Ham

Chapata works best with ripe summer tomatoes, but you can also use a hothouse tomato in the winter (I find them year-round—usually somebody is growing them indoors from heirloom tomatoes). The chapata itself is delicious, but I went on to top it with potatoes, eggs, and serrano ham. Serrano is a Spanish ham that is similar to prosciutto. If you can't find serrano, you can always substitute prosciutto.

2 small **russet (baking) potatoes**, peeled and cubed

2 **ciabatta rolls**, split horizontally

1 clove **garlic**, halved

1 **tomato**, halved

EVOO, for drizzling

Salt and **pepper**

Chicken stock

½ cup freshly grated **Manchego cheese**

½ teaspoon **sweet paprika**

A handful of **flat-leaf parsley**, finely chopped

4 slices **serrano ham** (about 1 ounce each)

2 **eggs**, cooked however you like (John likes his over easy)

Put the potatoes in a medium saucepan with cold water to cover. Bring to a boil and cook until fork-tender, about 10 minutes.

While the potatoes are cooking, preheat the broiler and toast the rolls.

Rub the toasted ciabatta with the garlic, then rub the halved tomato all over the bread. Drizzle with some EVOO and sprinkle with a little salt and pepper.

When the potatoes are done, drain them and mash with a little chicken stock to the desired consistency. Mash in the Manchego, paprika, parsley, and salt and pepper to taste. Pile the mashed potatoes on the rolls and top with the ham and an egg.

Serves 2

You can take a tomato that's a little past perfect or an underripe winter tomato and throw it into the oven just for a couple of minutes. Get it squishy and then halve it.

🕐 **NOVEMBER 6/DINNER**

I made **Jalapeño Poppers** (see April 26, page 30) and my friend **Jane Fox's Famous Tortilla Soup**. Her soup is made lightning-fast with rotisserie chicken. It figures; she *is* a Texan.

Jane Fox's Famous Tortilla Soup

12 **corn tortillas**
All-natural **cooking spray**
Salt and **pepper**
3 to 4 tablespoons **corn oil**
1 large **onion**, chopped
2 or 3 cloves **garlic**, chopped
A handful of **cilantro leaves**, coarsely chopped
2 **fresh bay leaves**
2 tablespoons **mild to medium chili powder** (such as Gebhardt's blend) or ground ancho chile powder
1 tablespoon ground **cumin**
1 (14.5-ounce) can **diced tomatoes with green chiles**
6 cups **chicken stock**
1 **rotisserie chicken**, skin and bones discarded, shredded or diced
2 **avocados**, diced
2 **limes**, cut into wedges
1 small **red onion**, finely chopped
2 large **jalapeño chiles**, seeded and chopped
Queso fresco, crumbled

Preheat the oven to 375°F. Cut 6 of the tortillas into 1-inch-wide strips. Arrange on a baking sheet in a single layer and coat with cooking spray. Bake to deeply golden and season with salt.

In a large Dutch oven or soup pot, heat the oil over medium-high heat. Chop the remaining 6 tortillas into 1- to 1½-inch squares. Add to the hot oil and cook, stirring, to brown, 2 to 3 minutes. Add the onion, garlic, cilantro, bay leaves, chili powder, cumin, and salt and pepper to taste.

Stir to toast the spices and cook until the onions are translucent, 7 to 8 minutes. Add the tomatoes and stock and bring to a boil. Add the chicken and reduce to a simmer until ready to serve.

To serve, place some avocado at the bottom of each soup bowl and douse with a healthy squeeze of lime juice, then fill the bowls with soup. At the table, top the soup with red onion, tortilla strips, jalapeño, and queso fresco.

Serves 4 to 6

🕐 **NOVEMBER 8/DINNER**

We had **Touchdown Chili** (see September 7, page 140).

🕐 **NOVEMBER 9/DINNER**

Wednesday we had pizza at Motorino on 12th Street, our favorite pizza place in New York City. My favorite pizzas there are the alici (I make an at-home version of this; see March 7, page 278), which is an anchovy pizza with raw tomato on top; the cremini mushroom pizza with house-made sausage and black olives (very yummy); and the pizza topped with hot sopressata.

🕐 **NOVEMBER 10/DINNER**

What we had for dinner could be two separate meals, but I had made them that day on the show, so I brought them home and served them both up.

Pumpkin Cheddar Mac & Cheese

Salt and **pepper**
1 pound **whole wheat** or **whole-grain short-cut pasta**, such as rigatoni or penne
4 tablespoons (½ stick) **butter**
3 slightly rounded tablespoons **flour**
1 cup **amber beer**

1 tablespoon **honey** or **maple syrup**
2 cups **whole milk**
A couple of pinches of **ground cloves** or ½ teaspoon allspice
About 1 teaspoon **dry mustard**
A pinch of **cayenne pepper**
Freshly grated **nutmeg**
1 (15-ounce) can **unsweetened pumpkin puree** or 2 cups pureed roasted fresh pumpkin or butternut squash
2½ cups shredded **sharp yellow Cheddar cheese**
Sweet paprika, for sprinkling
Chopped **parsley** or **chives**, for garnish

Preheat the broiler.

Bring a large pot of water to a boil. Salt the water and cook the pasta to al dente. Drain the pasta.

Meanwhile, in a medium saucepan, melt the butter over medium heat. Whisk in the flour and cook 1 minute. Increase the heat a bit and add the beer, cook until almost evaporated, then whisk in the honey, then the milk. Season with the cloves, mustard, cayenne, a little nutmeg, and some salt and pepper. Cook until thick enough to coat the spoon, a couple of minutes. Taste and adjust the seasonings.

Whisk in the pumpkin. Stir in about 2 cups of the cheese with a wooden spoon. Combine the sauce with the pasta and arrange in a 9 by 13-inch baking dish or individual ramekins and scatter the remaining ½ cup cheese on top. Sprinkle with a light dusting of paprika and broil until browned and bubbling. Garnish with chopped parsley or chives.

Serves 4 to 6

Sliced Steak Sliders

You need to make the pickles at least 1 day ahead.

1½ pounds **flat iron steaks** or **flank steak**
Vegetable oil, for drizzling
Salt and **pepper**
Bourbon BBQ Sauce (see June 24, page 71)
½ to ¾ cup **beef stock**
12 **soft slider rolls**, split
Pickled Onions, Peppers & Cucumbers (recipe follows)
Apple Slaw (recipe follows)

Coat the steak lightly with vegetable oil and season with salt and pepper. Let come to room temp.

Heat a cast-iron pan, griddle, or grill pan over medium-high to high heat. Add the steak and cook 4 minutes on each side. Let rest, then thinly slice the meat against the grain, on an angle. Thin the BBQ sauce with a little stock and add the meat to it. Serve the sliced meat on slider rolls with pickles and slaw.

Makes 12 sloppy sliders

PICKLED ONIONS, PEPPERS & CUCUMBERS

1 cup **white balsamic vinegar**
¼ cup **sugar**
1 rounded tablespoon **kosher salt**
1 small **red onion**, sliced
½ **seedless cucumber** or 3 medium kirby cucumbers, sliced
2 **red Fresno chiles**, sliced into rings
4 or 5 **fresh bay leaves**
A handful of fresh **dill tops**
A few sprigs of **flat-leaf parsley**
1 teaspoon **mustard seeds**
1 teaspoon **black peppercorns**
1 teaspoon **coriander seeds**

In a small saucepan, combine the vinegar, sugar, salt, and 1 cup water. Bring to a low boil to dissolve the salt and sugar, then reduce the heat to low.

Layer the onion, cucumber, chiles, herbs, and spices into a tight-fitting plastic or glass container, then douse with the brine. Cover the container tightly and refrigerate 24 hours or several days, turning occasionally.

Makes 2 cups

APPLE SLAW

Juice of ½ **lemon**
1 tablespoon **cider vinegar**
1 rounded tablespoon **Dijon mustard**
1 rounded tablespoon **honey**
⅓ cup **vegetable oil**
Salt and **pepper**
1 Gala **apple**, quartered and thinly sliced lengthwise
¼ medium head **red** or **green cabbage**, shredded

In a large bowl, combine the lemon juice, vinegar, mustard, honey, oil, salt, and pepper. Add the apple and cabbage and toss in the dressing.

Makes about 2 cups

🕐 **NOVEMBER 11/DINNER**

French Onion Soup with Wild Mushrooms

Instead of rubbing the toasts with garlic, you can spread them with roasted garlic (see Tip, page 114).

1 ounce **dried porcini mushrooms**
10 tablespoons (1¼ sticks) **butter**
6 medium **onions**, thinly sliced
2 **fresh bay leaves**
1 teaspoon **ground thyme**
1 pound **mixed mushrooms** (cremini, shiitake, oysters, or whatever blend you like), thinly sliced
Salt and **pepper**
1 cup **dry sherry**
4 cloves **garlic**, 3 finely chopped or thinly sliced, 1 cut in half
4 cups **beef stock**
4 slices thick-cut **crusty French** or **Italian bread**
1 cup freshly grated **Gruyère cheese**
1 tablespoon **fresh thyme** or chopped flat-leaf parsley

Put the porcini in a small saucepan with enough water to cover. Simmer until tender. Transfer the reconstituted mushrooms and the soaking liquid (all except the last few spoonfuls, because that's where grit tends to settle when you reconstitute dried mushrooms) to a food processor and puree. Set the puree aside.

In a large saucepan, melt 6 tablespoons of the butter over medium heat. Add the onions, bay leaves, and ground thyme and cook until the onions are caramelized and very sugary sweet and soft, 30 to 45 minutes. (Timing depends on how thick you cut the onions. If you slice them very thinly it can take as little 30 minutes; if they're a little thicker, they could take 40 to 45 minutes.)

Meanwhile, in a skillet, melt the remaining 4 tablespoons butter. Add the mushrooms and cook until browned. Season with a little salt and pepper.

Preheat the oven to 425°F. Deglaze the onions with the sherry. Add the sautéed mushrooms, porcini puree, and chopped garlic. Add the beef stock and let that simmer for about 20 minutes for the flavors to combine while you make your toast tops.

Toast the bread in the oven. Rub the toast with the garlic halves and top it with Gruyère cheese and fresh thyme or parsley, then bake until the Gruyère is golden and gooey. Serve the soup in bowls and float a cheese toast up on top (or go the traditional route; see Tip).

Serves 4

If you have onion soup crocks, you can fill them as is traditional with this soup, top them with the toasted bread, put the Gruyère up on top, pop it under the broiler, and let that brown right in the crock.

Pizzoccheri-Style Supper

Pizzoccheri is a whole-grain buckwheat pasta that's traditionally served with a lot of butter and crispy sage leaves, potatoes, white cabbage, and big pieces of cheese. It's a really hearty winter dish. I made a pizzoccheri-style dish that's hearty but not quite as heavy. You can top the dish, if you want to really ritz it up, with some toasted panko bread crumbs mixed with a little extra cheese.

> 12 to 14 very large **brussels sprouts**
> **Salt** and **pepper**
> 1 **russet (baking) potato**, peeled and finely diced
> 1 pound **whole wheat spaghetti** or linguine
> 6 tablespoons (¾ stick) **butter**
> 18 fresh **sage leaves**
> 3 cloves **garlic**, sliced
> ½ cup freshly grated **Parmigiano-Reggiano cheese**
> Freshly grated **nutmeg**

Core the brussels sprouts and separate into individual leaves. Bring a medium pot of water to a boil. Add salt and the brussels sprouts and cook for a minute or two to blanch. Remove with a slotted spoon. Add the potato to the boiling water and cook for 5 minutes; drain.

Bring a large pot of water to a boil. Salt the water and cook the pasta to al dente.

Meanwhile, in a skillet, melt the butter over medium heat. Add the sage leaves and let them cook until crispy. Remove the leaves, drain on paper towels, and crumble. Add the garlic to the butter and cook until translucent or just starting to brown.

Before draining the pasta, ladle out and reserve 1 cup of the starchy pasta cooking water. Drain the pasta and add to the garlic butter along with some of the cooking water. Add the brussels sprout leaves and the potato and toss that with the crumbled sage leaves, some Parm, salt and pepper to taste, and a little bit of grated nutmeg.

Serves 4

I made **Cheesy Chicken in Poblano Sauce,** which we served it up with tortillas. You could use charred corn or flour tortillas, whichever you prefer.

Cheesy Chicken in Poblano Sauce

I usually use poblanos here, but I happened to have some New Mexico chiles, which I got from my friend Emily, who gets them from her friend Sheila, and so on. It is "green chile contraband" that comes in once a year from New Mexico and we use them over months and months. We keep them in the freezer and they're a coveted, coveted possession.

> 1 cup **chicken** or **vegetable stock**
> 2 to 3 medium **poblano** or **New Mexico chiles**, seeded, stemmed, and chopped
> 1 small **onion**, chopped
> 2 cloves **garlic**, chopped
> 1 teaspoon ground **cumin**
> 1 teaspoon **Mexican herb blend** or dried oregano
> A small handful of **cilantro leaves**, plus a few leaves for garnish
> **Salt** and **pepper**

3 tablespoons **butter**
2 tablespoons **flour**
1 cup **whole milk**
½ cup **heavy cream** or Mexican crema
3 tablespoons **EVOO**
4 to 6 **boneless, skinless chicken breasts**
1½ cups shredded **Manchego cheese**
Tortillas, for serving
Thinly sliced **red onions**, for garnish

In a blender or food processor, combine the stock, chiles, onion, garlic, cumin, herb blend, cilantro, and salt and black pepper to taste.

In a saucepan, melt the butter over medium heat. Whisk in the flour, then add the milk and cream. Increase the heat a bit, add the poblano puree, and simmer to thicken and cook the sauce, 20 to 25 minutes.

Preheat the oven to 375°F.

While the sauce is cooking, place a large skillet over medium-high heat and add the EVOO (3 turns of the pan). Brown the chicken on both sides, about 3 to 4 minutes per side; shred. Place in a baking dish, top with the sauce and cheese, and bake until cooked through, about 15 to 20 minutes.

Serve with tortillas and garnish with cilantro sprigs and red onions.

Serves 4

Option: Spread shredded meat from 1 whole rotisserie (skinned & deboned) chicken in a baking dish and top with the poblano sauce and Manchego. Bake until browned on top and bubbling, 15 to 20 minutes.

🕐 **NOVEMBER 15/DINNER**

We had **Coq au Vin Blanc**, which I served simply with a warm baguette.

Coq au Vin Blanc

One 4- to 5-pound **chicken**, cut into 8 pieces
Salt and **pepper**
Flour, for dredging
8 tablespoons (1 stick) **butter**
EVOO, for drizzling
1 cup peeled fresh or drained thawed frozen **pearl onions**
3 to 4 cloves **garlic**, sliced
2 ribs **celery** with leafy tops, from the heart, finely chopped
1 **baby fennel** or ¼ small bulb, thinly sliced
1 **leek**, thinly sliced
1 large fresh **bay leaf**
1 (750 ml) bottle **dry white wine**, such as white burgundy
1 cup **crème fraîche**
2 to 3 cups **chicken stock** (optional)
¼ cup **Dijon mustard**
2 to 3 tablespoons chopped **fresh tarragon**
Baguette, warmed

Sprinkle the chicken with salt and pepper and dredge in flour. In a large Dutch oven, melt 2 tablespoons of the butter over medium-high heat. Working in batches, brown the chicken, and then transfer to a plate.

Add a drizzle of EVOO to the pot along with the remaining 6 tablespoons butter, the pearl onions, garlic, celery, fennel, and leek. Sprinkle the vegetables with some salt and pepper and cook until lightly browned, 7 to 8 minutes. Stir in the bay leaf and wine; return the chicken to the pot, and cook, partially covered, at a low simmer, 30 minutes.

Stir in the crème fraîche, reduce the heat to low, and cook 30 minutes longer. If the liquid gets too low, add the chicken stock. Transfer the chicken to a warm platter, and add the mustard and chopped tarragon to the sauce at the last minute. Serve with warm baguette.

Serves 4

🕐 **NOVEMBER 16/DINNER**

We had **Bolognese with Barolo Wine & Black Pepper** (see November 5, page 184).

🕐 **NOVEMBER 17/DINNER**

Again, by popular request; they cannot get enough of it: **Cider Beef** with **Mashed Potatoes & Parsnips with Cheddar** (see October 28, page 175). I also served up antipasto and my mother's **Country-Style Chicken Livers** (see April 20, page 18).

🕐 **NOVEMBER 19/DINNER**

Egg Tagliatelle with Truffle Butter (see August 27, page 129)

🕐 **NOVEMBER 21/DINNER**

Portuguese Soup

Serve with Portuguese rolls, which are slightly sweet, and butter, or any crusty bread and butter.

2 tablespoons **EVOO**
¾ pound **Spanish chorizo**, diced
2 **carrots**, chopped
2 ribs **celery** from the heart, chopped
1 **onion**, chopped
3 to 4 cloves **garlic**, chopped
1 **red Fresno chile**, seeded and chopped
Salt and **pepper**
2 **russet (baking) potatoes**, peeled and chopped
2 (14.5-ounce) cans **stewed tomatoes**
1 (15-ounce) can **garbanzo beans** (chickpeas), rinsed and drained
4 cups **chicken stock**
1 small bunch **lacinato kale** (also called black, Tuscan, or dinosaur kale), stemmed and finely chopped
2 tablespoons chopped fresh **thyme**
1 large **bay leaf**

In a soup pot, heat the EVOO (2 turns of the pan) over medium-high heat. Add the chorizo and render for 2 to 3 minutes. Add the carrots, celery, onion, garlic, chile, and salt and pepper to taste and let sweat out a few minutes partially covered. Add the potatoes, stir a couple of minutes more, then add the stewed tomatoes, breaking them up a bit with a spoon.

Add the garbanzos, stock, and 2 cups water and bring to a boil. Add the kale, thyme, bay leaf, and some black pepper. Bring to a bubble, reduce to a simmer, and cook 30 to 40 minutes to thicken. Adjust the seasonings and serve.

Serves 4

Here's what we had: **roasted turkey breast and legs (with a compound butter)**, **Elsa's Poulet Sauce**, a **stovetop gravy**, **Apple & Onion Stuffing**, **Roasted Butternut Squash** (see October 30, page 178; I made it with maple syrup instead of honey), **Mashed Potatoes & Parsnips with Cheddar** (see October 28, page 175), my mom's **Green Bean Casserole**, **peas with shallots**, and **Basic Cranberry Sauce** (page 167). We served a 2009 Morgon wine and that was it. I make basically the same dinner every year.

This year I **roasted 2 turkey breasts** (about 5 pounds each) and 6 legs. I covered the turkey with **compound butter** (softened butter, shallot, garlic, lemon juice, parsley, rosemary, thyme, chives, salt, and pepper) and roasted 15 minutes per pound at 325°F for the white meat and about 10 minutes longer per pound for the dark meat. I roasted the dark meat on a bed of root vegetables. After the turkey was in the oven for about an hour, I doused it with wine and basted it with stock. Be sure to save the pan drippings for Elsa's Poulet Sauce. I also made a stovetop gravy.

Elsa's Poulet Sauce

3 tablespoons **butter**
3 tablespoons **flour**
½ cup **white wine**
Pan drippings from a roast turkey
3 cups **chicken or turkey stock**
Salt and **pepper**
1 **egg yolk**

In a medium saucepan, melt the butter over medium heat. Add the flour and stir to cook it out. Cook, stirring constantly, until lightly golden in color, 2 to 3 minutes.

While that is cooking, place the roasting pan that you cooked your turkey in on a burner over medium-high heat. Once the pan gets hot, add the wine to deglaze, scraping up all the browned bits with a wooden spoon. Add the loosened pan juices to the flour and butter along with the stock, and season with salt and pepper.

When ready to serve, beat an egg yolk in a small bowl with a ladle of the hot sauce to warm it. Pour the warmed egg yolk mixture back into the pot of sauce and keep over very low heat. It will make a glossy, more stable gravy.

Serves 6

I also made a **stovetop gravy**. I melted 4 tablespoons butter (I used just a little of the compound butter I made for the turkey and then added plain butter to make up the difference) and stirred in ¼ cup flour. Then I added about 4 cups store-bought turkey or chicken stock, lots of black pepper, and salt to taste.

Apple & Onion Stuffing

2 tablespoons **EVOO**, plus extra for oiling the pan
4 tablespoons (½ stick) **butter**, softened
1 **fresh bay leaf**
4 ribs **celery** with leafy tops, from the heart, chopped
1 medium to large **yellow onion**, chopped
3 McIntosh **apples**, chopped
2 tablespoons **poultry seasoning**
Salt and **pepper**
¼ cup chopped **flat-leaf parsley leaves**
8 cups cubed **stuffing mix** (I like Pepperidge Farm)
4 to 5 cups **chicken stock**

Preheat the oven to 400°F.

Heat a large skillet over medium-high heat. Add the EVOO (2 turns of the pan) and the butter. When the butter melts, add the bay leaf, celery, onion, and apples. Season with the poultry seasoning and salt and pepper to taste. Cook until the vegetables and apples begin to soften, 5 to 6 minutes. Add the parsley and stuffing cubes to the pan and combine. Moisten the stuffing with chicken stock until all of the bread is soft but not wet. Remove the bay leaf and let cool either in the pan or in a bowl.

Brush a baking sheet or an oven-safe oval metal tray with EVOO. Form a loaf shape (see Tip) out of your stuffing and bake until set and crisp on top, 15 to 20 minutes.

Serves 12

You can also make this stuffin' into individual muffins: Brush a 12-cup muffin tin with 4 tablespoons softened butter. Add a beaten egg to the cooled stuffing mixture. Using an ice cream scoop, mound up the stuffing in the muffin tin. Bake until set and crisp on top, 10 to 15 minutes. Transfer the stuffin' muffins to a platter and serve hot or at room temperature.

Green Bean Casserole

2 pounds **green beans**, trimmed
2 tablespoons **butter**
1 bunch **scallions**, white and green parts thinly sliced, kept separate
1 (10-ounce) package **sliced fresh mushrooms**
Salt and **pepper**
3 tablespoons **flour**
1 cup **chicken broth**
1 cup **heavy cream**
½ cup crushed **potato chips**

Fill a medium skillet with enough water to reach a depth of ½ inch. Bring to a boil, then add the green beans, lower the heat, cover, and simmer until tender-crisp, about 4 minutes. Drain in a colander and rinse with cold water until cool. Transfer to a serving dish.

Using the same skillet, melt the butter over medium heat. Add the scallion whites and the mushrooms; season with salt and pepper; and cook, stirring, until golden brown, about 4 minutes. Sprinkle with the flour and stir for 1 minute (the mixture will be dry). Gradually stir in the chicken broth and cream and cook until thickened. Season with salt and pepper, sprinkle with the scallion greens, and remove from the heat.

Spoon the sauce over the green beans and sprinkle the potato chips on top.

Serves 6

Peas with shallots: Sauté sliced shallots in a little butter, add frozen peas, and stir until they're warmed through. Off the heat, toss them with lots of finely chopped mint, a little bit of thyme, lemon zest, and parsley.

🕐 NOVEMBER 25/BREAKFAST

We had **Almond Custard Brioche French Toast** (see June 24, page 70).

🕐 NOVEMBER 25/DINNER

We had one of our go-to dinners: **Cider Beef** and **Mashed Potatoes & Parsnips with Cheddar** (see October 28, page 175). I had also made a turkey soup with leftover Thanksgiving turkey, so we had that as an option.

Turkey soup: I pulled off all the breast meat from the turkey carcasses, then I simmered the carcasses with root vegetables (carrots, onion) and celery. I roasted up a head of garlic. I squeezed the garlic into the soup and added the pulled turkey meat and some fresh herbs (maybe ¼ cup mixed thyme, dill, and parsley). I added chicken stock to thin it out and then cooked some dumpling-like noodles directly in the soup.

November 26, Lunch. Hot turkey melts with sharp Cheddar: I mixed a cassis-flavored Dijon mustard with leftover cranberry sauce, slathered that on bread, put some thinly sliced shallot on there and supersharp white Cheddar and turkey. You can put that in a panini press or melt it in the oven.

🕐 NOVEMBER 26/DINNER

Roasted Garlic & Caramelized Onion Sauce with Homemade Turkey Sausage

1 head **garlic**, top cut off to expose the cloves
2 tablespoons **EVOO**, plus more for drizzling
Salt and **pepper**
4 tablespoons (½ stick) **butter**
2 large **onions**, thinly sliced
1 **bay leaf**
½ cup **dry white wine**
1 to 1½ cups **chicken stock**
½ cup **heavy cream**
1 pound **mezzi rigatoni**
Homemade **Turkey Sausage** (recipe follows)
Grated **Parmigiano-Reggiano cheese**, for serving

Preheat the oven to 400°F. Drizzle the garlic with some EVOO and season with salt and pepper. Wrap in foil and roast until tender and caramel in color, about 40 minutes.

Meanwhile, in a large skillet, melt the butter over medium heat. Add the onions and bay leaf and season with salt and pepper. Cook, stirring

occasionally, until the onions are caramel in color and very soft and sweet, about 30 minutes. Deglaze the pan with the wine. Discard the bay leaf.

Squeeze the roasted garlic into a food processor and add the onions and enough stock to smoothly puree the sauce. Transfer the puree to a saucepan and stir in the cream. Cook to reduce and thicken while the pasta cooks.

Bring a large pot of water to a boil. Salt the water and cook the rigatoni to al dente.

Meanwhile, in a large skillet, heat 2 tablespoons EVOO (2 turns of the pan) over medium-high heat. Add the sausage and brown, breaking it up as it cooks.

Drain the pasta and toss with the sausage and creamy sauce. Top with Parm.

Serves 4

HOMEMADE TURKEY SAUSAGE

1 pound **ground turkey** (dark and white meat) or ground chicken
3 cloves **garlic**, chopped
2 to 3 tablespoons chopped fresh **rosemary**
1½ teaspoons crushed **red pepper flakes**
1½ teaspoons **sweet paprika**
1½ teaspoons **fennel seeds**
1½ teaspoons **poultry seasoning**
Salt and **pepper**

Combine all the ingredients. Chill for several hours or overnight for flavors to combine.

Makes 1 pound

PIZZA NIGHT

NOVEMBER 27, DINNER

We had **sopressata pizza, pizza Margherita,** and **potato pizza with white truffle,** all made with our homemade **Pizza Crust** and two pizza sauces: **Homemade Marinara (with a Kick)** and **Blender Pizza Sauce.**

Sopressata pizza: We topped the dough with pizza sauce, thinly sliced fior di latte (a type of mozzarella), and thinly sliced hot sopressata. When it came out of the pizza oven, we topped it with a little freshly grated pecorino and served it with thinly sliced raw red onion and chopped parsley.

Pizza Margherita: We topped the dough with pizza sauce and fior di latte cheese. When it came out of the oven, we sprinkled it with Parm and garnished it with a couple of leaves of torn basil.

Potato pizza with white truffle: Mandoline-cut a small white or Yukon Gold potato (1 small potato per pie). Brush the rolled-out pizza dough with roasted garlic oil. Arrange a thin layer of the sliced potato; season with salt and pepper and torn sage (a few leaves per pie). Top with shredded Fontina Val d'Aosta. Bake to crispy. Top with shaved white truffle or drizzle with truffle oil.

Homemade Marinara (with a Kick)

2 to 3 tablespoons **EVOO**
¼ cup grated **onion**
2 to 3 cloves **garlic**, grated or pasted
1 **red Fresno chile**, finely diced
Salt and **pepper**
1 to 2 tablespoons **tomato paste**
½ cup **red wine**
1 (28- to 32-ounce) can **San Marzano tomatoes** (look for DOP on the label)
Leaves of 1 to 2 sprigs fresh **oregano**, finely chopped
1 tablespoon chopped fresh **thyme**
A small handful of **flat-leaf parsley**, finely chopped
2 **basil leaves**, torn or coarsely chopped

In a medium saucepan, heat the EVOO (2 to 3 turns of the pan) over medium-high heat. Add the onion, garlic, chile, and salt and pepper to taste and cook for a few minutes. Add the tomato paste and let cook out while stirring for another minute or two. Add the red wine to deglaze the pan, then stir in the tomatoes. Mash up the mixture using a potato masher or the back of a wooden spoon. Add the oregano, thyme, parsley, and basil and let cook out for 20 to 25 minutes.

Makes about 2 cups, enough for three or four 12-inch pizzas

Blender Pizza Sauce

1 (28- to 32-ounce) can **San Marzano tomatoes** (look for DOP on the label)
3 to 4 tablespoons grated **onion**
2 small cloves **garlic**, pasted or grated
½ teaspoon **ground fennel** or fennel pollen
A few torn fresh **basil leaves**
A few grinds of **sea salt** and **pepper**
½ teaspoon **sugar** (optional)

Combine everything in a food processor and blend until smooth. Adjust salt and pepper to taste.

Makes enough for eight 12-inch pizzas

Pizza Crust

This is our adaptation of a Mario Batali recipe for pizza dough—I use ½ cup less flour (and I omit the all-purpose flour called for in the original) and I go a bit heavier on all of the flavor elements (honey, wine, EVOO, salt). Also, the original recipe called for 1½ ounces of yeast—we didn't know if that was dry active, refrigerated, etc., so we experimented quite a bit. For every four 12-inch thin-crust pizzas, we use the following recipe. Feel free to Goldilocks around with the measurements we use as much as you like. The recipe is pretty forgiving of small adjustments.

¼ to ⅓ cup **dry white wine** (a 3-count in a slow stream)
1½ envelopes (about 3 teaspoons) **active dry yeast** (see Tip)
¾ cup **very warm tap water**
1½ tablespoons **honey**
1 rounded teaspoon **fine sea salt** or kosher salt
1½ tablespoons **EVOO** (1½ turns of the bowl), plus more for the bowl
2½ cups **OO flour** (our favorite pizza flour is Gran Mugnaio Farina Tipo 00 from Molino Spadoni)

In a bowl, combine the wine, yeast, and water and stir to dissolve the yeast. Add the honey, salt, and EVOO to the bowl, then stir in a cup of flour at a time to incorporate. Stir to combine as much flour as possible, then turn out onto a floured pastry board or marble counter and combine by hand. Knead for 6 or 7 minutes. Rinse the bowl, dry, and lightly oil. Return the dough to the bowl and cover with a clean towel. Let rise in a warm corner of the kitchen about 45 minutes or so.

Cut the dough into 4 pieces, knead each and cover again, and let stand 15 minutes more or until you're ready to make pizzas.

Preheat the oven (see Pizza in a Home Oven). Lightly flour a work surface and roll out each piece of dough to a round ⅛ inch thick and 12 inches across.

Top and bake the pizza. Depending on toppings, pizzas cook in 2 to 4 minutes in a very hot pizza oven. Crazy! The same effect can be achieved in any home oven with a little effort, once you get the system worked out.

Makes enough dough for four 12-inch pizzas

We like Fleischmann's Pizza Crust Yeast. We use 1½ envelopes for each batch of dough. Each envelope is ¼ ounce (7 grams). We buy the packets in multiples of 3 so there is always an even yield. We have messed about with the amount of yeast many times and these measurements make a crust that for us is just right.

Pizza in a Home Oven

Position a rack one notch higher than the center of the oven and preheat to 550°F (or your oven's highest setting). Put a baking sheet or pizza pan or pizza stone on the rack and heat the pan or stone for 10 to 15 minutes. Roll out the dough as described, then transfer to a cornmeal- or flour-dusted rimless baking sheet, top as you like, slide the pizza into the oven onto the preheated baking sheet (or pizza pan or stone), and bake 5 minutes. Switch the broiler on and brown the top, 3 to 5 minutes more. When you remove a pizza, switch the oven back to bake while you prepare the next pizza.

Winter Vegetable Sauce

Salt and **black pepper**
1 pound (small to medium) **eggplant**, cut into batons (thin sticks)
½ cup plus 3 to 4 tablespoons **EVOO**
1 bulb **fennel**, cored and thinly sliced
1 **red bell pepper**, quartered and thinly sliced
1 **cubanelle pepper**, halved and thinly sliced
1 **fresh chile**, seeded and chopped
1 **onion**, chopped or thinly sliced
2 or 3 cloves **garlic**, grated
Leaves from 2 sprigs **oregano** or marjoram, chopped
1 tablespoon chopped fresh **thyme leaves**
A small handful of **flat-leaf parsley**, chopped
2 tablespoons **tomato paste**
½ cup **red wine**
1 (28- or 32-ounce) can **San Marzano tomatoes** (look for DOP on the label)
15 to 20 fresh **basil leaves**, torn
1 pound **spaghetti**
Grated **Parmigiano-Reggiano cheese**, for serving

Salt the eggplant and let it drain on paper towels for a little bit.

In a saucepan, heat 3 to 4 tablespoons EVOO (3 to 4 turns of the pan) over medium to medium-high heat. Add the fennel, bell pepper, cubanelle pepper, chile, onion, garlic, oregano, thyme, parsley, and salt and black pepper to taste.

Cook until the vegetables are tender, then stir in the tomato paste and cook a minute or two. Deglaze with the wine. Add the canned tomatoes, torn basil, and salt and pepper to taste. Let that cook until the tomatoes break down. A whole can of tomatoes usually takes about 30 minutes or so to cook down and thicken.

Meanwhile, in a skillet, heat the remaining ½ cup EVOO (a thin layer) over medium-high heat. Add the eggplant and cook until golden brown and cooked through. Set aside until the sauce is done. (The eggplant gets tossed with the sauce right before serving so it doesn't fall apart.)

Bring a large pot of water to a boil. Salt the water and cook the pasta to al dente. Drain the pasta and toss with the eggplant and sauce. Serve the pasta topped with Parm.

Serves 4

Pasta with Golden Cauliflower

Here's my trick for prepping cauliflower. I cook it (using the method below) before I cut it into florets. It's great way to prepare it instead of making a mess with all those little bits of cauliflower all over the counter.

1 head **cauliflower**
2 cups **chicken** or **vegetable stock**
A good pinch of **saffron threads**
1 or 2 tablespoons **EVOO**
3 tablespoons **butter**
2 or 3 **anchovy fillets**
1 **onion**, finely chopped
3 or 4 cloves **garlic**, chopped
1 small **fresh chile**, seeded and finely chopped
½ cup **dry white wine**
1 pound **short-cut pasta**, such as penne rigate
½ cup grated **pecorino cheese**

Remove the core of the cauliflower with a sharp paring knife and put the whole head in a deep Dutch oven. Add ½ to ¾ cup water (or chicken stock, if you want) and bring it to a boil. Turn it down to a simmer and cover the pan to trap all the steam in there. Let the cauliflower cook until very tender. The time will depend on the size of the head of cauliflower. It can take anywhere from 10 to 12 minutes to as much as probably 15 to 18. When it gets fork-tender, you can just break it up into florets.

In a saucepan, combine the stock and saffron, bring to a simmer, and let it reduce by one-third to one-half; this intensifies the color and flavor and you end up with this really flavorful, bright orange-yellow saffron stock.

Bring a large pot of water to a boil.

Meanwhile, in a large skillet, heat the EVOO (1 or 2 turns of the pan) and melt the butter into it. Add the anchovies, cover the pan with a splatter screen or lid, and shake until the anchovies begin to break up. Reduce the heat a bit, uncover, and stir until the anchovies melt. Add the onion, garlic, and chile. Sauté that together. Deglaze with the wine.

Salt the boiling water and cook the pasta to al dente. Before draining, ladle out ½ cup of the starchy pasta cooking water and add to the sauce. Drain the pasta and add to the anchovy sauce along with the cheese, saffron stock, and cauliflower. Toss that together and then adjust the salt and pepper. Very yummy and very healthy dish.

Serves 4

DECEMBER

THURSDAY/1

DINNER
pasta & escarole soup

FRIDAY/2

DINNER
chicken curry, homemade rice pilaf

SATURDAY/3

DINNER
porcini & portobello ragu

SUNDAY/4

MONDAY/5

SUNDAY/11

BREAKFAST
breakfast chorizo & eggs, fresh salsa verde

MONDAY/12

TUESDAY/13

WEDNESDAY/14

DINNER
stuffed mushrooms, bull's-eye deviled eggs, short ribs & rigatoni

THURSDAY/15

DINNER
meatball party: Buffalo chicken meatballs, Danish meatballs, spaghetti & meatball meatballs

WEDNESDAY/21

DINNER
chicken & biscuits, creamy chicken & noodles, caponata

THURSDAY/22

DINNER
Grandpa's braised beef

FRIDAY/23

SATURDAY/24

DINNER
Christmas pasta 2011, shrimp with chile-lemon butter, Grandpa's stuffed artichokes, crab cakes, cocktail sauce and crab claws, pizza bites

SUNDAY/25

DINNER
Caesar salad, caponata, bull's-eye deviled eggs, country-style chicken livers, Christmas pasta

MONDAY/26

DINNER
roasted turkey breast with herb gravy, beef tenderloin with horse-radish sauce, basic cranberry sauce, green beans and almonds

TUESDAY/6

DINNER
Grandpa's braised beef

WEDNESDAY/7

DINNER
butternut squash
risotto

THURSDAY/8

DINNER
saffron fava bean soup

FRIDAY/9

DINNER
beef, pork & turkey
roasts, horseradish
sour cream sauce,
applesauce with fresh
thyme, Caesar pesto

SATURDAY/10

FRIDAY/16

DINNER
turkey mole chipotle
chili

SATURDAY/17

SUNDAY/18

MONDAY/19

DINNER
bean soup, bull's-eye
deviled eggs, peanut
butter cup–stuffed
ginger cookies, five
minute fudge wreath

TUESDAY/20

DINNER
coq au vin with cara-
melized pearl onions

TUESDAY/27

BREAKFAST
two-person ham &
mushroom omelet

WEDNESDAY/28

DINNER
mushroom soup,
rice pilaf, tenderloin
burgers, homemade
tots

THURSDAY/29

LUNCH
roast beef sandwiches
on ciabatta
DINNER
bucatini with sausage,
fennel, pepper &
onion sauce

FRIDAY/30

DINNER
caponata, bull's-eye
deviled eggs, cider
beef, country-style
chicken livers, mashed
potatoes & parsnips
with Cheddar

SATURDAY/31

BRUNCH
crab cakes with
cocktail sauce
DINNER
Jane Fox's famous
tortilla soup, jalapeño
poppers, vegetable
posole, fresh salsa
verde, bean dip,
zucchini & corn
fritters

DECEMBER 1, DINNER

Pasta & escarole soup: In a few tablespoons of EVOO (enough to coat the bottom of the soup pot, sauté ¼ pound diced pancetta and maybe a teaspoon of fennel seed. Add an onion, a couple of garlic cloves, a couple of small celery ribs, and a carrot— all finely chopped. I happened to have some leek left over, so you can add that in, too. Add about 4 cups stock, and some tomato sauce (I had some left over), and I thinned out the stock with 2 to 3 cups of water. I cooked the pasta in the liquid and I wilted in escarole at the end. Served it with an extra drizzle of olive oil and grated cheese on top.

🕐 DECEMBER 2/DINNER

I made my **Chicken Curry** that I served up with **Homemade Rice Pilaf** (see August 28, pages 130 and 131). I also added some roasted butternut squash (see Tip) to the curry.

To roast butternut squash, peel, seed, and cut into bite-size pieces. Toss with salt, pepper, EVOO, and nutmeg and roast in the oven at 425°F until tender, 20 to 30 minutes. This is a nice thing to do in the winter to stretch the curry.

🕐 DECEMBER 3/DINNER

Porcini & Portobello Ragu

We served the ragu with pappardelle, big wide ribbons of pasta. It's also nice with egg tagliatelle if you want it to be a little lighter. The red wine I used in the ragu was a Rosso di Montalcino.

3 cups **chicken stock**
¼ to ⅓ cup **dried porcini mushrooms**
¼ cup **EVOO**
¼ pound **pancetta**, finely diced
6 medium **portobello mushroom caps**, gills scraped and caps chopped
1 **carrot**, finely chopped
1 rib **celery**, finely chopped
1 **onion**, finely chopped
4 cloves **garlic**, finely chopped
1 tablespoon finely chopped fresh **sage**
2 tablespoons fresh **thyme leaves**, finely chopped
Small handful of **flat-leaf parsley**, finely chopped
2 tablespoons fresh **rosemary**, finely chopped
Salt and **pepper**
2 tablespoons **tomato paste**
1 cup **dry red wine**
1 (28- to 32-ounce) can **San Marzano tomatoes** (look for DOP on the label)
1 cup **whole milk** or half-and-half
Parmesan rind (optional; see Tip)

In a saucepan, combine the stock and porcini and let simmer gently until the mushrooms have

softened. You'll probably end up with about 2 cups of stock. It's going to reduce a little as the mushrooms reconstitute.

In a separate saucepan, heat the EVOO (4 turns of the pan) over medium to medium-high heat. Add pancetta and sauté that a few minutes to render it out, then stir for a couple of minutes until lightly crisp. Add the portobellos and brown those completely. Stir in the carrot, celery, onion, garlic, sage, thyme, parsley, and rosemary. Season with salt and pepper.

Stir in the tomato paste and stir that another minute until you can smell the tomato paste. Add the wine and reduce the wine by half.

Meanwhile, remove the reconstituted porcini from the soaking liquid and chop them. Add them to the sauce, then add the soaking liquid, tomatoes, and milk. Let that simmer to thicken, 40 minutes or so.

Makes enough for 1 pound pasta

You can also throw in the rind from Parmigiano-Reggiano if you have one on hand. That helps to flavor the sauce.

🕐 **DECEMBER 6/DINNER**

We had **Grandpa's Braised Beef**.

Grandpa's Braised Beef

I often brown the meat first, but I didn't do that this time.

EVOO
4 **onions**, very thinly sliced
6 cloves **garlic**, very thinly sliced
4 to 5 pounds **chuck**, **bottom round**, or **top sirloin**
Sea salt and **pepper**
1½ cups **red wine**
2 tablespoons chopped fresh **thyme**
4 or 5 **russet (baking) potatoes**, peeled and thinly sliced lengthwise into planks
Leaves from 2 sprigs fresh **rosemary**, finely chopped
A handful of grated **Parmigiano-Reggiano cheese**
1 (28- to 32-ounce) can **San Marzano tomatoes** (look for DOP on the label), lightly crushed with your hands or sliced, with their juices
A few **fresh basil leaves**, torn
1 loaf **ciabatta**, for serving

Preheat the oven to 325°F.

In a large skillet, heat a thin layer of EVOO over medium heat. Add the onions and garlic and sweat them until very soft and very light caramel in color, 20 to 30 minutes.

Season the meat very liberally with salt and pepper and place in a large Dutch oven with the wine.

Arrange half the onions over the top of the meat; season with salt, pepper, and half the thyme. Arrange half the potatoes over the onions and dress with a liberal drizzle of EVOO, the rosemary, Parm, and salt and pepper to taste. Top the potatoes with half the tomatoes and their juices and season with salt and pepper. Scatter in a few basil leaves. Repeat the layers, but do not add basil to the top layer of tomatoes.

Cover the pan and roast the meat in the oven for 2½ hours. Turn off the oven but leave the Dutch oven in, and let sit for 1 hour. To serve, cut into chunks and spoon sauce over the meat.

Serves 5 to 6

Butternut Squash Risotto

I made this by sautéing shredded butternut squash, but you can also make it with roasted butternut squash (see Tip).

6 cups **chicken stock**
A generous pinch of **saffron threads**
3 tablespoons **EVOO**
¼ pound **pancetta**, diced
1 **yellow onion**, finely chopped
2 to 3 cloves **garlic**, very finely chopped
3 to 4 cups shredded **butternut squash** (1 small to medium squash)
1 or 2 tablespoons fresh **thyme leaves**
Salt and **pepper**
Freshly grated **nutmeg**
1½ cups **carnaroli** or **arborio rice**
½ cup **dry white wine**
3 tablespoons **butter**
A few handfuls of grated **Parmigiano-Reggiano cheese**

Bring the chicken stock and the saffron to a boil in a saucepan, then reduce the heat and keep warm at a low simmer.

In a pot with a rounded bottom, heat the EVOO over medium-high heat. Add the pancetta and cook until some of the fat has rendered, about 5 minutes. Add the onion, garlic, and squash and sauté that out, 2 to 3 minutes. Add the thyme

and season with salt, pepper, and nutmeg. Add the rice and stir. Add the wine and cook, stirring, until the liquid has been absorbed. Begin adding the hot chicken stock, a few ladles at a time, stirring constantly and cooking until the liquid has been absorbed before adding more. Continue adding stock and cooking until the rice is al dente and has a starchy, creamy quality, about 18 minutes total. The last couple of minutes of cook time, stir in the butter and Parm. Serve in shallow bowls.

Serves 4

Halve a butternut squash lengthwise, brush it with olive oil, and roast it cut side down on a baking sheet in a 425°F oven until tender. Scoop the flesh out, puree it, and stir the puree into the risotto. Or if you want it to have more texture, you can dice the squash and roast it. Then you puree only half the roasted squash, add that to the risotto, and top the risotto with the remaining diced squash.

🕐 **DECEMBER 8/DINNER**

Saffron Fava Bean Soup

You can also serve the soup with pasta, or ladle it over toast with a drizzle of olive oil and Parm cheese up on top.

¾ pound **dried fava beans**
3 tablespoons **EVOO**
¼ pound **pancetta, bacon,** or **salt pork,** finely diced

1 **carrot**, chopped
1 rib **celery**, chopped
1 **onion**, chopped
2 or 3 cloves **garlic**, chopped
1 **red Fresno chile**, chopped
1½ to 2 tablespoons fresh **thyme leaves**, finely chopped
2 fresh **bay leaves**
2 pinches of **saffron threads**
4 cups **chicken stock**

Put the fava beans in a large bowl with salted water to cover by an inch or two and soak overnight. Drain and rinse the beans.

In a Dutch oven, heat the EVOO (3 turns of the pan). Add the pancetta and render that out a few minutes. Add the beans, carrot, celery, onion, garlic, chile, thyme, bay leaves, saffron, stock, and 4 cups water.

Cook for 2 hours at a low boil. Add more water if the pot looks as if it is becoming too dry. If you want a thicker or smoother soup, you can puree half of it and add the puree back to the pot. Fish out the bay leaves before serving.

Serves 4

🕐 DECEMBER 9/DINNER

Sandwich Party: I set up a **Sandwich Bar** with meat, bread, sauces, and all the fixin's. I made three different roasts (beef, pork, and turkey) for sandwiches, each paired with a different sauce: **Beef with Horseradish Sauce**, **Pork with Applesauce**, and **Turkey with Caesar Pesto**.

SANDWICH BAR

Set up a buffet line with the sliced meats paired with their sauces. Arrange the fixin's to follow the meats. Warm the bread in the oven once the meats are removed and are resting. Split the bread open for sandwich making and place the bread before the sliced meats on your buffet.

Bread: Warm French rolls or baguettes (2 rolls or 6 inches of baguette per person)

Meat-Sauce Pairs: Roast Beef + Horseradish Sauce; Pork + Applesauce with Fresh Thyme; Roast Turkey + Caesar Pesto

Fixin's
- Watercress (1 bunch for every 6 sandwiches)
- Romaine hearts, chopped (1 heart for every 6 sandwiches)
- Cornichons or mini gherkins
- Giardiniera, chopped in a food processor into a relish
- Assorted mustards
- Sliced sharp Cheddar cheese

Beef, Pork & Turkey Roasts

While the meat is in the oven, prepare all the sauces (recipes follow).

3 to 4 pounds trimmed **center-cut beef tenderloin**
3 pounds **pork loin roast**
EVOO, for drizzling
Kosher salt and **coarse pepper**
2 teaspoons **granulated onion**
2 teaspoons **granulated garlic**
2 teaspoons **fennel seeds**
1 (3-pound) **boneless turkey breast**, skin on
4 tablespoons (½ stick) **butter**, softened
3 to 4 tablespoons **minced fresh herbs** (parsley, chives, thyme)
1 small clove **garlic**, peeled
1 small **shallot**, grated
Juice of ½ **lemon**

Preheat the oven to 475°F.

Arrange the beef and pork roasts on 1 large rimmed baking sheet. Drizzle the meat with EVOO to coat. Season the beef aggressively with kosher salt and coarse pepper, and sprinkle on about 1 teaspoon each granulated onion and garlic. For the pork, season aggressively with salt and pepper, sprinkle with about 2 teaspoons fennel seeds, and season with 1 teaspoon each granulated garlic and onion. Place in the oven and roast 15 minutes.

Meanwhile, place the turkey breast on a wire rack over a rimmed baking sheet. In a food processor, combine the butter, herbs, garlic, shallot, and lemon juice and process. Pat the turkey dry and spread the butter over the breast. Season with salt and pepper.

Once the beef and pork have roasted 15 minutes, reduce the oven temperature to 350°F and add the turkey breast. Roast everything for 45 minutes. Remove all the meats from the oven and transfer to carving boards. Let stand 15 minutes, loosely covered with foil, before carving.

Thinly slice the beef and pork. Slice the turkey ⅛ to ¼ inch thick across the breast.

Serves 12

HORSERADISH SOUR CREAM SAUCE

1½ cups **sour cream**
⅓ cup **heavy cream**
3 rounded tablespoons **prepared horseradish**
6 tablespoons finely chopped **chives**
Salt and **coarse pepper**

Stir together all the ingredients, transfer to a serving bowl, and refrigerate to chill.

Makes about 2 cups

APPLESAUCE WITH FRESH THYME

4 large crisp **apples**, peeled and coarsely chopped
1 tablespoon **lemon juice**
2 cups cloudy **organic apple cider**
¼ cup **dark amber maple syrup**
A pinch of **salt**
2 tablespoons **fresh thyme**, finely chopped

In a medium saucepan, combine all the ingredients and bring to a boil. Reduce the heat to medium-high and cook, stirring frequently, until a sauce forms, about 20 minutes. Transfer to a serving dish.

Makes about 3 cups

CAESAR PESTO

1 cup packed dark leafy **romaine lettuce**, stemmed and coarsely chopped
1 rounded teaspoon **anchovy paste**
A generous handful of grated **Romano cheese**
1 tablespoon **Dijon mustard**
1 teaspoon **Worcestershire sauce**
Juice of 1 **lemon**
1 large clove **garlic**, grated or pasted
Coarse black pepper
3 tablespoons **pine nuts**, toasted
¼ to ⅓ cup **EVOO**

In a food processor, combine all of the ingredients except the EVOO. Pulse-chop them, then

add about ¼ cup EVOO and pulse the pesto into a thick sauce; stream in a few extra tablespoons EVOO if necessary. Transfer the pesto to a serving bowl and keep at room temperature.

Makes about 1 cup

🕐 **DECEMBER 11/BREAKFAST**

Breakfast Chorizo & Eggs

If you're making homemade salsa verde, roast the poblanos for this dish and the salsa at the same time. We had a side of refried beans to go with this.

3 tablespoon **EVOO**
¼ pound **fresh chorizo**, casings removed
½ small **onion**, chopped
2 cloves **garlic**, grated or minced
1 **poblano chile**, roasted (see Tip), peeled, and diced
Corn kernels cut from 1 ear corn
Salt and **pepper**
4 **eggs**
1 tablespoon chopped **mixed herbs**, such as parsley, thyme, and cilantro
½ cup **tomato sauce**
1½ teaspoons minced **chipotle in adobo** or **hot sauce** such as Frank's RedHot
½ cup **Fresh Salsa Verde** (recipe follows) or store-bought
½ cup crumbled **queso fresco**

In a medium skillet, heat 1 tablespoon EVOO (1 turn of the pan) over medium-high heat. Add the chorizo and cook while breaking up with a wooden spoon, until cooked through and browned, 4 to 5 minutes. Add the onion, garlic, poblano chile, and corn, and cook until the corn starts to brown. Season with salt and pepper and reserve.

In a small skillet, heat 1 tablespoon EVOO (1 turn of the pan) over medium heat. While the pan is heating, in a small bowl, beat the eggs and fresh herbs and season with salt and pepper. Pour half of the egg mixture into the skillet to make an omelet. Set the omelet on a plate, wipe out the skillet, add the remaining 1 tablespoon EVOO (1 turn of the pan), and make a second omelet.

In a small saucepan, combine the tomato sauce and chipotle and heat over low heat. Heat the salsa verde separately over low heat or in the microwave until warm.

To assemble, place an omelet on a plate, fill it with the chorizo mixture, and fold it over. Top it with the warm red sauce on one side and the warm salsa verde on the other side. Crumble the queso fresco down over the whole thing.

Serves 2

FRESH SALSA VERDE

I usually make this with fresh tomatillos, but I've also made it with canned and it was fine. See the recipe for July 11 (page 84).

1 large **poblano chile**, roasted and peeled (see Tip)
2 tablespoons **corn oil**
1 medium **onion**, chopped
2 or 3 cloves **garlic**, finely chopped
6 to 8 medium **fresh tomatillos**, husked and chopped
1 teaspoon ground **cumin**
Salt and **pepper**
1 tablespoon good-quality **honey**
Juice of 1 **lime**
Small handful of **cilantro leaves**

Coarsely chop the seeded roasted poblano and put it in a food processor.

In a skillet, heat the oil (2 turns of the pan) over medium to medium-high heat. Add the onion, garlic, tomatillos, and cumin; season with salt and pepper to taste. Cook until the tomatillos break down and their color has softened from bright green to light olive.

Transfer the onion-tomatillo mixture to the food processor. Add the honey, lime juice, and cilantro. Puree into a fairly smooth sauce. Adjust salt and pepper to your taste.

Makes about 2 cups

> To roast a pepper, char it all over on the stovetop over a gas flame or under the broiler in the oven. Place the blackened pepper in a bowl and cover tightly. When cool enough to handle, rub off the charred skins with a paper towel, then halve and seed the pepper.

🕐 DECEMBER 14/DINNER

Stuffed Mushrooms (see August 26, page 127) and **Bull's-Eye Deviled Eggs** (see April 24, page 29) to start, then **Short Ribs & Rigatoni**.

Short Ribs & Rigatoni

¼ cup **EVOO**
8 to 10 **whole bone-in beef short ribs**, trimmed of fat
Salt and **pepper**
2 **carrots**, finely diced
2 ribs **celery**, finely diced
1 large **onion**, finely diced
4 large cloves **garlic**, thinly sliced
2 large **fresh bay leaves**
¼ cup **tomato paste**

2 cups **dry red** or **white wine** (or 2 cups beef stock)
3 cups **beef stock**
1 (28- or 32-ounce) can **San Marzano tomatoes** (look for DOP on the label)
1 herb bundle of **sage**, **parsley**, and **thyme**
1 pound **rigatoni pasta**, regular or whole wheat
3 tablespoons **butter**, cut into pieces
Finely chopped **flat-leaf parsley**, for garnish
Freshly grated **Pecorino Romano cheese**

Preheat the oven to 325°F.

In a large Dutch oven, heat the EVOO (4 turns of the pan) over medium-high heat. Season the meat with salt and pepper and brown all over in batches. Remove the meat to a plate. Add the carrots, celery, onion, garlic, and bay leaves to the pot; season with salt and pepper. Cook to soften, 5 to 6 minutes. Stir in the tomato paste and cook for 1 minute, then add the wine. Reduce by half, then add the stock and tomatoes. Break up the tomatoes and slide the meat back in, along with the herb bundle. Bring to a simmer, cover, and transfer to the oven. Cook to tender, about 2½ hours.

Remove the meat and discard the herb bundle. Cover the meat to keep warm and simmer the sauce to thicken while you cook the rigatoni.

Bring a large pot of water to a boil. Salt the water and cook the pasta to al dente. Drain the pasta and toss with the butter and half to two-thirds of the sauce. Serve the pasta topped with the meat on or off the bone. Garnish with parsley. Pass extra sauce at the table with the cheese.

Serves 4

🕐 DECEMBER 15/DINNER

Thursday was the last tape day of 2011 and that night we had a Meatball Party. We had a gift swap at the house and we had 3 different types of meatballs: **Buffalo Chicken Meatballs**, **Danish Meatballs**, and **Spaghetti & Meatball Meatballs** (they have actual cooked spaghetti rolled into them).

Buffalo Chicken Meatballs

1 pound **ground chicken breast**
1 cup **fine dry bread crumbs**, moistened with a little water or milk
½ small **onion**, grated
2 cloves **garlic**, grated
½ cup chopped **flat-leaf parsley**
½ cup **hot sauce** (such as Frank's RedHot), plus more for the meatball mixture
Salt and **pepper**
EVOO, for drizzling
2 tablespoons **butter**
Good-quality store-bought **blue cheese dressing**, for dipping
3 **scallions**, thinly sliced
A couple of handfuls of **celery sticks**
A couple of handfuls of **carrot sticks**

Preheat the oven to 400°F.

In a large bowl, combine the chicken with the bread crumbs, onion, garlic, parsley, and a few shakes of hot sauce and season with salt and pepper. Flatten out the meat in the bowl and score it into four portions using the side of your hand. Shape each portion into 4 balls to give you 16 meatballs in total.

Arrange the meatballs on a nonstick baking sheet pan and drizzle them with EVOO. Bake until the meatballs are cooked through and golden brown, 10 to 12 minutes.

While the meatballs are baking, melt the butter in a large skillet over medium heat. Add the ½ cup hot sauce and whisk to combine. Toss the baked meatballs in this sauce to coat.

Transfer the meatballs to a serving platter and spike each one with a toothpick or serving fork. Place the blue cheese dressing in a small serving bowl and garnish with the scallions. Serve the meatballs with the celery and carrot sticks and the blue cheese dipping sauce.

Makes 16 meatballs

Danish Meatballs

1 pound **ground beef**, **pork**, or **veal**
1 small **onion**, grated (about ½ cup)
½ cup **fine dry bread crumbs**
1 teaspoon dried **marjoram**, lightly crushed in your palm
⅛ teaspoon freshly grated **nutmeg**
Salt and **pepper**
2 organic **eggs**, beaten
½ to ⅔ cup **whole milk**
6 tablespoons (¾ stick) **butter**
1 rounded tablespoon **flour**
1 (10.5-ounce) can **beef consommé**
¼ cup **heavy cream**
2 tablespoons **pickle relish**
Fresh dill, for garnish

Preheat the oven to 400°F.

In a large bowl, combine the meat with the onion, bread crumbs, marjoram, nutmeg, salt and pepper to taste, eggs, and milk.

In a small saucepan, melt 4 tablespoons of the butter and use some of it to butter a large baking sheet. Using a small scoop, roll the meat mixture into about 36 walnut-size meatballs. Arrange snugly on the baking sheet and brush with the remaining melted butter. Bake until cooked through, about 15 minutes.

In a medium saucepan, melt 2 more tablespoons butter. Whisk in the flour, then stir in the beef consommé and cook to thicken a bit. Stir in the heavy cream and relish.

Serve the meatballs in a shallow serving dish and douse with the sauce. Garnish with dill.

Makes 36 meatballs

Spaghetti & Meatball
Meatballs

1½ pounds **ground beef sirloin**
2 tablespoons **Montreal Steak Seasoning**
1 teaspoon ground **allspice**
2 small **onions**, 1 grated and 1 finely chopped
½ pound **spaghetti**, broken into small pieces,
  cooked, and cooled
4 tablespoons **EVOO**
3 cloves **garlic**, finely chopped or grated
Salt and **pepper**
1 (28-ounce) can **diced tomatoes**
¼ cup chopped **fresh basil**

Preheat the oven to 400°F.

In a large bowl, combine the sirloin, steak
seasoning, allspice, the grated onion, and spaghetti. Work the mixture together with your
hands until well combined. Roll the mixture into
12 to 15 meatballs, slightly larger than a golf
ball, and arrange them on a baking sheet. Drizzle
with about 2 tablespoons EVOO and pop into the
oven. Bake until deep golden brown and cooked
through, 15 to 18 minutes.

While the meatballs are baking, in a medium
skillet, heat the remaining 2 tablespoons EVOO
(2 turns of the pan) over medium-high heat. Add
the chopped onion and the garlic, season with salt
and pepper, and cook until tender, 5 to 6 minutes. Add the tomatoes and bring up to a bubble.
Add the basil to the pan and simmer the sauce
until thickened, about 5 minutes.

Serve the meatballs in a serving dish nestled in
the marinara sauce.

Makes 12 to 15 meatballs

Rachael shares
her seasonal
favorites.

Turkey Mole
Chipotle Chili

If you want, you could add cooked black or red
beans to the chili.

1 or 2 tablespoons **EVOO** or vegetable oil
¼ pound **smoky bacon**, chopped
1½ to 2 pounds **ground turkey** (white and dark
  meat combined)
1 tablespoon **unsweetened cocoa powder** (or
  mole powder, which is cocoa with toasted
  sesame seeds)
1 tablespoon ground **coriander**
1 tablespoon ground **cumin**
1 tablespoon **smoked sweet paprika** or regular
  paprika
1 teaspoon **dried Mexican oregano**
A couple of pinches of ground **cinnamon**
Salt and **pepper**
1 large or 2 small **red bell peppers**, roasted,
  peeled, and chopped
2 medium or 1 large **onion**, chopped
4 cloves **garlic**, finely chopped
2 tablespoons **tomato paste**
1 (12-ounce) bottle **beer**
2 or 3 **dried chipotle chiles**, seeded (see Tip)
3 cups **chicken stock**
Toppings: **Pico de Gallo** (page 32), toasted
  pumpkin seeds, diced **avocado**, **sour cream**,
  chopped **scallions** or **red onions**

In a large pot or Dutch oven, heat the oil (1 or
2 turns of the pan) and cook the bacon until
browned. Remove from the pan and set aside.

Add the ground turkey and cook until well
caramelized and evenly browned; break up the
meat as it browns. Add the cocoa, coriander,
cumin, paprika, oregano, and cinnamon. Season
with salt and pepper—heavy on the pepper and
easier on the salt because of the bacon drippings.
Stir to toast the spices. Add in the roasted red
pepper, onion, and garlic, and stir and cook that
over medium heat until the onion is tender. Stir
in the tomato paste and deglaze with the beer.

Meanwhile, in a saucepan, combine the dried chipotles and chicken stock. Simmer together to reconstitute the chiles and flavor the stock. When the chipotles are softened, transfer them with about 1 cup of the cooking liquid to a food processor and puree.

Add the chipotle puree and the remaining warm chicken stock to the chili. Then you just simmer the chili until it's thickened to your desired consistency.

To serve, top with the reserved bacon and any or all of the suggested toppings.

Serves 6

You could use canned chipotle peppers in adobo if you'd like. Use a little of the chicken stock to puree a 7-ounce can of chipotles and all the sauce. Measure out 3 tablespoons of puree for the chili, then take the leftover puree and pop it into the freezer in a plastic food storage bag. Just break off what you need on another occasion.

⏱ DECEMBER 19/ HOLIDAY PARTY PREP

For the holiday parties I attended, I made a **Five-Minute Fudge Wreath** and the **Peanut Butter Cup–Stuffed Ginger Cookies** from the Christmas issue (2011) of our magazine. The ginger cookies were from The *Cookiepedia*, a cool cookie encyclopedia by Stacy Adimando, who's one of our food editors at the magazine. And of course I made my **Bull's-Eye Deviled Eggs** (see April 24, page 29).

Five-Minute Fudge Wreath

Butter, softened, for greasing the pan
1 (12-ounce) package **semisweet chocolate chips**
9 ounces **butterscotch chips** (three-fourths of a 12-ounce bag)
1 (14-ounce) can **sweetened condensed milk**
1 teaspoon **vanilla extract**
8 ounces **walnut halves**
½ cup **dried currants**
Candied red and green cherries, cut to resemble holly berries and leaves, for garnish (optional)

Lightly grease an 8-inch round cake pan with softened butter.

Place a heavy pot on the stove and heat it over low heat. Add the chocolate and butterscotch chips and the condensed milk and stir until the chips are melted and the mixture is smooth. Save the empty condensed milk can. Stir in the vanilla and remove the fudge from the heat. Immediately stir in the nuts and currants.

Cover the empty condensed milk can with plastic wrap and center it in the greased cake pan. Spoon the fudge into the pan around the can, making sure to center the can if it drifts. The fudge will set up almost immediately. If you're garnishing the wreath, do it quickly before the fudge sets up too much. Decorate the wreath with "holly" made from cut candied red and green cherries. A wreath left plain can be garnished with a pretty fabric bow when serving.

Chill covered in the refrigerator. Slice the fudge very thin when ready to serve.

Makes 2 pounds (serves 32)

Peanut Butter Cup–Stuffed Ginger Cookies

3 cups **flour**
1 teaspoon **baking soda**
2 teaspoons ground **ginger**
1 teaspoon ground **cinnamon**
¼ teaspoon **pepper**
¼ teaspoon **salt**
2 sticks (8 ounces) unsalted **butter**, at room temperature
¼ cup **granulated sugar**
¼ cup light **brown sugar**
1 **egg**
⅓ cup **molasses**
36 **miniature peanut butter cups** (such as Reese's®), chilled
Confectioners' sugar, for rolling

In a medium bowl, whisk together the flour and baking soda. Whisk in the ginger, cinnamon, pepper, and salt.

Using an electric mixer, cream the butter, granulated sugar, and brown sugar on high speed until smooth, light, and fluffy, 2 minutes. Beat in the egg for 30 seconds, then mix in the molasses. Scrape down the bowl. Add the flour mixture in 2 batches, mixing on low speed until just combined. Turn out the dough onto a large piece of plastic wrap. Using the wrap to help, form the dough into a disk and seal tightly. Refrigerate the dough for at least 1 hour or up to 1 day.

Preheat the oven to 350°F. Line 3 cookie sheets with parchment paper.

Working with 1 tablespoon of dough at a time, mold the dough around each peanut butter cup to enclose completely. Place 12 dough balls on each of the prepared pans. Bake until the tops are just set and slightly cracked, 12 to 14 minutes. Using a spatula, transfer the cookies to a rack to cool for 5 minutes.

Roll the cookies in the confectioners' sugar, then return to the rack to cool completely. Roll the cookies in the confectioners' sugar again before serving.

Makes 36 cookies

Bean Soup

1 pound **dried borlotti beans**
¼ cup **EVOO**, plus extra for serving
2 **carrots**, chopped
2 or 3 ribs **celery** with leafy tops, chopped
1 large **onion**, chopped
4 or 5 cloves **garlic**, thinly sliced or chopped
1 large **fresh bay leaf**
2 tablespoons sliced fresh **sage**
2 tablespoons chopped fresh **thyme**
2 tablespoons chopped fresh **rosemary**
1 sprig fresh **oregano** or **marjoram**
3 tablespoons **tomato paste**
6 cups **chicken stock**
Salt and **pepper**
A couple of **basil leaves**, torn
Optional toppings: chopped **onion** and grated **pecorino** or **Parmigiano-Reggiano cheese**

In a large bowl of water, soak the beans overnight.

Drain the beans and place in a pot. Cover with water and bring to a boil over medium heat. Parboil for 15 minutes, then drain.

In a soup pot, heat the EVOO (4 turns of the pan) over medium to medium-high heat. Add the carrots, celery, onion, garlic, bay leaf, sage, thyme, rosemary, and oregano or marjoram. Stir that until the veggies are just tender, 7 to 8 minutes. Add the tomato paste and stir that until fragrant, 1 or 2 minutes.

In a food processor combine 2 cups of the stock and half of the beans. Puree that until smooth.

Add the bean puree, the remaining whole beans, and the remaining 4 cups stock to the soup pot. Bring to a bubble, add the basil, then simmer the soup gently until the flavors combine, the beans are tender, and the soup is the desired consistency.

To serve, drizzle EVOO on top. You can also garnish with finely chopped onion and grated cheese (pecorino if you want a tangy cheese or Parm if you want a more nutty flavor).

Serves 4

● **DECEMBER 20/DINNER**

Coq au Vin with Caramelized Pearl Onions

5 tablespoons **EVOO**
¼ pound **pancetta** or thick-cut uncured bacon, cut into ¼-inch-thick matchsticks
2 **chicken breasts**, halved (4 pieces total)
4 **chicken thighs** or drumsticks
Salt and **pepper**
3 to 4 tablespoons **flour**, plus more for dredging
6 tablespoons (¾ stick) **butter**, cut into small pieces
4 **carrots**, sliced or chopped
3 ribs **celery**, with leafy tops, thinly sliced on an angle
1 bulb **fennel**, thinly sliced
2 **leeks**, tough greens trimmed, white part thinly sliced and well rinsed
1 **onion**, thinly sliced
4 cloves **garlic**, thinly sliced
1 (750 ml) bottle **white burgundy wine**
1 cup **chicken stock**
Herb bundle: a few sprigs of parsley, sage, rosemary, thyme, and 1 fresh bay leaf tied together with twine
⅓ cup **crème fraîche**
3 tablespoons **Dijon mustard**
Grated zest and juice of 1 **lemon**
¾ pound **large white mushrooms**, larger ones quartered and smaller ones halved
½ cup **dry sherry** or brandy
1 tablespoon fresh **thyme leaves**, chopped

Caramelized Pearl Onions (recipe follows)
1 loaf **crusty baguette**, warmed

In a large Dutch oven, heat 4 tablespoons EVOO (4 turns of the pan) over medium-high heat. Add the pancetta or bacon and cook, stirring occasionally, until browned, about 10 minutes. Transfer from pan to a plate and set aside.

Season the chicken with salt and pepper, dredge in flour, and add to the Dutch oven. Brown the chicken on both sides, 3 to 4 minutes per side. Transfer to a plate. Wipe out the pan and add 4 tablespoons butter. When the butter is melted, add the carrots, celery, fennel, leeks, onion, and garlic. Season with salt and pepper, partially cover, and cook 5 to 7 minutes. Sprinkle the vegetables with 3 to 4 tablespoons flour and stir for a couple of minutes over medium heat. Stir in the wine and stock. Return the chicken to the pot and throw in the herb bundle. Bring that all to a boil, partially covered, and simmer for 30 minutes.

Remove the chicken from the pan and let the sauce reduce over medium-high heat. Once it is reduced and thickened a bit, reduce the heat to low, and stir in the crème fraîche and mustard and let cook for another 10 minutes or so. Slide the chicken back into the pan, add the lemon zest and juice, and let the chicken heat through.

While the sauce is simmering down, place a large skillet over medium-high heat; add the remaining 2 tablespoons butter and 1 tablespoon EVOO (1 turn of the pan). Add the mushrooms

to the pan and cook until browned, 5 to 7 minutes. Deglaze the pan with the sherry and let evaporate. Stir in the fresh thyme.

Garnish the coq au vin with the caramelized pearl onions and the mushrooms, and serve with a piece of nice crusty baguette.

Serves 4

CARAMELIZED PEARL ONIONS

1 tablespoon **butter**
1 tablespoon **EVOO**
1 bag **pearl onions**, fresh (see Tip) or peeled frozen
Salt and **pepper**
Sugar
Splash of **beef stock or beef consommé**

In a small skillet, heat the EVOO (1 turn of the pan) and butter over medium-high heat. When the butter foams, add the pearl onions and season with salt, pepper, and a little pinch of sugar. Cook until lightly caramelized and very golden in color, about 20 minutes. Make sure to shake the pan every few minutes or so. When golden, add a splash of beef stock and let reduce slightly.

If using fresh pearl onions, bring about 5 cups of water to a boil in a medium-size saucepan and season with salt. Once the water has come up to a boil, drop in the pearl onions. Cook until tender, 3 to 4 minutes. Once tender, dunk them into a large bowl of ice water to cool. Then you just hold them with the root facing out and give them a squeeze and they pop out of their little skins.

🕐 **DECEMBER 21/DINNER**

We started with **Caponata** (see April 24, page 27) and I guess we weren't sick of chicken yet, because I made both **Chicken & Biscuits** and **Creamy Chicken & Noodles** and let my guests decide which they wanted. I started by poaching chicken that I used for both dishes.

Chicken & Biscuits

Instead of using the biscuit dough to make dumplings, you can bake off biscuits, split them, and serve up on top of shallow bowlfuls of the filling.

1 (6-ounce) bag **pearl onions**, fresh (see Tip) or peeled frozen
1 to 2 tablespoons **EVOO**
3 to 4 tablespoons **butter**
2 or 3 **carrots**, chopped
2 or 3 small ribs **celery**, chopped
Salt and **pepper**
1 fresh **bay leaf**
2 to 3 tablespoons chopped fresh **dill**
2 to 3 tablespoons chopped fresh **thyme**
2 to 3 tablespoons **flat-leaf parsley**
3 tablespoons **flour**
3 cups **chicken stock** (reserved from poaching your own chicken, if you do that; see Tip)
2 to 3 cups **cooked chicken**, pulled or chopped (see Tip)
1 cup frozen **green peas**, thawed
1 recipe **biscuits** (homemade or from a mix), for 8 to 12 biscuits

In a small pot of boiling water, parboil the onions for 4 to 5 minutes. Drain. Peel if necessary.

In a Dutch oven, heat the EVOO (1 or 2 turns of the pan) and melt the butter into the oil. Add the pearl onions, carrots, and celery. Season them with salt and pepper and add the bay leaf. Sauté that until tender. Add the dill, thyme, and parsley. Sprinkle in the flour and stir that for a couple of minutes. Add in the chicken stock and cook until the sauce thickens, then add the chicken. Stir in the peas and bring to a simmer.

To make dumplings, drop clumps (a few tablespoons) of dough with a little space between them onto the surface of the simmering mixture. Cover the pan tightly so the steam cooks the dumplings on top of your chicken filling, 8 to 10 minutes.

Serves 4

For the chicken dishes, poach 2 full chicken breasts (4 halves) with a couple of coarsely chopped carrots, a couple of chopped celery ribs, a chopped onion, some chopped garlic, and an herb bundle of dill, parsley, thyme, rosemary, and a bay leaf. Then reserve the stock.

Creamy Chicken & Noodles

3 tablespoons **butter**
2 tablespoons **EVOO**
12 ounces **white mushrooms**, sliced
2 tablespoons fresh **thyme**, finely chopped
2 **leeks**, thinly sliced
1 small **carrot**, finely chopped
1 small rib **celery**, finely chopped
Salt and **pepper**
3 tablespoons **flour**
½ cup **dry white wine**
1½ to 2 cups **chicken stock**
½ cup **heavy cream**
Freshly grated **nutmeg**
2 to 3 cups **cooked poached chicken breast** (see Tip, this page) or rotisserie chicken, skin and bones removed, meat pulled or chopped
½ pound **extra-wide egg noodles**
2 tablespoons **Dijon mustard**
2 tablespoons chopped **fresh dill** or **tarragon**

In a large, deep skillet, heat the butter and EVOO (2 turns of the pan) over medium to medium-high heat. Add the mushrooms and lightly brown, 10 to 12 minutes. Stir in the thyme, leeks, carrots, and celery and sprinkle with salt and pepper. Cook, partially covered, until the vegetables soften, 10 minutes. Sprinkle in the flour and stir 1 minute, and then pour in the wine, letting it absorb. Add the stock and bring to a bubble. Stir in the cream, season with a little nutmeg, and let the sauce thicken a bit. Add the chicken and cook to heat through.

Bring a pot of salted water to a boil and cook the noodles to al dente. Drain. Stir the Dijon mustard into the creamy chicken, and then combine the sauce with the noodles and chopped herb.

Serves 4

🕐 DECEMBER 22/DINNER

We had **Grandpa's Braised Beef** (see December 6, page 205).

🕐 DECEMBER 23/DINNER

We went to John's family for Christmas Eve.

🕐 CHRISTMAS EVE DINNER

Feast of the Seven Fishes: My mom doesn't really care for a lot of seafood. John and I eat pretty much all types of seafood, but Mom likes only shrimp, crab, anchovies, and white flaky fish. So that's usually what we have, some variation of those things. We had **Shrimp with Chile-Lemon Butter**, **Crab Cakes** (see May 26, page 43), and cracked crab claws with my **Cocktail Sauce** (see September

ber 1, page 134). We also did **Grandpa's Stuffed Artichokes** (see November 4, page 182)—we made two of them and they looked like giant Christmas stars. And I tossed artichoke hearts with a little vinaigrette and made little **pizza bites**. I also prepared **Christmas Pasta**. We eat this on Christmas Day, but I prepared it on Christmas Eve so it would sit for a day.

> *Pizza bites:* When I go to the Harvest restaurant, I always get the pizza named after me, which is green peppers, onions, and hot peppers. We get it done on the crispy side and the next day we cut it into little triangles, reheat it in the oven, and use it as a little appetizer.

Shrimp with Chile-Lemon Butter

Serve this with crusty bread.

2 tablespoons **EVOO**
4 tablespoons (½ stick) **butter**, cut into pieces
5 or 6 cloves **garlic**, thinly sliced or chopped
1 **red Fresno chile**, thinly sliced
1 pound peeled, deveined **jumbo shrimp**
Sea salt and **pepper**
⅓ to ½ cup chopped **flat-leaf parsley**
½ cup **dry white wine** or ⅓ cup dry vermouth
Juice of 1 **lemon**

In a large skillet, heat the EVOO (2 turns of the pan) over medium to medium-high heat and melt the butter into it. Add the garlic, chile, and shrimp and toss them together in the pan until the shrimp are opaque and firm. Season with sea salt and pepper to taste. Stir in the parsley. Deglaze the pan with the wine or vermouth and douse it with the lemon juice.

Serves 4

Christmas Pasta 2011

6 tablespoons **EVOO**
¼ pound **pancetta**, diced
6 **bone-in beef short ribs** (about 1½ pounds)
Kosher salt and **pepper**
2 or 3 **carrots**, chopped
2 or 3 ribs **celery**, chopped
2 **onions**, finely chopped
7 or 8 cloves **garlic**, thinly sliced
2 tablespoons fresh **rosemary**, chopped
2 tablespoons fresh **thyme**, chopped
2 tablespoons chopped fresh **sage**
Leaves from 1 sprig fresh **oregano** or
  marjoram, chopped
A pinch of ground **cloves**
3 tablespoons **tomato paste**
2 cups Barolo or other **rich red wine**
1 (10.5-ounce) can **beef consommé**
1 (28- or 32-ounce) can **San Marzano tomatoes**
  (look for DOP on the label) or 2½ to
  3 pounds fresh tomatoes

¾ pound **bulk hot Italian sausage**
¾ pound **bulk sweet Italian sausage**
2 pounds **rigatoni pasta**
1 cup grated **pecorino cheese**

Preheat the oven to 325°F.

In a large Dutch oven, heat 4 tablespoons of the EVOO (4 turns of the pan) over medium-high heat. Add the pancetta and render out the fat until crisp. Remove the pancetta with a slotted spoon and drain on paper towels.

Season the short ribs generously with salt and pepper. Add to the pan and brown on all sides—you may need to do this in batches. Set aside. Stir in the carrots, celery, onions, garlic, rosemary, thyme, sage, oregano, and clove. Partially cover the vegetables and cook to soften a bit, 5 to 8 minutes. Once softened, add the tomato paste and stir for a minute or two to incorporate, then add the wine, consommé, and tomatoes. Return the short ribs and pancetta to the pot, stir everything together, bring up to a simmer, cover, and bake until the meat is tender to the touch or falls apart easily, 2 to 2½ hours. Cool and refrigerate overnight if making ahead.

The next day, remove the excess fat that has floated to the top and solidified. Take the meat off the bones and shred with two forks or with your fingers. Add the meat back into the sauce. Place the pot over medium heat to bring up to temperature.

Meanwhile, in a large skillet, heat the remaining 2 tablespoons EVOO (2 turns of the pan) over medium-high heat. Add the sausages to the pan and cook while breaking up with the back of a wooden spoon until browned, crisp, and crumbly, 8 to 10 minutes. Drain the sausage and then add it to the meat sauce. Stir together to combine.

While the meat sauce is coming together, bring a large pot of water to a boil for the rigatoni. Salt the boiling water and cook the rigatoni to al dente.

Toss the pasta with the sauce. Place pasta in bowls and sprinkle pecorino cheese on top.

Serves 8

For Christmas dinner, we started with **Caponata**, **Bull's-Eye Deviled Eggs** (see April 24, pages 27 and 29), and **Country-Style Chicken Livers** (see April 20, page 18). We also had **Caesar Salad** (see April 18, page 16) but because it was winter, I used all romaine lettuce instead of kale from my garden. And of course we had the **Christmas Pasta** that I had made the day before (page 219).

🕐 DECEMBER 26/CHRISTMAS, PART 2

We celebrate Christmas in many parts. On the eve of Christmas Eve, we go to John's family. On Christmas Eve, it's just Mom for the Feast of the Seven Fishes. Christmas Day was my brother, Manny; his baby, Viv; and Dad. The day after Christmas (today), my sister Ria, my niece Jessie, Mommy, John, and I all exchanged gifts. We had **Beef Tenderloin with Horseradish Sauce**, **Roasted Turkey Breast with Herb Gravy**, **Basic Cranberry Sauce** (see October 11, page 167), and **Green Beans & Almonds**.

Beef Tenderloin with Horseradish Sauce

I bought a whole tenderloin and saved the top and tail to grind for Tenderloin Burgers (which we had on December 28; see page 223).

- 2- to 3-pound **center-cut beef tenderloin**, well trimmed
- **EVOO**, for drizzling
- **Kosher salt** and **coarse pepper**
- 2 cups **sour cream**
- ¼ to ½ cup **prepared horseradish**
- 2 tablespoons **Dijon mustard**
- 30 **chives**, chopped

Preheat the oven to 425°F. Bring the meat to room temperature.

Place the beef on a baking sheet and drizzle the meat with a little EVOO; season very liberally with salt and pepper. Roast until dark golden brown, about 20 minutes. Reduce the oven temperature to 325°F (that's when the roast turkey had to go in) and roast for about 1½ hours. For medium, a thermometer should read 135° to 140°F. Let it rest before slicing

Meanwhile make the horseradish sauce. In a bowl, stir together the sour cream, horseradish, mustard, and chives. Season with salt and pepper to taste.

Serves 6 to 8

Roasted Turkey Breast with Herb Gravy

- 5- to 6-pound **skin-on, boneless turkey breast**
- 8 tablespoons (1 stick) **butter**, softened
- 1 small **shallot**, chopped
- 1 clove **garlic**, grated or pasted
- 1 teaspoon grated **lemon zest**
- 1 tablespoon **lemon juice**
- ¼ cup minced **fresh herbs** (such as parsley, chives, thyme, and rosemary)
- **Salt** and **pepper**
- 2 tablespoons **flour**
- 4 cups **chicken stock**
- 1 **egg yolk**
- **Worcestershire sauce**

Preheat the oven to 325°F. Place the turkey on a wire rack set over a baking sheet.

In a food processor, combine the butter, shallot, garlic, lemon zest, lemon juice, and herbs. Season it with salt and pepper and process until combined. Measure out ¼ cup and place in a small saucepan.

Slather the remaining garlic-herb butter over the turkey breast and sprinkle liberally with salt and pepper. Roast the turkey 15 minutes per pound, 1½ to 2 hours.

Right before serving the turkey, melt the reserved garlic-herb butter over medium heat. Whisk in the flour and cook for a minute or two. Add the stock and cook to thicken. Beat some of the warm stock into the egg yolk, then add the warmed egg yolk back into the pan. Season with Worcestershire sauce, salt, and pepper to taste.

Serves 6 to 8

Green Beans & Almonds

Salt and **pepper**
2 pounds **green beans**, trimmed
6 tablespoons (¾ stick) **butter**
1 large **onion**, sliced
1 cup **chicken stock**
½ to ¾ cup sliced **almonds**, toasted

In a large pot of boiling salted water, parboil the beans for 5 minutes. Drain them and cold-shock them in ice water.

In a large skillet, melt the butter over medium heat. Add the onion and cook until caramelized, about 30 minutes.

Add the chicken stock and simmer together for about 5 minutes. Add the beans and season with salt and pepper.

Serve topped with the toasted almonds.

Serves 6

Two-Person Ham & Mushroom Omelet

3 tablespoons **EVOO**
4 tablespoons (½ stick) **butter**
¼ pound **cremini** or **white mushrooms**, sliced
1 tablespoon fresh **thyme**, finely chopped
Salt and **pepper**
1 large **shallot**, finely chopped
¼ pound thin **asparagus** spears, very thinly sliced on an angle
¼ to ½ pound thick-cut **ham**, diced or chopped
6 **eggs**
2 tablespoons **Dijon mustard**
½ cup shredded **Swiss** or **Cheddar cheese**

In a skillet, heat 2 tablespoons EVOO (2 turns of the pan) over medium to medium-high heat and melt in 3 tablespoons butter. Add the mushrooms and thyme. Once the mushrooms are browned, season with salt and pepper to taste. Add the shallot and asparagus, and toss that around for another 2 to 3 minutes, then set aside.

In a separate pan, heat the remaining 1 tablespoon EVOO (1 turn of the pan) and 1 tablespoon butter. Add the ham and cook to brown it.

In a bowl, beat together the eggs, mustard, and salt and pepper to taste. Add the eggs to the skillet with the ham and combine. Cook until set, then top it with the mushroom and asparagus mixture and cheese, fold it over, and let the cheese melt.

Serves 2

⏱ **DECEMBER 28/DINNER**

We had **Mushroom Soup**, **Tenderloin Burgers**, and **Homemade Tots**.

Mushroom Soup

When I'm ready to serve, I stir in 3 cups of cooked rice pilaf. I cook the rice separately, so it doesn't overbloat in the soup. I also serve bread and butter alongside.

2 tablespoons **EVOO**
4 tablespoons (½ stick) **butter**
¾ pound **mushrooms**, sliced
½ cup **dry sherry**
1 large **leek**, sliced
1 **onion**, chopped
3 to 4 medium **carrots**, chopped
1 large **parsnip**, chopped
2 tablespoons chopped fresh **sage**
2 tablespoons **thyme leaves**, chopped
2 tablespoons chopped **flat-leaf parsley**
2 large cloves **garlic**, chopped
1 fresh **bay leaf**
Salt and **pepper**
2 cups diced **cooked turkey** or chicken
8 cups **chicken stock**
Rice Pilaf (recipe follows)

In a heavy soup pot, heat the EVOO (2 turns of the pan) over medium heat and melt the butter into it. Add the mushrooms and brown. Once the mushrooms are deeply browned, stir in the sherry and cook to reduce. Add the leek and onion. (I usually use leeks or onions. In this case it looks as if I had both on hand, so I used both.) Add carrots, parsnip, sage, thyme, parsley, garlic, and bay leaf. Season with salt and pepper to taste. Partially cover and sweat out the vegetables until tender. Add the turkey or chicken and the stock. Bring to a simmer. Just before serving, fish out the bay leaf and stir in the rice pilaf.

Serves 4

RICE PILAF

1 teaspoon **EVOO**
1 teaspoon **butter**
¼ small **onion**, chopped
Salt and **pepper**
1 cup long-grain **white rice**
2 cups **chicken stock** or water
2 or 3 tablespoons sliced **almonds**

In a small pot, heat the EVOO and butter over medium to medium-high heat. Add the onion and season with salt and pepper. Cook, stirring frequently, for 2 minutes.

Add the rice and stir to coat in the butter and oil, toasting the rice for 1 to 2 minutes. Add the stock and bring up to a bubble, then turn the heat down to medium and cover the pot. Cook until the rice is tender, about 18 minutes. Add the sliced almonds and fluff with a fork.

Makes 3 cups

Tenderloin Burgers

I cooked the burgers on a plancha. A plancha is like a really big griddle that they install in restaurants in order to cook a lot of burgers or other meats at once. You can get a cast-iron plancha for your stovetop. Basically it's just a cast-iron griddle with one side open and the other 3 sides with a cast-iron backsplash so the burgers don't splatter all over. My plancha is red and is quite large and heavy, like a big square skillet. I served the burgers with my Horseradish Sauce (see July 15, page 90) and ketchup.

1½ pounds **beef tenderloin**, cut into cubes
¼ cup very finely chopped **flat-leaf parsley**
¼ cup grated **onion**
1 large **egg yolk**, beaten
Kosher salt and **coarse pepper**
2 tablespoons **butter**
Sliced **mozzarella** or mild Cheddar (optional)
4 **brioche burger rolls**, split and lightly toasted

Using a grinder attachment for a stand mixer or pulsing in a food processor, coarsely grind the tenderloin meat. Transfer to a bowl. Add the parsley, onion, egg yolk, and salt and pepper to taste. Form 4 patties. Heat a cast-iron pan or large heavy skillet over medium-high heat. Add the butter and when it foams, add the burgers and cook 6 to 8 minutes for rare to medium-rare, turning once. For cheeseburgers, top with the cheese for the last minute of cooking. Serve on the rolls.

Serves 4

Homemade Tots

My buddy Tommy was there the first time we made these. He and John loved them so much their eyes popped out of their heads.

6 **medium starchy potatoes**, such as russets, peeled and cubed
Kosher salt and **pepper**
3 tablespoons finely grated **onion**

¼ cup **flour**, plus more for rolling
1 large **egg**
1 tablespoon minced fresh **rosemary**
Peanut oil or vegetable oil, for frying

Cook the potatoes in a large pot of well-salted boiling water until tender. Drain the potatoes well and pass them through a ricer into a large bowl. Add the grated onion (grate it right over the bowl), flour, egg, and rosemary; season with salt and pepper and mix well.

On a floured surface, roll the potato mix into 1-inch-thick logs and cut into tots.

Fill a countertop fryer with oil or pour a few inches of oil into a large Dutch oven. Heat the oil to 350°F. (The oil is ready when a 1-inch cube of white bread cooks to golden brown in 40 seconds.) Fry the tots in small batches until golden and crisp, about 4 minutes. Remove and drain on paper towels. Season the cooked tots with a little extra salt.

Makes 80 to 100 tots

🔴 DECEMBER 29/LUNCH

For lunch I made everyone roast beef sandwiches with tenderloin left over from a couple of nights before.

> **Tenderloin sandwiches:** I made the sandwiches with sliced tenderloin, but you could also make them with store-bought roast beef. I served them on ciabatta rolls with melted mozzarella over the top, and relish of chopped tomato and basil. I drizzled the roll with some olive oil as well.

Bucatini with Sausage, Fennel, Pepper & Onion Sauce

Salt and **pepper**
½ pound **bucatini**
2 tablespoons **EVOO**
½ pound **bulk Italian sweet sausage**
1 small **red or yellow onion**, finely chopped
2 large cloves **garlic**, finely chopped or grated
1 bulb **fennel**, trimmed, quartered, cored, and very thinly sliced
1 **red** and 1 **yellow bell pepper**, quartered lengthwise and thinly sliced
1 **cubanelle pepper**, halved lengthwise, then thinly sliced
½ to ¾ cup **white wine**
1 (28- or 32-ounce) can **San Marzano tomatoes** (look for DOP on the label)
A handful of **flat-leaf parsley**, chopped
A handful of **basil leaves**, torn or shredded
A handful of freshly grated **Parmigiano-Reggiano cheese**, plus more for serving

Bring a large pot of water to a boil. Salt the water and cook the pasta to al dente. Drain the pasta.

Meanwhile, in a large skillet, heat the EVOO (2 turns of the pan) over medium-high heat. Add the sausage and brown and crumble it, then add the onion and garlic and soften for a couple of minutes. Season with salt and pepper. Add the fennel and peppers and cook until tender, 7 to 8 minutes more. Deglaze with the wine. Add the tomatoes and cook for about 30 minutes.

Add the drained pasta to the pan and toss it with the parsley, basil, and Parm. Serve with more Parm at the table.

Serves 2 as an entrée or 3 to 4 as a side or starter

We had **Bull's-Eye Deviled Eggs**, **Caponata** (see April 24, pages 27 and 29), my mom's **Country-Style Chicken Livers** (see April 19, page 18), and **Cider Beef** and **Mashed Potatoes & Parsnips with Cheddar** (see October 28, page 175). I also served some cheese, fruit, and nuts.

Brunch was **Crab Cakes** (see May 26, page 43) with **Cocktail Sauce** (see September 1, page 134) and pink champagne.

We did a New Year's Eve Fiesta and I served the courses a few at a time over several hours to keep us all awake. The food was a motivator to stay awake! We had **Jalapeño Poppers** (see April 26, page 30), **Jane Fox's Famous Tortilla Soup** (see November 6, page 186), **Fresh Salsa Verde** (see December 11, page 209), **bean dip nachos** with **rajas**, and **Zucchini & Corn Fritters**. And for my friend Donna, I made a **Vegetable Posole**.

Bean dip nachos: I made my usual Bean Dip (page 44) and I served it with RW Garcia tortilla chips, which are gluten-free mixed vegetable chips. There's a carrot chip, a beet chip, and a spinach chip and it's a really delicious combination. So you spread the bean dip on any chips you like and top with shredded cheese that you melt down over it. Then I topped that with some rajas (see below) and any salsas you like and I put that out as one of the appetizers.

Rajas: Take about ¾ cup of crème fraîche and season it up with a little cumin and add grated garlic (1 large clove), salt and pepper, and about a tablespoon of lime juice. Roast 3 or 4 poblano chiles (see Tip, page 210) and cut into strips. Mix with the crème fraîche sauce.

Zucchini & Corn Fritters

1 small **zucchini**, chopped or shredded on the large holes of a box grater
Salt and **black pepper**
Kernels from 2 small ears **corn**
⅔ cup **flour**
2 large **eggs**
½ cup finely chopped **scallions**
About 1½ cups shredded cheese (I like to combine **sharp Cheddar with Monterey Jack or pepper jack**)
Corn oil, for shallow-frying

Preheat the oven to 250°F. Place a wire cooling rack over a baking sheet.

Place the zucchini in a strainer, salt it liberally, and allow it to drain for 15 to 20 minutes. Press out the excess liquid.

Transfer the zucchini to a food processor and add half of the corn. Pulse to finely chop. In a bowl, combine the flour, eggs, scallions, and cheese; season with salt and pepper. Add the remaining whole corn kernels as well as the finely chopped corn and zucchini. Stir to combine.

In a large skillet, heat about ¼ inch oil over medium to medium-high heat. Once the oil is hot and ripples, spoon in 2- to 3-inch mounds of the fritter mixture. Fry until deeply golden, 2 to 3 minutes on each side. Transfer to the rack to keep warm in the oven while you make the rest of the fritters.

Makes 10 to 12 fritters

Vegetable Posole

I made my homemade tomatillo salsa for this, and I had more than I needed for the posole, so I just put it out with chips as an app.

About 3 tablespoons **corn** or **vegetable oil**
1 pound **mixed mushrooms**, chopped or thinly sliced
Salt and **pepper**
1 teaspoon ground **cumin**
1 teaspoon ground **coriander**
1 teaspoon dried **Mexican oregano**, lightly crushed
1 teaspoon **dried epazote**, lightly crushed (optional)
½ bottle **Mexican beer**
1 cup **salsa verde**, homemade (pages 84, 209) or store-bought
1 (14-ounce) can **hominy**, drained
3 cups **vegetable stock**
Cilantro leaves and thinly sliced **scallions** or chopped red onion, for garnish

In a soup pot or Dutch oven, heat the oil over medium-high heat. Add the mushrooms and brown well, about 15 minutes. Season with salt and pepper. Stir in the cumin, coriander, oregano, and epazote (if using) and cook a minute more. Deglaze with the beer. Add the salsa, hominy, and stock, and simmer over low heat. Serve with the garnish.

Serves 4

JANUARY

SUNDAY/1

DINNER
New Year's lentil soup

MONDAY/2

DINNER
veal dumplings in broth with escarole, mushroom lasagna

TUESDAY/3

BREAKFAST
panettone French toast
LUNCH
creamy winter vegetable soup
DINNER
roast pork supper (with potato-parsnip pancakes)

WEDNESDAY/4

LUNCH
creamy winter vegetable soup, cheesy croutons

THURSDAY/5

BRUNCH
deviled ham melts
DINNER
chicken curry, homemade rice pilaf

WEDNESDAY/11

BREAKFAST
turkey stuffing hash and eggs

THURSDAY/12

FRIDAY/13

DINNER
puttanesca with red pepper spaghetti

SATURDAY/14

DINNER
lemon garlic guacamole, crabby guacamole, apple & almond guacamole, jalapeño poppers, bean dip, fresh salsa verde, zucchini and corn fritters. red pork posole

SUNDAY/15

DINNER
spaghetti & meatballs

SATURDAY/21

DINNER
beef bourguignon, assorted salumi and cheese, country-style chicken livers

SUNDAY/22

DINNER
chicken potpie/casserole

MONDAY/23

TUESDAY/24

WEDNESDAY/25

LUNCH
turkey tacos
DINNER
that's shallot-a flavor spaghetti

FRIDAY/6

DINNER
artichoke and
asparagus salad,
chicken chasseur

SATURDAY/7

LUNCH
soba bowls

SUNDAY/8

DINNER
stuffed cabbage with
rice pilaf

MONDAY/9

DINNER
cavatelli with sausage,
eggplant & saffron
cream

TUESDAY/10

MONDAY/16

TUESDAY/17

WEDNESDAY/18

DINNER
double-high patty
melts

THURSDAY/19

DINNER
egg tagliatelle with
Bolognese sauce,
Grandpa's stuffed
artichokes, vegetable
antipasto

FRIDAY/20

THURSDAY/26

DINNER
plum & ponzu short
ribs, soba bowls

FRIDAY/27

DINNER
portobello Bolognese

SATURDAY/28

SUNDAY/29

DINNER
apple-pear sauce,
light potato pancakes,
sauerbraten

MONDAY/30

TUESDAY/31

DINNER
pasta with sausage &
kale in roasted garlic
sauce, homemade
pork sausage

I made **Lentil Soup** because lentils are good luck. Because they look like little coins, they signify prosperity for the New Year.

New Year's Lentil Soup

Speck is a smoky prosciutto—or you can use pancetta.

¼ cup **EVOO**
¼ pound **speck**, diced (¼-inch cubes)
1 **onion**, finely chopped
2 **carrots** (see Tip), finely chopped
1 or 2 small ribs **celery** with leafy tops, finely chopped
4 cloves **garlic**, thinly sliced
Leaves from 1 or 2 sprigs fresh **rosemary**, chopped
1 to 2 tablespoons fresh **thyme** leaves, chopped
1 large fresh **bay leaf**
Salt and **pepper**
3 tablespoons **tomato paste**
1 cup **dry white wine**
4 cups **chicken stock**
1¼ cups **brown lentils**
1 small bunch **lacinato kale** (also called black, Tuscan, or dinosaur kale), stemmed and thinly sliced
Freshly grated **nutmeg**

In large soup pot, heat the EVOO (4 turns of the pan), add the speck, and render out the fat. Then add the onion, carrots, celery, garlic, rosemary, thyme, bay leaf, and salt and pepper to taste. Partially cover and cook 7 to 8 minutes to soften the vegetables, stirring occasionally. Stir in the tomato paste and cook until fragrant. Deglaze with the wine and reduce a minute. Add the stock and 2 cups water and bring to a boil. Add the lentils and cook to tender, 30 to 35 minutes.

Wilt in the kale, add a little nutmeg, and adjust the seasonings. Serve in shallow bowls.

Serves 4 to 6

> When I buy carrots I buy organic and I look for the ones with the green tops still on. I find that even if they're marked organic, bagged carrots can taste really musty, like a warehouse, so I always buy either bulk loose carrots with no tops or bunches of carrots with green tops.

Our friends Brooke and Marianna came upstate for a belated exchange of Christmas gifts, and good times and good tidings. Dinner was really fun because John got Christmas crackers that had sheet music and whistles in them, and you were assigned a number and John would conduct a song with us trying to play the whistles. It didn't sound too great but it was fun trying. I made a two-course dinner, starting with **Veal Dumplings in Broth with Escarole**, followed by **Mushroom Lasagna**.

Veal Dumplings in Broth with Escarole

2 slices good-quality **white bread**
1 cup **whole milk**
1¼ pounds **ground veal**
Freshly grated **nutmeg**
Kosher salt and **pepper**
10 to 12 medium **sage leaves**, very thinly sliced
2 cloves **garlic**, grated or pasted
About ⅓ cup **Gorgonzola dolce cheese**, crumbled
About ⅓ cup grated **Parmigiano-Reggiano cheese**
1 **egg**, lightly beaten
EVOO, for drizzling
8 cups **chicken stock**
1 head **escarole**, cleaned and chopped into
   2-inch pieces
4 ounces **extra-wide egg noodles**
Grated **lemon zest**

Soak the bread in the milk to soften. Place the veal in a bowl and season with a little nutmeg, salt, and pepper. Then add the sage, garlic, cheeses, and egg. Squeeze the liquid from the bread and crumble into fine crumbs between your fingertips as you add it to the veal mixture. Drizzle in a little EVOO and mix well to combine. Use a 2-ounce scoop or a warm water bath to keep your hands from sticking and roll out about 20 meatballs. Set them on a large plate.

In a large saucepan, combine the chicken stock and 2 to 3 cups water and bring to a low boil. Add the meatballs and cook for 8 to 10 minutes

to cook though. Wilt in the escarole in the last 1 or 2 minutes of cook time. (You can do this part ahead, cool, and then store until you're ready to serve. Reheat to a low boil before proceeding.)

Meanwhile, cook the egg noodles in salted water to al dente. Add the noodles to the soup, ladle into bowls, and top with a little lemon zest.

Serves 4

Mushroom Lasagna

SAUCE
2 tablespoons **butter**
2 tablespoons **flour**
1½ cups **milk**
Freshly grated **nutmeg**
Salt and **pepper**

LASAGNA
2 tablespoons **EVOO**
4 tablespoons (½ stick) **butter**
1½ to 2 pounds **mushrooms** (mixture of trumpets,
   lots of cremini, and some wood ears), sliced or
   quartered, depending on the mushroom
1 or 2 tablespoons chopped fresh **thyme**
Salt and **pepper**
4 cloves **garlic**, shaved or very thinly sliced
½ cup **Marsala**
2½ to 3 cups **fresh ricotta** (I like sheep's milk)
2 **eggs**, lightly beaten
1 cup grated **Parmigiano-Reggiano cheese** or a
   combination of Parm and Pecorino Romano
2 cups diced **fresh mozzarella** (I used fior de
   latte)
1 cup shredded **Fontina cheese**
1 (9-ounce) box **no-boil flat lasagna sheets** (I like
   Barilla; they taste the most like homemade
   fresh pasta sheets)

Make the sauce: In a saucepan, melt the butter over medium heat. Add the flour and whisk that together for a minute or two. Whisk in the milk and season with nutmeg, salt, and pepper. Cook that until it thickens up enough to coat the back of a spoon. Remove from the heat.

Make the lasagna: In a large skillet, heat the EVOO (2 turns of the pan) over medium heat.

Melt the butter into that and add the mushrooms. Let the mushrooms brown completely, then season them with the thyme and salt and pepper to taste. Add the garlic and stir that around for another 1 or 2 minutes. Deglaze the mushrooms with the Marsala. Set the mushrooms aside.

In a bowl, combine the ricotta, eggs, ½ cup of the Parm, 1 cup of the mozzarella, and salt and pepper to taste (see Tip). In a separate bowl, mix together the remaining ½ cup Parm, 1 cup mozzarella, and the Fontina.

Preheat the oven to 375°F.

Separate the lasagna sheets and soak them in hot water for 4 or 5 minutes. Then in a 9 by 13-inch baking pan, make layers in the following order: one-fourth of the sauce, 4 lasagna sheets, half the ricotta mixture, half the mushrooms, one-fourth of the sauce, half the mozzarella-Fontina, 4 lasagna sheets, the remaining ricotta mixture, the remaining mushrooms, one-fourth of the sauce, the remaining 4 lasagna sheets, the remaining sauce, and the remaining mozzarella-Fontina. That sounds complicated but it really isn't.

Cover the pan tightly with foil and place on a baking sheet as an underliner so it catches any spills. Bake for 45 minutes, uncover, and bake until browned and bubbling, 10 to 15 minutes.

Serves 4 to 6

You could add spinach to that ricotta mixture if you wanted to add some greens to this. Use a box of thawed chopped spinach, wrung dry in a kitchen towel.

JANUARY 3, BREAKFAST

Panettone French toast: I do this a lot around the holidays because we buy panettone. I get it at Buon Italia in Chelsea Market. (They ship anywhere and they have really authentic baked goods from great bakeries in Italy, and very lovely panettone.) Panettone is a fruited golden sweet bread, almost a cake. When making the French toast, I cut slices about an inch thick. You could substitute a thick-cut brioche. If I'm cooking for 4 people, I mix together 3 large eggs and 1½ cups half-and-half or whole milk and I season it with nutmeg and a little almond extract. I served it with warm syrup and I'm sure John wanted some Oscar's Smokehouse bacon to go along with it. It's really delicious. I love panettone French toast.

🔴 JANUARY 3/LUNCH

For lunch we had **Creamy Winter Vegetable Soup** and **Cheesy Croutons**.

Creamy Winter Vegetable Soup

You can make this ahead. Cool the soup and store in the fridge or freezer. To reheat, bring to room temp and heat over medium heat. Remove the herb bundle and bay leaves.

¼ cup **EVOO**
1 small **butternut squash**, peeled and cut into ½-inch pieces
2 medium **russet (baking) potatoes**, peeled and cut into ½-inch cubes
2 **carrots**, thinly sliced
2 **parsnips**, peeled and thinly sliced
1 bulb **fennel**, cut into ¼-inch dice
2 **leeks**, halved and cut into ¼-inch slices
2 ribs **celery** with leafy tops, cut into ¼-inch dice
3 or 4 cloves **garlic**, chopped or grated
Salt and **pepper**
2 large fresh **bay leaves**
Bundle of herbs such as parsley, sage, thyme, marjoram
½ cup **dry white wine**
About 2 cups **chicken** or **vegetable stock**
4 tablespoons (½ stick) **butter**
¼ cup **flour**
3 cups **whole milk**
Freshly grated **nutmeg**

CHEESY CROUTONS
2 tablespoons **EVOO**
4 tablespoons (½ stick) **butter**
2 large cloves **garlic**, smashed
4 cups diced stale **peasant-style white bread**
1 cup grated **Parmigiano-Reggiano cheese**

In a large soup pot or Dutch oven, heat the EVOO (4 turns of the pan) over medium-high heat. Add the vegetables as you chop them. Season with salt and pepper. Add the bay leaves and herb bundle, partially cover, and cook to soften the vegetables, stirring occasionally, about 10 minutes. Add the wine and cook until almost evaporated, then add the stock and bring to a boil.

Meanwhile, in a saucepan, melt the butter over medium to medium-high heat. Whisk in the flour for a minute. Whisk in the milk and season with salt, pepper, and nutmeg to taste. Cook until the sauce is thick enough to coat the back of a spoon, then stir the sauce into the soup.

Make the croutons: Preheat the oven to 350°F. In a large skillet, heat the EVOO (2 turns of the pan) and butter over medium to medium-high heat. Add the garlic and swirl a minute, then add the bread and toast to golden, stirring occasionally. Transfer to a baking sheet and sprinkle with the cheese. Bake to set the cheese and dry out the croutons, 10 to 12 minutes. Serve with the soup.

Serves 6

🕐 **JANUARY 3/DINNER**

Roast pork supper: It was **Roast Pork with Potato-Parsnip Cakes**, **Red Cabbage with Apples & Onions** (see October 7, page 165), and **Apple-Pear Sauce** (see January 29, page 246).

Roast Pork with Potato-Parsnip Cakes

The fennel salt I use is from a company called Volterra. You can order from them online. Or you could just make fennel salt with salt and fennel pollen or ground fennel.

4-pound **pork loin roast**
Fennel salt
Pepper
1 cup **dry white wine**
2 large **potatoes**
2 **parsnips**, peeled and shredded
½ cup grated **onion**
1 **egg**, beaten
3 to 4 tablespoons **flour**
Salt
Vegetable oil or olive oil, for shallow-frying

Preheat the oven to 375°F.

Score the fat layer on the roast in a crisscross pattern, about an inch apart. Rub it liberally with fennel salt and lots of black pepper. Place it in a roasting pan and roast for 45 minutes. Add the wine. Continue roasting until the internal temperature reaches 140°F, 35 to 45 minutes (depending on your oven). The roast will continue to cook as it rests out of the oven. Loosely cover the roast with foil (I also put a dish towel on top) and just let it sit so the juices can redistribute. (I probably leave it there a good 20 minutes or so.) Then slice it and set it back in its own juices in the pan.

When the roast comes out, turn the oven down to 275°F. Place a wire rack in a rimmed baking sheet.

Meanwhile, make potato-parsnip pancakes: grate the potatoes, salt them, and let them drain. Then squeeze out all the liquid.

In a bowl, combine the potatoes with the parsnips, onion, egg, and flour. Season with salt and pepper. In a large skillet, heat about ¼ inch oil. When it shimmers, add the potato mixture to make pancakes 3 to 4 inches wide. As you make the pancakes, transfer them to the rack on the baking sheet to keep them nice and crisp.

Serves 6 to 8

🕐 **JANUARY 4/DINNER**

We had **Creamy Winter Vegetable Soup** (see January 3, page 231), back by popular demand.

🕐 **JANUARY 5/BRUNCH**

Deviled Ham Melts

1 bundle thin **asparagus spears**, trimmed
½ pound **deli-sliced imported ham**, coarsely chopped
3 to 4 tablespoons grated or finely chopped **red onion**
1 clove **garlic**, grated or pasted
1 small **red Fresno chile**, seeded and chopped
1 small **celery rib** from the heart, coarsely chopped
A small handful of **flat-leaf parsley leaves**
2 tablespoons **yellow mustard**
1 tablespoon **Frank's RedHot hot sauce**
2 teaspoons **Worcestershire sauce**
1 teaspoon **sweet paprika**
Salt and **pepper**
4 large slices **good-quality pumpernickel bread**
About 1 cup shredded **Gruyère cheese**
About 1 cup shredded **sharp white Cheddar cheese**

In a skillet, bring a couple of inches of water to a boil. Add the asparagus and cook 3 minutes. Remove from the skillet and pat dry.

Preheat the oven to 375°F.

Place the ham, onion, garlic, chile, celery, parsley, mustard, hot sauce, Worcestershire, and paprika in the food processor, season with salt and pepper, and pulse into a spread.

Arrange the bread on a baking sheet, top with an even thick layer of ham, set spears of asparagus across the ham, cover with the cheeses, and bake until golden and the bread is toasted, 10 to 12 minutes.

Serves 4

JANUARY 5/DINNER

We had **Chicken Curry**, a dish I make all the time. And I served it up with **Homemade Rice Pilaf** (see August 28, pages 130 and 131).

JANUARY 6/DINNER

We went out to the movies, but I had made dinner, which was **Chicken Chasseur**, ahead of time. We also had an **artichoke and asparagus salad** with Dijon vinaigrette.

Artichoke and asparagus salad:
I combined artichoke hearts, steamed asparagus tips, romaine hearts, tomato, and red onion and served it with a Dijon vinaigrette. Whenever I make vinaigrette I put a little bit of finely grated shallot in a small bowl and I add the acid (lemon juice or vinegar or a combination of the two) and some salt and let that sit for a bit and the shallot flavor bleeds out into the acid. Then I add a spoonful of Dijon and stream in enough EVOO for the dressing to come together. I season that with salt and pepper (or when I make a salad with fennel maybe I'll add a little ground fennel or fennel pollen to the dressing).

Chicken Chasseur

You could serve this with a warm, crusty baguette or with egg noodles.

6 tablespoons **EVOO**
1 whole 4- to 5-pound **chicken**, cut into skin-on, bone-in serving pieces (thighs, drumsticks, wings, and breasts cut in half)
Salt and **pepper**
1 cup **flour**
¾ pound **button mushrooms**, sliced
1 large **shallot**, finely chopped
¼ cup **cognac**
½ cup **white wine**
1 cup **chicken stock**
1 (15-ounce) can **diced** or **crushed tomatoes**
2 tablespoons chopped fresh **tarragon**
3 tablespoons **butter**, cut in pieces

Preheat the oven to 325°F.

In a large high-sided skillet, heat 3 tablespoons of the EVOO (3 turns of the pan) over medium-high heat. While the oil is heating, liberally season the chicken with salt and pepper and dredge in the flour. Add the chicken to the pan and brown on both sides, 3 to 4 minutes per side. If the pan is oven-safe, place in the oven to finish cooking through, about 20 minutes. If the pan is not oven-safe, place the chicken on a rack set over a baking sheet and place in the oven (in this case, reserve the skillet for the next step). Transfer the cooked chicken to a plate. Tent the plate with foil to keep warm.

Heat the remaining 3 tablespoons EVOO

(3 turns of the pan) in the skillet and add the mushrooms. Cook until browned, then add the shallot and cook for 3 minutes. Deglaze the pan with the cognac and stir until the liquid is almost evaporated. Add the wine and cook for 1 minute, then add the chicken stock, tomatoes, and tarragon and stir to combine. Let cook for a few minutes to reduce and then whisk in the butter. When the butter has melted, turn the heat to medium and add the chicken back to the pan. Stir gently until the chicken is heated through, 4 to 5 minutes.

Serves 4

If you wanted a more vegetable-laden chasseur, you could add leeks (instead of shallots), carrots, and a little bit of celery, all finely chopped (that's the way my mom likes it). My husband likes it with just the shallots.

⏱ JANUARY 7/LUNCH

Soba Bowls

When I made soba bowls the first time at home, it was with soba noodles that we got from Eric, John's best friend, who speaks fluent Japanese and loves Japanese cuisine. He sent us a beautiful collection of flavored soba noodles. The first noodles I tried were mountain yam–flavored soba (called *yamaimo soba*), but you can use regular soba, which are buckwheat-based pasta. You can find them right in the regular grocery store. But if you can't find them, then use whole wheat spaghetti or thin spaghetti.

¼ cup **vegetable oil** for frying, such as safflower or canola
About ½ pound **shiitake mushrooms**, stems discarded, caps thinly sliced
About ¼ pound **maitake** (hen of the woods) mushrooms, thinly sliced

2 **carrots**, peeled and cut into matchsticks
1 large **parsnip**, cut into matchsticks
2 medium **leeks**, cut into matchsticks, washed, and well drained
2 inches fresh **ginger**, peeled and grated
3 or 4 cloves **garlic**, thinly sliced
1 **red Fresno chile**, halved, seeded, and thinly sliced
Salt and **black pepper**
8 cups **chicken** or **vegetable stock**
4 to 6 tablespoons **tamari**
1 (8-ounce) package **soba** or 8 ounces whole wheat spaghetti or thin spaghetti
¼ pound **enoki mushrooms**, trimmed and separated
Chopped **shiso leaf** or cilantro, for garnish
Chopped **scallion greens**, for garnish

In a soup pot or Dutch oven, heat the oil (4 turns of the pan) over medium-high to high heat. Add the shiitake and maitake mushrooms. Cook the mushrooms until nutty and fragrant; then add the vegetable matchsticks, ginger, garlic, and chile; season lightly with salt and liberally with black pepper; and stir-fry 1 to 2 minutes. Add the stock and bring the soup to a boil. Season with tamari to taste. Add the soba or spaghetti and cook to just tender. Stir in the enoki.

Using tongs, fill bowls with the noodles, mushrooms, and vegetables. Ladle the broth over the top and garnish with shiso and scallion greens. Serve with chopsticks and a large spoon for slurping.

Serves 4

⏱ JANUARY 8/DINNER

Stuffed Cabbage with Rice Pilaf

You can stuff the cabbage rolls and get them in the baking pan but not bake them until later. I let them come to room temperature before baking. If you bake them straight from the fridge, they will take about 15 minutes longer in the oven.

1 small head **savoy cabbage**
Salt and **pepper**
2 tablespoons **butter**
About ⅓ cup **orzo or broken spaghetti**
1 cup **long-grain white rice**
4 cups **chicken stock**
3 tablespoons **dried currants**
3 tablespoons **EVOO**
1 pound **meat loaf mix** (ground beef, pork, and veal combined)
2 tablespoons chopped fresh **sage**
⅛ teaspoon freshly grated **nutmeg**
1 **onion**, finely chopped
2 large cloves **garlic**, grated or finely chopped
¼ pound **pancetta**, finely diced
1 fresh **bay leaf**
1 (14- to 15-ounce) can **diced** or **crushed tomatoes**
1 (8-ounce) can **tomato sauce**
3 tablespoons **pine nuts**, toasted
¼ cup **flat-leaf parsley leaves**, finely chopped
⅔ to ¾ cup grated **Parmigiano-Reggiano cheese**
1 large **egg**, lightly beaten

Bring a large pot of water to a boil. Separate 12 large leaves of cabbage. Salt the water, boil the leaves for 2 to 3 minutes, drain, and cool in a single layer on kitchen towels. From the remaining uncooked cabbage, finely chop about 1 cup and set aside.

In a medium saucepan, melt the butter over medium heat. When the butter foams, add the orzo or broken spaghetti. Toss the pasta until very fragrant, deeply brown, and nutty. Stir in the rice and add 2½ cups chicken stock and the currants.

Bring to a boil, reduce to a simmer, cover, and cook until the rice is tender, about 18 minutes. Cool and set the pilaf aside.

In a large skillet, heat 1 tablespoon of the EVOO (1 turn of the pan) over medium-high heat. When the oil is hot, add the ground meat, breaking it up into crumbles as it browns. Add the sage and season with the nutmeg and salt and pepper to taste. Add half the onion, the reserved chopped cabbage, and two-thirds of the garlic, and cook 5 to 6 minutes. Adjust the seasoning to taste. Remove from the heat.

In a small saucepan, heat the remaining 2 tablespoons EVOO (2 turns of the pan) over medium to medium-high heat. Add the pancetta and render for 2 to 3 minutes. Add the remaining onion and the bay leaf, and cook the onion 5 to 6 minutes. Add the remaining 1½ cups chicken stock, the canned tomatoes, and tomato sauce, and season the sauce with salt and pepper. Simmer 20 minutes.

Preheat the oven to 350°F.

In a large bowl, combine the rice pilaf, the cooked meat, about ½ cup of the tomato sauce (fish out the bay leaf), the pine nuts, parsley, Parm, and egg. Wrap and roll each leaf of cabbage burrito-style by placing a mound of filling in a log shape to one edge of each leaf, tuck in the sides, and roll the stuffed cabbage into logs. Arrange the stuffed cabbage logs in a baking dish large enough to hold them in a single layer and top with the rest of the tomato sauce. Bake until hot and bubbling, about 45 minutes.

Serves 4

Cavatelli with Sausage, Eggplant & Saffron Cream

I like to make this dish with a dry pasta called gnocchetti di Sardi. Any small, short-cut pasta will do.

Salt and **black pepper**
1 pound **cavatelli** or cavatappi pasta
¼ cup **EVOO**
2 pinches of **saffron threads** or saffron powder
¾ teaspoon **fennel seeds**
¾ pound **ground pork**
3 or 4 cloves garlic, finely chopped
¼ teaspoon crushed **red pepper flakes**
1 **eggplant**, half-peeled and cut into small dice (leave on half the skin for the color and texture it gives the dish)
Leaves from 3 or 4 **sprigs of fresh thyme**, finely chopped
1 cup **chicken broth**
½ cup **heavy cream**
½ cup freshly grated **Parmigiano-Reggiano** or **Pecorino Romano cheese**, plus more for serving

Bring a large pot of water to a boil. Salt the water and cook the pasta to al dente. Before draining, ladle out and reserve 1 cup of the starchy pasta cooking water. Drain the pasta.

While the pasta is working, in a large, deep skillet, heat 3 tablespoons of the EVOO (3 turns of the pan), the saffron, and fennel seeds over medium-high heat. Add the pork, breaking it up into crumbles as it browns, 3 to 4 minutes. Add the garlic and red pepper flakes and season with salt and black pepper to taste.

Push the meat to the side of the pan. Add the remaining 1 tablespoon EVOO (1 turn of the pan) and the eggplant to the center of the pan; season with salt. Cook the eggplant until just tender, about 5 minutes. Combine with the meat. Add the thyme and toss, then stir in the broth and bring to a boil. Stir in the cream and reduce the heat to low. Adjust the seasoning to taste.

Add the pasta to the sauce and toss with ½ cup cheese until well combined, adding the reserved pasta cooking water to loosen if it gets too thick.

Serve with more cheese passed around the table.

Serves 4

JANUARY 11, BREAKFAST.
Turkey stuffing hash and eggs: Brown 1 pound mild turkey sausage in a little EVOO and drain. Transfer to a plate. Add a couple of tablespoons butter to the skillet. When it foams, add 1 chopped apple, a couple of ribs of chopped celery, and 1 chopped red onion; season with a little poultry seasoning, fresh parsley, bay leaf, salt, and pepper. When the vegetables are tender, deglaze with apple brandy. Return the sausage to the pan along with 2 slices of brioche bread (toasted and chopped into 1/2-inch dice) and a splash of stock to soften it a bit. It basically tastes like sausage stuffing. Top that with over-easy eggs.

Puttanesca with Red Pepper Spaghetti

There is a store in New York City called Buon Italia. They carry all my favorite dried pastas, including a pepperoncini spaghetti with ground peppers incorporated into the pasta itself. When I don't have this on hand I just cook up a pound of any good-quality Italian dried pasta. Puttanesca is one of the few sauces I enjoy with long- and short-cuts of pasta, linguine to penne—it's all fine, just no cut thinner than spaghetti.

¼ cup **EVOO**
7 or 8 good-quality **anchovy fillets**
4 cloves **garlic**, very thinly sliced
1 **red Fresno chile**, thinly sliced, or 1 teaspoon crushed red pepper flakes
¼ to ⅓ cup **dry vermouth**
1 (28- or 32-ounce) can **San Marzano tomatoes** (look for DOP on the label)
A handful of **flat-leaf parsley**, finely chopped
A couple of **basil leaves**, torn
½ cup **oil-cured black olives**, pitted and chopped
3 tablespoons **capers**, drained
Salt
1 pound **red pepper spaghetti** or other dried pasta of choice

In a large skillet, heat the EVOO (4 turns of the pan) over medium-low heat. Add the anchovies, cover the pan with a splatter screen or lid, and shake until the anchovies begin to break up. Reduce the heat a bit, uncover, and stir until the anchovies melt into the oil. Stir in the garlic and chile and cook 1 or 2 minutes. Add the vermouth and stir a minute more. Add the tomatoes and gently break up with a potato masher or wooden spoon. Increase the heat a bit; stir in the parsley, basil, olives, and capers. Bring the sauce to a bubble and cook to thicken while the pasta water comes to a boil and pasta cooks.

Bring a large pot of water to a boil. Salt the water and cook the pasta to al dente. Before draining, ladle out and reserve ½ cup of the starchy pasta cooking water. Drain the pasta and add to the sauce. Add a splash of starchy cooking water and toss the pasta a minute or two for the flavors to absorb. Serve in shallow bowls.

Serves 4

Had friends over for a Mexican Fiesta Night. We had **Red Pork Posole** (see August 21, page 122), **Bean Dip** (see May 27, page 44) that I added some of the pulled-pork cooking juices to, **Fresh Salsa Verde** (see December 11, page 209), **Jalapeño Poppers** (see April 26, page 30), **Zucchini & Corn Fritters** (see December 31, page 225), **Guacamole 3 Ways** (see April 26, page 31, and July 11, page 82)—big shout-out to La Condesa in Austin, Texas. They make an amazing guacamole sampler. Because I visit Austin only once or twice a year, I had to come up with my own knockoffs for the other 363 nights of the year.

Spaghetti & Meatballs

I shave my garlic with a truffle shaver (see page 154) and it comes out Paulie (from *Goodfellas*) thin.

SAUCE
¼ cup **EVOO**
1 **onion**, grated
3 or 4 cloves **garlic**, shaved or thinly sliced
1 **red Fresno chile**, seeded and finely chopped, or 1 teaspoon crushed red pepper flakes
1 tablespoon finely chopped fresh **marjoram** or **oregano**, or 1 teaspoon dried, lightly crushed
Salt and **pepper**
2 tablespoons **tomato paste**
1 cup **dry white wine**
1 cup **beef stock**
1 (28- or 32-ounce) **San Marzano tomatoes** (look for DOP on the label)
A handful of **flat-leaf parsley**, finely chopped
A few leaves of **basil**, torn

MEATBALLS
2 slices good-quality **white bread**, crusts trimmed
1 cup **whole milk**
1 pound **meat loaf mix** (ground beef, pork, and veal combined)
Salt and **pepper**
1 teaspoon **fennel seeds**
A handful of grated **Parmigiano-Reggiano cheese**
A handful of grated **Pecorino Romano cheese**
1 large **egg**, lightly beaten

2 or 3 cloves **garlic**, grated or pasted
2 tablespoons **EVOO**

1 pound **spaghetti**
2 tablespoons **butter**
Grated **Parmigiano-Reggiano** or **Pecorino Romano cheese**, for serving

Make the sauce: In a large Dutch oven, heat the EVOO (4 turns of the pan) over medium-low heat. Add the onion and its juice, the garlic, chile, and marjoram or oregano. Season with salt and pepper to taste. Let cook out slowly, 10 to 12 minutes.

Stir in the tomato paste and cook until very fragrant and well combined, 1 to 2 minutes. Stir in the wine; increase the heat to medium to medium-high; and cook to reduce the wine by half, 3 to 4 minutes. Stir in the stock. Add the tomatoes and crush with a potato masher. Stir in the parsley and basil. Bring the sauce to a bubble, then reduce to a simmer.

Meanwhile, make the meatballs: Preheat the oven to 375°F. Arrange a wire cooling rack over a baking sheet.

Tear up the bread and place in a small bowl and cover with the milk. Let stand 5 minutes. Place the meat in a large bowl. Gently squeeze out the excess liquid from the bread as you add it to the meat, crumbling the bread with your fingertips as you work. Season the meat with salt and pepper. Add the fennel seeds, grated cheeses, egg, garlic, and the EVOO (2 turns around the bowl). Combine all the ingredients thoroughly, then roll into 2-inch balls.

Place the meatballs on the rack in the baking sheet and roast until browned, about 15 minutes. Gently add the meatballs to the simmering sauce and cook, partially covered, for 20 minutes.

Meanwhile, bring a large pot of water to a boil. Salt the water and cook the pasta to al dente. Before draining, ladle out and reserve 1 cup of the starchy pasta cooking water. Drain the pasta, return to the hot cooking pot, and add the butter.

Remove the meatballs from the thickened

sauce. Add half of the sauce to the cooked pasta and toss to combine with a splash of the reserved starchy cooking water. Serve the pasta in shallow bowls, topped with the remaining sauce and 3 meatballs. Top with grated Parmigiano-Reggiano (if you like a nutty flavor) or Pecorino Romano (if you prefer a tangy flavor).

Serve 4

🕐 **JANUARY 18/DINNER**

Double-High Patty Melts

These were turkey and portobello patty melts—they were insanely delicious (and I used Amy's bread).

TURKEY BURGERS
1½ pounds **ground turkey**
2 to 3 tablespoons grated **onion**
2 tablespoons chopped **chives**
2 tablespoons chopped **flat-leaf parsley**
2 tablespoons **Dijon mustard**
1 tablespoon **Worcestershire sauce**
1 tablespoon **poultry seasoning**
1 tablespoon **EVOO**

PORTOBELLOS
3 tablespoons **EVOO**
4 large **portobello mushrooms**, cut into ¼-inch slices
1 large **shallot**, sliced
2 tablespoons chopped **fresh thyme**
Salt and **pepper**
¼ cup **dry sherry or Marsala**

Softened **butter**
8 slices **Pullman** or **sourdough bread**
8 slices **Jarlsberg** or **Emmentaler cheese**

Make the turkey burgers: In a bowl, combine the turkey, onion, chives, parsley, mustard, Worcestershire, and poultry seasoning. Form into 4 thin patties. In a skillet, heat the EVOO (1 turn of the pan). Add the patties and cook, turning once, until cooked through, 8 to 10 minutes.

Cook the portobellos: In another skillet, heat the EVOO (3 turns of the pan) over medium-high heat. Add the mushrooms and brown for 10 minutes. Add the shallot, thyme, and salt and pepper to taste; cook to soften, 5 to 10 minutes. Deglaze with the sherry.

Wipe out the skillet and place over medium-high heat. Spread some butter on 1 side of each bread slice. Lay 4 bread slices, buttered side down, on a work surface. Top with a cheese slice, then a turkey burger, then some mushrooms, another cheese slice, and another bread slice, buttered side up. Fry the melts in the skillet (in batches if you have to) over medium heat until golden brown on both sides.

Serves 4

🕐 **JANUARY 19/DINNER**

Regis Philbin and Joy came to supper, and I made **Egg Tagliatelle with Bolognese Sauce** at Reeg's request. I ordered lean meat because I was frankly a little nervous about feeding Reeg beef. He had had heart surgery and I wanted to keep his arteries working, so I got lean beef and veal for the pasta dish. I also put out **Grandpa's Stuffed Artichokes** (see November 4, page 182), a vegetable antipasto, and a couple of healthy salads.

Egg Tagliatelle with Bolognese Sauce

2 tablespoons **EVOO**
1 pound **coarsely ground beef**
1 pound **coarsely ground veal**
1 **carrot**, finely chopped
1 rib **celery**, finely chopped
1 **onion**, finely chopped
2 or 3 large cloves **garlic**, preferably rocambole (I get it from Keith's at the Union Square Greenmarket in NYC), very thinly sliced
1 **bay leaf**

Salt and pepper
¼ cup minced **fresh herbs** (a combination of parsley, sage, rosemary, and thyme)
2 tablespoons **tomato paste**
1 cup **dry white** or **red wine**, preferably Italian
1 (28- or 32-ounce) can **San Marzano tomatoes** (look for DOP on the label)
1 cup whole **milk**
Pinch of ground **cloves**
1 pound **egg tagliatelle noodles** (I like Delverde brand)
1 cup grated **Parmigiano-Reggiano cheese**
½ cup **flat-leaf parsley leaves**, chopped

In a large Dutch oven, heat the EVOO (2 turns of the pan) over medium-high heat. Add the meats and cook, breaking it up into crumbles as it browns; get the meat very, very, dry. When the meat gets deeply browned, stir in the carrot, celery, onion, garlic, bay leaf, and salt and pepper. Add the parsley, sage, rosemary, and thyme (I know, it's a Simon and Garfunkel song, but there ya go, that's what I had on hand in the fridge). Stir that around, let the little bits of vegetables sweat out a couple of minutes, then stir in the tomato paste. Add the wine and tomatoes. Mash the tomatoes up a little bit with your potato masher. Add the milk and ground cloves. Put that on a simmer (between low and medium-low) and let that hang out, stirring occasionally, for a good 45 minutes.

Bring a large pot of water to a boil. Salt the water and cook the pasta to al dente. Drain the pasta and toss with about half of the sauce, a good healthy handful of Parm, and some parsley.

Ladle it up into shallow bowls and top with a little more of the sauce.

Serves 4

🕐 **JANUARY 21/DINNER**

I put out assorted salumi and Fontina Val d'Aosta, my favorite cheese, and I made my mom's **Country-Style Chicken Livers** (see April 20, page 18) and **Beef Bourguignon**, my version of the fantastic Julia Child recipe.

Beef Bourguignon

I serve this up with a nice warm, crunchy baguette and butter or egg noodles or even rice pilaf with smoked almonds mixed into it. If I do egg noodles I toss them with a little butter and minced fresh herb or even a little parsley. It's absolutely delicious.

4 pounds **beef stew meat**
4 cups good-quality **red burgundy wine**
About ⅓ cup **EVOO**
8 slices **lean bacon**, chopped
1 cup **flour**
Salt and pepper
3 tablespoons good-quality **butter**, cut into small pieces
2 or 3 large **carrots**, sliced on an angle
1½ pounds **white mushrooms**, halved
2 fresh **bay leaves**
4 ribs **celery**, sliced
4 large cloves **garlic**, chopped
2 cups **beef stock**
2 (10.5-ounce) cans **beef consommé**
1 (16-ounce) bag frozen **pearl onions**, thawed
½ cup **flat-leaf parsley leaves**, chopped

Preheat the oven to 325°F. (You can also make this recipe on the stovetop.)

Combine the beef and the wine in a resealable plastic bag or in a container with a lid. Marinate the beef in the wine for at least 3 and up to 8 hours, giving the beef a stir every now and then so that it marinates evenly. Strain the beef from the wine, reserving the wine, and pat the beef dry.

In a large Dutch oven, heat 2 tablespoons of the EVOO (2 turns of the pan) over medium-high heat. Add the bacon and cook until all the fat has rendered out and it is crispy. Remove with a slotted spoon to drain on paper towels.

Scatter the flour out onto a plate and season it with salt and pepper. Coat the beef in the flour, making sure to shake off any excess. Working in batches, add the beef to the fat remaining in the pan, adding more EVOO as necessary. Once the beef is browned on all sides, remove and set aside (see Tip).

Once all of the meat is deeply browned and out of the pan, wipe out any little grit from the flour that's stuck in the corners of the pan to keep it from smoking up too much. Reduce the heat a bit and add the butter. Once the butter foams up, add the carrots and cook for a couple of minutes. Add the mushrooms and bay leaves and cook until golden brown, 8 to 10 minutes. Add the celery and garlic, and cook for another 4 to 5 minutes. Season with salt and pepper. Deglaze the pan with the wine reserved from marinating the beef, scraping up all the browned bits from the bottom of the pan. Add the beef stock and beef consommé, bring to a boil, and cook for 5 minutes.

Return the browned beef to the pan with the pearl onions and bring the pot up to a simmer. Cover and pop it in the oven and bake until the beef is tender, 2 hours to 2½ hours. To check and see if the beef is tender, poke a piece with a fork—the beef should easily pull apart.

If the sauce is not thick enough for your liking, put it on the stovetop, turn the heat up to high, and reduce the liquid until it reaches the desired consistency. Fish out and discard the bay leaves, then taste and adjust the seasonings. Pour into a serving bowl and garnish with the crispy bacon and chopped parsley.

Serves 8 to 10

In Julia Child's recipe, the meat goes in and out of the oven at a bunch of different temperatures. I think it's just easier the way I do it. I prefer to brown the beef on the stovetop in batches in olive oil and the drippings from the bacon. I add a little more oil as necessary to keep a thin coating on the bottom of the pan.

Chicken Potpie/ Casserole

4 **skin-on, bone-in chicken breast halves**
3 small **onions**, 2 halved, 1 chopped
2 **bay leaves**
Herb bundle: a small handful each of flat-leaf parsley and thyme sprigs, tied with twine
2 tablespoons **EVOO**
5 tablespoons **butter**, plus melted butter for the crust
¼ pound **button mushrooms** or cremini, chopped (your choice; I use white when it's potpie)
2 **carrots**, chopped
3 ribs **celery**, chopped
2 **parsnips**, peeled and chopped
Salt and **pepper**
3 tablespoons **flour**
½ cup **white wine** (optional)
1 cup **milk**
1 cup **chicken stock**
Leaves from 5 or 6 sprigs **fresh tarragon**, chopped
3 tablespoons **Dijon mustard**
1 cup **frozen peas**
Simple Piecrust (recipe follows) or 1 sheet puff pastry or pie dough, thawed if frozen
1 **egg**, lightly beaten with a splash of water

Preheat the oven to 375°F.

Place the chicken, halved onions, bay leaves, and the parsley-thyme bundle in a large pot and cover with cold water. Place the pot over medium-high heat and bring up to a simmer. Reduce the heat to medium and simmer until the chicken has cooked through, about 45 minutes. Remove the chicken from the pot and let cool. Reserve about 1 cup of the cooking liquid and discard the remainder.

While the chicken cools, in a large Dutch oven, heat the EVOO (2 turns of the pan) over medium-high heat. Melt in 3 tablespoons of the butter. Add the chopped onion, mushrooms, carrots, celery, and parsnips, then season with salt and pepper and cover. Cook, stirring occasionally, until softened, 7 to 8 minutes.

the egg wash. Continue baking until the filling is bubbling and the crust is golden brown, about 15 minutes longer.

Serves 4 to 6

SIMPLE PIECRUST

When I make this for a chicken potpie, I add ground sage to the dough.

1½ cups **flour** plus more for rolling the dough
2½ teaspoons **baking powder**
1½ teaspoons ground **sage**
Sea salt
3 tablespoons cold **butter**, cut into small pieces
About ½ cup **whole milk**

In a bowl, combine the flour, baking powder, sage, and a good pinch of salt. Add the butter and work that together with your fingertips. Add the milk a little at a time and work it in just until a nice dough comes together. Scatter a little flour on a work surface and knead up the dough, then roll it out ¼ inch thick. (If I'm going to make it ahead, I store it between sheets of parchment paper, wrapped in plastic wrap and folded in half.)

Makes enough for a single crust

While the veggies are cooking, remove the skin from the chicken and the meat from the bones and shred the meat. When the veggies are tender, scoot them over to the side of the pan and add the remaining 2 tablespoons butter to the center of the pot. Once the butter has melted, add the flour and cook for a minute. Whisk in the wine (if using), milk, chicken stock, and reserved poaching liquid. Bring up to a simmer, then add the tarragon, mustard, peas, and shredded chicken. Bring back up to a simmer; season with salt and pepper; and cook until the sauce has thickened, 2 to 3 minutes.

Transfer to a casserole dish (2 quarts or larger) and cover with the pastry, trimming it as needed to cover the entire surface. Make a few slits in the dough to allow steam to escape. Place the dish on a baking sheet (in case the filling bubbles over) and brush the crust with some melted butter. Bake the potpie for 15 minutes, then brush with

⬤ JANUARY 25/LUNCH

I spent the day with Michelle Obama. We were celebrating the Healthy, Hunger-Free Kids Act. It was a big milestone for kids in this country. We were at the Park Lawn School in Alexandria, Virginia, and had our own Yum-o! **Turkey Tacos** with spicy **corn and black bean salad**. This recipe has been adapted for an at-home version.

Turkey Tacos

BLACK BEAN AND CORN SALAD
1 tablespoon **EVOO**
2 cloves **garlic**, grated or minced
½ **red onion**, finely diced

½ **red bell pepper**, finely diced

1 (10-ounce) box **frozen corn kernels** or the kernels from 2 to 3 ears fresh **corn**

Juice of 1 **lime**

1 (15.5-ounce) can **black beans**, rinsed and drained

2 **scallions**, thinly sliced

YUM-O! SOUTHWEST RANCH

1 cup **store-bought low-fat ranch dressing**

3 **red bell peppers**, roasted and peeled (see Tip, page 210), or pimientos

2 teaspoons **chili powder**

1 teaspoon ground **cumin**

Juice of 1 **lime**

1 tablespoon coarsely chopped **cilantro**

1 to 2 **scallions**, finely sliced

Black pepper

TACOS

2 or 3 tablespoons **EVOO**

1¼ pounds **ground turkey breast**

Salt and **pepper**

1 yellow **onion**, small diced

2 cloves **garlic**, minced

1 **jalapeño chile**, finely chopped (optional)

1 tablespoon **chili powder**

1½ teaspoons ground **cumin**

8 (6-inch) **whole-grain tortillas** or **hard taco shells**

1 cup shredded **Cheddar cheese** (regular or reduced-fat)

1 **romaine lettuce heart**, shredded

Make the bean and corn salad: In a medium or large skillet, heat the EVOO (1 turn of the pan) over medium-high heat. Add the garlic, onion, and bell pepper and cook until slightly tender, 3 to 4 minutes. Add the corn and cook until heated through and lightly golden brown, 3 to 4 minutes. During the last minute of cooking, add the lime juice, black beans, and scallions and toss to combine. Set aside.

Make the Yum-o! Southwest ranch: In a food processor, combine the ranch dressing, roasted peppers, chili powder, cumin, lime juice, and cilantro and pulse to combine until the peppers are pureed. Empty the flavored ranch into a bowl and stir in the scallions. Season with black pepper to taste. Set aside.

Make the tacos: In a medium nonstick skillet, heat 2 tablespoons EVOO (2 turns of the pan) over medium-high heat. Add the turkey; season with salt and pepper; and cook, breaking it up into crumbles as it browns, 6 to 7 minutes. Add another tablespoon EVOO (1 turn of the pan) if the mixture is dry. Add the onion, garlic, and jalapeño (if using) and cook for 3 to 4 minutes. Add the chili powder and cumin and cook for another couple of minutes. If the mixture seems dry, add a couple of tablespoons of water to loosen it up. Turn the heat off and set aside to keep warm.

Serve the turkey with the tortillas or hard taco shells (heat them before filling), Cheddar, and lettuce. Drizzle with the Yum-o! Southwest ranch and serve the black bean and corn salad alongside.

Makes 8 tacos

🕐 JANUARY 25/DINNER

I came home after spending the day in Virginia and made a simple supper. I made my **That's Shallot-a Flavor Spaghetti.** The shallots I had on hand in the kitchen were so beautiful (I had just bought a ton of them). I didn't count them, but I guess I ended up using 14 shallots (I usually use about 12). It is delicious and very nutritious. Lots of protein; lots of fiber; excellent, excellent meal. One of our favorites.

That's Shallot-a Flavor Spaghetti

¼ cup **EVOO**

2 cloves **garlic**, finely chopped

14 **shallots**, halved and thinly sliced

Salt and **pepper**

1 pound Italian **farro spaghetti** (you can substitute whole wheat spaghetti)

½ cup **flat-leaf parsley leaves**, chopped

1 cup grated **Grana Padano cheese**

In a high-sided skillet, heat the EVOO (4 turns of the pan) over medium-low heat. Add the garlic and shallots to the warm EVOO. Season with salt and pepper, then gently cook to caramelize them, stirring occasionally, about 20 minutes.

Bring a large pot of water to a boil. Salt the water and cook the pasta to al dente. Before draining, ladle out 1¼ cups of the starchy pasta cooking water, add to the shallots, and stir. Drain the pasta and add to the shallots. Add the parsley and cheese and more black pepper, to taste. Toss 1 to 2 minutes for the liquid to absorb and serve.

Serves 4

🕐 JANUARY 26/DINNER

We made **Plum & Ponzu Short Ribs**. I pulled the meat off the bones and used it in **Soba Bowls** (see January 7, page 234). For the soba bowls, I added some of the leftover cooking liquid and a couple of pieces of the pulled short rib meat, and I used plum-flavored soba noodles.

Plum & Ponzu Short Ribs

3 pounds **bone-in short ribs**, at room temperature
Salt and **pepper**
¼ cup **peanut oil**
¼ cup **ponzu sauce**
3 tablespoons **plum preserves**

2 tablespoons **Worcestershire sauce**
1 **onion**, thinly sliced
2 cups **beef stock**

Preheat the oven to 325°F.

Pat the short ribs dry and season with salt and pepper. In a large Dutch oven, heat the oil. Add the short ribs and brown them.

In a small bowl, stir together the ponzu sauce, plum preserves, and Worcestershire. Top the browned ribs with the onion, plum-ponzu sauce, and beef stock, bring to a simmer, cover, and bake until fork-tender, about 2½ hours. Let cool to room temperature, then pull the meat off the bones and discard the bones. (I actually reserved one of the bones for soup flavoring.) Once the liquid has cooled off in the fridge, the fat will rise to the top, allowing you to skim it very easily.

Serves 4

🕐 JANUARY 27/DINNER

We made one of my winter favorites, **Portobello Bolognese**. It's a thick, meat-free portobello ragu that's similar in taste and heartiness to a Bolognese, but you're not having a beef-based sauce so technically it's a little lighter. John really loves it.

Portobello Bolognese

1 ounce **dried mushrooms**, such as porcini or mixed wild mushrooms
2 cups **chicken stock** or water
2 tablespoons **EVOO**
3 tablespoons **butter**, cut into pieces
4 **portobello mushroom caps**, cut into ¼-inch dice
1 medium **onion**, chopped
1 small **carrot**, chopped
1 small rib **celery**, chopped
2 large cloves **garlic**, finely chopped
1 **bay leaf**, fresh or dried
Freshly grated **nutmeg**
Salt and **pepper**
2 tablespoons **tomato paste**
1 cup **dry red wine**

1 (14- or 15-ounce) ounce can **crushed tomatoes** or tomato puree
1 cup **whole milk**
1 pound **fettuccine**
A handful of **flat-leaf parsley leaves**, finely chopped
Grated **Pecorino Romano cheese**

Place the dried mushrooms in a small pot and cover with the water or chicken stock. Bring to a boil, then reduce the heat to low and let steep for about 10 minutes.

In a heavy pot, heat the EVOO (2 turns of the pan) over medium to medium-high heat. Melt in the butter, then add the portobellos, onion, carrot, celery, garlic, bay leaf, and nutmeg to taste. Cook until tender, about 15 minutes. Season with salt and pepper. Stir in the tomato paste and cook until fragrant, about 1 minute. Stir in the wine and cook 2 minutes to evaporate. Add the tomatoes and stir. Reduce the heat.

Reserving the soaking liquid, remove the dried mushrooms and chop. Stir into the sauce. Add the soaking liquid, taking care not to add the last few spoonfuls in the pot as any grit on the mushrooms will have settled there. Stir in the milk. Simmer over low heat for 20 to 30 minutes to thicken.

Bring a large pot of water to a boil. Salt the water and cook the fettuccine to al dente. Drain the fettuccine and toss with the sauce. Serve in shallow bowls, topped with parsley and pecorino.

Serves 4

🕐 **JANUARY 29/DINNER**

It was German Night. We had **Sauerbraten** with **Light Potato Pancakes** and **Apple-Pear Sauce.** We always have to plan ahead for this, because the sauerbraten has to brine for 3 days.

Sauerbraten

1 **beef round roast** (3½ to 4 pounds), at room temperature
Vegetable oil, to coat
Salt and **black pepper** or Montreal Steak Seasoning
2 large **bay leaves**
4 whole **cloves**
1 tablespoon **juniper berries** (you can find them in the spice aisle)
1½ teaspoons **mustard seeds**
1½ teaspoons **coriander seeds**
1½ teaspoons **dill seeds**
2 cups **cider vinegar**
1 cup cloudy **organic apple cider**
1 large **carrot**, thickly sliced on an angle
1 **onion**, quartered with root end left attached
2 or 3 ribs **celery**, thickly sliced on an angle
3 tablespoons **light brown sugar**
2 tablespoons **tomato paste**
16 **gingersnaps**, ground

Heat a large Dutch oven over medium-high heat. Rub the roast with vegetable oil and season liberally with salt and pepper. Brown in the hot pan on all sides, 10 to 12 minutes. Remove from the heat.

In a tea filter sack, coffee filter, or piece of cheesecloth, bundle together the bay leaves, cloves, juniper berries, mustard seeds, coriander seeds, and dill seeds. In a large pot or Dutch oven, combine the flavor pouch (I secure mine with kitchen twine to the handle of the pot), vinegar, cider, 2½ cups water, the carrot, onion, and celery. Bring to a boil, then turn off the heat and let cool. Combine the brine and meat in the pot and refrigerate for 3 days, turning the meat occasionally.

Preheat the oven to 325°F. Let the meat return to room temperature.

Sprinkle the sugar into the pot and combine with the brine. Roast for 3½ to 4 hours. (The meat may also be cooked in a slow cooker on high for 4 hours or low for 7 hours.)

Remove the roast to a carving board and cover with foil. Let rest for 30 minutes. Discard the flavor pouch. Strain out the vegetables or puree the sauce in a food mill and return the sauce to the

pot. Whisk in the tomato paste and the ground gingersnaps—if the gingersnaps do not dissolve completely, pass them through the food mill or a sieve. Adjust the black pepper to taste.

Thinly slice the meat and serve with potato pancakes and apple/pear sauce alongside.

Serves 6

Light Potato Pancakes

Salt and **pepper**
12 **medium russet potatoes** (about 4 pounds)
1 large **onion**
1 tablespoon **ground thyme**
3 **eggs**
½ teaspoon **baking powder**
¼ cup **flour**
Vegetable oil, for frying

Set up a bowl of cold salted water. Peel the potatoes, and as you peel them, put them in the bowl of salted water.

Drain the potatoes, grate them, and place them in a sieve set over another bowl. Let them drain over the bowl, collecting all of that liquid, for a good 20 to 30 minutes. Then press on the potatoes to get out more liquid.

Transfer the grated potatoes to another bowl. Slowly pour the liquid out of the bowl that was under the strainer until you can see the potato starch collected in the bottom. Add the starch to the grated potatoes. Grate the onion into the bowl of potatoes and season the mixture with salt, pepper, and thyme.

Preheat the oven to 275°F. Place a wire cooling rack in a baking sheet.

Beat the eggs with the baking powder and flour. Pour that over the potatoes and stir to combine.

In a large skillet, heat a thin layer of vegetable oil over medium to medium-high heat. Add ¼ cup batter per pancake and cook until nicely browned on both side. Keep the pancakes warm in the oven as you make more pancakes.

Serves 10 to 12

Apple-Pear Sauce

4 to 5 **Gala apples**, diced
2 ripe **Bosc pears**, diced
2 cups cloudy **organic apple cider**
Lemon juice
Sea salt
Freshly grated **nutmeg**

In a saucepan, combine the apples, pears, cider, a splash of lemon juice, a pinch of sea salt, and a little freshly grated nutmeg. Bring to a bubble, reduce the heat to low, and let cook for about an hour. Put it through a coarse food mill.

Makes 3 to 4 cups

JANUARY 31, DINNER. I made a variation on my pasta with sausage and roasted garlic sauce. On this night I added kale because we had eaten at the fabulous Maialino (in the Gramercy Park Hotel in New York City) and the chef there made a beautiful house-made sausage and cream pasta that John and I had with a little bit of kale. We liked it so much we decided to add kale as a riff on this recipe of mine where the sauce tastes sort of similar. Incidentally, our favorite dish at Maialino is their malfatti al Maialino, which is suckling pig with a house-made pasta torn into irregular pieces and tossed with arugula, fresh lemon, and shaved pecorino cheese. It is outstanding. (P.S. Maialino means "suckling pig" in Italian.)

Pasta with Sausage & Kale in Roasted Garlic Sauce

You need to make the sausage in the morning so it has time to develop flavor.

1 head **garlic**, top cut off to expose the cloves, plus 3 cloves garlic, chopped
2 tablespoons **EVOO**, plus more for drizzling
Salt and **pepper**
1 bunch (about ½ pound) **lacinato kale** (also called black, Tuscan, or dinosaur kale), stemmed and thinly sliced
4 tablespoons (½ stick) **butter**
2 large **onions**, thinly sliced
1 **bay leaf**
½ cup **dry white wine**
1½ cups **chicken stock**
½ cup **heavy cream**
1 pound **rigatoni pasta**
Homemade Pork Sausage (recipe follows)
Freshly grated **nutmeg**
½ cup grated **Parmigiano-Reggiano cheese**, for topping

Preheat the oven to 400°F. Drizzle the head of garlic with some EVOO and season with salt and pepper. Wrap in foil and roast until tender and caramel in color, about 40 minutes.

Meanwhile, in a pot of boiling salted water, cook the kale for a few minutes to take the bitterness out. Drain it and wring it out in a kitchen towel so it's perfectly dry. Set aside.

In a large skillet, melt the butter over medium heat. Add the onions and bay leaf and season with salt and pepper. Cook, stirring occasionally, until the onions are caramel in color, very soft and sweet, about 30 minutes. Deglaze the pan with the wine and discard the bay leaf.

In a food processor, combine the roasted garlic (squeezed out of the skins), the onions, and enough stock to smoothly puree the sauce. Transfer to a saucepan and stir in the cream. Cook to reduce and thicken while the pasta cooks.

Bring a large pot of water to a boil. Salt the water and cook the pasta to al dente.

Meanwhile, in a large skillet, heat 2 tablespoons EVOO (2 turns of the pan) over medium-high heat. Add the sausage, breaking it up into crumbles as it browns.

Combine the sausage, kale, and creamy sauce. Adjust the salt and pepper, and add nutmeg to taste. Drain the pasta and toss with the sauce. Serve topped with Parm.

Serves 4 to 6

HOMEMADE PORK SAUSAGE

1 pound **ground pork**
1 teaspoon **ground sage**
½ teaspoon **ground red pepper** (I get that at the Italian market)
1 teaspoon **fennel seed**
½ teaspoon **fennel pollen**, fennel flour, or ground fennel
2 cloves **garlic**, finely chopped
Salt and **pepper**, to taste

Mix everything together and let it hang out all day in the fridge so that the flavors in the sausage combine. Or you can even make it a day or two ahead.

Makes 1 pound

FEBRUARY

WEDNESDAY/1

BREAKFAST
egg BLT sandwiches
with arugula
DINNER
swordfish cutlets,
tomato relish, roasted
eggplant pasta,
Sicilian-style orange
salad

THURSDAY/2

DINNER
coq au vin rouge

FRIDAY/3

DINNER
meat lasagna,
basic hummus

SATURDAY/4

LUNCH
croque monsieur
DINNER
pissaladière, French
country lentil soup

SUNDAY/5

DINNER
Siena-style garlic
sauce with fat spa-
ghetti

SATURDAY11

DINNER
pici with fennel, onion
& cream sauce

SUNDAY/12

BREAKFAST
eastern egg sand-
wiches with bacon
DINNER
mulligatawny,
poached chicken

MONDAY/13

DINNER
enchiladas suizas,
green rice, refried
beans

TUESDAY/14

DINNER
beef Milanese with
tomato & arugula raw
sauce, pasta with baby
broccoli, chiles, and
garlic

WEDNESDAY/15

DINNER
saffron chicken & rice

TUESDAY/21

DINNER
cacio e pepe,
balsamic cipollini,
rib-eye steaks with
celery salad

WEDNESDAY/22

THURSDAY/23

DINNER
tabbouleh, red
lentil soup with mint
yogurt

FRIDAY/24

SATURDAY/25

DINNER
lazy Bolognese
lasagne, lazy lasagna
with butternut squash
& escarole

MONDAY/6	TUESDAY/7	WEDNESDAY/8	THURSDAY/9	FRIDAY/10

DINNER
creamy mushroom
& Marsala fettuccine
with garlicky bread-
crumb topping

DINNER
veal meatball–stuffed
peppers

DINNER
pasta with gremolata,
soup for mommy, veal
meatballs

DINNER
creamy mushroom
& herb sauce with
whole-grain pasta

THURSDAY/16	FRIDAY/17	SATURDAY/18	SUNDAY/19	MONDAY/20

DINNER
that's shallot-a flavor
spaghetti

DINNER
fennel-roasted pork,
butternut squash
and potato mashers,
balsamic cipollini

DINNER
chicken Vesuvio

DINNER
veal chops with Gor-
gonzola, gnocchi with
spinach & garlic

DINNER
double-high patty
melts

SUNDAY/26	MONDAY/27	TUESDAY/28	WEDNESDAY/29	

DINNER
touchdown chili,
Isaboo's puppy dog
chili, jalapeño popper
dip

DINNER
macaroni & cheese
with fennel

FEBRUARY 1, BREAKFAST

Egg BLT sandwiches with arugula: They were egg sandwiches with bacon, lettuce, tomato, arugula, red pepper jelly, and aged goat cheese. Delicious sandwich.

🕐 FEBRUARY 1/DINNER

Swordfish Cutlets with tomato relish and **Sicilian-style orange salad** (see June 2, pages 55 and 56). For the side pasta I made **Roasted Eggplant Pasta** (see August 13, page 114)—though I usually serve **Aglio e Olio** (see June 2, page 56), which is equally delicious.

🕐 FEBRUARY 2/DINNER

Coq au Vin Rouge

My friend Tommy loves this red wine coq au vin. Serve it with a warm baguette.

1 tablespoon **EVOO**, plus more for drizzling
⅓ pound **uncured thick-cut bacon**, cut into 2-inch pieces
2 skinless, **bone-in chicken breasts**, halved (4 pieces)
4 skinless, **bone-in chicken thighs**
2 **chicken drumsticks**
Salt and **pepper**
4 tablespoons (½ stick) **butter**
10 medium-large **shallots**, halved, with the root end attached
2 **carrots**, thinly sliced or chopped
4 cloves **garlic**, sliced
1 tablespoon **tomato paste**
2 rounded tablespoons **flour**
2 shots **Armagnac** or cognac
3 cups **red burgundy wine**
1 cup **chicken stock**
1 **bundle mixed herbs** (thyme, rosemary, parsley, fresh bay leaves) tied with twine
¾ pound **mushrooms**, quartered

Preheat the oven to 325°F. (You can also make this recipe on the stovetop.)

In a large Dutch oven, heat the EVOO (1 turn of the pan) over medium-high heat. Add the bacon (mine was very mild, not smoky, not too salty) and cook until nice and crisp. Transfer the bacon to paper towels.

Pat the chicken dry and season with salt and pepper. Working in batches, add it to the rendered bacon fat and cook until deep golden. Add another drizzle of EVOO if necessary for the second batch. Remove the chicken from the pan.

Reduce the heat a little bit and melt 3 tablespoons of the butter over medium heat. When it foams up, add the shallots, carrots, garlic, and salt and pepper to taste. Cook partially covered, stirring occasionally, for about 10 minutes. Stir in the tomato paste for 1 minute until you can

smell it and it's very fragrant. Add the flour and stir that for another minute to cook it out. Deglaze the pan with Armagnac or cognac (we used Armagnac). Then add the wine, stock, and herb bundle.

Return the chicken to the pan, cover, and bake for 1½ hours. (Or cook on the stovetop: partially cover and cook for about an hour over low heat at a low bubble. I prefer just throwing it into the oven.)

Meanwhile, in a medium skillet, melt the remaining 1 tablespoon butter. Add the mushrooms and cook until browned. Season with salt and pepper.

Transfer the chicken to the platter and reduce the sauce a little bit if you need to (mine was thick enough to serve as is). Serve garnished with the sautéed mushrooms.

Serves 4

🕐 FEBRUARY 3/DINNER

We had a nice **Meat Lasagna** and while that was in the oven, I made a little **Basic Hummus** for a snack.

Meat Lasagna

WHITE SAUCE
4 tablespoons (½ stick) **butter**
¼ cup **flour**
3 cups **milk** (let the milk sit at room temperature a few minute before using)
Salt and **pepper**
Freshly grated **nutmeg**

LASAGNA
¼ cup **EVOO**
¾ pound **meat loaf mix** (ground beef, pork, and veal combined)
Kosher salt and **pepper**
½ to 1 teaspoon **fennel seeds**
1 tablespoon **butter**
1 **carrot**, finely chopped
1 rib **celery** with leafy top, finely chopped
1 small **onion**, finely chopped
2 cloves **garlic**, very thinly sliced
2 tablespoons finely chopped fresh **sage**
Ground **cloves** or freshly grated nutmeg
2 tablespoons **tomato paste**
1 cup **whole milk**
1½ cups **dry white wine**
1 (28- or 32-ounce) can **San Marzano tomatoes** (look for DOP on the label)
1 (9-ounce) box **no-boil flat lasagna sheets** (I like Barilla)
¾ to 1 cup grated **Parmigiano-Reggiano cheese**

Make the white sauce: In a small saucepan, melt the butter over medium heat. Whisk in the flour, then the milk. Bring to a boil, then reduce the heat to a simmer. Season with salt, pepper, and nutmeg to taste. Cook a few minutes until the sauce is thick enough to coat a spoon. Turn it off and just let it hang out at room temperature.

Make the lasagna: In a Dutch oven or heavy pot, heat the EVOO (4 turns of the pan) over medium-high heat. Pat the meat dry and season it generously with kosher salt, pepper, and fennel seeds. Add the meat to the pan and cook until lightly browned. Make a well in the center of the meat and add the butter. When butter foams, add the carrot, celery, onion, garlic, and sage. Cook to

soften the carrot and onion, 8 to 10 minutes. Add a pinch of cloves or nutmeg. Add the tomato paste and stir until fragrant. Stir in the milk, partially cover, and simmer over low heat for about 20 minutes. The milk will cook almost completely out. Add the wine and simmer for 20 minutes more. Add the tomatoes and break them up with a potato masher. Let simmer partially covered for another 20 minutes, so you end up with a thick sauce that's not too acidic.

Soak the lasagna sheets in very hot tap water for about 5 minutes (I drop them in one at a time so they don't stick together). When I'm ready to build the lasagna, I remove them and wipe off the excess liquid.

Preheat the oven to 400°F.

Put a little of the meat sauce on the bottom of a 9 by 13-inch pan; just spread it around so the pasta is not sitting directly on the bottom of the pan. Then build the lasagna in this order: a layer of pasta, half the meat sauce, one-third of the white sauce; then a layer of pasta, the remaining meat sauce, one-third of the white sauce; a last layer of pasta and the remaining white sauce alone. Sprinkle the entire top with Parm.

Place the pan on a baking sheet to catch drips. Cover the pan with foil and bake for 45 minutes and then uncovered until the top is nice and browned and the lasagna is bubbling, about another 15 minutes or so.

Serves 4 to 6

Basic Hummus

Serve the hummus with pita crisps and cucumber sticks.

> 1 (15-ounce) can **chickpeas**, drained
> Juice of 1 **lemon**
> Leaves from 1 sprig **oregano**
> 1 clove **garlic**, finely chopped
> **Salt**
> 2 rounded tablespoons **tahini paste**
> ¼ teaspoon **ground red pepper** or ½ teaspoon crushed red pepper flakes
> A handful of **flat-leaf parsley leaves**

In a food processor, combine the chickpeas, lemon juice, and oregano. Mash the garlic into paste with some salt, pressing under the flat part of your knife, then add the garlic paste to the processor along with the tahini, ground red pepper, and parsley. Process the hummus until smooth (add a splash of water if too thick), then transfer to a bowl.

Makes about 1½ cups

🕐 **FEBRUARY 4/LUNCH**

Croque Monsieur

If you want, you could make a Croque Madame (see April 16, page 13), which is more or less this recipe, but you top it with eggs.

> 4 tablespoons (½ stick) **butter**
> 4 scant tablespoons **flour**
> 2 cups **whole milk**
> **Salt** and **white pepper** or finely ground black pepper
> Freshly grated **nutmeg**
> 1 rounded tablespoon **Dijon mustard**
> 6 slices **brioche bread** or white bread
> 12 to 18 thin slices **French-style ham** (mild, sweet and buttery—not smoky)
> 1⅓ to 2 cups shredded **Comté** or **Gruyère cheese** (see Tip)

Preheat the oven to 375°F.

In a saucepan, melt the butter over medium heat. Whisk in the flour and cook for a minute, then whisk in the milk and season with salt, pepper, and nutmeg to taste. Simmer at a low bubble until thick enough to coat a spoon; stir in the mustard.

Arrange the bread on a baking sheet and top with the sauce, ham, and cheese and bake to deep golden on top. The sandwiches can be made in a single or double layer, finishing the top layer with sauce and cheese: i.e., bread, sauce, ham, cheese, bread, sauce, cheese.

Serves 6

Sometimes I sort of make this French dish Italian. I use prosciutto cotto instead of French ham and I substitute Fontina Val d'Aosta for the Gruyère.

🕐 **FEBRUARY 4/DINNER**

We had **Pissaladière** (which we made in our wood-burning pizza oven) and **French Country Lentil Soup**.

Pissaladière

Pissaladière is a French tart, but I think it's more akin to a French pizza. We made this in our wood-burning oven, which gets very hot, but to make it in a home oven, see "Pizza in a Home Oven," page 199. (You can also make this with store-bought bread; see the Tip.)

DOUGH
2¼ cups **bread flour**, plus more for the work surface
1 teaspoon **instant yeast**
1 teaspoon **sea salt**
A good heavy tablespoon **EVOO**, plus more for the bowl
1 cup **warm water**

TOPPINGS
3 tablespoons **EVOO**
6 **anchovy fillets**
3 large or 4 medium **onions**, sliced
1 teaspoon **fennel seeds**
4 cloves **garlic**, chopped or thinly sliced
1½ teaspoons **light brown sugar**
1 tablespoon **fresh thyme leaves**, chopped, or 1 teaspoon ground thyme
1 **bay leaf**
Salt and **pepper**
½ cup **dry white wine**
½ to ¾ cup **niçoise olives**, pitted and chopped
Chopped **flat-leaf parsley**

Make the dough: Combine all the ingredients in a food processor fitted with the dough blade—make sure you switch out the metal blade for the dough blade. Pulse that together until it forms a rough dough. Turn it out onto a flour surface and knead it. Then put it into an oiled bowl and let it rest about 1½ hours.

Make the onion topping: In a large skillet, heat the EVOO (3 turns of the pan) with the anchovies over medium heat until the anchovies are melted. Add the onions, fennel seeds, and garlic. Season with the sugar, thyme, bay leaf, and pepper. Increase the heat a bit and cook the onions, stirring frequently, until light caramel in color, about

30 minutes. Add the wine and season with salt.

Divide the dough into 4 pieces. Flour your hands and flour the board you're working on. Stretch each piece of dough into an 8-inch-long oval: Hold it above your board and just let it keep stretching down. Once you get the shape you want (the 8-inch oblong), pat it with your fingertips and cover it with the onion topping, leaving a border around the edges. Cover the border with the chopped olives. (On John's and mine we put extra anchovy fillets in little crisscross patterns on top of the individual pies so you have anchovy in it and anchovy on it.)

Bake the pissaladières until they're nice and crispy, 10 to 12 minutes in a home oven (it was 3 or 4 minutes in our 900°F pizza oven). When they come out and right before you serve them top with lots of chopped flat-leaf parsley.

Serves 4

If you don't want to make your own dough, you can make this with a 24-inch loaf crusty French bread, halved lengthwise and crosswise (or buy 2 smaller loaves) to yield 4 individual foot-long sections. Preheat the oven to 325°F, and toast the bread on a baking sheet in the oven for 8 to 10 minutes while you make the onion topping. Preheat the broiler. Top the toasted bread evenly with the onion topping and 2 cups shredded Gruyère or Fontina Val d'Aosta cheese and ½ cup grated Parmigiano-Reggiano cheese. Brown under the broiler for 1 to 3 minutes.

French Country Lentil Soup

2 tablespoons **EVOO**
1 medium **onion**, chopped
1 **carrot**, chopped
1 rib **celery**, chopped
3 or 4 **anchovy fillets**
2 cloves **garlic**, sliced
1½ cups **Puy green lentils**
2 to 3 tablespoons **tomato paste**
¼ cup mixed **minced fresh herbs**: parsley, sage, rosemary, and thyme
1 **bay leaf**
½ cup **dry white wine**
4 cups **chicken** or **vegetable stock**
Salt and **pepper**
Grated **Parmigiano-Reggiano cheese**, for serving
Crusty bread, for mopping

In a large saucepan, heat the EVOO (2 turns of the pan) over medium-high heat. Add the onion and let it sweat out until light caramel in color. Add the carrot, celery, and anchovies and sauté until the anchovy melts out. Add the garlic and cook for 5 minutes more. Add the lentils, tomato paste, fresh herbs, bay leaf, wine, and stock and simmer for 30 minutes (add a couple of cups of water to stretch the stock out if the mixture starts to lose too much liquid). Season with salt and pepper to taste.

Serve piping hot with grated cheese sprinkled on top and crusty bread alongside.

Serves 4

 Rachael's tips on entertaining.

It was Super Bowl, so we just had a big bowl of **Siena-Style Garlic Sauce with Fat Spaghetti**. John had lots of antipasti while the game was going on. The Giants won so John was pretty happy about that.

Siena-Style Garlic Sauce with Fat Spaghetti

¼ cup **EVOO**
5 to 6 cloves **garlic**, very thinly sliced
1 **fresh red chile**, thinly sliced with seeds, or
  1 teaspoon crushed red pepper flakes
1 (28- or 32-ounce) can **San Marzano tomatoes**
  (look for DOP on the label)
Sea salt
1 pound **pici** or **bucatini pasta**
Grated **Parmigiano-Reggiano** or **Pecorino Romano cheese**, for serving

In a saucepan, heat the EVOO (4 turns of the pan) over medium heat. Add the garlic and chile and stir until very fragrant and the garlic is light golden in color at the edges, 3 to 4 minutes. Add the tomatoes and break up with a potato masher. Season with sea salt, partially cover, and cook over low heat at a bubble for 30 minutes, stirring occasionally.

Bring a large pot of water to a boil. Salt the water and cook the pasta to just shy of al dente. Before draining, ladle out and reserve 1 cup of the starchy pasta cooking water. Drain the pasta. Toss with the sauce, using a little starchy cooking water to incorporate the two; toss vigorously for 1 to 2 minutes. Serve with either grated pecorino (tangy) or grated Parmigiano-Reggiano (nuttier in flavor).

Serves 4

We were all out all day and we came home and had some mushrooms in the fridge we had to use up, so I made my **Creamy Mushroom & Marsala Fettuccine with Garlicky Bread-Crumb Topping**.

Creamy Mushroom & Marsala Fettuccine with Garlicky Bread-Crumb Topping

3 tablespoons **EVOO**
6 tablespoons (¾ stick) **butter**
1 pound **cremini mushrooms**, sliced
3 **shallots**, halved and thinly sliced
2 tablespoons **fresh thyme leaves**, finely chopped
Salt and **pepper**
1 rounded tablespoon **flour**
⅓ to ½ cup **Marsala**
1 cup **chicken stock**
½ cup **heavy cream**
1 pound **whole wheat** or **semolina fettuccine**
1 cup **panko bread crumbs**
4 cloves **garlic**, finely chopped or grated
½ cup grated **Parmigiano-Reggiano cheese**
¼ cup chopped **flat-leaf parsley**

Bring a large pot of water to a boil for the pasta.

In a large skillet, heat 1 tablespoon of the EVOO (1 turn of the pan) over medium-high heat. Add 3 tablespoons of the butter and melt until it foams. Add the mushrooms and cook until golden, about 12 minutes.

Add the shallots, thyme, and salt and pepper to taste. Stir 3 minutes more, sprinkle with the flour, add the Marsala, and reduce 1 minute. Add the stock and cream and simmer to thicken a couple of minutes more.

When you add the shallots, salt the pasta water and cook the fettucine to al dente. Before draining, ladle out and reserve 1 cup of the starchy pasta cooking water. Drain the pasta.

Meanwhile, in a medium skillet, heat the remaining 2 tablespoons EVOO (2 turns of the pan) and melt in the remaining 3 tablespoons butter. Add the panko and garlic and cook until nutty and fragrant. Remove from the heat, let cool a couple of minutes, then add the Parm and parsley; season with pepper.

Toss the pasta with the creamy mushroom sauce and serve topped with the bread crumbs.

Serves 4

FEBRUARY 7, DINNER. We went to Motorino Pizza on 12th Street, just off 1st Avenue. We absolutely love Motorino. We always get a red wine called Pin from La Spinetta. One of our favorite pizzas is the alici pizza, which is anchovy oil, fresh tomatoes, and bufala mozzarella on top, and I always get onions and parsley as well. We like the cremini pizza with sausage and we like the spicy soppressata pizza. Their oven burns at 1,000 degrees and it used to be Uno Pizza Napoletana, a guy who made only Neapolitan-style pizza—period. He wouldn't make anything else; he was sort of like the Pizza Nazi. And then our friend Mathieu Palombino bought it—he also owns a really cool diner, Bowery Diner. Motorino started in Brooklyn. We used to have to drive all the way out there, but now we get it here in Manhattan.

🕑 FEBRUARY 8/DINNER

Veal Meatball–Stuffed Peppers

4 tablespoons **EVOO**, plus more for drizzling
6 cloves **garlic**, 2 thinly sliced, 4 minced or finely chopped
1 small **onion**, halved and left attached at the root end
1 **bay leaf**
1 (28- to 32-ounce) can **San Marzano tomatoes** (look for DOP on the label)
1 (14-ounce) can **crushed tomatoes**
Pinch of **sugar**
Salt and **pepper**
A few leaves of **basil**, torn
4 **red bell peppers**, tops removed, seeds scraped, and bottoms trimmed to sit upright
4 (½-inch-thick) slices good-quality **white bread** or Italian bread, crusts trimmed
1 to 1½ cups **whole milk**
1 pound **ground veal**, **lamb**, or **meat loaf mix** (beef, pork, and veal)
2 **eggs**, lightly beaten
1 (10-ounce) box **frozen chopped spinach,** thawed, wrung out in a kitchen towel, and finely chopped
Freshly grated **nutmeg**
½ cup freshly grated **Parmigiano-Reggiano cheese**, plus more for topping peppers

Preheat the oven to 425°F.

In a saucepan, heat 2 tablespoons of the EVOO (2 turns of the pan). Add the sliced garlic and stir 1 to 2 minutes. Add the onion, bay leaf, and San Marzano and crushed tomatoes, breaking the whole tomatoes up with a potato masher. Season with the sugar and salt and pepper to taste. Simmer for 25 to 30 minutes at a low bubble to thicken and break down the tomatoes.

Remove the onion and bay leaf and stir in the basil. If the sauce thickens too quickly, add a splash of water.

Meanwhile, drizzle the peppers with some EVOO and season with salt and pepper. Roast for 20 minutes, then set aside to cool. Leave the oven on.

In a small bowl, cover the bread with milk and let soak.

In a skillet, heat the remaining 2 tablespoons EVOO (2 turns of the pan) over medium to medium-high heat. Add the meat and chopped garlic and cook, breaking the meat up into crumbles as it browns. Transfer to a bowl to cool.

Wring out the bread and crumble into crumbs into the bowl with the meat. Add the eggs and spinach. Season with a few grates of nutmeg and salt and pepper to taste. Add the ½ cup Parm and 1 cup of the tomato sauce, and mix to combine. Fill the peppers with the meat mixture and smooth off the tops. Place in a square baking dish and pour the remaining sauce around and over the peppers. Sprinkle with a little more cheese and bake until bubbling and heated through, 20 to 25 minutes.

Serves 4

🕐 **FEBRUARY 9/DINNER**

My mom loves soup over pasta, so that's what I did. I made a **Pasta with Gremolata** and then I poured **Soup for Mommy** over it. I also had a little ground veal left over from the show that day, so I made little meatballs and dropped those into the soup, too.

Soup for Mommy

To serve this up, ladle some of the Pasta with Gremolata into a soup bowl, then ladle the soup over it.

¼ cup **EVOO**
2 **carrots**, finely chopped
3 ribs **celery** with leafy tops, from the heart, finely chopped
1 **onion**, finely chopped
2 or 3 cloves **garlic**, chopped
Salt and **pepper**
1 large head **escarole**, chopped
Freshly grated **nutmeg**

1 (15-ounce) can **cannellini (white) beans**, drained
4 cups **chicken stock**
Veal Meatballs (recipe follows; optional)

In a large soup pot, heat the EVOO (4 turns of the pan). Add the carrots, celery, onion, and garlic. Season with salt and pepper and sweat that out. Wilt in the escarole and season with a little bit of nutmeg. Add the white beans and chicken stock. Bring up to a simmer and let cook out for a few minutes. Stir in the meatballs, if desired.

Serves 4

Pasta with Gremolata

I always cook the noodles separately so they don't get too tender in the soup. You can do any kind of pasta: little ditalini, extra-wide egg noodles, or whichever cut of pasta you prefer.

Salt
1 pound **pasta** (ditalini, extra-wide egg noodles)
Grated zest of 1 **lemon**
½ cup **flat-leaf parsley leaves**, very finely chopped
2 small cloves **garlic**, very finely chopped
1 tablespoon **EVOO**
1 tablespoon **butter**

Bring a large pot of water to a boil. Salt the water and cook the pasta to al dente.

Meanwhile, for the gremolata, combine the lemon zest on a cutting board with the parsley and garlic. Mix it all together.

Drain the pasta and toss it with the gremolata, EVOO, and butter while the pasta is still hot.

Serves 4

VEAL MEATBALLS

1¼ pounds **ground veal** or chuck
2 teaspoons **Worcestershire sauce**
1 **egg**, beaten
½ cup **fine dry bread crumbs**
¼ cup grated **Parmigiano-Reggiano** or **Pecorino Romano cheese**
2 cloves **garlic**, chopped
Salt and **pepper**

Preheat the oven to 425°F.

In a bowl, combine the meat, Worcestershire, egg, bread crumbs, Parm, garlic, and salt and pepper to taste. Roll into 1½-inch meatballs and place on a nonstick baking sheet (or grease a baking sheet with EVOO). Bake until no longer pink inside, 10 to 12 minutes.

Makes 15 to 18 meatballs

🕐 **FEBRUARY 10/DINNER**

Creamy Mushroom & Herb Sauce with Whole-Grain Pasta

Both long and short cuts of pasta work with this sauce. I enjoy linguine with it.

3 tablespoons **EVOO**
2 tablespoons **butter**
1 pound **cremini mushrooms**, thinly sliced
2 large **shallots**, finely chopped
4 cloves **garlic**, finely chopped
About 2 tablespoons finely chopped **fresh thyme**
Leaves from 2 sprigs **rosemary**, finely chopped
1 large fresh **bay leaf**
Salt and **pepper**
About 2 tablespoons **double-concentrated tomato paste** (from a tube)
About ½ cup **dry sherry** or **Marsala wine**
1 cup **heavy cream**
Freshly grated **nutmeg**
1 pound **whole wheat** or **whole-grain pasta**
A couple of handfuls of grated **Parmigiano-Reggiano cheese**, plus more for serving

GARNISHES (OPTIONAL)
Chopped toasted **hazelnuts**
Chopped **flat-leaf parsley** or watercress

Bring a large pot of water to boil for the pasta.

In a large, deep skillet, heat the EVOO (3 turns of the pan) over medium to medium-high heat. Melt in the butter, then add the mushrooms and cook until well browned, 10 to 12 minutes.

Add the shallots, garlic, herbs, and salt and pepper to taste, and stir a few minutes more until very fragrant. Stir in the tomato paste and cook out for a minute or two. Stir in the sherry or Marsala, then stir in the cream and reduce the heat to low. Season with a few grates of nutmeg and let the sauce gently reduce at a low bubble while you cook the pasta.

Add salt and pasta to the boiling water and cook the pasta to al dente. Before draining, ladle out and reserve ½ cup of the starchy pasta cooking water. Drain the pasta.

Stir the Parm into the sauce. Add the drained pasta to the sauce and toss to coat, using a little starchy water to incorporate if necessary. Serve in shallow bowls with more cheese to pass at the table. Add texture and more flavors to the dish by topping with toasted chopped hazelnuts and parsley or watercress.

Serves 4

🕐 **FEBRUARY 11/DINNER**

Pici with Fennel, Onion & Cream Sauce

Maria was craving pici pasta again, but she requested a sauce different from what we have had in the past.

Salt
1 pound **pici pasta**
3 tablespoons **EVOO**

3 tablespoons **butter**
1 large bulb **fennel**, trimmed, quartered, cored, and very thinly sliced
1 large **onion**, very thinly sliced
3 to 4 cloves **garlic**, thinly sliced
2 or 3 tablespoons **fresh thyme**
1 cup **dry white wine**
1 cup **chicken stock**
⅓ cup **heavy cream**
Freshly grated **nutmeg**
A couple of handfuls of **walnut halves**, toasted and finely chopped
Shaved **aged pecorino cheese**

Bring a large pot of water to a boil. Salt the water and cook the pasta to al dente. Before draining, ladle out and reserve 1 cup of the starchy pasta cooking water. Drain the pasta and reserve.

Meanwhile, in a large skillet, heat the EVOO (3 turns of the pan) over high heat. Melt the butter into the olive oil. Add the fennel, onion, garlic, and thyme and cook until they're light golden in color, about 20 minutes. When they start to caramelize (don't let them go too far, just light caramel in color), stir in the wine. Reduce that by about half, then add the chicken stock and cream. Season the sauce with nutmeg to taste.

Toss the pasta and some of the starchy cooking water with the fennel-onion cream sauce. Serve topped with walnuts and shaved pecorino. It was out of this world!

Serves 4

Eastern Egg Sandwiches with Bacon

I served these sandwiches on "white and wheat" bread from Whole Foods. It's a mixture of white and wheat in the same loaf. My mom loves it.

2 tablespoons **EVOO**
2 tablespoons **butter**, plus some for buttering the bread
1 **cubanelle pepper**, diced
½ **red onion**, sliced
8 large **eggs**
1 rounded teaspoon **Dijon mustard**
1 teaspoon **Tabasco sauce**
½ teaspoon **sweet paprika**
Salt and **pepper**
8 slices **bread**, toasted and buttered
8 slices **bacon**, baked (see Tip)

In a large skillet, heat the EVOO (2 turns of the pan) over medium heat. Melt in the butter. Add the cubanelle and onion and let sweat for 5 minutes.

In a bowl, whisk the eggs, mustard, Tabasco, paprika, and salt and pepper to taste. Pour the mixture into the hot skillet and cook over medium heat to a loose scramble, about 2 minutes.

Place a heaping spoonful of eggs on a piece of toast, top with 2 pieces of bacon, crisscrossed, and top with another piece of bread.

Makes 4 sandwiches

Arrange the bacon on a slotted broiler pan or on a wire rack over a baking sheet and bake at 375°F until crisp.

For dinner, I made **Mulligatawny**, a delish soup from India with lots of exotic flavor. I started by making my own **Poached Chicken** so I'd have homemade stock for the mulligatawny.

Mulligatawny

1 tablespoon **EVOO**
4 tablespoons (½ stick) **butter**
4 cloves **garlic**, grated
2 medium **onions**, chopped
2-inch piece of fresh **ginger**, grated
2 **green apples**, peeled and grated
Kosher salt and **pepper**
1 tablespoon ground **coriander**
1 tablespoon ground **cumin**
1 tablespoon **turmeric**
1 teaspoon **dry mustard**
3 tablespoons **flour**
6 cups **chicken stock** (from Poached Chicken; recipe follows)
4 cups **shredded Poached Chicken** (recipe follows)
1½ cups **basmati rice**
Mint or cilantro, finely chopped

In a Dutch oven, heat the EVOO (1 turn of the pan) over medium-high heat. Melt in the butter. Add the garlic, onions, ginger, and half the apple, and season with salt and pepper. Cook until tender, 7 to 8 minutes. Add the coriander, cumin, turmeric, and dry mustard and cook, stirring, until fragrant. Add the flour and cook,

stirring, for 1 minute. Add the stock and simmer until thickened to the consistency of a light sauce, about 20 minutes. Stir in the chicken.

To serve, prepare the rice according to the package directions. (I keep the rice separate from the soup so that it doesn't get too soft in the soup.) When ready to serve, stir the rice into the soup. Garnish with finely chopped mint and/or cilantro, and the remaining grated apple.

Serves 4

POACHED CHICKEN

4 full **skin-on, bone-in chicken breasts** (for all white meat) or 1 whole 4-pound chicken (for a mix of white and dark meat)
1 tablespoon whole **black peppercorns**
8 cloves **garlic**, smashed
4 large **bay leaves**
4 **carrots**, coarsely chopped
4 ribs **celery**, coarsely chopped
2 **lemons**, sliced
2 **onions**, quartered
Herb bundle of fresh parsley, rosemary, and thyme tied with kitchen twine
Kosher salt

Put the chicken in a very large stockpot or divide between 2 pots if necessary. Add the peppercorns, garlic, bay leaves, carrots, celery, lemons, onions, and herb bundle and sprinkle with salt. Add enough water to cover the chicken. Bring to a boil, then reduce the heat to low and cook at a rolling simmer for 1½ hours.

Remove the chicken from the liquid and let cool. Strain the stock. (You should have 5 to 6 quarts stock.)

Remove the skin and bones from the chicken. Chop, dice into bite-size pieces, or shred the meat using your hands or 2 forks. (Of course I probably gave one breast to my dog, Izzy.)

Makes about 8 cups

We had **Enchiladas Suizas**, **Green Rice**, and **refried beans**.

Enchiladas Suizas

Make the Green Rice while the enchiladas are in the oven.

- 2 large **poblano chiles**
- 4 **skinless boneless, chicken breast halves**
- 2 tablespoons **EVOO**
- 1 **onion**, chopped
- 2 cloves **garlic**, finely chopped
- 1 **jalapeño chile**, seeded and chopped
- 8 medium-large **tomatillos**, husked, rinsed, and chopped
- ¼ cup packed **cilantro leaves**
- Juice of 1 **lime**
- 2 teaspoons **honey**
- **Salt** and **pepper**
- 8 (6-inch) **flour tortillas** or 12 (5-inch) corn tortillas
- **Vegetable oil** (optional)
- 1 cup **crème fraîche, Mexican crema,** or **sour cream**
- 1 cup shredded **Swiss cheese**
- 1 cup shredded **Monterey Jack cheese**
- **Red onion**, cut into rings, and **cilantro**, for garnish
- **Green Rice** (recipe follows)

Preheat the broiler to high. Place the poblanos under the broiler and char until blackened an all sides, 10 to 12 minutes. Leave the door of the oven cracked open to allow the steam to escape. Place the peppers in a bowl and cover tightly with plastic wrap. Allow the peppers to cool enough to handle. Switch the oven to bake at 375°F.

Meanwhile, place the chicken in a medium saucepan and add enough water to come up to the top of the meat but do not submerge completely. Bring to a boil, then reduce to a simmer, and poach 10 to 12 minutes.

While the chicken is poaching, in a skillet, heat the EVOO (2 turns of the pan) over medium-high heat. Add the onion, garlic, and jalapeño, and cook to soften, 5 minutes.

Place the tomatillos, cilantro, and lime juice in a food processor with the onion mixture. Peel and seed the poblanos, give them a coarse chop, and add to processor. Process until an almost-smooth sauce forms, 1 minute. Pour the sauce into a skillet and stir to combine. Stir in the honey, season with salt and pepper, and simmer 10 minutes.

Shred the cooked, poached chicken with 2 forks.

Blister flour tortillas in a dry skillet or over an open flame to soften. If using corn tortillas, warm a thin layer of vegetable oil in a small skillet over medium-low heat. Pass the corn tortillas through the warm oil to soften them, stacking them on a paper towel–lined plate to drain.

Pour a little sauce into the bottom of a 7 by 11-inch baking dish or 4 individual casseroles. Fill the corn tortillas with shredded chicken, roll them up, and arrange them side by side in the baking dish. Top with the remaining sauce. Dot the enchiladas with crème fraîche and top with the two cheeses. Bake until browned on top and bubbling, 25 to 30 minutes.

Garnish the enchiladas with red onion and cilantro. Serve the Green Rice alongside.

Serves 4

GREEN RICE

1¾ cups **chicken stock**
1 cup packed **fresh spinach leaves**
½ cup packed **cilantro leaves**
1 **jalapeño chile**, seeded and chopped
3 to 4 **scallions**, chopped
1 tablespoon **butter**
1 cup **long-grain white rice**

In a food processor, combine ¼ cup of the stock, the spinach, cilantro, jalapeño, and scallions and process into a finely chopped, thick paste.

In a saucepan, bring the remaining 1½ cups stock and the butter to a boil. Stir in the rice, reduce to a simmer, cover, and cook until tender, 17 to 18 minutes. When the rice has been cooking for 15 minutes, stir in the spinach mixture, cover, and cook 2 to 3 minutes more. Turn off the heat and let stand 5 minutes.

Serves 4

Refried beans:

If you want beans, I start with canned spicy refried beans and I mix in a little bit of sautéed onion and garlic seasoned with cumin, salt, and pepper. I add a little water (½ cup per can of beans) to thin them. When I serve this with the enchiladas and green rice, I put the refried beans in small side-dish cups and top them with the green rice so the beans are sort of a surprise underneath the rice.

⏱ FEBRUARY 14/ VALENTINE'S DAY DINNER

I made **Beef Milanese with Tomato & Arugula Raw Sauce**. My sister and mom were with us, so it was a family Valentine's Day. My sister doesn't eat a lot of red meat, so I made her chicken cutlets (following the same recipe). To go along with it we had **pasta with organic baby broccoli**.

Beef Milanese with Tomato & Arugula Raw Sauce

RAW SAUCE
1 cup **arugula leaves**
½ cup **basil leaves**
1 large clove **garlic**, grated or pasted
Juice of 1 **lemon**
Salt and **pepper**
⅓ cup **EVOO**
2 cups chopped, seeded **vine-ripened tomatoes**
½ small **red onion**, finely chopped

BEEF CUTLETS
4 (3-ounce) thin-cut slices **beef top round** or sirloin (¾ pound)
Kosher salt and **pepper**
1 cup **flour**
1 teaspoon ground **sage**
2 large **eggs**
1 cup **fine dry bread crumbs**
½ cup **panko bread crumbs**
½ cup grated **pecorino cheese**
Olive oil, for shallow-frying
4 **lemon** wedges

Preheat the oven to 275°F. Place a wire rack over a rimmed baking sheet and place in the oven to warm.

Make the raw sauce: In a food processor, combine the arugula, basil, garlic, and lemon juice; season with salt and pepper. Turn the processor on and stream in the EVOO to form a pesto-like

sauce. Toss the sauce with the tomatoes and onion and set aside.

Make the beef cutlets: Pound the meat ⅛ inch thick and season with salt and pepper. Line up 3 shallow bowls on the counter: Spread the flour out in one and season with the sage; beat the eggs in the second; and mix together the two bread crumbs and the pecorino in the third.

In a skillet, heat a thin layer of oil (about ¼ cup) over medium to medium-high heat.

Coat 2 pieces of beef in the flour, then in egg, and finally in the bread-crumb mixture, pressing to make sure the coating sticks. Fry to a deep golden in color, 2 to 3 minutes on each side. Transfer to the oven to keep warm. Repeat with the remaining beef.

Serve the beef cutlets with the lemon wedges and top with the raw sauce.

Serves 4

Pasta with baby broccoli, chiles, and garlic: I bought 2 bunches of organic baby broccoli at Whole Foods—it was on sale. (You could also use 1 bundle broccoli rabe or 2 bundles broccolini.) Parboil the baby broccoli (chopped into florets) in salted boiling water for about 5 minutes to cook the bitterness out. Drain it. Heat up about ¼ cup EVOO (4 turns of the pan) over medium heat, add 4 cloves garlic (shaved Goodfellas thin), and 1 red Fresno chile, seeded and finely chopped. Stir the olive oil until the garlic is very lightly golden in color and very fragrant. Add the baby broccoli to the pan; season with a little sea salt, pepper, and nutmeg. Cook up some short-cut pasta (we used penne). Right before you drain the pasta, add some of that starchy liquid to the broccoli mixture. Drain the pasta and toss all together. Top with pecorino if you want a sharp, salty flavor. Top with Parm if you want a milder, nuttier flavor.

Everybody just kept wanting chicken this week. My mom and my sister were still staying with us, so I made **Saffron Chicken & Rice.**

Saffron Chicken & Rice

My sister likes a little flavor of cinnamon in her saffron rice. You could throw in a cinnamon stick and pull it out later, or you could add in a little pinch of ground cinnamon to your saffron rice as it's cooking.

½ teaspoon (about 2 pinches) **saffron threads**
5 to 6 cups **chicken stock**
1 tablespoon **EVOO**
3 tablespoons **butter**
8 **skin-on, bone-in chicken thighs** or 4 skin-on, bone-in chicken breast halves, cut in half (8 pieces)
Salt and **pepper**
⅓ to ½ cup broken **spaghetti**
1 cup **long-grain white rice**
1 medium **onion**, chopped
2 cloves **garlic**, finely chopped or grated
A handful of **golden raisins**
1 **bay leaf**
1 pinch of ground **cinnamon** or a cinnamon stick
1 pinch **turmeric**
Optional toppings: Toasted slivered **almonds** and **gremolata** (see Tip)

In a medium saucepan, combine the saffron and chicken stock and bring to a simmer over medium heat. Keep warm.

In a large, high-sided skillet, heat the EVOO (1 turn of the pan) over medium-high heat. Melt in 1 tablespoon of the butter. Season the chicken with salt and pepper and cook until golden brown, 4 to 5 minutes per side. Remove the chicken to a plate and set aside, covered with foil.

Melt the remaining 2 tablespoons butter in the skillet. Add the pasta and cook until toasted and golden brown, 2 to 3 minutes. Add the rice to the pan, tossing to coat in the butter, along with the onion, garlic, and raisins.

Add the bay leaf, cinnamon, turmeric, saffron-infused stock, and reserved chicken to the pan. Bring the liquid up to a bubble, cover the pan, then reduce the heat to medium and simmer until the chicken is cooked through and the rice is tender, 15 to 18 minutes. Remove and discard the bay leaf (and cinnamon stick, if that's what you used).

Serve topped with almonds and gremolata, if you want.

Serves 4

> A gremolata is a mixture of citrus zest and herbs that is used as a flavorful topping for lots of dishes. On a cutting board, chop together some parsley, fresh thyme, and orange or lemon zest.

We had **That's Shallot-a Flavor Spaghetti** (see January 25, page 243) and a nice green salad.

We had **fennel-roasted pork**, **butternut squash and potato mashers**, and **balsamic cipollini**.

Fennel-roasted pork: I took a 4-pound pork roast (a boned leg), scored the thin layer of fat on top, and rubbed it with fennel seed, fresh or dried thyme, sea salt, and pepper. We started that at 425°F until well browned and then we reduced the heat to 300°F, added a bed of vegetables and some wine, and roasted it until the internal temperature reached 155°F. Let it rest, covered with foil, for 20 to 30 minutes, then slice.

Butternut squash and potato mashers: I diced the squash and potatoes and boiled about 15 minutes together. Then I drained them, put them back in the hot pot, and mashed them with milk (or half-and-half), grated Parm, grated orange zest (or lemon zest), freshly grated nutmeg, salt, and pepper.

Balsamic cipollini: I parboiled some cipollini onions about 5 minutes so I could peel them. I cooled them and popped them out of their skins. I caramelized them in browned butter over medium-low heat for 7 or 8 minutes on each side. Added ½ cup chicken stock and a drizzle of aged balsamic vinegar (my Balsamic Drizzle would be good here) and I garnished with a little chopped parsley.

🕐 **FEBRUARY 18/DINNER**

Chicken Vesuvio

⅓ to ½ cup **EVOO**
6 cloves **garlic**, thinly sliced
2 **russet (baking) potatoes**, peeled and cut into wedges
1 teaspoon dried **oregano**, lightly crushed
Leaves from 2 or 3 sprigs of **rosemary**, finely chopped
Leaves from 2 or 3 sprigs of **thyme**, finely chopped
Salt and **pepper**
2 pounds **skinless, boneless chicken breast**, cut into large chunks
Flour, for dredging
½ cup **dry white wine**
½ cup **chicken stock**
½ cup fresh **peas** or thawed frozen
¼ cup finely chopped **flat-leaf parsley**
Crusty bread, for mopping

Preheat the oven to 375°F.

In a skillet, heat ¼ cup EVOO (4 turns of the pan) over medium-high heat. Add the garlic, potatoes, oregano, rosemary, and thyme; season liberally with salt and pepper. Cook until browned, turning occasionally, about 15 minutes.

Meanwhile, in a large ovenproof skillet, heat a couple of tablespoons EVOO over medium-high heat. Season the chicken liberally with salt and pepper and dredge in flour. Add to the pan and cook until golden, 3 to 4 minutes per side. Deglaze the pan with the wine and add the stock.

Transfer the potatoes and garlic to the chicken pan and place in the oven. Roast until the chicken is cooked through, 10 to 12 minutes. Add the peas during the last few minutes of cooking. Serve topped with parsley and with crusty bread for mopping.

Serves 4

🕐 FEBRUARY 19/DINNER

We had **Veal Chops with Gorgonzola** (see August 14, page 116) and a side dish of **Gnocchi with Spinach & Garlic**.

Gnocchi with Spinach & Garlic

Pan-roasting the garlic takes a third of the time it would take in the oven. It's just delicious.

¼ cup **EVOO**
4 large cloves **garlic**, peeled and smashed
A couple of bundles of **fresh spinach**, coarsely chopped, or 1 bag
Salt and **pepper**
Freshly grated **nutmeg**
1 pound store-bought **spinach gnocchi**
1 tablespoon **butter**
Grated **Parmigiano-Reggiano cheese**, for serving

In a large skillet, heat the EVOO (4 turns of the pan) over medium-low heat. Add the garlic

and slowly cook until a light caramel color, 10 to 15 minutes. Once the garlic is nice and soft and caramel in color you can just mash it into the oil with the back of a wooden spoon or puree it with the warm oil in a blender. Reserve half of the oil for another use and return the remaining oil to the pan. Wilt the spinach into the garlic oil and season with salt, pepper, and a few grates of nutmeg.

Bring a large pot of water to a boil for the gnocchi. Add salt and cook the gnocchi until they float to the top of the pan. Drain the gnocchi and toss with the butter, spinach mixture, and Parm.

Serves 4

🕐 FEBRUARY 20/DINNER

We had the delicious **Double-High Patty Melts** (see January 18, page 239), which are turkey burgers piled high with sautéed portobellos.

🕐 FEBRUARY 21/DINNER

Tonight's meal was inspired by Il Buco's recipe for the short ribs they make there, which are amazing. We had such a delicious meal there, I had to re-create it. I adapted their short-rib recipe to make **Rib-Eye Steaks with Celery Salad**, which we had with a side dish of **balsamic cipollini** (see February 17, page 265). We started off with a first course of **Cacio e Pepe**.

Cacio e Pepe

Salt
1 pound **spaghetti**
¼ cup **EVOO**
2 tablespoons **butter**
2 teaspoons **coarse black pepper**
¾ to 1 cup grated **pecorino cheese**
¾ cup grated **Grana Padano** or **cacio de Roma cheese**

Bring a large pot of water to a boil. Salt the water and cook the pasta to al dente. Before draining, ladle out and reserve 1 cup of the starchy pasta cooking water. Drain the pasta.

In a large skillet, heat the EVOO (4 turns of the pan) over medium-low heat. Melt in the butter. Add the black pepper and stir for a couple of minutes. Add the starchy cooking water to the pan. Let that come up to a boil.

Toss the pasta, sauce, and half the cheeses. Keep tossing to coat evenly. It will become a sauce on the spaghetti. Serve it in shallow dishes with the remaining cheese on top. Pass more pepper at the table.

Serves 4 to 6

Rib-Eye Steaks with Celery Salad

I'm also going to try this in the future as Il Buco does, with a big giant beef rib.

6 or 8 ribs **celery** with leafy tops, very thinly sliced on an angle
6 to 7 tablespoons **EVOO**, plus more for the steaks
Juice of 1 **lemon**
Kosher salt and **coarse black pepper**
2 large **rib-eye steaks**, at room temperature
1½ teaspoons **coriander seeds**, toasted and crushed
6 **anchovy fillets**
3 cloves **garlic**, finely chopped
½ cup **Cerignola olives** (the bright green, buttery olives), pitted and coarsely chopped
A handful of **walnuts**, toasted
½ cup shaved **pecorino cheese**
A little chopped **flat-leaf parsley**

Preheat the oven to 325°F.

To make the salad, in a bowl, toss the celery with 3 to 4 tablespoons EVOO, the lemon juice, and salt and pepper to taste. Set aside.

Pat the steaks dry and rub them with EVOO. Make a crust on them of coriander, coarse black

pepper, and salt. Heat a cast-iron skillet over medium-high heat until screaming hot. Add the steaks and once they're crusted on both sides and edges, finish them in the oven, cooking them to medium-rare, about 125°F on an instant-read thermometer, about 3 to 5 minutes per side.

In another skillet, heat 3 tablespoons EVOO (3 turns of the pan) over low heat. Add the anchovies and stir until they melt into the oil. Stir in the garlic.

When the steaks come out of the oven, pour the anchovy oil over them. Let the steaks rest on a cutting board, then slice them.

Serve the steaks garnished with the olives, walnuts, pecorino, and a little parsley. Serve the celery salad alongside.

Serves 4

🕐 **FEBRUARY 23/DINNER**

We started with **Tabbouleh** and then we had **Red Lentil Soup with Mint Yogurt**, which I served with pieces of naan brushed with melted butter.

Red Lentil Soup with Mint Yogurt

About 2 tablespoons **EVOO** or **butter**
2 **carrots**, finely diced
2 ribs **celery**, chopped
1 **onion**, finely chopped
4 cloves **garlic**, chopped
1 **red Fresno chile**, very thinly sliced
Salt and **pepper**
1 tablespoon ground **cumin**
1 tablespoon **turmeric**
1 tablespoon ground **coriander**
1 tablespoon **ancho chile powder**
1 teaspoon ground **cardamom**
2 tablespoons **tomato paste**
1½ cups **red lentils**
6 cups **chicken** or **vegetable stock**

½ pound **spinach leaves**, stemmed and coarsely chopped
½ cup **mint leaves**
¼ cup **cilantro leaves**
1 cup plain **Greek yogurt**

In a soup pot, heat the EVOO (a couple of turns of the pan) or butter over medium to medium-high heat. Add the carrots, celery, onion, garlic, and chile; season liberally with salt and lightly with black pepper. Cook to soften, 8 to 10 minutes.

Add the spices and stir 1 or 2 minutes, then stir in the tomato paste and cook until fragrant, about 1 minute. Add the lentils and stock and bring to a boil. Lower the heat and simmer until the lentils are very tender, 40 minutes or so. Wilt in the spinach and remove from the heat.

While the soup cooks, combine the mint, cilantro, and yogurt in a food processor or blender and process into a sauce. Add salt to taste.

Serve the soup in shallow bowls topped with the cool yogurt sauce.

Serves 4

Tabbouleh: Cooked bulgur tossed with tomatoes, mint, scallions, parsley, dill, garlic, lemon, salt, and pepper.

I made two lasagnas: **Lazy Bolognese Lasagna** and **Lazy Lasagna with Butternut Squash & Escarole**. For dessert I made a limoncello tart adapted from a British cooking magazine. It came out picture-perfect. I was shocked.

Lazy Bolognese Lasagna

Salt and **pepper**
1 pound **ruffle-edge lasagna noodles**, broken into irregular pieces
2 tablespoons **EVOO**
1½ pounds **ground beef**
1 **onion**, finely chopped
2 or 3 large cloves **garlic**, finely chopped
1 small **carrot**, finely chopped or grated
2 tablespoons **mixed chopped fresh herbs** (rosemary, oregano, marjoram, and thyme)
A sprinkle of ground **cloves**
¼ cup **tomato paste**
1 cup **white wine**
2 cups **beef stock**
3 tablespoons **butter**
2 rounded tablespoons **flour**
2 cups **whole milk**
Freshly grated **nutmeg**
Freshly grated **Parmigiano-Reggiano cheese**

Bring a large pot of water to a boil. Salt the water and cook the pasta to about 2 minutes shy of al dente. Drain the pasta.

In a Dutch oven, heat the EVOO (2 turns of the pan) over medium-high heat. Add the beef and brown well. Add the onion, garlic, carrot, herbs, cloves, and lots of salt and pepper and cook until tender, 7 to 8 minutes. Stir in the tomato paste for 1 minute, then stir in the wine for 1 minute. Stir in the stock and simmer for a few minutes longer.

Preheat the broiler and position a rack in the center of the oven. In a saucepan, melt the butter over medium heat. Whisk in the flour, then the milk, and let the white sauce thicken enough to coat a spoon; season with salt, pepper, and nutmeg.

Toss the pasta with the meat sauce and arrange in a 9 by 13-inch baking pan. Pour the white sauce over the top in an even layer. Top with a layer of Parm and broil to brown the top.

Serves 6

Lazy Lasagna with Butternut Squash & Escarole

1 medium **butternut squash**, peeled and chopped into 1-inch pieces
2 tablespoons **EVOO**, plus more for drizzling
Salt and **pepper**
1 pound **ruffle-edge lasagna noodles**, broken into irregular shapes
4 cloves **garlic**, finely chopped
1 medium head **escarole**, chopped
About 1 cup **chicken** or **vegetable stock**
1½ cups fresh **ricotta cheese**
A small handful of **sage leaves**, thinly sliced
½ cup grated **Parmigiano-Reggiano cheese**
2 tablespoons **butter**
2 tablespoons **flour**
2 cups whole **milk**
Freshly grated **nutmeg**
⅓ pound **Italian Fontina** or **Gruyère cheese**, shredded (about 1½ cups)

Position a rack in the center of the oven and preheat to 400°F. Arrange the squash on a baking sheet and lightly dress with a drizzle of EVOO,

salt, and pepper. Roast until golden at the edges and tender, 35 to 45 minutes. Leave the oven on.

Bring a large pot of water to a boil. Salt the water and cook the pasta to about 2 minutes shy of al dente.

Meanwhile, in a skillet, heat 2 tablespoons EVOO (2 turns of the pan) over medium heat. Add the garlic and stir a minute, then wilt in the escarole. Season with a little salt and pepper, add the stock, and simmer gently until ready to use.

In a small bowl, stir together the ricotta, sage, Parm, and salt and pepper to taste.

In a saucepan, melt the butter over medium heat. Whisk in the flour, then the milk, and let the white sauce thicken enough to coat a spoon; season with salt, pepper, and nutmeg.

Drain the lasagna noodles and return them to the hot pot. Stir in the ricotta mixture, combine evenly, then fold in the roasted squash and escarole. Transfer to a 9 by 13-inch baking dish and pour the white sauce evenly over the top. Cover with the Fontina or Gruyère cheese and place in the oven. Switch the oven to broil and broil until the lasagna is browned and bubbling all over, about 4 minutes.

Serves 6

🕐 FEBRUARY 26/DINNER

We had **Jalapeño Popper Dip** and **Touchdown Chili** (see September 7, page 140), which I served with a bunch of toppings: pepitas, thinly sliced fresh chiles, pickled jalapeño rings, and sour cream. And I made a **Puppy Dog Chili** for Isaboo.

Jalapeño Popper Dip

We put this out with potato chips and RW Garcia's gluten-free tortilla chips. They're lovely, and they come in beet and carrot and spinach flavors. Really, really delicious product. You can use any whole-grain tortilla chip or flaxseed chip or any good-quality potato chip for this dip.

1 cup **crème fraîche** or sour cream (we prefer crème fraîche)
1 **jalapeño chile**, minced
1 teaspoon grated **lime zest**
1 tablespoon fresh **lime juice**
Salt and **pepper**
¼ cup grated **Parmigiano-Reggiano cheese**
¼ cup very finely chopped **scallions**
1 small clove **garlic**, grated or pasted
2 tablespoons very finely chopped **cilantro**

Stir that all together and that's your Popper Dip. It's delicious!

Makes about 1½ cups

> 🦴 *Isaboo's puppy dog chili:* Throw 1 cup beef stock, ¼ cup masa harina (cornmeal), ½ cup long-grain white rice, ⅔ pound ground beef chuck, ¼ teaspoon sweet paprika, and 1 tablespoon Worcestershire sauce into a pot. Bring it up to a boil, turn it down to low, keep the lid on it, mash it all up with a potato masher. Keep an eye on it. It should cook until the rice is all plump and mixed in well with the beef, 15 to 18 minutes. If the pan starts to get a little bit dry, add a splash of water.

I ate dinner out at Tertulia, a restaurant that serves what the chef calls "hero foods." The chef, Seamus Mullen, works with us on our site (www .rachaelray.com). He learned to control his disease, which is severe rheumatoid arthritis, by eating these things he calls "hero foods" in the right combination. His restaurant, one of the faves in New York, offers all hero foods, so it's a great place to dine out because you're doing something good for your body while you're enjoying a nice meal.

⏱ **FEBRUARY 29/DINNER**

Macaroni & Cheese with Fennel

- 1 tablespoon **EVOO**
- 3 tablespoons **butter**
- 1 bulb **fennel**, trimmed and quartered, thinly sliced, with a handful of fronds reserved and chopped
- 1 large **onion**, quartered and thinly sliced
- 4 cloves **garlic**, sliced
- **Salt** and **pepper**
- 3 tablespoons **flour**
- About ½ cup **dry white wine**
- 1 cup **vegetable** or **chicken stock**
- 2 cups **whole milk**
- Freshly grated **nutmeg**
- 1 pound Italian **macaroni** or ziti
- 1½ to 2 cups shredded **Fontina Val d'Aosta** or **Gruyère cheese**
- 1 cup freshly grated **Grana Padano** or **Parmigiano-Reggiano cheese**, plus some for topping
- **Fennel pollen** (optional)
- **Crispy fried onions**, homemade or store-bought, for garnish

Preheat the oven to 375°F. Bring a large pot of water to a boil for the macaroni.

Meanwhile, in a medium saucepan or deep skillet, heat the EVOO (1 turn of the pan) over medium heat. Melt in the butter. When the butter begins to foam, add the fennel, onion, garlic, and salt and pepper to taste. Partially cover and cook, stirring occasionally, until light caramel in color, about 20 minutes. If the fennel and onion brown too quickly at the edges, reduce the heat.

Once very soft and sweet, sprinkle the flour over the vegetables and stir for 1 minute. Deglaze with the wine. Stir in the stock and milk and cook to thicken, 5 to 7 minutes. Season the sauce with salt, pepper, and nutmeg to taste.

Salt the pasta water and cook the macaroni to al dente. Drain.

Stir the Fontina and ½ cup of the Grana Padano into the fennel sauce in a figure-8 motion until melted. Toss the sauce with the pasta and top with the remaining grated cheese; sprinkle with fennel pollen (if using) and the fennel fronds.

Scrape into a 9 by 13-inch baking pan and bake until browned and bubbling, 10 to 12 minutes. Top with crispy onions.

Serves 6

MARCH

THURSDAY/1

FRIDAY/2

DINNER
basic hummus, blood orange salad, sword-fish cutlets, pasta with roasted garlic & eggplant

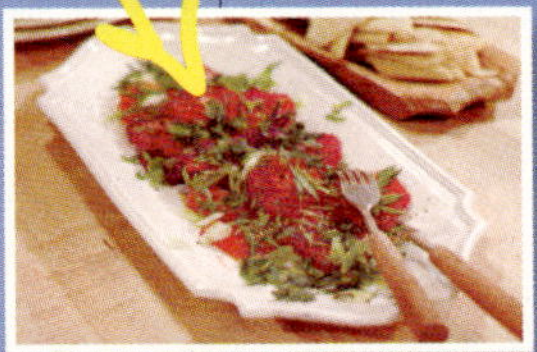

SATURDAY/3

BREAKFAST
deviled ham on toast with cheese and asparagus

LUNCH
vegetable soup

DINNER
paella

SUNDAY/4

BREAKFAST
pecan waffles with maple-apple topping

DINNER
pasta with broccoli rabe

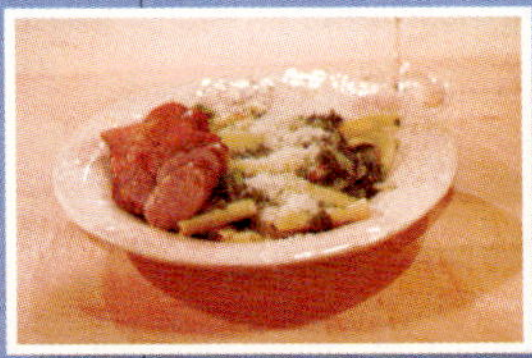

MONDAY/5

LUNCH
pan bagnat

DINNER
carbonara with spring onions & peas

SUNDAY/11

BREAKFAST
deviled ham on toast (with eggs)

DINNER
spaghetti with creamy spring pea pesto & mini meatballs

MONDAY/12

DINNER
cream of chicken & leeks on buttered toast

TUESDAY/13

DINNER
corned beef with veggies

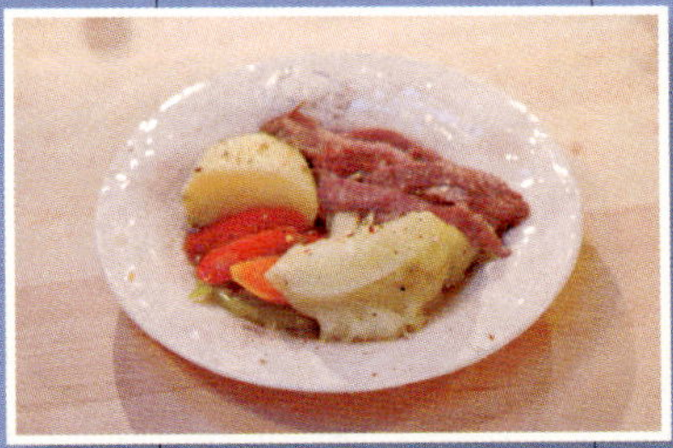

WEDNESDAY/14

DINNER
that's shallot-a flavor spaghetti

THURSDAY/15

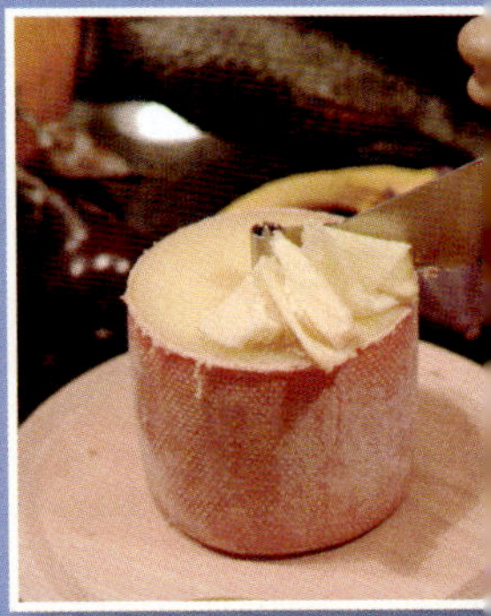

WEDNESDAY/21

DINNER
lemon–poppy seed egg tagliatelle, bull's-eye deviled eggs, roast leg of lamb, tomato & mint jam

THURSDAY/22

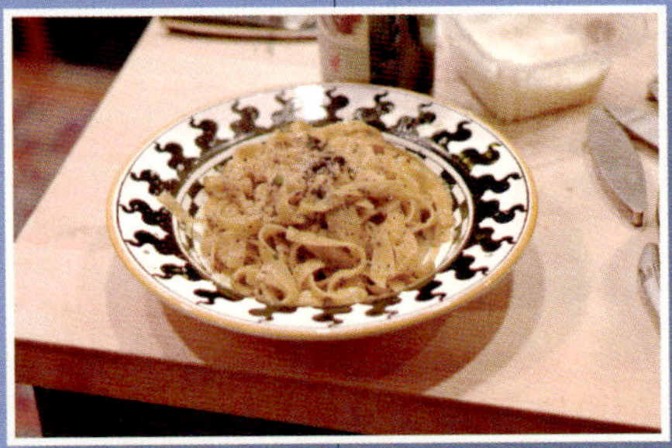

FRIDAY/23

SATURDAY/24

LUNCH
lamb and tomato jam sandwiches

DINNER
pici pasta with fava pesto & asparagus

SUNDAY/25

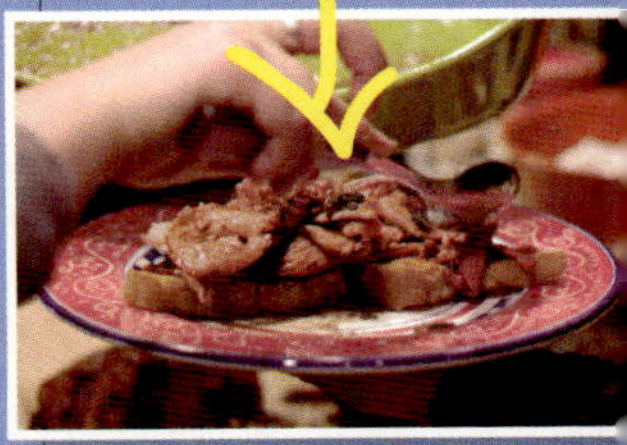

| TUESDAY/6 | WEDNESDAY/7 | THURSDAY/8 | FRIDAY/9 | SATURDAY/10 |

WEDNESDAY/7

DINNER
alici pizza,
all'Amatriciana pizza,
pizza capricciosa,
Italian marinated
mushrooms, roasted
garlic oil, eggplant
with roasted garlic
and sage, roasted pep-
pers in garlic oil

FRIDAY/9

DINNER
oven fish fry on a bed
of not-so-mushy peas

SATURDAY/10

DINNER
chicken croquettes
with gravy, mashed
potatoes & parsnips
with Boursin, green
beans with caramel-
ized onions

| FRIDAY/16 | SATURDAY/17 | SUNDAY/18 | MONDAY/19 | TUESDAY/20 |

| MONDAY/26 | WEDNESDAY/28 | THURSDAY/29 | FRIDAY/30 | SATURDAY/31 |

WEDNESDAY/28

DINNER
spring risotto

THURSDAY/29

DINNER
fava bean spread,
lemon spaghetti with
ramps

FRIDAY/30

DINNER
chicken curry,
homemade rice pilaf

SATURDAY/31

BREAKFAST
breakfast potato
pancakes with Tex-
Mex eggs

DINNER
springtime
minestrone, grilled
cheese with spinach,
calzone-style

I made my **Basic Hummus** (see February 3, page 252), but I threw in a little ground cumin. We had **Swordfish Cutlets** and a tomato relish (see June 2, page 55) and **Pasta with Roasted Garlic & Eggplant** and **Blood Orange Salad** on the side.

Pasta with Roasted Garlic & Eggplant

2 heads **garlic**, tops cut off to expose the cloves
EVOO, for liberal drizzling
Salt and **pepper**
1 medium-large firm **eggplant**
1 pound **short-cut pasta**
A handful each of grated **Parmigiano-Reggiano** and **Pecorino Romano cheese**
A few leaves of **basil**
A small handful of **flat-leaf parsley**

Preheat the oven to 400°F. Drizzle the garlic with some EVOO and season with salt and pepper. Wrap in foil and roast until tender and caramel in color, 40 to 45 minutes. At the same time, roast the eggplant: Pour a few tablespoons of EVOO onto a baking sheet and spread a thin layer around the pan with a pastry brush. Halve the eggplant lengthwise and score the flesh in a crosshatch pattern, with rows 1 inch apart; score the edges near the skin. Season the eggplant with salt and pepper. Place cut side down on the baking sheet and roast until tender, 30 to 35 minutes. Set aside to cool.

Bring a large pot of water to a boil. Salt the water and cook the pasta to al dente.

Scrape the eggplant off the skin into a food processor. Squish the garlic from the skins into the processor. Add the cheeses, basil, and parsley.

Just before draining the pasta, ladle out 1 cup of starchy cooking water and add to the food processor. Pulse the mixture into a thick sauce.

Drain the pasta and toss with the sauce; adjust the salt and pepper to taste.

Serves 6 to 8

Blood Orange Salad

4 **blood oranges**
2 to 3 **scallions**, chopped
1 small **red Fresno chile**, very thinly sliced
Sea salt and **black pepper**
EVOO, for liberal drizzling
A small handful of **flat-leaf parsley**, coarsely chopped

Trim tops and bottoms of oranges; then remove the peel in strips, working top to bottom around the oranges with a sharp paring knife. Thinly slice the peeled oranges into disks, arrange on a platter, top with the scallions and chile, and dress with salt, pepper, and EVOO. Garnish with parsley.

Serves 4

MARCH 3, BREAKFAST
Deviled ham on toast with cheese and asparagus: I topped toast with my Deviled Ham (see May 29, page 46), then with sautéed asparagus tips, and then with Cheddar or Gruyère. I baked them at 375°F. until golden. Then I topped them with over-easy eggs.

MARCH 3, LUNCH

Vegetable soup: I cooked up rainbow carrots (different-colored carrots from the farmers' market), fennel, onions, garlic, and celery. Seasoned with bay leaf and chopped thyme. Then I added 8 cups stock and 2 cups water. I cooked 1 cup short-cut whole wheat pasta right in the soup itself, but if you're making the soup to be eaten over a couple of days or you want leftovers, you should cook the pasta separately (so it doesn't get too soft when you reheat). It had a sprinkle of dill pollen (you can use chopped fresh dill) and a sprinkle of fennel pollen and salt and pepper.

🕐 **MARCH 3/DINNER**

Paella

½ cup **flat-leaf parsley**
4 cloves **garlic**, chopped or thinly sliced
Zest and juice of 1 **lemon**
2 tablespoons **fresh thyme leaves**
Leaves from 1 or 2 sprigs **oregano** or marjoram, finely chopped
4 cups **chicken stock**
2 generous pinches of **saffron threads**
1 pound large **shrimp**, peeled and deveined
1 tablespoon **seafood seasoning**
Sea salt and **pepper**
4 **skin-on, bone-in chicken thighs**
4 **skin-on chicken drumsticks**
1 tablespoon **poultry seasoning**

4 to 5 tablespoons **EVOO**
½ pound **Spanish chorizo**, casings removed, sliced on an angle into thick ovals
1 **Spanish onion**, chopped
1 **red Fresno chile**, finely chopped
4 to 5 **water-packed piquillo peppers**, finely chopped, or 2 large roasted red peppers, finely chopped
2 **tomatoes**, seeded and chopped
1½ teaspoons **sweet paprika** or smoked sweet paprika
2 large fresh **bay leaves**
½ cup **dry sherry**
2¼ cups **paella rice**, such as Bomba or Calasparra (half a 1-kilo sack)
16 to 20 **mussels**, scrubbed and debearded
1 cup **frozen peas**, thawed

On a cutting board, chop together the parsley, 2 cloves garlic, the lemon zest, thyme, and oregano. Set the gremolata aside.

In a medium saucepan, combine the stock, 2 cups water, and the saffron. Warm the mixture to steep the saffron threads and flavor the stock; keep warm over low heat.

Toss the shrimp with the seafood seasoning; add salt and pepper if not included in the seasoning blend. Season the chicken with poultry seasoning; add salt and pepper if not included in the seasoning blend.

In a very large shallow pan, heat 2 tablespoons of the EVOO (2 turns of the pan) over medium-high heat. Add the shrimp and cook 2 minutes

on each side. Transfer to a plate. Add a little more oil to the pan. Add the chicken and cook until golden all over, 8 to 10 minutes. Transfer to a plate. Add the chorizo ovals and cook 1 or 2 minutes on each side. Transfer to a plate.

Add another 1 tablespoon EVOO (1 turn of the pan) to the pan and add the onion, the remaining 2 cloves garlic, and salt and pepper to taste. Stir 2 to 3 minutes; then add the chile, piquillo peppers, tomatoes, paprika, and herb gremolata and stir 2 to 3 minutes; then add the bay leaves. Deglaze with the sherry. Add the saffron stock to the pan and scatter the rice around the pan. Nestle the chicken and chorizo into the rice and cook, without stirring, for 12 to 15 minutes. Reduce the heat to low, add the mussels (hinge side set into the rice), and cook 5 minutes without stirring. Add the shrimp and peas and cook 5 minutes more. Douse the pan with the lemon juice; turn off the heat; and let stand, covered with foil, for 5 to 10 minutes. Discard any unopened mussels and the bay leaves before serving.

Serves 6

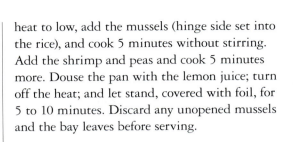 **MARCH 4/BREAKFAST**

We had one of our faves, **Pecan Waffles with Maple-Apple Topping** (see September 17, page 144).

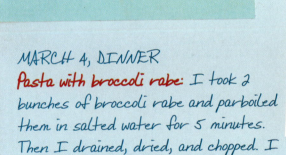

MARCH 4, DINNER

Pasta with broccoli rabe: I took 2 bunches of broccoli rabe and parboiled them in salted water for 5 minutes. Then I drained, dried, and chopped. I melted 6 good-quality anchovy fillets into ¼ to ⅓ cup EVOO (just eyeball it) and added in 6 cloves of garlic and 2 thinly sliced red Fresno chiles. Stir that together and add your rabe. Cook up some pasta and before you drain it, ladle 1 cup of the cooking water into the broccoli rabe along with some grated Parm or pecorino or a combination of the two. Toss with the pasta to combine.

Pan Bagnat

Juice of 2 **lemons**
1 **red onion**, finely chopped
3 tablespoons **capers**, rinsed
2 cloves **garlic**, pasted
1 **red Fresno chile**, seeded and finely diced
1 tablespoon fresh **thyme leaves**, finely chopped
2 ribs **celery**, finely chopped
¼ cup **niçoise olives**, pitted and chopped
2 (6-ounce) cans line-caught **tuna**, drained
1½ teaspoons **seafood seasoning**, such as Old Bay
Black pepper
1 **baguette**, cut into 3 (8-inch) subs, split and lightly toasted
2 **tomatoes**, seeded and diced
¼ cup **EVOO**

In a medium bowl, combine the lemon juice, onion, capers, garlic, chile, thyme, celery, olives, tuna, seafood seasoning, and black pepper to taste and gently stir. Divide the mixture evenly among the toasted baguette pieces. Top with diced tomatoes and olive oil and squeeze the bread together to let it soak up the olive oil and juices. Cut each sandwich in half and serve.

Serves 3

Carbonara with Spring Onions & Peas

Salt and **pepper**
1 cup shelled **fresh peas**
1 pound **egg tagliatelle** (I like Delverde brand)
3 tablespoons **EVOO**
⅓ pound **uncured bacon** or pancetta, chopped or sliced
4 cloves **garlic**, very thinly sliced or chopped
4 **spring onions** with green tops or 1 bunch scallions, thinly sliced, white and greens kept separate
½ cup **white wine**
1 tablespoon grated **lemon zest**

3 organic **egg yolks**
½ cup **flat-leaf parsley leaves**, finely chopped
½ cup grated **Pecorino Romano cheese**
½ cup grated **Grana Padano** or **Parmigiano-Reggiano cheese**

In a small pot of boiling salted water, cook the peas for 5 minutes. Drain and set aside.

Bring a large pot of water to a boil. Salt the water and cook the pasta to al dente.

Meanwhile, in a large skillet, heat the EVOO (3 turns of the pan) over medium heat. Add the bacon or pancetta and render to crisp. Add lots of pepper, the garlic, and the whites of the onions or scallions and stir 2 to 3 minutes. Add the wine and lemon zest.

When the pasta is about done, ladle out and set aside ½ cup starchy cooking water. Ladle out another ¼ cup of the starchy water and beat into the egg yolks to warm them.

Add the onion greens and parsley to the sauce. Drain the pasta and add to the sauce, along with the peas, warmed eggs, and half the cheeses. Toss 1 to 2 minutes to combine, using a little of the reserved starchy cooking water if the pasta tightens up too much before a glossy coating forms. Top with the remaining cheeses and serve immediately.

Serves 4

Pizza Night: Started with an antipasto of **eggplant with roasted garlic and sage** and **roasted peppers in garlic oil**. Then we had **pizza capricciosa** (one of my favorites, which you can usually get only in Italy), **all'Amatriciana pizza**, and **alici pizza**. My favorite pizza in NYC is from Motorino on 12th Street and we eat there once a week when we are in town. Mathieu, the chef, makes me a crazy-good alici pizza brushed with anchovy oil, topped with white anchovies, grape tomatoes, fior di latte cheese, parsley, and red onions. When I'm upstate, I am 4 hours outside the delivery zone, so I had to start making my own.

Pizza

Pizza capricciosa: Capricciosa pizza is artichoke, ham, marinated mushrooms, and hard-boiled egg all on a pizza. It's kind of a crazy pizza. But even if you don't want to make the pizza, you can make the delicious Italian Marinated Mushrooms (page 279) just to put on an antipasto platter. Capricciosa is my Pizza Crust (page 198) topped with shredded Fontina Val d'Aosta, sage leaves, cracked olives, artichoke hearts, and sliced marinated mushrooms. When the pizza comes out of the oven, you top it with prosciutto cotto, hard-boiled egg, and a drizzle of EVOO all over it. Some people like to bake this pizza with the ham on—it's really up to the pizza maker.

All'Amatriciana pizza: You make a raw tomato sauce in the food processor with chiles, Italian canned tomatoes, a little grated onion, grated garlic, a few leaves of basil, salt, pepper, and drizzle of EVOO. You then spread the raw sauce on the Pizza Crust (page 198), top it with lots of rendered smoky bacon—don't cook the bacon all the way; I take it about halfway—and then with lots of pecorino cheese. When the pizza comes out of the oven, top with thin slices of red onion and lots of parsley.

Alici (anchovy) pizza: Roast halved cherry or grape tomatoes dressed with a drizzle of EVOO, salt and pepper, and thyme, on a wire rack over a baking sheet in a low oven, 275° to 300°F, for about an hour. Then melt good-quality anchovy fillets into EVOO (2 fillets to 2 tablespoons EVOO) over medium-low heat and add 2 large cloves garlic, thinly sliced or chopped, and ½ fresh chile, finely chopped or thinly sliced, per pizza. Stir the garlic and chiles 1 to 2 minutes in the oil, then remove from the heat. Bake the Pizza Crust (page 198) to crisp. Remove from the oven and baste liberally with the anchovy-garlic-chile topping. Top the pizza with lots of oven-dried tomatoes, a handful of flat-leaf parsley leaves, a small handful of thinly sliced red onions, chopped oil-cured black olives, and diced fior di latte or other fresh mozzarella.

Italian Marinated Mushrooms

1 cup **white wine vinegar** or white balsamic vinegar

¼ cup **sugar**

1 tablespoon **sea salt**

1 pound **white mushrooms**

1 small **red onion**, sliced

1 fresh **chile** (a red Fresno or Italian chile pepper), halved or sliced

1 or 2 cloves **garlic**, smashed

A handful of **flat-leaf parsley**

A handful of **celery leaves**

A few **bay leaves**

About 1 teaspoon **mustard seeds**

About 1 teaspoon **black peppercorns**

In a small saucepan, combine the vinegar, 1 cup water, the sugar, and salt. Heat until the sugar and salt dissolve.

In a container with a tight-fitting lid, combine the mushrooms, onion, chile, garlic, parsley, celery leaves, bay leaves, mustard seeds, and peppercorns. Pour the marinade over the top, cover, and refrigerate. You can serve them whole as part of an antipasto or slice them up for pizza capricciosa.

Makes 2 to 3 cups

Roasted garlic oil: This is one of my kitchen staples. I make roasted garlic in large batches. It freezes beautifully and is delicious on charred bread. Cut off the tops of whole heads of garlic to expose the cloves, drizzle with EVOO, and season with salt and pepper. Wrap in a foil pouch, then roast in a 425°F oven until soft and golden, 40 to 45 minutes. Squish the roasted garlic cloves out of their skins, mash the garlic into a paste, and cover with EVOO.

Eggplant with roasted garlic and sage: Salt thin slices of eggplant and let drain on paper towels. Arrange a rack over a baking sheet, brush the eggplant slices with roasted garlic oil, and bake at 425°F until the eggplant is charred at the edges, 10 to 15 minutes. Top with torn sage and a few grinds of pepper.

Roasted peppers with garlic oil: Char peppers over an open flame on the stovetop or under the broiler on high heat. When blackened, place in a bowl and cover to cool. Remove the blackened skins with a paper towel. Halve and seed the peppers. Cut them into thin strips, drizzle with roasted garlic oil, and top with chopped thyme and sea salt.

Oven Fish Fry on a Bed of Not-So-Mushy Peas

I used cod, but any thick-cut chunks of white fish will do.

5 tablespoons **butter**
3 cups **panko bread crumbs**
1 tablespoon **seafood seasoning**, such as Old Bay or Szeged fish spice
1 tablespoon **granulated onion**
1 tablespoon **granulated garlic**
Grated zest of 1 **lemon** or **lime**
1 to 2 tablespoons chopped fresh **thyme leaves**
1 to 2 tablespoons finely chopped **chives**
1½ to 2 pounds **cod**, cut from the thickest part of the fillets, shaped into 8 rectangular batons
Salt and **pepper**
2 extra-large **egg whites**, beaten to frothy
1 cup packed **flat-leaf parsley leaves**
1 cup packed fresh **mint leaves**
3 cups shelled fresh **peas** or thawed frozen peas, patted dry
1 tablespoon **EVOO**
2 large **shallots**, finely chopped
2 cups **chicken stock**
Malt vinegar or fresh lemon juice

Position a rack in the center of the oven and preheat to 400°F. Place a wire rack over a baking sheet.

In a small saucepan, melt 4 tablespoons of the butter over low heat. Put the panko in a shallow dish, douse with the melted butter, and toss to combine. Stir in the seafood seasoning, granulated onion, granulated garlic, citrus zest, thyme, and chives.

Pat the fish dry, then season with salt to taste. Coat the fish in the egg whites, then gently press them into the bread crumbs to coat evenly. Arrange them on the wire rack. Bake until the fish is white and flaky and the crumbs are golden, about 20 minutes.

Meanwhile, in a food processor, combine the parsley and mint and pulse to finely chop. Scrape into a bowl and set aside. Return the work bowl to the processor (no need to rinse), add the peas, and pulse until very finely chopped.

In a medium saucepan, heat the EVOO (1 turn of the pan) and the remaining 1 tablespoon butter over medium heat. Add the shallots and cook for 5 minutes. Add the stock and peas and bring to a bubble over medium-high heat. Cook the fresh peas for about 10 minutes or the frozen peas for 6 to 7 minutes. When most of the liquid has evaporated, season with salt and pepper to taste. Stir in the parsley-mint mixture. Remove from the heat.

Spoon pools of not-so-mushy peas onto each dinner plate and top with crispy fish batons. Douse the fish with lots of malt vinegar or lemon.

Serves 4 to 6

This meal was the special request of my sister, Maria, for her birthday. We had **Chicken Croquettes with Gravy**, **Mashed Potatoes & Parsnips with Boursin**, and **Green Beans with Caramelized Onions**. For many years my mom managed a group of restaurants, which included some franchise Howard Johnson's. Back in the day, HoJo's hired Pierre Franey, famed French chef, to develop signature recipes for Howard Johnson's, which included chicken croquettes.

This is my version of the Franey great based on my mom's recollection of seeing the original recipe in print, and on research I've done over the years. My additions include a little more garlic, ground thyme, Parmesan cheese, and nutmeg.

Chicken Croquettes with Gravy

POACHED CHICKEN
1 **onion**, quartered with root end attached
2 **carrots**, thick-cut on an angle
2 ribs **celery**, thick-cut on an angle
2 large fresh **bay leaves**
2 full **skin-on, bone-in chicken breasts**
Salt

CROQUETTES
4 tablespoons (½ stick) **butter**
1 small **onion**, very finely chopped
2 large cloves **garlic**, minced
½ teaspoon **ground thyme**
A pinch of **cayenne pepper**
Salt and **black pepper**
Freshly grated **nutmeg**
6 tablespoons **flour**
2 cups **chicken stock**
¼ to ⅓ cup **heavy cream**
4 large **egg yolks**, lightly beaten
1 cup **fine dry bread crumbs**
Frying oil
1 extra-large **egg**
½ cup **panko bread crumbs**
A small handful of **flat-leaf parsley**, very finely chopped
About ⅓ cup grated **Parmigiano-Reggiano cheese**

GRAVY
3 tablespoons **butter**
¼ cup **flour**
2½ cups **chicken stock**
2 tablespoons **Worcestershire sauce**
Salt and **pepper**
1 extra-large **egg yolk**, beaten

Make the poached chicken: In a large pot, combine the onion, carrots, celery, bay leaves, and chicken. Cover with water, bring to a boil, season with salt, and reduce to a simmer. Poach at a gentle, low rolling boil for 1 hour. Remove the chicken to cool. Strain the stock, return to the pan, and simmer 30 minutes more. Strain again.

Discard the chicken skin and bones and coarsely chop the chicken meat. Add it to a food processor and pulse to fine-chop. You should get about 2½ cups chopped meat. Chill in the refrigerator in a large bowl.

Make the croquettes: In a large skillet, melt the butter over medium heat. Add the onion, garlic, thyme, and cayenne and season with salt, black pepper, and nutmeg to taste. Stir 5 to 6 minutes to soften. Add the flour and whisk 1 minute, then whisk in the chicken stock, then the cream. Stir some of the hot liquid into the egg yolks to warm them, then add them to the sauce and stir until thickened. Remove from the heat and stir in about ½ cup of the fine bread crumbs. The sauce should be very thick. Let cool to room temp, then pour the sauce over the cold chicken. Stir to combine and chill at least 1 hour more.

Preheat the oven to 275°F. Place a wire rack in a rimmed baking sheet.

Fill a countertop fryer with oil or pour a few inches of oil into a large Dutch oven. Heat the oil to 360° to 365°F.

Line up 2 shallow bowls on the counter: Beat the whole egg in the first, and mix together the remaining ½ cup fine bread crumbs, the panko, parsley, and Parm in the second.

Using a conical ice cream scoop to form pyramid shapes or your damp hands to roll balls, form 12 to 15 croquettes. Turn the croquettes in the beaten egg, then gently press breading mixture evenly all over the croquettes. Fry them 3 to 4 at a time until deeply golden, turning conical shapes gently as they cook to evenly brown, 5 to 6 minutes per croquette. Keep the croquettes warm in the oven.

Make the gravy: In a small saucepan or skillet, melt the butter over medium to medium-high heat. Whisk in the flour, 1 to 2 minutes; then whisk in the stock and cook to thicken. Stir in

the Worcestershire and salt and pepper to taste. Stir some hot liquid into the egg yolk to warm it, then add it to the gravy. Adjust the seasoning to taste and reduce the heat to low.

Serves 4 to 6

Mashed Potatoes & Parsnips with Boursin

3 or 4 **russet potatoes**, peeled and chopped
2 **parsnips**, peeled and chopped
Salt and **pepper**
½ to ¾ cup **chicken stock**, for mashing
¼ cup **heavy cream** or half-and-half
1 (5.4-ounce) wheel **Boursin with garlic and herbs** (or other soft herb cheese)
½ cup grated **Parmigiano-Reggiano cheese**
Freshly grated **nutmeg**

In a saucepan, combine the potatoes and parsnips with cold water to cover. Bring to a boil, salt the water, and cook until fork-tender, 10 to 12 minutes. Drain and return to the pot, mash with the stock, then mash in the cream. Stir in the cheeses and season with salt, pepper, and nutmeg to taste.

If you're making this ahead, hold covered over simmering water in a larger pot.

Serves 4 to 6

Green Beans with Caramelized Onions

1½ pounds **green beans**, trimmed
Salt and **pepper**
4 tablespoons (½ stick) **butter**
1 large **onion**, chopped
1 cup **chicken stock**

In deep skillet, bring 2 to 3 inches water to a boil. Add the beans, season with salt, and parboil until they are bright green in color but still have

a bite to them, 3 to 5 minutes, depending on the thickness of the beans. Drain and cool under cold running water; reserve in a strainer.

In the same skillet, melt the butter over medium heat. Stir in the onion, reduce the heat to medium-low, and cook, stirring occasionally, until caramelized, 25 to 30 minutes; reduce the heat if it browns too quickly at the edges.

Add the stock and beans and turn with tongs to combine. Season with salt and pepper to taste.

Serves 4 to 6

🕐 MARCH 11/BREAKFAST

We had **Deviled Ham on Toast** (see September 4, page 138) with over-easy eggs. It's John's favorite thing now.

Spaghetti with Creamy Spring Pea Pesto & Mini Meatballs

I used chitarra spaghetti, which gets its name from the contraption used to make this specific cut of pasta—it has wires that resemble guitar strings.

Grated zest of 1 **lemon**
½ cup flat-leaf **parsley tops**
3 large cloves **garlic**, finely chopped
1 pound **ground pork** or veal
1 cup **panko** or fresh bread crumbs
1 large **egg**
¼ cup **whole milk**
Grated **Parmigiano-Reggiano cheese**
2 tablespoons **EVOO**, plus more for pesto
Salt and **pepper**
2 cups shelled fresh **peas** or thawed frozen peas
1 cup **chicken stock**
1 cup chopped **mixed fresh herbs**: tarragon, parsley, basil, and mint
½ cup **crème fraîche**
1 pound **spaghetti** (I used chitarra spaghetti)

Preheat the oven to 350°F.

Make a gremolata: On a cutting board, combine the zest with the parsley and 2 cloves of the garlic and finely chop together.

Place the meat in a bowl. Add the gremolata, panko, egg, milk, ¼ to ⅓ cup Parm, 2 tablespoons EVOO, and salt and pepper to taste. Combine thoroughly and roll into walnut-size balls. Arrange them on a nonstick baking sheet and roast until cooked through, about 15 minutes.

Bring a large pot of water to a boil for the spaghetti.

In a small saucepan, combine the peas and stock, cover, and simmer for 5 minutes for fresh peas, 2 minutes for frozen. Set aside to cool to room temperature.

In a food processor, combine 1 cup of the peas, the remaining garlic, the herbs, and ¼ to ⅓ cup Parm and pulse-chop. Turn the machine on and stream in enough EVOO to make a pesto.

Return the remaining unprocessed peas and stock to the heat, bring to low simmer, and stir in the crème fraîche. Cook over low heat to keep warm and thicken.

Salt the pasta water and cook the pasta to al dente. Before draining, ladle out and reserve ½ cup of the starchy pasta cooking water. Drain the pasta.

Stir the pesto into the creamy peas and combine with the pasta and the reserved starchy pasta cooking water. Serve the meatballs alongside.

Serves 4

Cream of Chicken & Leeks on Buttered Toast

1½ pounds **skinless, boneless chicken breast halves**
Salt and **pepper**
1 **carrot**, coarsely shopped
1 rib **celery**, coarsely chopped
1 small **onion**, halved with root end attached
1 **lemon**, sliced
1 **bay leaf**

A few sprigs of fresh **thyme**

Half a bunch of **flat-leaf parsley**

2 tablespoons **butter**

1 tablespoon **EVOO**

3 medium **leeks**, trimmed, halved lengthwise, cut crosswise into ½-inch slices, and thoroughly rinsed

1 tablespoon **flour**

½ cup **dry white wine**

½ cup **heavy cream**

2 to 3 tablespoons chopped **fresh tarragon**

1 tablespoon **Dijon mustard**

4 slices good-quality **white bread**, toasted, lightly buttered, and halved into triangles

Place the chicken in a deep skillet and season with salt. Add the carrot, celery, onion, lemon, bay leaf, thyme, parsley, and just enough water to cover the chicken. Bring to a boil, then reduce the heat to a low boil and poach the chicken for 15 minutes. Remove the chicken and shred or slice. Strain the stock.

Meanwhile, in another deep skillet, heat the butter and EVOO (1 turn of the pan) over medium heat. Add the leeks and cook until softened, 6 to 7 minutes. Season with salt and pepper. Sprinkle with flour and stir for a minute. Add the white wine and ladle in 1 cup of chicken poaching stock. Stir in the cream for about 5 minutes to thicken. Stir in the tarragon and mustard. Add the shredded or sliced chicken and cook until heated through.

Align the toast triangles on plates point to point, with the cut sides facing out. Top with the cream of chicken and leeks.

Serves 4

🕐 **MARCH 13/DINNER**

Corned Beef with Veggies

Serve with pumpernickel bread, Irish soda bread, butter, and mustard.

IRISH SPICE DUST

¼ cup **caraway seeds**

¼ cup **coriander seeds**

¼ cup **black peppercorns**

1 tablespoon **coarse sea salt**

1 tablespoon rubbed **sage**

1 tablespoon dried **dill**

BRINE

½ cup **kosher salt**

½ cup **light brown sugar**

1 fresh **bay leaf**

Stems from ¼ bunch **flat-leaf parsley**

3 **garlic cloves**, unpeeled, smashed

1 tablespoon **juniper berries**, lightly crushed

6-pound **beef brisket** (see Tip)

CORNED BEEF AND VEGGIES

2 (12-ounce) bottles **Guinness stout**

1 **green** or **white cabbage**, cut into 6 wedges with the core in (to hold the wedges together)

9 medium **russet potatoes**, peeled and halved

3 large **carrots,** cut into quarters on an angle

3 ribs **celery**, cut into quarters on an angle

3 small **onions**, quartered, with root end attached

Chopped **flat-leaf parsley leaves**, for garnish

Make the Irish spice dust: In a medium skillet, combine the caraway seeds, coriander seeds, and peppercorns and toast over medium heat until fragrant, 1 to 2 minutes. Set aside half of the toasted spices for the brine. Place the remaining half in a spice grinder with the sea salt, sage, and dill and grind into a fine dust.

Make the brine for the corned beef: In a 12-quart stockpot, combine 2 cups water with the

reserved toasted spices, the kosher salt, sugar, bay leaf, parsley stems, garlic cloves, and juniper berries and bring to a boil. Stir until the sugar and salt have dissolved. Remove from the heat and add 6 cups ice-cold water.

Submerge the brisket in the liquid, then top with a heavy platter to weight it down and keep it completely submerged. Cover and refrigerate for a minimum of 3 days or as long as 5 days.

Remove the beef from the brine; discard the brine. Rinse the beef under cold water to remove any spices that may have stuck to it. Return it to the stockpot, add enough fresh water to cover the beef (about 4 quarts), then top it off with the Guinness. Bring to a bubble, then turn it down slightly to a gentle simmer, cover, and cook for 5 hours. During the last 45 to 60 minutes of cooking, add the cabbage, potatoes, carrots, celery, and onions. Cover and simmer until the vegetables are tender.

Cut the beef against the grain into ½-inch slices and arrange on a platter with the vegetables alongside. Sprinkle with the Irish Spice Dust and chopped parsley.

Serves 6 to 8

You can also make this with a 10-pound shank ham, bone-in and skin removed. When you go to cook the ham, you'll need about 7 quarts of water.

🕐 MARCH 14/DINNER

We had **That's Shallot-a Flavor Spaghetti** (see January 25, page 243).

MARCH 15 THROUGH MARCH 19

We went out of town. ✈

🕐 MARCH 21/DINNER

We had dinner with our friend Jordan Salcito and her husband, Robert. We had **Bull's-Eye Deviled Eggs** (see April 24, page 29), **Lemon–Poppy Seed Egg Tagliatelle**, and **Roast Leg of Lamb** (see July 30, page 104) with **Tomato & Mint Jam**. Jordan brought wine.

Lemon–Poppy Seed Egg Tagliatelle

1 cup **chicken** or **vegetable stock**
1 pinch of **saffron threads**
½ cup **flat-leaf parsley leaves**
2 cloves **garlic**, finely chopped
Grated zest of 2 small organic **lemons** and juice of ½ lemon
2 tablespoons **EVOO**
3 tablespoons **butter**
2 large **shallots**, minced
Salt and **pepper**
3 tablespoons **poppy seeds**
½ cup **dry white wine**
½ cup **heavy cream**
1 pound **egg tagliatelle** or fettuccine
1 cup freshly grated **Parmigiano-Reggiano cheese**

Bring a large pot of water to a boil for the pasta. In a small saucepan, combine the stock and saffron and heat to warm.

Make a gremolata: On a cutting board, chop the parsley, garlic, and lemon zest together.

In a large skillet, heat the EVOO (2 turns of the pan) over medium heat. Melt in the butter. When the butter foams, add the shallots, season with salt and pepper, and stir 2 to 3 minutes. Add the poppy seeds and stir 1 or 2 minutes. Add the gremolata and stir 1 or 2 minutes. Add the wine and cook until almost evaporated. Add the warm saffron stock and the cream and cook to reduce while the pasta cooks.

Salt the water and cook the pasta to al dente. Before draining, ladle out and reserve ½ cup of the starchy pasta cooking water. Drain the pasta and toss with the sauce, cheese, and enough cooking water to help the cheese turn into a thick coating on the pasta. Add the lemon juice. Adjust the salt and pepper.

Serves 4

Tomato & Mint Jam

1 (28- or 32-ounce) can **San Marzano tomatoes** (look for DOP on the label), or 3 pounds fresh Roma tomatoes, peeled
½ cup **sugar**
½ cup fresh **mint leaves**, chopped
1 **shallot**, grated or minced
2 teaspoons **Worcestershire sauce** or aged balsamic vinegar
1 rounded teaspoon **kosher salt**
Pepper

In a saucepan, combine all the ingredients and bring to a boil. Reduce the heat to medium and mash, then cook until thick and jam-like, about 20 minutes.

Makes 2 to 3 cups

MARCH 24, LUNCH. Lamb and tomato jam sandwiches: Thin slices of leftover lamb, with radicchio mixed with thinly sliced red onion and chile dressed with lemon juice, olive oil, and my 24/7 seasoning or salt and pepper to taste. You can add a little sprinkle of superfine sugar if you want to sweeten it up a bit and it makes a really tasty sandwich. John loved it.

🕐 **MARCH 24/DINNER**

Pici Pasta with Fava Pesto & Asparagus

To peel the favas, parboil them briefly to loosen the skins. I also blanch the asparagus tips in a pot of boiling water before sautéing them.

FAVA PESTO
½ cup peeled fresh **fava beans**
½ cup flat-leaf **parsley leaves**
½ cup fresh **mint leaves**
¼ cup **tarragon leaves**
½ cup **pine nuts**
Juice of 1 **lemon**

⅓ cup grated **Parmigiano-Reggiano cheese**
   or pecorino, or a combination
⅓ cup **EVOO**
Salt and **pepper**

PASTA
Salt and **pepper**
1 pound **pici pasta**
2 to 3 tablespoons **EVOO**
2 **shallots**, finely chopped
½ cup **dry white wine**
1½ to 2 cups **asparagus** tips (about 2-inch
   pieces), blanched

Make the pesto: In a food processor, combine
the favas, parsley, mint, tarragon, pine nuts,
lemon juice, and Parm. Pulse-chop to combine. With the machine running, stream in the
EVOO to make a pesto. Season with salt and
pepper to taste.

Make the pasta: Bring a large pot of water to a
boil. Salt the water and cook the pasta to al dente.
Before draining, ladle out and reserve 1 cup of the
starchy pasta cooking water. Drain the pasta.

In a skillet, heat the EVOO (2 to 3 turns of the
pan) over medium heat. Add the shallots and salt
and pepper to taste and cook 3 minutes. Deglaze
with the wine. Add the asparagus, the cup of
starchy cooking water, the pesto, and the drained
pasta and toss everything together.

Serves 4

🕐 MARCH 28/DINNER

My good buddy Chef Adam Perry Lang came over
and he made a sliced lamb loin cooked in a cast-
iron skillet. We served up the lamb on buttered
toast with more of our **Tomato & Mint Jam** (see
March 21, page 286). We just can't get enough of
it. I garnished with a radicchio slaw (with chiles,
red onion, lemon, sugar, salt, pepper, and olive
oil). We also had **Spring Risotto** (see April 18,
page 16).

MARCH 29/DINNER

Started with **Fava Bean Spread** (see May 26, page 42) and then had **Lemon Spaghetti with Ramps** and merguez sausages.

Lemon Spaghetti with Ramps

I served this with merguez (spicy lamb sausages) on top or on the side. The lemon spaghetti in the title is lemon-flavored spaghetti that I get at Buon Italia market.

2 bunches **ramps** (see Tip)
3 tablespoons **EVOO**
3 or 4 small cloves **garlic**, finely chopped
1 **red chile**, such as Fresno, finely chopped
Grated zest of 2 **Meyer lemons**, juice of 1
Salt and **pepper**
½ cup **dry white wine**
1 pound **spaghetti** or **lemon spaghetti**
3 tablespoons **butter**
½ cup grated **pecorino cheese**, plus more for serving
½ cup **flat-leaf parsley** and **mint leaves** combined, finely chopped

Bring a large pot of water to boil for the pasta.

Soak the ramps to remove grit. Trim the roots and cut the ramps across where the whites meet the green tops. Finely chop the whites. Chop the greens into 1-inch pieces.

In a large skillet, heat the EVOO (3 turns of the pan) over medium heat. Add the whites of the ramps, the garlic, chile, and lemon zest; season with salt and pepper to taste. Stir 5 or 6 minutes, then add the wine and reduce the heat to low.

Salt the pasta water and cook the pasta to al dente. Before draining, ladle out and reserve ½ cup of the starchy pasta cooking water. Drain the pasta.

Raise the heat on the sauce again to medium and add the lemon juice. Melt in the butter, add the starchy cooking water, the pecorino, drained spaghetti, and green ramp tops, and toss to combine. Serve in shallow bowls with more cheese, parsley, and mint on top.

Serves 4

Since ramps are seasonal and not that easy to find, you could make this with leeks instead; you'll need 4 or 5 medium. Trim the tough tops and roots, halve the leeks lengthwise, and cut crosswise into ½-inch pieces. Wash well to get rid of sand.

MARCH 30/DINNER

We had one of our all-time faves: **Chicken Curry** and **Homemade Rice Pilaf** (see August 28, pages 130 and 131).

MARCH 31, BREAKFAST. Breakfast potato pancakes with Tex-Mex eggs: I grated 2 large starchy potatoes and soaked them in cold salted water, then drained them and pressed out all the liquid. I combined them with 2 small or 1 large parsnip, peeled and grated. I added ¼ cup grated onion, my Rachael Ray 24/7 Seasoning or salt and pepper, about ¼ cup flour, and 1 large beaten egg. I shallow-fried the pancakes in a little oil over medium to medium-high heat. Then I topped the potato pancakes with chipotle mustard. I made Tex-Mex eggs to go with them: I fried up some eggs with garlic, chile, and red onion and stirred in cilantro and extra-sharp Cheddar (I like XXX Cheddar from Oscar's Smokehouse).

🕐 MARCH 31/DINNER

We had **Springtime Minestrone**. I also made **Grilled Cheese with Spinach**, **Calzone-Style** (see April 21, page 19), but everyone was so full from the soup that no one touched the sandwiches.

Springtime Minestrone

This hearty but very healthy minestrone gets its springtime boost from fresh favas and peas.

½ pound **dried Italian cannellini beans**
1 **onion**, halved with the root end attached, plus 2 small onions, chopped
3 fresh **bay leaves**
Salt and **pepper**
5 cups **chicken stock**
¼ cup **EVOO**
4 or 5 bulbs **baby fennel**, thinly sliced, or 1 small bulb regular fennel, quartered and thinly sliced
4 cloves **garlic**, thinly sliced or chopped
3 or 4 **carrots**, thinly sliced or chopped
2 **parsnips**, peeled and thinly sliced or chopped
3 or 4 ribs **celery** with leafy tops, chopped
3 tablespoons **rosemary**, chopped
2 tablespoons **thyme leaves**, chopped
2 cups **vegetable stock**
1 cup **ditalini**
1 to 2 tablespoons **butter**
Small handful of grated **Parmigiano-Reggiano cheese**
1 cup fresh peeled **fava beans**
1 cup shelled **spring peas**
Grated zest and juice of 1 **lemon**

Soak the cannellini in water to cover overnight.

Drain, place in a saucepan, and add the halved onion and 1 bay leaf. Add water to cover and bring to a boil. Salt the water and parboil for 15 minutes.

Drain the beans and transfer half of them to a food processor. Add 1 cup of the chicken stock and puree until it's pretty smooth. Set aside.

In a soup pot, heat the EVOO (4 turns of the pan) over medium to medium-high heat. Add the fennel, chopped onions, garlic, carrots, parsnips, celery, 2 bay leaves, the rosemary, thyme, and salt and pepper. Partially cover and cook until they start to become tender. Add 4 cups chicken stock and the vegetable stock. Stir in the bean puree and the whole beans, and cook until the beans are fully tender, 15 to 20 minutes.

Meanwhile, in a pot of boiling salted water, cook the pasta to al dente. Drain and toss with the butter and cheese.

Stir the favas, peas, lemon zest, and lemon juice into the soup. Put a little bit of pasta in the bottom of a bowl and top it with your soup.

Serves 4

acknowledgments

Thank you, Boxer and Kappy, for formatting a dozen paper notebooks into a keepsake for our family and for those who make the recipes for their families.

Thank you to Jill Armus for designing our gorgeous cover. Thanks to Judith Curr, publisher of Atria Books, and her spectacular team: my editor, Johanna Castillo; Sybil Pincus; Dana Sloan; and every person involved in this project.

index

(Titles of dishes that are capitalized refer to structured recipes. Titles that are lower case refer to less formal recipes written on recipe cards or notebook pages.)

Green Harissa, 137

Green Pastitsio, 23

Green Rice, 262

   with Beans, 64

gremolata (topping), 177, 264

   Pasta with, 257

   Spring Herb, 68

grilled. *See also* slow-smoked;

   smoked

   artichoke hearts, 137

   baby back ribs, 70

   Bistecca, 66–67

   cedar planks for, 129

   Chicken Spiedies with Sesame

     Sauce, 66

   Chicken & Steak with Italian

     Marinade, 94–95

   corn on the cob, red, 90

   Corn with Chipotle Cream &

     Cotija, 45

   flank steaks, 77

   Flat Iron Steaks with Tre Colore

     Pesto & Quick-Roasted To-

     matoes, 45

   portobellos, 39

   prosciutto-wrapped figs, 48

   Shrimp, 86

   Snapper with Pesto, 128

   steaks, 39, 99

   Surf & Turf, 72–73

Grilled Cheese with Spinach,

   Calzone-Style, 19

Gruyère cheese:

   Croque Madame, 13

   Croque Monsieur, 252–53

   Croque Monsieur with Mush-

     rooms, 147

   Deviled Ham Melts, 232

   French Onion French Bread

     Pizzas, 118

   French Onion Soup with Wild

     Mushrooms, 189

   Macaroni & Cheese with Fennel,

     271

   onion frittata, 109

guacamole:

   Apple & Almond, 83

   Crabby, 82

   Lemon-Garlic, 31

   Roasted Onion, Chile & Garlic,

     160

guanciale, in Carbonara with

   Spring Herb Gremolata, 68

H

ham. *See also* prosciutto

   Croque Madame, 13

   Croque Monsieur, 252–53

   Croque Monsieur with Mush-

     rooms, 147

   Deviled, 46

   Deviled, Melts, 232

   Deviled, on Toast, 138

   Deviled Eggs &, 34–35

   & Eggs Crêpes, 86–87

   & Mushroom Omelet, Two-

     Person, 221

   pizza capricciosa, 278

   Serrano, Chapata with Man-

     chego Potatoes, Eggs &,

     185–86

Harvest (New York City), 218

hash:

   Popper, 56–57

   turkey stuffing, and eggs, 236

   wild boar sausage, 121

herb(s). *See also* specific herbs

   Butter, 178

   chile butter, 79

   Egg Noodles, Buttered, 173

   Gravy, 220–21

   Mixed, Pesto Penne, 59

   and Mushroom Sauce, Creamy,

     with Whole-Grain Pasta, 258

   Spring, Gremolata, 68

heroes or hoagies. *See* submarine

   sandwiches (heroes, hoagies,

   or Italian sandwiches)

holiday parties, prepping for,

   213–14

hominy:

   Red Pork Posole, 122–24

   Vegetable Posole, 225

Horseradish Sauce, 90, 220

   Sour Cream, 208

hot dogs, in Sloppy Dawgs, 60–61

Howard Johnson's, 280–81

Huevos Rancheros, Smoky, 8

Hummus, Basic, 252

I

Indian flavors:

   Chicken Vindaloo, 14

   Mulligatawny, 260

   Raita, 86

Irish Spice Dust, 284

Isaboo's puppy dog chili, 270

Italian and Italian-American cook-

   ing. *See also* frittatas; pasta;

   pizza; ragu; risotto; sub-

   marine sandwiches (heroes,

   hoagies, or Italian sandwiches)

   Beef Milanese with Tomato &

     Arugula Raw Sauce, 262–63

   Bistecca, 66–67

   Caponata, 27

   Chicken Saltimbocca with Ta-

     gliatelle, 32–33

   Chicken Vesuvio, 265–66

   Deviled Crab Arancini, 92–93

   Gazpacho Italiano, 95

   Grilled Cheese with Spinach,

     Calzone-Style, 19

   Marinade, 95

   Marinated Mushrooms, 279

   Osso Buco, 176–77

   piadinas, 41, 115

   Polenta, 177

   Potato Cake with Roast Sau-

     sages & Crispy Kale, 10–11

   Red Pepper Minestrone Soup,

     110–11

   Semifreddo, 73

   Sicilian-style orange salad, 56

   Sort of Cioppino, 143